The Association of
Accountants and
Financial Professionals
in Business

T0311075

Management Accounting Case Book

Cases from the IMA Educational Case Journal

Raef A. Lawson

About IMA®

IMA, the association of accountants and financial professionals in business, is one of the largest and most respected associations focused exclusively on advancing the management accounting profession. Globally, IMA supports the profession through research, the CMA(R) (Certified Management Accountant) program, continuing education, networking, and advocacy of the highest ethical business practices. IMA has a global network of more than 80,000 members in 140 countries and 300 professional and student chapters. Headquartered in Montvale, N.J., USA, IMA provides localized services through its four global regions: The Americas, Asia/Pacific, Europe, and Middle East/Africa. For more information about IMA, please visit www.imanet.org.

About the CMA®

IMA's globally recognized CMA (Certified Management Accountant) is the leading certification for management accountants and financial professionals in business. Earning the CMA requires a mastery of advanced-level knowledge in four critical areas: financial planning, analysis, control, and decision support. For more information about the CMA certification program, please visit www.imanet.org/certification.

© 2016 Institute of Management Accountants

All rights reserved.

ISBN: 978-0-9967293-4-5 (paper)
ISBN: 978-1-119-72452-0 (ePub)
ISBN: 978-1-119-72455-1 (ePDF)

Cover Design: Wiley
Cover Image: © Peter Grosch/Shutterstock

Teaching notes for the Management Accounting Case Book are available upon request to accounting academics and practitioners. Requests can be sent to research@imanet.org.

Preface

As the field of management accounting evolves, management accountants are required to have a mastery over an ever-widening body of knowledge, including such areas as risk management, strategic cost management, process management, and more. They must also be able to apply that knowledge in an integrated manner to situations often involving uncertainty.

A useful way to develop such competency is through the use of case studies. Besides making mastery of important concepts more interesting, case studies can enhance one's grasp of management theory by facilitating broad discussion designed to challenge one's thinking and helping to foster critical thinking skills.

Management Accounting Case Book: Cases from the IMA Educational Case Journal (MACB) offers may cases that have been through a rigorous review process to ensure high quality of both case and teaching notes and have been used at dozens of schools. Some cases are intended for a certain academic level (e.g., principles, undergraduate, graduate, MBA), but most are usable for multiple audiences and can be adapted to the objectives of the instructor. MACB can be used to supplement a textbook or as a standalone text for using the case method.

The cases in this book were chosen from cases published in the IMA Educational Case Journal (IECJ ®). The IECJ is a high-quality online journal with the mission to publish teaching cases for management accounting and related fields. The IECJ aims to provide an educational resource rich in detail to reflect current business problems. Through publication of these case studies, IMA (Institute of Management Accountants) is pursuing its goal of enhancing the teaching of management accounting worldwide to help develop the global management accounting profession.

The *Management Accounting Case Book* is organized into five sections, each dealing with a specific area of management accounting:

- Business Leadership and Ethics (including the role of the management accountant, ethical situations, IMA Guidelines, whistleblowing, organizational culture, and employee engagement)
- Operations, Process Management, and Innovation (including flexible budgeting, standard costs, variance analysis, nonfinancial performance indicators, quality control, lean, and innovation governance)
- Planning and Decision Making (including cost estimation, CVP analysis, budgeting, decision making, capital investments, target costing, and TOC)
- Risk Management and Internal Controls (including sustainability, performance evaluation and indicators, responsibility centers, balanced scorecard, transfer pricing, compensation, and incentives)
- Strategic Cost Management (including product and service costing, cost allocation, and strategy implementation)

I want to thank the Associate Editors of the IECJ, the members of the IECJ Advisory & Review Board, and the authors of the cases included in this volume for their many years of support of our journal. Their efforts have been instrumental to the development of this great resource.

I wish you success and hope you enjoy these cases!

Raef Lawson, Ph.D., CMA, CPA, CFA
Editor, *IMA Educational Case Journal*
Professor-in-Residence and Vice President of Research & Policy
Institute of Management Accountants

Table of Contents

I. Business Leadership and Ethics

Trust May Breed Trouble: Fraud Opportunities and Ethics at Saintly Church

Cecily Raiborn, Janet B. Butler, Nathan H. Cannon, and Randall F. Young, Texas State University

SAINTLY CHURCH IS EXPERIENCING DECLINING REVENUES AND increasing expenses, and several fraud risk factors are present. Do these fraud risk factors indicate fraudulent activity by one or more of the key persons in the case, or could there be reasonable and legitimate explanations? The purpose of this case is to allow students to explore the IMA Statement of Ethical Professional Practice within the context of a nonprofit institution by examining the role of Sandy Withers, CMA, as she attempts to help the church address these issues. By completing the case, students will identify potential underlying causes (both fraudulent and legitimate) of the declining revenues and increasing expenses, highlight weaknesses in internal controls, and discuss Withers's responsibilities and approaches to communication under the IMA Statement of Ethical Professional Practice.

This case is an ideal assignment for an undergraduate or graduate accounting course that discusses internal controls, the fraud triangle, and potential organizational fraud. It is also a good assignment to integrate toward the end of a fraud prevention class that employs a case-based teaching methodology since most fraud cases have a primary objective of identifying the fraud or the fraud risk factors.

Keywords: ethical standards, church fraud, not-for-profit fraud, fraud triangle, internal controls.

The Association of
Accountants and
Financial Professionals
in Business

Trust May Breed Trouble: Fraud Opportunities and Ethics at Saintly Church

Cecily Raiborn, Ph.D., CMA, CPA, CFE
McCoy Endowed Chair in Accounting
Texas State University

Nathan H. Cannon, Ph.D., CPA
Assistant Professor of Accounting
Texas State University

Janet B. Butler, Ph.D., CGMA, CITP
Professor of Accounting
Texas State University

Randall F. Young, Ph.D.
Assistant Professor of Accounting
Texas State University

INTRODUCTION

Light twinkled through the stained glass windows as Pastor Peter Lang walked through Saintly Church. He had just met with Sandy Withers, a CMA® (Certified Management Accountant) and two-year member of the church's governing board. Lang and Withers had been discussing the fact that the church was perennially short of funds—although what church wasn't these days?—and the possibility of instituting some new internal controls for oversight.

As a board member, Withers was part of the group responsible for managing Saintly Church's overall business and nonbusiness affairs. Such responsibility included implementing policies regarding church administrative policies and procedures. Although the church had grown significantly over the past 20 years, board members had made few of the administrative policy changes suggested by advisers and the church's denomination headquarters.[1] The church was primarily operating under a system of trust. The following passage illustrates the majority viewpoint of the board: "Trust is the emotional glue that binds a team together and produces confidence…. High-achieving churches have a high level of trust among the staff. It means the lead pastor trusts the staff, the staff trusts the pastor, and the staff trusts one another."[2]

While Withers agrees with the basic sentiment, she also believes that too much trust could create problems. She explained to Pastor Lang that trust is simply not a valid internal control. She referenced a recently-read article stating that the environments of not-for-profit organizations (including churches) often make them more vulnerable to fraud and abuse than for-profit businesses because of the reasons listed in Figure 1. Pastor Lang can see the point Withers was trying to make, but he could also see that putting in internal controls would likely mean additional work for him and other church workers. He asked Withers to please discuss with him any recommendations she is considering before taking those recommendations to the board.

THE CHURCH

Saintly Church was formed about 20 years ago in a small suburb of a metropolitan area. As the city grew, so did the suburb and the church. A large proportion, but definitely not all, of the members would be classified as having middle-to-high income. To meet the needs of its membership and others in the community, the church operates Little Saints Daycare five days a week. Church operating funds are raised from the Little Saints Daycare tuition, collection plate donations, online donations through Secure Spirits (the church denomination's giving website), and a monthly bingo game. The church also has two large community rooms that may be rented out for nonchurch events. The community rooms are constantly under renovation to make them more attractive for rental activities.

In addition to a small petty cash fund in the church secretary's desk drawer, a larger cash "benevolent fund" is available to pay for food for the occasional homeless person or to provide less-affluent church members with financial assistance for small emergencies. If there is insufficient cash in the benevolent fund to help someone in need, the pastor can ask the governing board for additional money.

THE PEOPLE

Pastor Lang has been with the church for three years, having moved halfway across the country just prior to taking the position. He showed up at the right time. The previous pastor retired and moved to Florida a year previously, and the church had just finished its discernment and transition process, which generated recommendations for interview candidates and sought to preserve continuity between the leaving and incoming pastors. After wowing the governing board in his interview, Lang (with an undergraduate degree in accounting and graduate degree in theology) passed his background check and was hired. In addition to his salary and a credit card to be used for church business, Lang is provided with a housing and car allowance. He was slightly disappointed by the salary offered, but stated that he could manage on that amount since he is single and his accounting major made him good at budgeting. His background has also made him a favorite with some of the elderly parishioners because he is able to help them with their finances.

Sabrina Louis, the church secretary, had been hired eight years ago by the previous pastor. That pastor, being concerned about privacy issues related to congregants' contributions, made Louis solely responsible for counting collection plate offerings rather than the more typical approach of having rotating teams of congregation members perform that task. Over the years, Louis has been given more and more responsibilities. Today she is in charge of much of the bookkeeping, including recording contributions and pledges, preparing financial statements, and making purchases authorized by Lang or, in the case of purchases more than $2,000, by the board. Because of her multiple job duties and her dedication to the church, Louis tends to work long hours and takes few vacation days. She says that vacations aren't really important to her since she is not married and few family members live close by.

GENERAL FINANCIAL PROCESSES

The church has a checking and savings account at a local bank. Two tellers and one manager from the bank are church members. Bank statements are sent to the church address and are reconciled monthly by Lang. In addition to Lang, one member of the governing board has authority to sign checks for the church; only one signature is required on a check. Lang typically makes bank deposits on Monday. Cash and checks from the Sunday collection plate are stored in a small safe that Lang, Louis, and one member of the governing board have the combination for. Cash offerings have decreased significantly over the past few years since many church members prefer to contribute by check or online on a monthly basis.

Daycare tuition can be paid on a daily, weekly, or monthly basis depending on how regularly a child attends. Daily and weekly tuitions are generally paid by check, but some people do pay in cash. Monthly tuition is billed by Louis and remitted to her by check. The number of people working at Little Saints Daycare varies based on the number of children. Lang interviews and hires daycare workers. There are three "regular" workers, and substitutes are available to fill in when needed. One of the regular workers provides Lang with information about the daily number of children attending (and those who paid in cash) as well as who worked and for how long. Lang reviews the attendance records and forwards the attendance records and any tuition payments to Louis. Louis records the tuition payments received then sends the checks or cash to Lang to deposit into the bank. Daycare employees' timesheets are also reviewed, and the information is given to Louis. She writes the payroll checks, and Lang signs them. One of the other regular workers is in charge of purchasing snack and meal items for the daycare center and turns the receipts over to Lang, who approves them and submits them to Louis to provide payment.

Although Louis is in charge of checking the calendar for availability of community rooms, Lang meets with individuals wanting to rent the room. There is no set fee for room rental. The amount Lang charges depends on whether the person who wants to rent is a church member or nonmember, what the purpose of the rental is, how long the rental will be, and what (if any) church furniture or fixtures will be used. Lang collects a deposit and tells Louis the remaining amount to bill.

The monthly bingo game is scheduled on a Saturday night and is a cash-only event. Both Lang and Louis sell the bingo cards, and Lang pays out the winnings from the proceeds. Volunteers call the games and help with the event. Lang uses bingo proceeds to pay for the volunteers' drinks and snacks as a thank you for donating their time. The net cash is then deposited into the bank on Monday along with the Sunday offerings. Bingo proceeds have been declining substantially although most church members still attend and socialize.

THE CIRCUMSTANCES

Three days after her discussion with Pastor Lang, Withers gathered with the rest of the church's governing board for the monthly meeting. A major focal point of the meeting was the financial statements provided by Louis.[3] (Tables 1 and 2 present portions of the 2014 budget and excerpts from the three-year Statement of Activities prepared for the Board.) While they may not have been considered dismal, the financials did not provide good news compared to the budget. Offerings were lower than expected, as were tuition, rental, and bingo revenue. Expenditures for benevolences, daycare worker wages, daycare snacks and meals, and community room improvements were higher than budgeted. The situation has been getting worse over the last 18 months, and the board members were concerned. One board member who had recently become the victim of employee fraud at his business remarked that things had financially gone downhill since Lang had become pastor. The board member then mused aloud that Lang could easily be stealing from the church. After all, had the other board members seen Lang's new car?

Table 1: 2014 Budget Excerpt

Unrestricted Revenues:		
Contributions/Offerings		$200,000
Daycare Tuition		155,000
Bingo Revenue		18,000
Building Use		5,500
Total Unrestricted Revenues		$378,500
Expenses:		
Pastor Compensation		$ 80,000
Church Employees Compensation		75,500
Daycare:		
Employee Wages	130,000	
Snacks and Meals	13,000	
Utilities and Miscellaneous	8,200	151,200
Maintenance & Utilities (incl. Community Room)		30,000
Benevolences		18,500
Church Council		4,000
Youth Ministry		5,100
Worship and Music		4,300
Outreach and Advertising		1,000
Total Expenses		$369,600
Excess of Revenues over Expenses		$ 8,900

Table 2: Statement of Activities Excerpts for Three Years Table 2: Statement of Activities Excerpts for Three Years

STATEMENT OF ACTIVITIES
FOR YEAR ENDED DECEMBER 31

	2014		2013		2012	
Contributions/Offerings		$195,000		$198,000		$202,000
Auxiliary Service Revenue:						
Daycare Tuition		150,000		154,000		158,000
Bingo Revenue		15,000		18,000		19,500
Building Use		5,000		5,300		5,800
Total Unrestricted Revenue		$365,000		$375,300		$385,300
Pastor Compensation		$80,000		$78,000		$77,000
Church Employees Compensation		75,000		74,500		74,000
Daycare:						
Employee Wages	$135,000		$130,000		$129,000	
Snacks and Meals	15,000		14,500		14,000	
Utilities and Miscellaneous	8,000	158,000	8,100	152,600	8,000	137,000
Maintenance & Utilities (incl. Community Room Improvements)		32,000		29,000		27,500
Benevolences		19,000		18,700		18,200
Church Council		4,000		3,900		3,900
Youth Ministry		5,000		5,100		5,000
Worship and Music		4,000		4,000		3,900
Outreach and Advertising		1,000		950		900
Total Expenses		$378,000		$366,750		$347,400
Excess of Revenues over Expenses		($13,000)		$8,550		$37,900

The board members turned to Withers. Surely her knowledge of accounting and budgeting could help them understand what might be happening. Withers thought carefully about everything that was going on. On one hand, logical explanations could be given for all of the unfavorable variances between the budget and actual amounts. On the other hand, internal controls were weak, and the potential for fraud is high.

Given the *IMA Statement of Ethical Professional Practice*, Withers knows that she has a responsibility to be honest, fair, and objective in addressing the church's financial issues with the rest of the board members. A CMA has a competence responsibility to "provide decision support information and recommendations that are accurate, clear, concise, and timely." Additionally, a CMA has a credibility responsibility to "communicate information fairly and objectively" and to "disclose all relevant information that could reasonably be expected to influence [a] user's understanding of…analyses or recommendations." Finally, even though the church had no stated internal control policies, Withers knew that she had a responsibility to disclose the control problems that could lead to inappropriate behaviors.

CASE QUESTIONS

1. Who are the stakeholders of Saintly Church?
2. A system of internal controls should be designed to protect assets and ensure compliance with organizational policies and procedures. Do you believe that the church has a reasonable system of internal controls? Explain why or why not.

3. Prepare a flowchart of the sources and uses of the church funds. Indicate within the flowchart where documentation is being prepared and by whom. Use this flowchart to identify points of weakness in the current system of internal controls for question 4.

4. Fraud, waste, and/or abuse may occur when an organization has no, or ineffective, internal controls.

   a. In what ways might Pastor Lang commit fraud in the church? If the pastor is stealing from the church, what rationalizations might he use for his actions?

   b. In what ways might Sabrina Louis commit fraud in the church?

   c. What types of waste and abuse could be occurring in the church by persons other than Pastor Lang or Sabrina Louis?

   d. What recommendations should Withers supply to the board about the church's internal controls?

5. Assuming that no theft is occurring at the church, discuss the human resource issues that the lack of internal controls places on church employees.

6. Organizational governance reflects the manner in which management (in this case, the church's board and pastor) is directed, administered, and controlled toward the achievement of mission and vision. It appears that the appropriate level of governance is not being provided by the board at Saintly Church. What legal and ethical issues might arise related to the various stakeholders given the lack of good organizational governance?

7. What rational and legitimate explanations could be given for each of the line item budget variances?

8. Review the standards of competence, confidentiality, integrity, and credibility within the *IMA Statement of Ethical Professional Practice*.

   a. How should Withers proceed relative to (1) the situation and (2) her communications with the board and others?

   b. Given the responsibility of confidentiality, how should Withers broach the subject (if at all) of the potential for Louis committing fraud?

ENDNOTES

[1] See, for example, http://www.kybaptist.org/wp-content/uploads/2012/06/27-Handling-Money-in-Church-Internal-Controls.pdf , http://download.elca.org/ELCA%20Resource%20Repository/Internal_Control_Best_Practices.pdf , http://www.churchmanagementsolutions.com/kb/KnowledgebaseArticle50270.aspx.

[2] Warren, R., "How to Build Trust Within Your Staff," *Pastors.com* (September 3, 2012); http://pastors.com/how-to-build-trust-within-your-staff/.

[3] Churches are not-for-profit organizations. Not-for-profit entities typically use fund accounting rules and principles and prepare financial statements in accordance with FASB Statement of Financial Accounting Standards (SFAS) Nos. 116 and 117. At the time this case was written, SFAS 117 was under review. See http://www.fasb.org/cs/ContentServer?c=FASBContent_C&pagename=FASB%2FFASBContent_C%2FProjectUpdatePage&cid=1176159286112 for an update of the current status of this standard and the review process.

Diamond Foods, Inc.

Jomo Sankara and Deborah L. Lindberg, Illinois State University

THIS CASE EXAMINES A REAL-LIFE OCCURRENCE OF ALLEGED financial statement fraud by Diamond Foods, Inc. Specifically, the company purportedly understated walnut costs in order to falsify earnings to meet estimates by stock analysts. The facts of this case are drawn from Securities & Exchange Commission (SEC) accounting and auditing enforcement releases and administrative proceedings releases. Learning objectives specific to this case include increased awareness of real-life ethical dilemmas, understanding the reasons for earnings management, understanding the costs of earnings management, and greater awareness of appropriate auditing responses to potential earnings management fraud.

The case is within the grasp of introductory undergraduate students and is also appropriate for graduate students. The case can be used in either an auditing course or a managerial course. You can pick relevant questions from the case to assign to students as deemed appropriate based on the class.

Keywords: Diamond Foods, Inc., managed earnings, analyst expectations, ethics, auditors, budgetary control.

The Association of
Accountants and
Financial Professionals
in Business

Diamond Foods, Inc.

Jomo Sankara
Illinois State University

Deborah L. Lindberg
Illinois State University

INTRODUCTION

This case examines an interesting real-life occurrence of
alleged financial statement fraud by Diamond Foods, Inc.
Specifically, the company purportedly understated walnut
costs in two fiscal years in order to falsify earnings to meet
estimates by stock analysts. The facts of this case are drawn
from Securities & Exchange Commission (SEC) accounting
and auditing enforcement releases and administrative
proceedings releases.

OVERVIEW

The SEC filed separate actions in January 2014 against
Diamond Foods, Inc., its former Chief Executive Officer
Michael Mendes, and its former Chief Financial Officer
Steven Neil for their roles in a scheme to understate walnut
costs in order to falsify earnings to meet estimates by stock
analysts.[1] The SEC contends that Diamond materially
falsified its financial statements in fiscal years 2010 and
2011.[2] Diamond has since restated its financial results for
those periods. The company's reported earnings decreased
by $10.5 million for its 2010 fiscal year and by $23.6 million
for its 2011 fiscal year.[3] Additional specific information is
provided in the following sections of the case.

DIAMOND FOODS: MORE THAN NUTS

Diamond Foods, Inc., based in San Francisco, Calif., has
a significant line of business that involves buying walnuts
from growers and then selling the walnuts to retailers. The
company diversified into potato chip and microwave popcorn
product lines, introducing these lines after Diamond became
a publicly traded company in 2005. Diamond first entered
the microwave popcorn business when it acquired the Pop
Secret popcorn brand from General Mills in 2008. Two
years later, Diamond Foods expanded into potato chips by
acquiring the Kettle Foods potato chip company. The potato
chips are sold under the Kettle Brand label in the United
States and Kettle Chips brand in the United Kingdom.[4] As
of August 31, 2011, Diamond had issued 22,011,196 shares of
common stock.

Although Diamond Foods diversified into other product
lines, walnuts remained its primary product. In 2010,
a significant increase in the cost of walnuts threatened
Diamond's financial results, and, as described in the
following paragraphs, two of Diamond's top officers allegedly
manipulated financial information.

THE ACCOUNTING SCHEMES

In fiscal year 2010, there were significant increases in the
average prices demanded by walnut growers.[5] Accordingly,
Diamond needed to pay significantly more to its growers in
2010, compared to prior years. Yet an increase in the cost of
walnuts would decrease net income at a time when Neil,

Diamond's then-CFO, was facing pressure to meet or exceed the earnings estimates of Wall Street analysts.[6] Neil gave "extra" payments to Diamond's walnut growers but allegedly improperly excluded portions of these payments from the cost of walnuts by instructing his finance team to consider the payments as advances on crops that had not yet been delivered. Mendes, Diamond's then-CEO, was not only involved in the decision to make special payments to growers but also was aware of the way these payments were recorded in the financial statements.[7] By allegedly falsifying the financial statements for fiscal years 2010 and 2011, Diamond was able to hit quarterly earnings per share (EPS) targets and exceed analysts' estimates.[8] The SEC also alleges that both Neil and Mendes personally benefited from the alleged fraud by receiving cash bonuses and other compensation based on reported EPS in both fiscal years 2010 and 2011.[9]

FISCAL YEAR 2010: "CONTINUITY" PAYMENTS

Diamond began manipulating the financial statements by understating its walnut cost in the second quarter of fiscal year 2010. In accordance with Diamond's accounting policy, the cost of the 2009 walnut crop is reported in the 2010 financial statements. Diamond had previously recorded an estimated average walnut cost of $0.82 per pound in the first quarter of fiscal year 2010 based on the 2009 crop. But in order to beat the analysts' consensus second quarter EPS forecast, Neil reduced the walnut cost estimate to $0.72 per pound.[10] The resultant increase in stock price from beating analysts' forecasts supported Diamond's expansion into potato chips and the imminent acquisition of the Kettle Foods potato chip company.

Diamond subsequently paid a final minimum price to the walnut growers of $0.71 per pound, which was significantly lower than market price for the 2009 crop. Therefore, Neil created a scheme to "close the gap" between the final minimum price and the market price, which was to pay the walnut growers extraordinary payments of approximately $0.10 per pound, termed as a "continuity" payment. Only the final minimum price of $0.71 per pound was included in the 2010 financial statements. To avoid including the continuity payment in the 2010 financial statements, Neil instructed his finance team that the payment was an advance for the 2010 walnut crop. But the growers were paid the continuity payment and final 2009 crop payment in one check, the continuity payment went to growers not under contract to deliver the 2010 crop, and continuity payments were made to growers who ultimately did not deliver a 2010 crop. Mendes reviewed and approved correspondence sent to the growers related to this matter. Excluding the continuity payments from the 2010 financial statements resulted in Diamond beating its EPS forecasts and reporting a 52% growth in earnings.[11]

FISCAL YEAR 2011: "MOMENTUM" PAYMENTS

Neil also allegedly manipulated walnut costs in the 2011 fiscal year, resulting in the continuation of the trend of beating analysts' earnings estimates. A competitive price for the 2010 walnut crop was approximately $1 per pound. Diamond paid the walnut growers an average first installment payment of $0.57 per pound and agreed to pay a final payment of $0.08 per pound. Diamond subsequently recorded the final 2010 crop walnut cost as $0.74 per pound. The cost of the 2010 walnut crop is recorded in 2011 fiscal year's financial statements.

Neil knew that Diamond's "final" price for the 2010 crop of walnuts, not including the "momentum" payment, was about $0.40 per pound below prices being paid by Diamond's competitors. This gap was considered unusual and unprecedented.[12] To close the gap in payments to the walnut growers, Neil issued an extraordinary and unusual payment to growers of $0.30 per pound, termed the "momentum" payment. This payment was treated by the finance team as an advance for the 2011 crop and therefore was excluded from 2011 fiscal year's reported earnings. The payment, however, was paid to all growers who delivered the 2010 walnut crop to Diamond, including those not under contract to deliver a 2011 crop and those who ultimately did not deliver a 2011 crop.

The fiscal year 2010 "continuity" payments and the fiscal year 2011 "momentum" payments could be termed "earnings management" activities. As noted in this case, the SEC took exception to the earnings management methods used by Diamond. But not all methods used to increase net income are unethical.

EARNINGS MANAGEMENT METHODS

Earnings management is the purposeful intervention in the external financial reporting process with the intent of obtaining some private gain.[13] Several methods may be used to manage earnings. Accruals management (AM) is the manipulation of accounting accruals (or prepayments) in order to manage earnings. AM is relatively common and relatively easy to justify since it is based on accounting estimates and assumptions. Real transaction management (RTM) involves the timing and structuring of actual business activities in order to achieve a desired financial reporting result.[14] Non-GAAP earnings management is another type of earnings management where GAAP (Generally Accepted Accounting Principles) is violated in order to manipulate the reported earnings number. Although both AM and RTM do not generally violate GAAP, there may be instances when AM does violate GAAP.[15]

In his article "Overvaluation and the Choice of Alternative Earnings Management Mechanisms," Brad Badertscher argues that there is a pecking order to managing earnings. He argues that firms are likely to first use AM because it does not affect business operations and therefore is the least costly form of earnings management. But use of AM is limited because of the reversing nature of accruals. RTM generally follows AM but is more costly than AM because it impacts the company's long-term performance. In addition, companies will eventually run out of RTM opportunities and either stop managing earnings or transition to the most costly form of earnings management.[16] Companies use non-GAAP earnings management because it is difficult to detect and enables large-scale changes to reported earnings. Yet Badertscher argues that non-GAAP earnings management is the most costly form of managing earnings because of legal fees and capital market costs once the GAAP violation has been revealed. Therefore, non-GAAP earnings management is generally the last method used to manage earnings.

Auditors have the responsibility to conduct their audit to provide reasonable assurance that there are no material misstatements in the financial statements. This responsibility includes ascertaining that any "earnings management" techniques do not violate GAAP.

THE AUDITORS

Neil approved the walnut cost and determined the accounting for walnut payments. He supervised Diamond's finance and accounting team ("finance team") and the team that managed relationships with growers ("grower relations team"). As the CFO, Neil directly interacted with Diamond's external auditors. Neil prepared an internal memorandum each quarter that justifyed the quarterly estimated cost of walnuts and a memorandum to the external auditors that justifyed the final walnut costs. The SEC notes that the auditors relied on the memos when issuing their opinions about Diamond's financial statements.[17]

FISCAL YEAR 2010

During the audit of the 2010 financial statements, the auditors asked Neil for information to justify his decision to account for the "continuity" payment as an advance on the next year's crop of walnuts. The SEC contends that Neil made material misrepresentations to the auditors and withheld material information from them. Specifically, he falsely stated that walnut growers had asked for an advance payment for next year's crop and omitted the fact that he and other Diamond representatives had assured growers a competitive price for the current year.[18] Further, the auditors relied on a "management representation letter" that Neil signed, which stated that the "continuity" payment was for the 2010 crop and did not represent a payment for 2009 walnut costs. Mendes was cognizant of representations made to the external auditors and signed the related management representation letter related to the 2010 financial statements audit.[19]

FISCAL YEAR 2011

Neil continued to manipulate walnut costs during fiscal year 2011. In e-mails, Neil referred to the walnut costs as a "lever" to manage earnings in Diamond's quarterly financial statements. As a result of the cost manipulations, Diamond reported EPS that met or exceeded analysts' expectations for every quarter in 2011. It should be noted that Diamond's stock price was central to a proposed acquisition of a major potato chip business unit in spring 2011.[20] The company's stock price reached approximately $92.50 per share in September 2011.

EPILOGUE

DIAMOND FOODS

As a result of media speculation of accounting irregularities and an internal investigation, Diamond Foods issued restatements on November 14, 2012. Around the time of the announcement, the price of Diamond's stock declined to approximately $15.40 per share.

Diamond Foods, Inc., without admitting or denying the allegations, agreed to pay $5 million to settle the charges filed against it by the SEC.[21] Diamond also consented to the entry of a permanent injunction against future violations of the relevant securities laws.[22]

MICHAEL MENDES

Michael Mendes, Diamond's former CEO, agreed to settle charges against him by paying a civil money payment of $125,000 to the SEC and agreeing to "cease and desist" from committing or causing any future violations of Sections 17(a)(2) and (a)(3) of the Securities Act as well as other Sections and Rules of the Exchange Act.[23] In addition, Mendes returned or forfeited more than $4 million in bonuses and other benefits he received as a result of Diamond's allegedly fraudulent financial reporting.[24]

STEVEN NEIL

The SEC's litigation against Steven Neil, Diamond's former CFO, continues and, at the time of this writing, is still pending.[25] The SEC is seeking several things from Neil, including:

- Permanently enjoining Neil from directly or indirectly violating certain rules of federal securities laws;
- Prohibiting Neil from serving as an officer or director of any entity having securities registered with the SEC pursuant to the Exchange Act;
- Surrendering any wrongfully obtained benefits (Neil received $1.18 million in bonuses, including $687,043 tied to meeting EPS goals);
- Reimbursing Diamond for all compensation received or obtained during the relevant statutory time period established by Section 304 of the Sarbanes-Oxley Act (SOX); and
- Paying civil penalties.[26]

GENERAL QUESTIONS:

1. In this case, Diamond Foods was accused of "managing earnings" in an unethical manner. Provide two specific examples of how a company could *ethically* improve net income.

2a. Why do you think accounting personnel (the "finance team") seemed to "go along" with the schemes to understate the cost of walnuts in both fiscal year 2010 and fiscal year 2011? Provide as many possible reasons you can think of.

2b. Instead of agreeing to record the extra payments to growers as "advances" and, in effect, helping the company falsify the financial statements, what other alternative actions were available to the finance team? Consider professional standards, such as the *IMA® (Institute of Management Accountants) Statement of Ethical Professional Practice* or the AICPA (American Institute of Certified Public Accountants) Code of Professional Conduct, when answering this question.

3. At the time of this writing, charges against Steven Neil, the former CFO of Diamond Foods, were still pending. Conduct research to determine the status of these charges. In your opinion, why do you think Michael Mendes, the former CEO of Diamond Foods, chose to settle charges with the SEC, whereas Neil is disputing the charges?

AUDITING QUESTIONS:

4. Describe the "fraud triangle." Discuss the components of the fraud triangle in the context of this case.

5a. The auditors were misled by both Michael Mendes and Steven Neil. Neil even signed a "management representation letter." Describe what a "management representation letter" is. Do you believe that it, and other representations by management, constituted sufficient appropriate audit evidence in this case? Defend your answer. (Hint: Review the requirements of Statement on Auditing Standards (SAS) No. 99, paying particular attention to the concept of fraud risk factors ("red flags") in an auditing context.)

5b. Describe what the terms "analytical procedures" and "professional skepticism" mean in an auditing context. Do you think the auditors *should have* discovered the alleged fraud perpetrated in the financial statements in fiscal year 2010 and fiscal year 2011? Defend your answer.

5c. Conduct research as to (1) who the auditors were during the timeframe of this case and (2) the current status of any litigation against the auditors. Discuss any allegations against the auditors, including your opinion as to the merits of the allegations.

6. If the auditors *had* discovered the alleged fraud, what is the appropriate action, or series of actions, for an audit firm of a publicly traded company (such as Diamond) that becomes aware of illegal acts by the client's management?

COST/MANAGERIAL ACCOUNTING QUESTIONS:

7. How could management accounting tools, such as variance analysis, benchmarking, and Cost-Volume-Profit analysis, have been used to highlight Diamond's profitability challenges?

8. How could the budgeting process have been used to help Diamond achieve its targets *without* resorting to the alleged financial statement irregularities?

9. Reconcile the 2010 walnut cost payments with the final walnut cost of $0.74 per pound recorded in the 2011 financial statements.

10. Why was the 2010 "momentum" payment larger than the 2009 "continuity" payment? If the earnings management was not exposed, do you believe the earnings management could have continued? If the earnings management did continue, how would it likely have been done?

11. Describe the different reasons for managing earnings.

12. What are the disincentives for managing earnings?

13. Which IMA ethical guideline(s) was violated by Diamond's CFO?

ENDNOTES

[1]The material presented in this case was drawn from several SEC accounting and auditing enforcement releases, litigation releases, and administrative proceedings. Since some of the information from these sources is overlapping, endnotes include the primary sources where the information is located.

[2]U.S. Securities & Exchange Commission (SEC), Litigation Release No. 22902, January 9, 2014, www.sec.gov/litigation/litreleases/2014/lr22902.htm.

[3]SEC, Administrative Proceeding File No.3-15674, In the Matter of Michael Mendes, Respondent, January 9, 2014, www.sec.gov/litigation/admin/2014/33-9508.pdf.

[4]Learn more about Diamond Foods at www.diamondfoods.com/about.

[5]Fiscal year 2010 ended July 31, 2010.

[6]SEC, Litigation Release No. 22902.

[7]SEC, Administrative Proceeding File No. 3-15674.

[8]Fiscal year 2011 ended July 31, 2011.

[9]SEC, Litigation Release No. 22902, and SEC, Administrative Proceeding File No. 3-15674.

[10]SEC, Litigation Release No. 22902.

[11]Ibid.

[12]SEC, Complaint relating to Case 3:14-cv-00122, Securities and Exchange Commission v. Steven Neil, January 9, 2014, www.sec.gov/litigation/complaints/2014/comp-pr2014-4-neil.pdf.

[13]Katherine Schipper, "Commentary on Earnings Management," Accounting Horizons, December 1989, pp. 91-102.

[14]Amy Zang, "Evidence on the Trade-Off between Real Activities Manipulation and Accrual-Based Earnings Management," The Accounting Review, March 2012, pp. 675-703.

[15]Brad A. Badertscher, "Overvaluation and the Choice of Alternative Earnings Management Mechanisms," The Accounting Review, September 2011, pp. 1,491-1,518.

[16]Michael Ettredge, Susan Scholz, Kevin R. Smith, and Lili Sun, "How Do Restatements Begin? Evidence of Earnings Management Preceding Restated Financial Reports," Journal of Business Finance & Accounting, April/May 2010, pp. 332-355.

[17]SEC, Securities and Exchange Commission v. Steven Neil.

[18]Ibid.

[19]SEC, Administrative Proceeding File No. 3-15674.

[20]SEC, Securities and Exchange Commission v. Steven Neil.

[21]SEC, Litigation Release No. 22902, and SEC, Complaint relating to Case 3:14-cv-00123, Securities and Exchange Commission v. Diamond Foods, Inc., January 9, 2014, www.sec.gov/litigation/complaints/2014/comp-pr2014-4-diamond.pdf.

[22]SEC, Litigation Release No. 22902.

[23]SEC, Administrative Proceeding File No. 3-15674.

[24]SEC, Litigation Release No. 22902.

[25]Ibid.

[26]SEC, Securities and Exchange Commission v. Steven Neil.

Sunk Costs: What Costs Do You Sea?

Marty Stuebs and Cari Edison, Baylor University; Katy Hurt, Independent External Auditor

COMPANIES' RESPONSIBILITIES FOR SAFETY ARE IMPORTANT SOCIAL AND ENVIRONMENTAL CONCERNS. This fictional case—inspired by recent actual events—presents a capital investment intended to improve cruise ship safety. Both managerial accounting investment analyses and ethical recognition of responsibilities play necessary roles in the safety investment decisions. The case also refers to and encourages use of the *IMA® Statement of Ethical Professional Practice*.

The case blends managerial accounting and ethics, so it is suitable for a number of managerial accounting and accounting ethics courses. It was written for students in an undergraduate, advanced undergraduate, or graduate managerial or cost accounting course. It should be used after students have practiced NPV and payback period capital investment techniques. Since the case integrates capital investment analyses within a larger analysis and considers professional responsibilities (in particular, the IMA Statement of Ethical Professional Practice) in the presence of incentives, it can be used in an accounting ethics course as well. The case can also be simplified and adapted for use in lower-level managerial accounting classes.

Keywords: capital budgeting, capital investments, safety investments, ethics, responsibility, managerial and cost accounting analysis, decision making.

Sunk Costs: What Costs Do You *Sea*?

Marty Stuebs
Baylor University

Cari Edison
Baylor University

Katy Hurt
Independent External Auditor

BACKGROUND

Festival Cruise Lines (FCL), a publicly traded company on both the New York Stock Exchange (NYSE) and London Stock Exchange, is the largest cruise company in the world. FCL serves as the parent company for four primary subsidiaries—a broad spectrum of cruise line brands that cater to a variety of cruise vacationers. At the low end, the first FCL subsidiary, Festival, offers an affordable cruise experience to a wide variety of cost-conscious customers. Other FCL subsidiaries, like Goddess Cruise Lines, American Swiss Cruise Lines, and Dranuc Cruise Lines, offer progressively higher-quality cruise experiences for correspondingly higher price premiums. FCL is domiciled internationally and has two headquarters located in Doral, Fla., an industrial area of Miami, and Southampton, England.

FCL's Festival subsidiary began entertaining passengers on its Happy Boats in 1972. Today, it employs upwards of 90,000 crew members who serve more than 3.5 million cruise passengers annually on a fleet of 24 ships. Cruises generally range from three to 18 days in duration, and the one-week cruise is the most common. Ships venture to a wide variety of world-wide destinations, including New Zealand, Tahiti, New England, Alaska, the Mexican Riviera, Caribbean, Mediterranean, and many more.

Festival finds itself in an industry that has evolved over the last century. The cruise ship industry was born in 1844. Focus shifted from carrying cargo to pleasing customers, and superliners were being developed by the early 20th Century. These ships provided an abundance of fine dining and leisure activities to affluent passengers and generally were not designed to cater to the general population. In the 1960s, cruise ship companies began shifting operations to attract a broader spectrum of middle-income clientele. While premium ships were still available, the days of the affluent Titanic-style voyages were becoming a thing of the past. Price competition began to slowly enter the market and dramatically increased in recent years. Call it the "Walmart-ization" of the cruise ship industry. The recent downturn in the economy put real pressure on potential passengers' discretionary income and, as a result, cruise ship prices. Containing and controlling costs in this environment is critical to a cruise ship company's success.

The cruise industry is also a high-fixed-cost industry. A typical cruise ship can cost $500 million, and larger and larger ships are being built. Given the enormous fixed costs, one of the greatest challenges facing the cruise ship industry today is utilizing capacity—filling ships with passengers and generating revenue. Festival's bottom line is extremely dependent on cruise ship passengers and ship occupancy levels. Projecting a healthy reputation to attract customers and maintain occupancy levels is important.

Festival generally has an impeccable history of safety. But increased competition and economic pressures in the industry recently created an additional bottom-line focus on cost control. Many safety repairs and investments had been tabled and delayed to increase ship turnaround, time at sea, revenue utilization, and ultimately profits. In1998, Festival ran into its first instance of trouble with a passenger-filled ship. Since that time, more than five ships have encountered disconcerting incidences—four incidences attributable to fires in engine rooms, laundry rooms, and a generator room.

INTRODUCTION

The office was quiet. The sunny spring weather in Miami, Fla., had lured many Festival Cruise Line (FCL) personnel to take an enjoyable Friday afternoon off. But Linda Wright, a senior accountant at FCL, and some of her accounting staff were still busy at work. It was late Friday afternoon; Linda took a brief pause to reflect on her career at FCL.

Linda Wright's name suited her perfectly. She did not like being wrong—carried herself with integrity and seldom made bad decisions. She had been attracted to Festival's culture and mission—to the happiness, joy, laughter, and entertainment FCL generated and brought to passengers on its Happy Boats. Miami also provided Linda and her family a picturesque destination to call home. FCL had been a great career choice for Linda. When she joined Festival, she was the sole female in the accounting department. Over the years, she had become a skilled accountant and excelled within the company.

Linda and her staff were busy putting together capital budgeting analyses for investment proposals and projects that had been submitted to the corporate office. Among the submitted proposals, Linda and a few of her colleagues—Matt Dennison and Evan Truett—were analyzing a capital investment proposal to improve the safety of the cruise ship fleet for FCL's Festival subsidiary. This capital investment analysis posed a real challenge to delicately balance bottom-line income considerations of controlling costs with adequate safety investment considerations for protecting cruise ship personnel and passengers and minimizing safety risks.

Linda recognized a few challenges with the safety investment proposal, and two were prominent. First, the developing analysis was based on many—often slippery—estimates. Although accounting can be perceived as black-and-white and relatively straightforward, Linda found herself in murky waters, collecting data and performing analyses that were largely based on educated estimates. What was the cost of an accident? What value should be placed on human injury? The team's estimates could influence analysis of the safety investment's viability and eventually influence FCL passenger and crew safety.

Second, Linda wondered how receptive executive management would be to a significant capital outlay designed to generate safety improvements but potentially offer little bottom-line benefit. Would the proposal be passed over for projects promising larger potential boosts to profits?

Bottom-line considerations were becoming a primary focus in executive decisions because of increasing price competition in the cruise industry and the increasingly tight economy.

Linda pondered her concerns: "How can I handle the uncertain estimates included in my analysis? What are my responsibilities to passenger and crew safety? How do I balance these responsibilities with controlling costs and profitability?" Linda Wright could not get this one wrong.

THE TURBULENCE

"What are you having for lunch today?" David asked with a jovial smile.

"Dave! Do you even have to ask? A spinach salad with smoked salmon and veggies," Linda replied.

"A creature of habit! You're a typical accountant," David nodded. "You need to live a little; try something different—even delicious. They're serving filet mignon today and look at these desserts!" David exclaimed as he took a bite of tiramisu.

Linda was having lunch in Festival's corporate cafeteria with David Santana, the head of Corporate Risk Management at Festival. David was a colleague and friend who Linda had known and respected for years—even if their dietary preferences were strikingly different. David was a bright, hard-working Peruvian immigrant who had worked his way up through the Festival ranks over the years. The capital investments in safety improvements were his brain child, and now he was audaciously championing the latest proposal.

In fact, the capital proposal for safety improvements had been a main topic of conversation during several lunches Linda and David shared over the last couple of months. David's concern for these safety improvements went beyond the professional; it was also personal. A few years earlier, an engine fire on the Festival ship Victory had created serious safety concerns. Mario Venasquez, one of David's Peruvian childhood friends, was a Festival employee on the ship. In fact, David was able to get Mario the job on the Victory so that he could help his family in Peru. Mario valiantly took action to fight the fire, and his responsive and courageous actions contained it, resulting in limited damage and minimal interruptions. The engine fire incident went virtually unnoticed to passengers. But Mario sacrificed his life to contain the engine fire—a tragic blow for David. This incident became the "canary in the coal mine" for David—a signal that Festival needed to change course and take corrective action to improve ship safety.

So conversation quickly returned to the safety investment topic as Linda and David started lunch. "Did you get our actuarial estimates on the probabilities and magnitudes of cruise ship safety accidents?" David queried.

"Yes, we did. Thank you. Matt and Evan added them into our capital investment analyses. In fact, we also finished extensive conversations with Festival's legal counsel," Linda replied.

"Oh? Great! Let me know if you have any questions or need any more data. What did legal have to say?" asked David.

"Well, according to the lawyers, Festival is currently meeting all international maritime safety standards. The safety improvements would go well beyond current international legal standards and requirements but would protect Festival in the future if laws change and safety requirements become more rigorous," Linda said.

"Well, that isn't all that surprising. The cruise ship industry has consistently lobbied lawmakers for years to keep safety regulation to a minimum," David revealed, "but Festival needs to be different." David's face reflected the passion resulting from the loss of his friend and his recent experiences.

"You're right. This is important for Festival," Linda affirmed.

"Our crew members, valued passengers, and shareholders need to be protected and reassured that we care about the safety of our people. I'm concerned that the Board of Directors is favoring cost control and financial considerations a little too much. Their minds are wrapped up in the current year's bottom line. I have championed safety investments for several years now and have been repeatedly turned down due to limited financial resources. Corporate needs to extend its vision beyond a myopic focus on the bottom line. This is about more than just profits; it's about people," David concluded.

Linda nodded empathetically. David was right. Festival executives selected capital investments primarily on the basis of a project's contribution to economic return and bottom-line impact. The lunch conversation continued and slowly meandered into casual chit-chat. Linda appreciated David as a Festival employee.

THE NUMBERS

"I just got an e-mail from John. Corporate is now breathing down our necks for the capital investment analysis information. We really need to wrap this up soon," Linda relayed as she rallied Matt and Evan during a brief powwow in her office. John Cary was Festival's current hard-charging CEO. Projects including the safety investment proposal had made it through the initial screening phase. Now executives wanted analysis information to rank proposals for possible selection and funding during the preference phase of analysis.

Linda's team had begun putting together the capital investment analyses for the safety investment proposal.

Linda decided to develop three estimates: one for what she viewed as the minimum investment required by adding emergency generators to each ship; one for installing the emergency generators and high-pressure water mist systems (an intermediate-level proposal); and one to fully fund all the recommended changes, including upgrading the engine rooms. Using these three alternatives, Evan and Matt began calculating the total number of annual cruise line passengers Festival can carry.

If Festival chooses not to invest in the expenditures, each ship has an available passenger capacity of 3,500. But under Festival's current operations, the ships are only at 90% capacity. Additionally, Festival's fleet of 24 ships cruise an average of 48 weeks out of the year. In order to make the minimal changes, the cruise schedule must remain the same to minimize the effect on capacity. The emergency generators will be installed during each of the ships' four weeks of dock time (52 weeks in a year – 48 weeks), so total passenger capacity will remain unchanged for this alternative.

If the midrange alternative is selected, substantial effects will be seen. Average available passenger capacity will remain unchanged at 3,500, but the utilization rate will be 90% for year one, 91% for year two, and 92% for years beyond year two. In order to install the generators and sprinkler systems, the ships will need to be docked for the repairs. Therefore, only 36 cruises can be operated in year one, 40 in year two, and 49 in years beyond year two.

If all repairs and upgrades are performed, the utilization rate will be 90% for year one, 93% for year two, and 96% for years beyond year two. On average, 30 one-week-long cruises will operate in years one and two, and 50 one-week-long cruises will operate each year after year two. Evan and Matt's findings and calculations are shown in Table 1.

Without any expenditures, Festival's cruise ships can carry approximately 3.629 million passengers per year on its fleet of 24 ships. Each passenger will generate $1,700 of revenue (sales price plus onboard spending). The variable costs are approximately $300 per passenger, and the fixed costs are around $3.6 billion per year. Linda's team also collected the information on the actuarial estimates, probabilities, and costs of possible expected accidents from David Santana. This information can be used to calculate an estimated expected value of the cost of accidents. The operating costs, total passenger capacity, and potential accident costs depend on which parts of Linda's recommendations are funded. In all three cases, Linda decided to leave the $1,700 selling price and onboard spending and $300 variable cost estimates in place. None of

Table 1: Festival Cruise Lines, Inc.: Annual Passenger Factors

	Current Operations	Minimum Funding	Midrange Funding			Complete Funding		
	(All Years)	(All Years)	Year 1	Year 2	After Year 2	Year 1	Year 2	After Year 2
1. Capacity Utilization Factor:								
Average available passenger capacity/cruise	3,500	3,500	3,500	3,500	3,500	3,500	3,500	3,500
Capacity utilization rate (average actual capacity/available capacity)	90.00%	90.00%	90.00%	91.00%	92.00%	90.00%	93.00%	96.00%
Capacity utilization factor (Number of passengers/1 week cruise)	3,150	3,150	3,150	3,185	3,220	3,150	3,255	3,360
2. Turnover Factor (Number of 1 week cruises/year)	48	48	36	40	49	30	30	50
3. Fleet Factor (Number of Cruise Ships/year)	24	24	24	24	24	24	24	24
Total Annual Festival Cruise Line Passengers	**3,628,800**	**3,628,800**	**2,721,600**	**3,057,600**	**3,786,720**	**2,268,000**	**2,343,600**	**4,032,000**

the changes were likely to impact those two figures. Total passenger capacity, investment costs, and fixed operating costs, however, are another story.

Making the minimum required changes would cost $100 million. Such minimal changes will have little impact on continuing capacity or efficiency, and during and after the repair process, total passenger capacity would remain unchanged. The investment would, however, somewhat reduce the probability of an accident. Linda and her team collected data on the likelihood and costs of accidents based on historical data in the industry. This information is included in Table 2.

Adding the emergency generators and installing high-pressure water mist systems on all ships will cost approximately $250 million. Linda expects these changes to improve efficiency enough to increase post-project annual passenger capacity to 2.722 million in year one, 3.058 million in year two, and 3.787 million in years following year two. Once the upgrades are made, the net annual fixed costs will decrease slightly to approximately $3.384 billion. The investments will also reduce the probability and projected costs of expected accidents.

If the Board of Directors will allow upgrades to the engine room as well, Linda estimates the upfront cost will be $300 million. Post-implementation annual passenger capacity will be approximately 2.268 million in year one, 2.344 million in year two, and 4.032 million in all years following year two. In addition, annual fixed costs will drop to around $3.240 billion, and the projected probabilities and costs of expected accidents will decrease as well.

Matt and Evan estimate that all of the capital investments will have a useful life of 15 years with no salvage value. Additionally, they conservatively assume that all capital investment outlays occur and begin to depreciate at the same time (i.e., time 0) even though complete installation of some considered alternatives will occur after the start of capital investment outlays (i.e., time 0).

Linda, with the help of Matt and Evan, input the information into a spreadsheet (see Table 2) in order to calculate the net present value (NPV) and payback period of the different funding options. For tax purposes, it is Festival's policy to depreciate capital investments using the straight-line method, and Festival's marginal tax rate (combined federal, state, and local) is about 40%. The hurdle (discount) rate is 10% after tax for all capital expenditures.

Festival's policy states that the company will only consider investing in capital projects with a positive NPV within five years to satisfy certain profitability thresholds. Also, it will only invest in capital projects with an unadjusted payback period of five years or less. Linda and her team used these standards to evaluate the different alternatives.

LINDA'S SITUATION

The analysis was coming together, but Linda began to replay executives' potential responses over and over in her head. Because of Festival's large size in the market, the public's eye is always on its stock price. CEO John Cary was well aware of this and never let anyone forget the importance of the bottom line. Even though Festival seeks to please its passengers, John and the rest of the top executives put pleasing shareholders as their first priority.

These thoughts left Linda somewhat anxious. Her analysis affected a significant number of people. What were her responsibilities to the executives and the Board of Directors, shareholders, Festival employees, Festival cruise ship personnel and passengers, and David? How could she balance and meet all of these responsibilities?

Table 2: Festival Cruise Lines, Inc.: Cruise Ship Safety Repairs and Upgrades Data
(All numbers shown in thousands except Variable Costs per Ticket and Sales Price per Ticket + Onboard Spending)

Initial Investment

Complete funding	$ 300,000
Midrange funding	$ 250,000
Minimum funding	$ 100,000

Depreciable life of investment	15

Operations Information:

Original Operations		With Capital Expenditures	
Costs:		**Costs:**	
Sales price per ticket + onboard spending	$ 1,700	Sales price per ticket + onboard spending	$ 1,700
Variable costs per ticket	$ 300	Variable costs per ticket	$ 300
Fixed costs	$3,600,000	Fixed costs	
		Complete funding	$3,240,000
		Midrange funding	$3,384,000
		Minimum funding	$3,600,000
Total Passengers (from table 1, rounded in the thousands)	3,629	**Total Passengers** (from table 1, rounded in the thousands)	
		Year 1, Midrange funding	2,722
		Year 1, Complete funding	2,268
		Year 2, Midrange funding	3,058
		Year 2, Complete funding	2,344
		Thereafter	
		Complete funding	4,032
		Midrange funding	3,787
		Minimum funding	3,629

Expected Accident Costs	Probability	Cost	Expected Accident Cost	Probability	Cost
			Complete funding		
Significant Accident/Event	3%	$ 160,000	Significant Accident/Event	1%	$ 100,000
Moderate Accident/Event	4%	$ 120,000	Moderate Accident/Event	1%	$ 80,000
Minor Accident/Event	5%	$ 80,000	Minor Accident/Event	1%	$ 60,000
No Accident	88%	0	No Accident	97%	0
			Midrange funding		
			Significant Accident/Event	1%	$ 120,000
			Moderate Accident/Event	2%	$ 100,000
			Minor Accident/Event	1%	$ 70,000
			No Accident	96%	0
			Minimum funding		
			Significant Accident/Event	1%	$ 160,000
			Moderate Accident/Event	2%	$ 120,000
			Minor Accident/Event	1%	$ 80,000
			No Accident	96%	0

Other Information					
Income Tax Rate:		40%	Hurdle (Discount) Rate:		10%

FESTIVAL CRUISE LINES CASE QUESTIONS

Would you do the right thing if you were Linda Wright? Answer the following case questions by preparing an analysis to guide Festival Cruise Line's decisions. Help Festival decide whether it should fully fund all of the recommended upgrades.

1. What are Linda's responsibilities in this situation? NOTE: You can apply the general standards in the *IMA Statement of Ethical Professional Practice* (available in Appendix A to help you identify specific responsibilities for Linda in this situation).

2. Complete the net present value (NPV) analysis and payback-period analysis required for Linda's report and prepare a discussion of your findings. Remember to use Festival's required five-year time horizon for your analyses. (The NPV and payback period analyses can be organized neatly in an appendix to your case analysis. A reader of your conclusions should be able to follow your work and computations. You can use an Excel spreadsheet. The results of your appendix analyses can be referenced in the body of your case to support your decision.) Based solely on the economics, what course of action should Linda recommend?

3. As Linda, what is your final decision and why? Assess the impacts of your final decision:
   a. What benefits/harms result and to whom?
   b. What rights are being exercised (denied) and by (to) whom?
   c. Do these impacts modify or change your decision? How?

APPENDIX A: IMA® STATEMENT OF ETHICAL PROFESSIONAL PRACTICE

STATEMENT OF ETHICAL PROFESSIONAL PRACTICE

Members of IMA shall behave ethically. A commitment to ethical professional practice includes: overarching principles that express our values, and standards that guide our conduct.

PRINCIPLES

IMA's overarching ethical principles include: Honesty, Fairness, Objectivity, and Responsibility. Members shall act in accordance with these principles and shall encourage others within their organizations to adhere to them.

STANDARDS

A member's failure to comply with the following standards may result in disciplinary action.

I. COMPETENCE

Each member has a responsibility to:
1. Maintain an appropriate level of professional expertise by continually developing knowledge and skills.
2. Perform professional duties in accordance with relevant laws, regulations, and technical standards.
3. Provide decision support information and recommendations that are accurate, clear, concise, and timely.
4. Recognize and communicate professional limitations or other constraints that would preclude responsible judgment or successful performance of an activity.

II. CONFIDENTIALITY

Each member has a responsibility to:
1. Keep information confidential except when disclosure is authorized or legally required.
2. Inform all relevant parties regarding appropriate use of confidential information. Monitor subordinates' activities to ensure compliance.
3. Refrain from using confidential information for unethical or illegal advantage.

III. INTEGRITY

Each member has a responsibility to:
1. Mitigate actual conflicts of interest, regularly communicate with business associates to avoid apparent conflicts of interest. Advise all parties of any potential conflicts.
2. Refrain from engaging in any conduct that would prejudice carrying out duties ethically.
3. Abstain from engaging in or supporting any activity that might discredit the profession.

IV. CREDIBILITY

Each member has a responsibility to:
1. Communicate information fairly and objectively.
2. Disclose all relevant information that could reasonably be expected to influence an intended user's understanding of the reports, analyses, or recommendations.
3. Disclose delays or deficiencies in information, timeliness, processing, or internal controls in conformance with organization policy and/or applicable law.

RESOLUTION OF ETHICAL CONFLICT

In applying the Standards of Ethical Professional Practice, you may encounter problems identifying unethical behavior or resolving an ethical conflict. When faced with ethical issues, you should follow your organization's established policies on the resolution of such conflict. If these policies do not resolve the ethical conflict, you should consider the following courses of action:

1. Discuss the issue with your immediate supervisor except when it appears that the supervisor is involved. In that case, present the issue to the next level. If you cannot achieve a satisfactory resolution, submit the issue to the next management level. If your immediate superior is the chief executive officer or equivalent, the acceptable reviewing authority may be a group such as the audit committee, executive committee, board of directors, board of trustees, or owners. Contact with levels above the immediate superior should be initiated only with your superior's knowledge, assuming he or she is not involved. Communication of such problems to authorities or individuals not employed or engaged by the organization is not considered appropriate, unless you believe there is a clear violation of the law.

2. Clarify relevant ethical issues by initiating a confidential discussion with an IMA Ethics Counselor or other impartial advisor to obtain a better understanding of possible courses of action.

3. Consult your own attorney as to legal obligations and rights concerning the ethical conflict.

The A-12 Stealth Bomber: Escalating Commitment to a Failing Project

David S. Christensen and Robin Boneck, Southern Utah University

THE A-12 WAS THE NAVY'S TOP AVIATION PRIORITY. The carrier-based stealth bomber was designed to replace the aging and crippled A-6 Intruder. In 1991 the program was cancelled due to cost overruns, schedule delays, technical problems, and a culture that suppressed bad news about the A-12 from Congress. To increase moral awareness, students are required to reflect, write about, and discuss the facts and moral implications of an ethical dilemma experienced by a cost analyst whose cost estimate about the A-12 was suppressed by supervisors in her chain of command.

Students use the IMA® Statement of Ethical Professional Practice as a framework to explore applicable values, standards, and actions. The case is designed for a graduate cost accounting course for both MBA and accounting students.

Keywords: moral awareness, ethics, values, escalation of commitment.

The A-12 Stealth Bomber:
Escalating Commitment to a Failing Project

David S. Christensen
Southern Utah University

Robin Boneck
Southern Utah University

INTRODUCTION

On January 7, 1991, Defense Secretary Richard Cheney announced that the Navy's A-12 stealth bomber project was terminated, citing severe schedule, cost, and performance problems as the reasons. It was the largest weapons system contract cancellation in the history of the Pentagon. In cancelling the program, a result of an investigative report conducted by Navy Principal Deputy General Counsel Chester Beach, Cheney claimed that no one could tell him how much the program was going to cost. In reality, there were many estimates of the final cost; some were more accurate than others. In an effort to save the program, the information forwarded to top military and civilian leadership was unreasonably optimistic.

For more information, read Brian Montgomery's article "How the A-12 Went Down," in the April 1991 edition of Air Force Magazine.

BACKGROUND

The A-12 was needed to replace the aging A-6E aircraft. The A-6A aircraft was first introduced in 1963 as the Navy's only day/night, all weather, medium-attack aircraft. A later version of the A-6, the A-6E, was also used to refuel other carrier-based aircraft. In the early 1980s the mission of the A-6E was greatly reduced due to wing cracks discovered in many of the aircraft. Defense Secretary Richard Cheney had recently grounded the A-6E due to cracks in its wings. Replacing the A-6E with the A-12 was the Navy's top aviation priority.[1]

According to the Government Accountability Office (GAO), on January 13, 1988, "the Navy awarded General Dynamics and McDonnell Douglas Aerospace corporations a $4.8 billion fixed-price incentive contract for the full-scale development of the A-12. The Navy expected that the A-12 will be significantly more capable and survivable against increasingly sophisticated air defense systems being deployed by the Soviets and third-world countries."[2]

Navy Captain Larry Elberfeld was designated as the program manager (PM). He was responsible for managing the A-12 program, including reporting on the program's cost, schedule, and technical progress in *Defense Acquisition Executive Summary* (DAES) reports. Elberfeld was required to complete a quarterly DAES report and provide it to the Navy Secretary of Defense, the Under Secretary of Defense for Acquisition, and the Assistant Secretary of Defense. In addition to periodically summarizing the cost, schedule, and technical status of a major defense acquisition program, its purpose was to provide early-warning information about actual and potential problems and corrective action plans. Chester Beach, Navy Principal Deputy General Counsel, conducted an investigation into the A-12 program and provided a description of Elberfeld's qualifications:

> "The PM (Elberfeld) is an Aviation Engineering Duty Officer, with three advanced degrees and a career path which would be a model in any of the new Service Acquisition Corps. He has been on-station for more than four years and was assigned

with the understanding that he would remain through first flight. In short, the PM (Elberfeld) in this case is the archetype of the well-trained, highly motivated professional, fully empowered to fulfill his responsibility and be accountable for cost, schedule, and performance of his program that we are seeking to develop under the acquisition corps plans and matrix management approach reflected in the Defense Management Report."[3]

Elberfeld had a civilian employee—Debbie D'Angelo—who had graduated with a Bachelor's degree in business from the University of Arizona. In August1988 she was cleared into the A-12 program and assigned as its lead cost analyst. She received the monthly *Cost Performance Reports* (CPRs) from the contractors. The CPRs were prepared by the contractors and showed actual cost incurred, the schedule status of the project, and estimates of final cost. The Navy needed this information to assess the cost and schedule status of the project. D'Angelo's job was to analyze the CPRs and provide findings, conclusions, and recommendations to Elberfeld and others higher in the chain of command. She had quarterly meetings with Elberfeld, where she provided A-12 program cost estimates developed from her examination of the monthly CPRs.

Initially the contractors estimated the total cost to complete the program would be $3.981 billion. This amount was well below the Navy's ceiling price of $4.8 billion, the maximum amount that may be paid by the Navy to the contractors. Using this information in November 1988, the A-12 Program Office released DAES report No. 1, consistent with the contractors' estimates. By the next month, however, the estimated final cost began to rise. D'Angelo regularly informed Elberfeld of the ever-increasing cost estimates. Per office policy, her official reports were to contain the required lowest estimate she could provide, but she also provided a range of other estimates she thought were more accurate.

Department of Defense experience in more than 400 programs since 1977 indicated that a range of estimated final costs can be computed using cost and schedule performance indices derived from the monthly CPR. The minimum value in this range was computed using a cumulative cost performance index. Larger and more accurate estimates of final cost are usually derived from indices of shorter periods, especially when performance on a program is deteriorating.

A Beach investigation review of D'Angelo's cost reports to Elberfeld showed that they

"contained a single point estimate based upon the cumulative cost performance index (CPI), rather than the Cost Analyst's best professional judgment. This comported with the standard practice of

her office, but facilitated reliance by the Program Manager upon the single written cumulative CPI-based estimate as her best estimate. Her supervisor stated that the practice of providing the cumulative CPI-based estimate as the written estimate, rather than the Cost Analyst's best estimate, was intended to afford the Program Manager maximum flexibility in representing his program."[4]

In early 1989, D'Angelo provided Elberfeld with a report estimating the final cost at $4.575 billion. She warned that if performance continued to decline, cost would go through the ceiling. In the worst-case scenario she estimated the final cost would be around $5 billion. Furthermore, she indicated that the first flight of the A-12 would be delayed by at least three months.

In February 1989, Elberfeld released DAES Report No. 2 with an estimated final cost at $4.12 billion, well below D'Angelo's more realistic estimates. Concerned that Elberfeld was ignoring her estimates, D'Angelo began complaining to her immediate supervisor, Robert Patterson. As far as she could tell, no action was taken on her several complaints. In spite of her warnings that cost would exceed ceiling by $200 million, Elberfeld released DAES report No. 3 in May 1989, using the much lower estimate of $4.415 billion.

In July 1989, D'Angelo again provided a report to Elberfeld that indicated cost would exceed ceiling by over $200 million, placing the total cost over $5 billion. Throughout the summer she continued reporting that costs were escalating, the weight of the aircraft was exceeding specifications by more than 3,800 pounds, and that no further weight savings were possible without altering other aircraft specifications.

In August 1989, Elberfeld produced DAES Report No. 4 by using the same low-ball numbers used in the prior report. Elberfeld chose to use the lowest estimate provided to him irrespective of higher estimates available and contrary to D'Angelo's professional judgment. According to the Beach investigation report, "his justification for this action was based upon other information which he believed would result in an improvement in the contractor team's cumulative cost performance."

Meanwhile, in August 1989, Tom Hafer, a senior budget analyst on Navy programs at the Department of Defense Comptroller's Office, visited McDonnell Douglas to review the status of the A-12 for budget planning purposes. He was in for a shock. Not only was there no production taking place, but the contractor hadn't even completed half the tooling to start production.

During his plant tour he received word that, upon returning to the Pentagon, Vice Admiral Richard Dunleavy wanted to see him. In his meeting with Dunleavy, Hafer revealed that he was going to recommend adjusting the military services budget upward to reflect cost and production schedule problems in a formal document known as a *Program Budget Decision* (PBD). This information would jeopardize the continuation of the A-12 project.

As part of the process of preparing the A-12 PBD, Hafer sent approximately six pages of questions to the A-12 Program Office. The office refused to send him written responses using the justification that this was a "special access" project. In order to obtain responses to his questions he was required to visit the office and review the written responses on location. He was not allowed to remove the written responses or take any notes. During his office visits he met with D'Angelo, who presented him with cost data but was under strict orders not to discuss the information with him.

Even with this limited access Hafer determined that the program was at least two years behind schedule and cost would exceed ceiling by at least $500 million. Being under hush orders, D'Angelo was unable to verbally acknowledge his concerns and understanding of the numbers. She did give a slight nod of her head, however, which he took as an indication of her agreement with him. Hafer's draft PBD was later withdrawn by Comptroller Sean O'Keefe due to heavy opposition from Elberfeld and others in higher authority in the Department of Defense.

According to a 1990 GAO report, in December 1989 Cheney ordered a review of four major aircraft programs in development: the B-2 bomber, F-22 fighter, C-17 cargo plane, and the A-12. This study, known as the Major Aircraft Review (MAR), was to validate the necessity for these programs in light of changing world threats, including the diminishing Soviet threat.[5]

The Office of the Secretary of Defense (OSD) Cost Analysis Improvement Group (CAIG) was charged with the duty of completing the MAR. Among other duties, the CAIG helps ensure that the costs of Department of Defense programs are presented accurately and completely. Jo Ann Vines, a cost analyst with the CAIG, was assigned to collect performance data on the A-12 program. D'Angelo was instructed to provide Vines with only the official program costs and exclude all other estimates. The official estimates showed the lowest possible final cost. D'Angelo provided Elberfeld with a range of higher estimates, however, that predicted severe cost overruns and schedule delays. At the official briefing, Vines asked D'Angelo if there were other cost estimates available other than the official CPRs.

D'Angelo responded in the positive, however, she did not offer to provide Vines with them, nor did Vines request to see them.

In March 1990, the OSD authorized an independent analysis of the cost and schedule status of the A-12, which was to be conducted by OSD Cost Analyst Gary Christle. Christle's analysis indicated that the program's estimated final cost would be $1 billion over ceiling and at least one year behind schedule. By this time the contractors' cost reports to D'Angelo showed growing cost overruns, and her analysis was consistent with Christle's.

On March 28, 1990, Christle briefed the A-12 Program Office on his analysis. He requested that D'Angelo be present in the briefing, which included Elberfeld, and D'Angelo's immediate supervisor, Patterson. Yet D'Angelo was purposefully excluded from the meeting—she believed it was at the request of Elberfeld, which he later denied. Shortly thereafter, on two occasions, Christle's report was briefed to the Under Secretary of Defense for Acquisition, John A. Betti. Yet, the Under Secretary did not consider the analyst's projections to be credible and did not pass the estimates on to the Secretary of Defense. According to a 1995 *Washington Post* article, on April 26, 1990, Cheney advised the House Armed Services Committee: "We think we ought to go forward with the A-12, that it's a good system, and that the program appears to be reasonably well-handled at this point."[6]

It wasn't until June 1, 1990, that the contractors publicly acknowledged that the scheduled first-flight would be significantly delayed, the contract cost would significantly exceed the contract ceiling (and could not be absorbed by the contractors), and the aircraft would not meet certain critical performance requirements (e.g., weight) specified in the contract. Cheney was outraged by this news and later testified to Congress that he had "gone forward to the Congress in good faith and presented the best information that was available to us then and then subsequently found that the information we'd been presented was not accurate."[7]

In July 1990, Navy Secretary Lawrence Garrett ordered an inquiry to investigate how and why the adverse information about the cost, schedule, and technical status of the A-12 failed to be reported to him and others. The Beach investigation resulted and determined that the earlier estimates supported by the contractors and the Navy were unrealistic and suggested that adverse information about the A-12 project may have been suppressed from Congress. The Beach investigation lasted three months. His team collected about 9,000 documents and interviewed 60 government and contractor employees. In his report, Beach concluded that,

"The PM (Elberfeld) erred in judgment by failing to anticipate substantial additional cost increases. His projections of completion at or within ceiling were unreasonably optimistic and not supported by the facts available to him. The PM (Elberfeld) also erred by failing to anticipate greater risk to schedule than was briefed at the Major Aircraft Review."[8]

In December of 1990, Secretary Cheney ordered the Navy to justify the A-12 program. He was unconvinced by their arguments, and on January 7, 1991, he cancelled the program. He later commented on his decision to cancel the program, saying:

"The A-12 I did terminate. It was not an easy decision to make because it's an important requirement that we're trying to fulfill. But no one could tell me how much the program was going to cost, even just through the full-scale development phase, or when it would be available. And data that had been presented at one point a few months ago turned out to be invalid and inaccurate."[9]

In the end, Elberfeld was denied a promotion to rear admiral. His promotion had been approved by the Senate on October 27, 1990. After the Beach report, Navy Secretary Garrett had second thoughts, denied the promotion, and assigned Elberfeld to other duties. Two admirals above Elberfeld—Vice Admiral Richard Gentz and Rear Admiral John Calvert—received letters of reprimand, and Under Secretary of Defense Betti resigned. According to Congressional investigators, cost analysts Hafer and D'Angelo did not escape unscathed. Each received downgraded performance ratings. Hafer was reassigned to missile programs, and D'Angelo left the Department of Defense for public health service. Christle left OSD a few years later. He was awarded the Defense Distinguished Service Medal, in part for his analysis of the A-12's cost difficulties. Additionally, the Navy sought to recover approximately $2 billion in payments to the contractors, which the contractors disputed in federal court.

REQUIREMENTS

Write an essay (three pages, double-spaced, one-inch margins) that analyzes the ethical issue that Debbie D'Angelo faced.

Include a brief description and explanation of the (1) ethical issue, (2) stakeholders, (3) alternatives with related consequences, and (4) an appropriate course of action for D'Angelo. Make specific references to relevant principles (values), standards, and actions recommended in the *IMA® Statement of Ethical Professional Practice* and excerpts from the Department of Defense's *Joint Ethics Regulation* (see appendices for statements).

Consider the following questions and be prepared to discuss your answers in class:

1. Did Debbie D'Angelo have an ethical duty to ensure that her cost estimate was not suppressed?
   i. Assuming D'Angelo was a CMA® (Certified Management Accountant), which overarching ethical principles (values) in the *IMA Statement* clarify her duty?
   ii. Assuming D'Angelo was a CMA, which responsibilities in the Standards section of the *IMA Statement* clarify her duty?
   iii. Which additional values listed in *Joint Ethics Regulation* are relevant to her situation?

2. How should D'Angelo have made her concerns known about the program manager's decision to suppress her cost estimate? How can the *IMA Statement*'s Resolution of Ethical Conflict section be applied to this case? Does it have any shortcomings?

3. In general, does a supervisor's escalating commitment to a failing project create a moral issue for the management accountant? Why or why not?

APPENDIX A: IMA STATEMENTS ON ETHICS

ETHICAL BEHAVIOR FOR PRACTITIONERS OF MANAGEMENT ACCOUNTING AND FINANCIAL MANAGEMENT (INTRODUCTION)

Practitioners of management accounting and financial management have an obligation to the public, their profession, the organizations they serve, and themselves to maintain the highest standards of ethical conduct. In recognition of this obligation, the Institute of Management Accountants has promulgated the following standards of ethical professional practice. Adherence to these standards, both domestically and internationally, is integral to achieving the Objectives of Management Accounting. Practitioners of management accounting and financial management shall not commit acts contrary to these standards nor shall they condone the commission of such acts by others within their organizations.

IMA STATEMENT OF ETHICAL PROFESSIONAL PRACTICE

Members of IMA shall behave ethically. A commitment to ethical professional practice includes overarching principles that express our values, and standards that guide our conduct.

Principles

IMA's overarching ethical principles include Honesty, Fairness, Objectivity, and Responsibility. Members shall act in accordance with these principles and shall encourage others within their organizations to adhere to them.

Standards

A member's failure to comply with the following standards may result in disciplinary action.

Section I. Competence

Each member has a responsibility to:

1. Maintain an appropriate level of professional expertise by continually developing knowledge and skills.
2. Perform professional duties in accordance with relevant laws, regulations, and technical standards.
3. Provide decision support information and recommendations that are accurate, clear, concise, and timely.
4. Recognize and communicate professional limitations or other constraints that would preclude responsible judgment or successful performance of an activity.

Section II. Confidentiality

Each member has a responsibility to:

1. Keep information confidential except when disclosure is authorized or legally required.

2. Inform all relevant parties regarding appropriate use of confidential information. Monitor subordinates' activities to ensure compliance.
3. Refrain from using confidential information for unethical or illegal advantage.

Section III. Integrity

Each member has a responsibility to:

1. Mitigate actual conflicts of interest. Regularly communicate with business associates to avoid apparent conflicts of interest. Advise all parties of any potential conflicts.
2. Refrain from engaging in any conduct that would prejudice carrying out duties ethically.
3. Abstain from engaging in or supporting any activity that might discredit the profession.

Section IV. Credibility

Each member has a responsibility to:

1. Communicate information fairly and objectively.
2. Disclose all relevant information that could reasonably be expected to influence an intended user's understanding of the reports, analyses, or recommendations.
3. Disclose delays or deficiencies in information, timeliness, processing, or internal controls in conformance with organization policy and/or applicable law.

Resolution of Ethical Conflict

In applying the Standards of Ethical Professional Practice, you may encounter problems identifying unethical behavior or resolving an ethical conflict. When faced with ethical issues, you should follow your organization's established policies on the resolution of such conflict. If these policies do not resolve the ethical conflict, you should consider the following courses of action:

1. Discuss the issue with your immediate supervisor except when it appears that the supervisor is involved. In that case, present the issue to the next level. If you cannot achieve a satisfactory resolution, submit the issue to the next management level. If your immediate superior is the chief executive officer or equivalent, the acceptable reviewing authority may be a group such as the audit committee, executive committee, board of directors, board of trustees, or owners. Contact with levels above the immediate superior should be initiated only with your superior's knowledge, assuming he or she is not involved. Communication of such problems to authorities or individuals not employed or engaged by the organization is not considered appropriate, unless you believe there is a clear violation of the law.

2. Clarify relevant ethical issues by initiating a confidential discussion with an IMA Ethics Counselor or other impartial advisor to obtain a better understanding of possible courses of action.

3. Consult your own attorney as to legal obligations and rights concerning the ethical conflict.

APPENDIX B: DEPARTMENT OF DEFENSE'S STATEMENT ON ETHICS

EXCERPT FROM THE DEPARTMENT OF DEFENSE'S JOINT ETHICS REGULATION

SECTION 4. ETHICAL VALUES

12-400. General. Ethics are standards by which one should act based on values. Values are core beliefs such as duty, honor, and integrity that motivate attitudes and actions. Not all values are ethical values (integrity is; happiness is not). Ethical values relate to what is right and wrong and thus take precedence over non-ethical values when making ethical decisions. DOD employees should carefully consider ethical values when making decisions as part of official duties.

12-401. Primary Ethical Values

a. **Honesty.** Being truthful, straightforward and candid are aspects of honesty.

   1. Truthfulness is required. Deceptions are easily uncovered and usually are. Lies erode credibility and undermine public confidence. Untruths told for seemingly altruistic reasons (to prevent hurt feelings, to promote good will, etc.) are nonetheless resented by the recipients.

   2. Straightforwardness adds frankness to truthfulness and is usually necessary to promote public confidence and to ensure effective, efficient conduct of Federal Government operations. Truths that are presented in such a way as to lead recipients to confusion, misinterpretation, or inaccurate conclusions are not productive. Such indirect deceptions can promote ill-will and erode openness, especially when there is an expectation of frankness.

   3. Candor is the forthright offering of unrequested information. It is necessary in accordance with the gravity of the situation and the nature of the relationships. Candor is required when a reasonable person would feel betrayed if the information were withheld. In some circumstances, silence is dishonest, yet in other circumstances, disclosing information would be wrong and perhaps unlawful.

b. **Integrity.** Being faithful to one's convictions is part of integrity. Following principles, acting with honor, maintaining independent judgment and performing duties with impartiality help to maintain integrity and avoid conflicts of interest and hypocrisy.

c. **Loyalty.** There are many synonyms for loyalty: fidelity, faithfulness, allegiance, devotion and fealty. Loyalty is the bond that holds the nation and the Federal Government together and the balm against dissension and conflict. It is not blind obedience or unquestioning acceptance of the status quo. Loyalty requires careful balancing among various interests, values and institutions in the interest of harmony and cohesion.

d. **Accountability.** DOD employees are required to accept responsibility for their decisions and the resulting consequences. This includes avoiding even the appearance of impropriety because appearances affect public confidence. Accountability promotes careful, well thought-out decision-making and limits thoughtless action.

e. **Fairness.** Open-mindedness and impartiality are important aspects of fairness. DOD employees must be committed to justice in the performance of their official duties. Decisions must not be arbitrary, capricious or biased. Individuals must be treated equally and with tolerance.

f. **Caring.** Compassion is an essential element of good government. Courtesy and kindness, both to those we serve and to those we work with, help to ensure that individuals are not treated solely as a means to an end. Caring for others is the counterbalance against the temptation to pursue the mission at any cost.

g. **Respect.** To treat people with dignity, to honor privacy and to allow self-determination are critical in a government of diverse people. Lack of respect leads to a breakdown of loyalty and honesty within a government and brings chaos to the international community.

h. **Promise Keeping.** No government can function for long if its commitments are not kept. DOD employees are obligated to keep their promises in order to promote trust and cooperation. Because of the importance of promise keeping, it is critical that DOD employees only make commitments that are within their authority.

i. **Responsible Citizenship.** It is the civic duty of every citizen, and especially DOD employees, to exercise discretion. Public servants are expected to engage personal judgment in the performance of official duties within the limits of their authority so that the will of the people is respected in accordance with democratic principles. Justice must be pursued and injustice must be challenged through accepted means.

Pursuit of Excellence. In public service, competence is only the starting point. DOD employees are expected to set an example of superior diligence and commitment. They are expected to be all they can be and to strive beyond mediocrity.

ENDNOTES

[1] U.S. Government Accountability Office, "Navy A-12: Cost and Requirements," December 31, 1990.

[2] *Ibid.*

[3] Chester P. Beach, *A-12 Administrative Inquiry: Memorandum to the Secretary of the Navy*, Washington, D.C., Department of the Navy, November 28, 1990.

[4] *Ibid.*

[5] U.S. GAO, 1990.

[6] George C. Wilson and Peter Carlson, "Stealth Albatross," *The Washington Post*, October 29, 1995.

[7] *Ibid.*

[8] Beach, 1990.

[9] James Perry Stevenson, *The $5 Billion Misunderstanding: The Collapse of the Navy's A-12 Stealth Bomber Program*, U.S. Naval Institute Press, Annapolis, Md., 2000.

Jensen Pharma: A Governance Role Play

J. Kay Keels, Coastal Carolina University; Norman T. Sheehan, University of Saskatchewan

JENSEN PHARMA IS A role play that explores governance and ethical issues where shareholder demands and stakeholder considerations are in direct conflict. Board members and the members of the firm's management team attending the meeting are asked to act out a broad range of issues, including concern for Jensen Pharma's shareholders, its stakeholders, their personal values, career progression, and personal wealth. Learning objectives include learning about the role of governance and applying best practice guidelines to improve governance, while recognizing the ethical leadership responsibilities of the board of directors. The role-play has been tested several times and 99% of masters students and managers recommended that instructors at other universities adopt the role play. The two most common reasons for recommending the role-play case were that users found it to bea fun, interesting, and engaging way to learn about governance, while others said it was a good way to see what boards do and learn about governance.

The role play is meant for undergraduate and graduate accounting capstone courses, as well as, management control, auditing, and governance courses to expose students to the challenges of governing organizations and making ethical decisions at the board level.

Keywords: governance, boards, ethics, agency theory, and pharmaceutical industry.

Jensen Pharma: A Governance Role-Play

J. Kay Keels
Coastal Carolina University

Norman T. Sheehan
University of Saskatchewan

INTRODUCTION

It is January 2012, and a special meeting of the Jensen Pharma board has been called. Jensen has a relatively small board in order to enhance its decision-making responsiveness and cohesiveness, which means that each board member must serve on several committees. Jensen's directors are compensated with Jensen stock options, which can only be exercised and sold at certain periods. A director can be expected to be awarded anywhere from 20,000 to 100,000 stock options each year depending on the number of committees he/she serves on and how many times these committees meet during the year.

Jensen is a relatively small, unlisted corporation. To date, Jensen has successfully delivered on its mission to help its patients live longer, pain-free lives through the use of effective pharmaceutical treatments. With sales of $300 million, Dekanor is Jensen's largest seller. It is a "blockbuster drug" that accounts for one-third of Jensen's annual revenues. Dekanor is an analgesic (i.e., painkiller) that is in the alpha-suppressing neural class of drugs. Dekanor was introduced over three years ago and quickly rose to be doctors' favorite prescription for patients suffering from acute chronic migraine pain. Jensen's current director of research, H. Phillips, led the team that brought Dekanor to the market, and Dekanor is seen to be a "career-maker" for Phillips and the other team members, such as the CIO, who were instrumental in getting the drug through the U.S. Food and Drug Administration (FDA) clinical trials in record time.

This special board meeting has been called to discuss a rumor that the FDA is considering banning Dekanor. The board meeting documents, which were sent out the day prior to meeting, include many financial, legal, and medical terms with which some board members may not be familiar. These documents are summarized here:

- Dekanor went through a total of six years of development, which is two to three years less than most other drugs, due to Jensen's skill in managing the FDA approval process. Dekanor's efficacy was tested on 1,100 patients, which is the minimum number the FDA will accept, at a cost of $675 million. The drug passed through the FDA clinical trials without any issues, so Dekanor is currently sold with the same drug product label information as other analgesic drugs (i.e., the drug label information outlines potential side effects of taking Dekanor, but does not mention the risk of death).
- Many patients report very high satisfaction with Dekanor, as it is more effective in combating chronic migraine pain than rival medications.
- Since being introduced, however, Dekanor has been associated with a large number of adverse cardiovascular events (typically heart attacks), some of which have resulted in death.
- An independent study found evidence to suggest that Dekanor may have contributed to some of these deaths; however, the number of patients studied was not large enough to be conclusive. The researcher who led the study, a prominent scientist from an Ivy League school, called for more studies of Dekanor, arguing that Dekanor "could very well be a ticking time bomb."
- Since the independent study was published, some doctors have publicly refused to prescribe Dekanor to their patients. Since Jensen has no alternative drug, these doctors began prescribing a rival's pain reliever for their patients, even though it is less effective.

- In response to the controversy surrounding Dekanor, some websites have emerged in support of Dekanor. Many of these websites are filled with Dekanor users pleading with Jensen and the larger medical community to keep Dekanor on the market. The document distributed to board members provides quotes from several websites carrying messages such as, "Dekanor has allowed me to live my life again. I can now play with my children and volunteer in the community. Thanks Dekanor!!!" and "Please keep Dekanor for me. I need it to survive my headaches." Still, there are also comments such as, "Dekanor stole my mother from me. Dekanor is a KILLER!!!"
- It is estimated that it will take a minimum of three years and $12 million for a large-scale, independent clinical trial to prove that Dekanor is a safe drug.
- Other pharmaceutical firms that have been found to knowingly sell drugs that harmed patients have faced lawsuits and been assessed fines between $50 million and $5 billion, depending on the number of deaths and culpability (i.e., how much blame could be assigned to the company for the deaths).
- Dekanor currently produces about half of Jensen's yearly profits of $250 million, and Jensen Pharma has no other drugs in its product development pipeline that have the potential to replace Dekanor's profits if it is banned.
- It is estimated that adding a drug warning label that clearly specifies the heart attack risk could result in a 50% drop in sales. On the other hand, the remaining 50% of existing patients are very satisfied with Dekanor and are not likely to switch to a rival's drug.
- A rival pharmaceutical firm has just announced that it plans to introduce a drug next month that also treats migraine symptoms with no proven fatal side effects.
- As Jensen is currently an unlisted corporation, its shares are publicly traded on the over-the-counter market. When the results of the independent study became public, Jensen's stock price decreased by 22%. Jensen's current over-the-counter stock price is $17 per share, which is down from a high of $30 a year ago. There are 53 million shares of Jensen Pharma outstanding.
- Jensen's board recognizes that it needs to spend even more on research if it is to successfully develop and bring new drugs to the market. To that end, the board has been in discussions about whether Jensen should be listed on the New York Stock Exchange (NYSE), so that the proceeds from an initial public offering (IPO) could be used to generate the much needed research funds.

In order to provide additional information to the board, Jensen's senior management team has been asked to attend the meeting to decide Dekanor's fate. The board chair (also the CEO) plans to open the meeting by proposing three alternatives for Dekanor. The board must select one of these alternatives by the end of the meeting:

1. Stop sales of Dekanor immediately and recall all inventory until an independent clinical trial has satisfactorily proven that Dekanor is not causing patients to die prematurely.
2. Add a warning label that clearly states that taking Dekanor may lead to adverse cardiovascular events that may result in death, and stop all direct advertising to consumers and promotion of Dekanor to doctors, but continue to sell it to those doctors who request it.
3. Continue efforts to market Dekanor aggressively and take any necessary legal, political, and other actions to prevent the FDA from banning Dekanor.

INSTRUCTIONS TO STUDENTS:

1. Read the case background information and the assigned readings prior to the class.
2. Roles for the 14 role-players and understudies will be assigned by the instructor in advance of class or in the class when the role-play is to be discussed.
3. As a designated role-player, you should meet with your understudy, read your assigned role, and prepare notes on points your character should emphasize during the board's discussion of Dekanor. Do not share any of the private information contained in your role with other role-players prior to the board meeting.
4. Acting as you think your assigned character would, be prepared to state your preferred alternative during the board meeting and explain why you support that alternative. During the board discussion, you may consult with your understudy (who should sit near you), but be discreet so as not to interrupt or distract other board members.
5. The board meeting will be timed, and the board must reach a decision before adjournment.

ROLES FOR EACH OF THE 14 ROLE-PLAYERS

Note to instructors: Students should receive copies of their assigned roles only. No role-player should be given any information or description about any of the other role-players' roles.

Jensen's Board Members and Senior Management Team Members Attending the Special Dekanor Board Meeting

1. **C. Jensen, M.D., CEO and chairperson of the board (ex-officio member of all board committees):** C. Jensen is concerned about the effect that a reduction in Dekanor's sales will have on Jensen's future share price (C. Jensen owns the single largest block of Jensen shares, worth $90 million at the current over-the-counter market share price), and its ability to raise funds through an initial public offering. Still, as the only child of the founder, C. Jensen is also very concerned about preserving his image and the image of Jensen Pharma.

2. **M. Jensen, offspring of C. Jensen, member of the board (member of ARCo and Nominating Committees):** M. Jensen operates a consulting firm, MJ Associates, which does most of its business with Jensen Pharma. M. Jensen owns almost 4% of Jensen stock, which was given by the parent, C. Jensen. M. Jensen has been pushing the board to execute an initial public offering (IPO) quickly in order to fund the development of new drugs. Concerned about the current management team's lack of responsiveness to Jensen's shareholders, M. Jensen was recently quoted in The Wall Street Journal saying, "Jensen's management team needs to be reminded that they were hired by Jensen's shareholders, NOT its stakeholders."

3. **L. Vayan, member of the board (chair of Governance Committee, member of Compensation Committee):** With 28 years of experience in the pharmaceutical industry, Vayan knows that all drugs carry some risk. Vayan is the CEO of RAV Pharmaceuticals, a pharmaceutical supply company that is one of Jensen's largest suppliers. Vayan has 300,000 stock options.

4. **D. Charles, retired, member of the board (chair of ARCo and Nominating Committees and member of Governance Committee):** As a retired insurance executive, Charles is very concerned about the liability implications of the Dekanor issue. At the last board meeting, Charles requested that Jensen increase its liability coverage on its directors and officers (D&O) insurance policy to $10 million per director, but this request has not been honored yet. Charles owns a considerable amount of Jensen stock and stock options.

5. **B. Garrison, M.D., member of the board (chair of Compensation Committee, member of Nomination and ARCo Committees):** As a practicing physician, Garrison has been prescribing Dekanor to patients for years without any issues. The fact that the doctors that Garrison talks to have been using Dekanor for over three years indicates that it has value. Garrison owns 50,000 shares of Jensen stock as well as 300,000 stock options.

6. **Y. Boiki, member of the board (member of ARCo, Compensation, and Governance Committees):** This is Boiki's first board meeting with Jensen Pharma. Last year, Boiki's firm built the mansions that C. Jensen, CEO and chair of Jensen, and his offspring now occupy. C. Jensen was so impressed with Boiki's business acumen and ability to handle the municipal authorities that he recently recruited Boiki to Jensen's board.

7. **H. Phillips, M.D., Ph.D., director of research:** Phillips was instrumental in getting Dekanor on the market in record time and under budget. For that reason alone, Phillips was named director of research three years ago. Phillips is aware of the deaths linked to Dekanor but often says, "It is a very safe drug when compared to alcohol and tobacco; it is even safer to take Dekanor than texting while driving!" Phillips has a significant number of stock options.

8. **J. Vance, J.D., corporate legal counsel:** Vance is a high profile litigator and attorney who is well-versed in lobbying and fighting the FDA. Vance has a significant number of shares and share options that will be used to fund his/her retirement.

9. **E. Rollins, M.D., Ph.D., assistant director of research:** Rollins is the youngest research scientist ever to hold to such a high corporate position. Rollins earned a stellar reputation as one of the pharmaceutical industry's brightest young stars while working as an assistant to Dr. John Lee, a former head of the FDA. One of Dr. Lee's strongest beliefs was that the medical profession and pharmaceutical industry should never do anything that would endanger people's lives. Given that Rollins recently joined Jensen, Rollins does not own any shares or share options.

10. **D. Stone, director of public relations:** Stone is responsible for shaping the company's public image and has been invited to the meeting to be certain that Jensen can "spin" whatever option the board chooses in a positive way. Stone has 200,000 share options.

11. **R. Johnson, CMA, vice president and CFO:** Johnson's principal concern is for the company's financial performance. Johnson constantly reminds the board that any significant drop in the sales of Dekanor would significantly hurt Jensen's future profitability. Johnson will also remind the board that the patents on Jensen's other two best-selling drugs will expire in the next two years. Johnson has a significant number of shares and options.

12. **L. Goodson, vice president of human resources:** Goodson is widely recognized as a humanist, meaning the values of compassion, integrity, and justice play a central role in Goodson's dealings with others. Goodson is known to be uncomfortable with the argument that Jensen must place shareholders' demands above stakeholders' concerns.

13. **N. Greene, vice president of marketing:** Greene has led a very successful marketing campaign for Dekanor since it was introduced to the market three years ago. Greene is very confident that Jensen's marketing group can continue to generate strong revenue numbers as long as the company continues to market Dekanor aggressively.

14. **T. Garcia, chief information officer:** Garcia is an excellent CIO, meticulously keeping every file relating to Jensen's drug testing trials, some of which have never been released to the FDA or the public. Garcia has a number of shares and share options.

ROLE OF C. JENSEN, M.D.
CEO and chairperson of the board, Jensen Pharma

As Jensen's board chair and CEO, you will be responsible for directing the discussion and ensuring that everyone is heard. You must lead the board to a decision by the end of the time available, since some board members have to leave immediately after adjournment to make a scheduled flight.

Your general philosophy about meetings is to try to allow for various sides of the issue to be discussed before a decision is reached. Legally speaking, a majority vote is required to reach a decision. You prefer a consensus decision, but in any case, a formal vote must be taken at the end of the meeting. As board chair, you do not vote unless there is a tie, at which time your vote will break the tie. The board's decision, whether by consensus or by majority vote, must be formally recorded in the meeting's minutes to be available to stockholders at a later date.

Personally, you are of two minds: (1) You are concerned about the effect that a reduction in Dekanor's sales will have on Jensen's future share price (you own the single largest block of Jensen shares, which are worth $90 million at the current over-the-counter market share price) and the firm's ability to raise funds through an initial public offering. (2) On the other hand, you are also committed to having this company—which you have led through its period of greatest growth—maintain its image of honesty and integrity. To honor this commitment, Jensen must act in ways that convince the public that it is devoted to its patients' well-being, not just the wealth of its shareholders. Ultimately, you know that is how you and your family (which founded the company) will be judged in history.

As chair of the Jensen Pharma board, you will:

1. Call the special board meeting to order when indicated by the instructor;
2. Review each option for Dekanor;
3. Ask each individual at the meeting to introduce him/herself and explain what option he/she thinks the board should choose (i.e., option 1, 2, or 3) and why he/she supports this option;
4. Ensure that everyone has a chance to speak; and
5. Call for a vote of the board when time expires or when directed to do so by the instructor. (NB: Only the five board members are allowed to vote. The chair does not vote unless there is a tie.)

ROLE OF M. JENSEN
Offspring of C. Jensen (board chair), member of Jensen's board of directors and president of MJ Associates, consultants

You operate a consulting firm, MJ Associates, which does most of its business with Jensen Pharma. You own almost 4% of Jensen stock, which was given to you by your parent, C. Jensen. As you repeatedly remind the other board members, you own the second largest block of stock, worth $36 million at the current share price. You also own 300,000 stock options that you earned during your tenure as a board member, which are worth several more millions. The value of your shares and options have dropped over $30 million in the last year, so you are very concerned about the potential effects that the FDA's ban of Dekanor could have on Jensen's future share price and the firm's ability to execute an initial public offering. Having been closely involved in the drug industry since birth, you are acutely aware of Jensen's need to invest funds into the development of new drugs if it is to survive in the longer term, and thus you have been pushing the board to list Jensen on the NYSE quickly, and then do an initial public offering (IPO).

You have recently become increasingly disturbed about management's apparent responsiveness to stakeholders' demands. In a well-publicized statement that appeared in The Wall Street Journal, you stated, "Jensen's management team needs to be reminded that they were hired by Jensen's shareholders, NOT its stakeholders."

A suggestion was recently sent to you by a corporate lobbyist in Washington. He suggests that it might be possible to bring political pressure to bear on the FDA by securing the cooperation of the current secretary of the Department of Health and Human Services (of which the FDA is an agency). The secretary might be willing to postpone the FDA ban until independent testing can show Dekanor is safe, a result that is anticipated within three to four years. In the best case, the secretary might even be persuaded to overrule any ban proposed by the FDA, since the ban would represent a major precedent that increases the power of the FDA at the expense of drug companies and their rights to free enterprise. Getting the secretary to go along with this plan might require some major financial contributions to the president's re-election campaign. Either way, these tactics would buy Jensen the time it needs to complete an IPO, the proceeds from which would allow the firm to develop some new blockbuster drugs to replace Dekanor.

ROLE OF L. VAYAN
Member of Jensen's board of directors and CEO of RAV Pharmaceuticals

You have 28 years of experience in the pharmaceutical industry, having served 12 years as a senior manager in several large international pharmaceutical companies, and the last 8 years as a CEO of a pharmaceutical supply company, RAV Pharmaceuticals. Jensen is one of your larger customers, making up almost 10% of RAV's sales. Due to cash flow problems, Jensen has not paid its invoices for six months and now owes RAV $8 million. You have served on the board for four years and have 300,000 stock options, but, to date, you own no stock.

You have heard from several industry insiders that prescription drugs kill more people in North America than illegal drugs. Given that all drugs carry some risk, you favor permitting patients and their doctors to decide what is best for them. Although you are unsure of the board's legal exposure, you feel that the best path for Jensen is to maintain pressure on the FDA, to continue to aggressively market Dekanor, and to do whatever the firm can to avoid having the drug banned. Otherwise, you fear that your Jensen stock options will be worthless, and the $8 million owed to RAV will never be paid.

ROLE OF D. CHARLES
Member of Jensen's board and retired CEO of an insurance company

You were first elected to Jensen's board 12 years ago when you were the CEO of a well known insurance company. As chair of Jensen's ARCo (Audit, Risk, and Compliance) Committee, you were annoyed when this meeting was called, for two reasons: First, while you have heard allegations that Dekanor is not safe, you have nonetheless been told repeatedly by management that it is safe. And second, you were supposed to play golf with your usual foursome today and had to cancel at the last minute in order to attend this meeting.

As a retired insurance executive, you are well aware of the liability implications of the Dekanor issue. At the last board meeting, you requested that Jensen increase its liability coverage on its directors and officers (D&O) insurance policy to $10 million per director, but this request has not been honored yet. Still, even if the board votes to add a warning to Dekanor's product label, you doubt that $10 million in D&O insurance will be enough to cover the personal liability if Jensen's directors are later found negligent.

Given this, your professional experience indicates a conservative approach should be considered. You want to bring up these issues in the meeting, as well as the fact the board has never discussed its risk tolerance level. How much risk is the board comfortable with, and how much risk is too much? You want to ensure that Jensen's board makes the right decision, as you own a considerable amount of its stock and stock options, and you are counting on the proceeds from these holdings to fund the rest of your retirement.

ROLE OF B. GARRISON, M.D.
Member of Jensen's board of directors and practicing physician

You are aware of the bad publicity surrounding Dekanor. As a practicing physician, you have been prescribing Dekanor to your patients for three years, and you have seen nothing wrong with it. At the last American Medical Association meeting, other doctors with whom you have spoken reported similar experiences. Your thought is that an appeal should be sent to all doctors to protest the FDA's threat to ban Dekanor on the grounds that a ban would be violating a physician's right to prescribe the most effective drugs. The fact that some of the doctors you talked to have been using Dekanor for over three years indicates that it has value.

You have been a member of the board of directors for eight years and own 50,000 shares of Jensen stock as well as 300,000 stock options that you have been awarded for serving on Jensen's board. When you checked Jensen's over-the-counter share price this morning, you saw that 120,000 of these stock options are still exercisable at prices lower than the current stock price of $17, so you are eager to avoid any imprudent decisions regarding Dekanor at this meeting.

ROLE OF Y. BOIKI
Member of Jensen's board of directors and CEO of a property development firm

You have just been summoned to your first board meeting with Jensen Pharma. You are the CEO of a successful local property development firm. Last year, your firm developed the land and built the mansions that C. Jensen, CEO and chair of Jensen Pharma, and his offspring now occupy. C. Jensen was so impressed with your business acumen and ability to handle the authorities that he recently recruited you to fill the position as an independent director on Jensen's board. You have been since informed you that you will be appointed to Jensen's ARCo (Audit, Risk, and Compliance), Compensation, and Governance Committees.

As this is your first introduction to Jensen Pharma's board and its senior management team, you want to make a good impression. If pushed, you would admit to feeling very nervous, as you are ill prepared to vote on such an important issue. Given that your background is in civil engineering and construction, you feel as unprepared as a university student walking into a final exam without ever having opened the text. You regret that you have not had more education and exposure to the pharmaceutical industry and its legal issues before joining the board.

You have come to the special meeting with very positive impressions of Dekanor, as your mother-in-law uses it and speaks very highly of it. You are, of course, worried about the personal liability issues as a director and do not want to be associated with any product that causes harm to humans. At the end of the day, however, you just want to fit in, so you will "go along, to get along."

ROLE OF H. PHILLIPS, M.D., PH.D.
Director of research, Jensen Pharma

You were instrumental in getting Dekanor on the market in record time and under budget. For that reason alone, you were named director of research three years ago, the position you currently hold. As head of Jensen's research division, you are aware of the deaths linked to Dekanor. As you often tell anyone who will listen, however, "It is a very safe drug when compared to alcohol and tobacco; it is even safer to take Dekanor than texting while driving!"

Although it is the only product of its kind that Jensen produces to help lessen migraine symptoms, you know there are negative side effects. You feel that it is only because of Jensen's superior marketing, its direct advertising to consumers, and its aggressive sales force pushing it on physicians that Dekanor has fared so well against rival migraine drugs. You want to remind the board again that it has become increasingly difficult for companies with smaller research budgets, like Jensen, to develop and bring new products to the market because of the lengthy and exhaustive testing requirements of the FDA. It now requires almost $1 billion to develop and bring a new drug to market. Drug companies typically test 5,000 to 10,000 compounds for their ability to treat a disease, and of these only 4 to 5 make it to the next phase, which is clinical testing on human subjects. Typically, only one of the compounds tested on humans will be approved by the FDA and then brought to market. You will tell the board that without the profits from Dekanor, Jensen will not have the resources to finance new drug research unless Jensen quickly does an initial public offering to raise the needed research funds.

You have been awarded a significant amount of Jensen stock options since being named director of research and would like to have a chance to exercise these so you can fund your children's educations.

ROLE OF J. VANCE, J.D.
Corporate legal counsel, Jensen Pharma

You want to present two legal options to the board. The first is to negotiate with the FDA to place a black box warning on Dekanor in lieu of banning Dekanor. Black box warnings, the strongest issued by the FDA, are placed on a drug's label to alert patients to life-threatening risks associated with the drug. Requiring a black box warning label is the last step that the FDA will take before banning that drug from the market. You feel the FDA can be persuaded to accept this option with some arm twisting.

A second, much more aggressive option was suggested to you by another Jensen attorney. She has seen the Dekanor issue develop over the past year, and she thinks that it would be possible to delay any action by the FDA using legal means. She suggests that Judge Kent of Atlanta (someone you know personally) would be willing to serve an injunction on any FDA action. This injunction would prohibit the FDA from banning Dekanor until a formal hearing could be held. The results of the hearing, if unfavorable, could be appealed. In effect, the case could be tied up in the courts for three to five years, allowing Jensen time to execute an initial public offering to fund the development of new drugs. You have been given a significant number of shares and options that you hope will fund a prosperous retirement in a few years.

ROLE OF E. ROLLINS, M.D., PH.D.
Assistant director of research, Jensen Pharma

You are the newest member of the management team and the youngest research scientist ever to be promoted to such a high corporate position. You earned an international reputation as one of the brightest young stars in the pharmaceutical industry very early in your career when you worked as the assistant to Dr. John Lee, a highly respected member of the scientific community and former head of the FDA. One of Dr. Lee's strongest beliefs was that, above all, the medical profession—and, by extension, the pharmaceutical industry—should never do anything that would endanger people's lives. He was also a fervent advocate of the FDA and the important role that it plays in maintaining the nation's health and welfare. As your mentor, Dr. Lee instilled those same values in you.

You have not been with Jensen very long, so you do not own any stock options. Your highly regarded reputation, however, practically ensures that you will have a very long and highly lucrative career. Therefore, you do not want to do anything that would displease your mentor or damage your standing in the scientific community. You studied with the researcher at the Ivy League university who led the study that indicated that taking Dekanor may increase the risk of heart attacks. You know this individual is an outstanding researcher with impeccable standards, and if she found evidence that Dekanor is dangerous, it is based on solid, scientific research.

In your opinion, you do not feel the board fully understands the risks involved with keeping Dekanor available for sale. You want to remind the board, in a way that will not alienate your boss, H. Phillips (whom you have every reason to suspect will strongly support continuing the sale of the drug), that the ultimate purpose of Jensen Pharma is to make people's lives better, not to make money.

ROLE OF D. STONE
Director of public relations, Jensen Pharma

As the company's primary interface with the public and most especially with the press, you are responsible for shaping the company's image. Since the issues to be discussed at the special meeting are so sensitive and the decision will have such a huge impact on Jensen, you have been invited to the meeting to be certain that you can "spin" whatever option the board chooses in a positive way.

You have two ideas to help place a favorable spin on each option. If the board goes with Option 1, to remove Dekanor from the market, you will use Johnson & Johnson's (J&J) experience with Tylenol as a guide. Once J&J found that an individual was tampering with Tylenol and individuals were being harmed, it immediately removed all Tylenol from the market. This decision was very costly for J&J in the short term, but this action built J&J's reputation as being a company that puts its patients' well being ahead of profitability; a reputation that J&J effectively leveraged for years. You feel that by removing Dekanor at this point, Jensen could make a strong case that the company cares for its patients more than profits, and Jensen could then leverage this reputation to market its other drugs effectively.

If the board decides to proceed with Option 2 or 3, then you will propose a two-pronged attack. First, you will begin a campaign designed to smear the reputation of the independent researcher at the Ivy League school. Second, you plan to attack the premise of the research study, perhaps by arguing that the study did not adequately control for pre-existing heart conditions, which may explain why Dekanor was found to be associated with a higher incidence of heart attacks. If you can convince the public to believe that the researcher is incompetent and her study is flawed, this will significantly lessen the pressure on the FDA to ban Dekanor.

ROLE OF R. JOHNSON, CMA
Vice president and CFO, Jensen Pharma

As CFO of the corporation, your principal concern is for the company's financial performance (although you also own a significant number of Jensen stock options, which you are relying on to fund your retirement). You are not a member of the board; nonetheless, you attend all board meetings in order to speak to the effect any board decisions may have on the company's bottom line. You will remind the board that any significant drop in the sales of Dekanor would reverse the trend of strong growth in profits that has been characteristic of Jensen's performance under the leadership of its current CEO. In addition, any such adverse trend would further drive down Jensen's share price and significantly hurt its ability to execute an initial public offering (IPO). You also want to make the board understands that the ability to fund R&D is the key to Jensen's long-term success, as there are no drugs in the pipeline to replace the lost revenue if Dekanor's sales slump. In addition, the patents on the other two of Jensen's best-selling drugs will expire in the next two to three years, which means the income from these drugs will fall significantly.

If you are feeling grumpy, you may also add that the research director, H. Phillips, whom you dislike, has not successfully introduced any new drugs to the market since Dekanor three years ago, meaning the research director is a "one-hit wonder." You can also use this opportunity to point out to the board that if Jensen is to survive, it needs to hire a new research director, as its future lies in bringing new drugs to market. Since your bonus, the value of your stock options, and also your job depend upon the well-being of the company's financial condition, you have a substantial personal stake in rejecting or delaying any action that would remove Dekanor from the market.

ROLE OF L. GOODSON
Vice president of human resources, Jensen Pharma

As head of human resources, your primary concern is for the company's employees. You are widely known as a humanist; the values of compassion, integrity, and justice are very important to you as a person and as an HR professional. You are extremely uncomfortable with the argument that Jensen must place shareholders' concerns for profits above stakeholders' concerns for patients' well-being. Even though you have 40,000 stock options, you personally can see a clear answer to the debate of shareholder versus stakeholder. If it were left to you, you would live Jensen's mission and place patients' health concerns over the shareholders' desire for profits.

You are not a member of the board, but you attend all board meetings in order to provide advice as to how board decisions may impact the well-being of Jensen's employees. You know that a decision to remove Dekanor from the market immediately would create a human resources nightmare, as the decision would mean closing one or more of Jensen's production facilities as well as one of its R&D labs. As a result, several hundred people would lose their jobs, and it would fall to you to decide who has to go. While you will inform the board of the negative impact a decision to stop selling Dekanor would have on many of Jensen's employees, you would like to see Dekanor removed from the market immediately, and you feel that it should only be re-introduced when it has been proven safe.

ROLE OF N. GREENE
Vice president of marketing, Jensen Pharma

As vice president of marketing, you have led a very successful marketing campaign for Dekanor since it was introduced to the market three years ago. You have every confidence that your marketing group can continue to turn in a strong performance as long as the company continues to market Dekanor aggressively. Given the negative publicity currently surrounding Dekanor, you favor instituting a new advertising campaign aimed directly at consumers and physicians.

You are not a member of the board, but you attend all board meetings to provide input on marketing issues when called upon. At today's meeting, you will begin by reminding the board that a new migraine drug is due to be released by a rival firm shortly, and you fear that if Jensen recalls Dekanor at this time to conduct independent testing, or if Jensen even stops aggressively promoting it, the rival's new drug will steal most, if not all, of Dekanor's market share. Given this, you want to make an especially strong case to keep Dekanor on the market and to launch a new marketing campaign. You know that you are on the short list of CEO candidates at a well-known firm in another industry, and if you are to be considered as a finalist for this position, you need to make a strong impression right now.

ROLE OF T. GARCIA
Chief information officer, Jensen Pharma

As chief information officer, you have worked diligently to protect Jensen Pharma's information systems. Competing in the pharmaceutical industry requires the very best in corporate information security. New and unpatented drugs are the frequent targets of those who seek to steal company secrets because the next big blockbuster drug can be worth billions.

You have meticulously kept every file relevant to Dekanor since the early days of its initial development, and you feel very confident that all of the Dekanor computer files are safe from any sort of illegal hacking. If the FDA begins formal investigations, however, your careful preservation of the Dekanor records could end up harming the company, since there were some troubling findings of side effects in the early testing of Dekanor that were never released to the FDA or made public. You are thinking that it might be a good idea to very quietly put together a small team that would be prepared to take immediate and decisive action to destroy any potentially damaging files. You realize that you could end up being the ultimate scapegoat, regardless of which way things go.

II. Operations, Process Management, and Innovation

General Lab

Oriol Amat and Martí Guasch, Universitat Pompeu Fabra

GENERAL LAB IS A CASE STUDY that shows the current situation of a European company operating in the healthcare industry. In particular, General Lab has conducted clinical analysis and managed clinical laboratories in Spain since the early 1990s and has expanded its operations in Europe in the past decade. The case presents information from different corporate areas (strategy, quality, human resources, control, and internationalization) so that students obtain information from many different perspectives. The appendices at the end of the case provide financial information that's compared to General Lab's main competitor, Laboratorio Dr. F. Echevarne. The purpose of the case is for students to identify the factors that explain General Lab's success.

The target audience of the case is MBA students. But, it can be used in a variety of environments, from a meeting with senior executives to undergraduate students in the final years of their degree.

Keywords: business strategy, growth, mergers, healthcare industry.

The Association of
Accountants and
Financial Professionals
in Business

General Lab

Oriol Amat
Universitat Pompeu Fabra

Martí Guasch
Universitat Pompeu Fabra

INTRODUCTION

General Lab is a corporation created in 1991 that is dedicated to conducting clinical analysis and managing clinical laboratories. Since 2005, it has been the leading laboratory group in Spain and has been profitable since its beginning. The company's headquarters is in Barcelona.

The idea to create General Lab arose from the desire to launch a large private laboratory using the latest techniques in business management. The mission was to become the leading clinical laboratory company in Catalonia, Spain, in two years and eventually become a leader in Europe. To do so, the company needed to provide the best service to the prescribing physician and the patient at a controlled and efficient cost. It was a matter of modernizing the clinical laboratory industry, or clinical analysis as a business, from the standpoints of production, quality, and efficiency, as well as that of a service firm.

Josep Ignasi Hornos Vila, clinical analysis specialist and PDD of IESE, and Jesús Mª Martínez Larrañaga, industrial engineer and PADE of IESE, developed a business plan that included three stages of activity: (1) treat 1,000, (2) 2,000, and (3) then 4,000 patients daily. The initial break-even point for the company stood at an annual net revenue of €4.2 million. Vila, future general manager of General Lab, contacted Carles Sumarroca Coixet, future president of General Lab, to obtain financial partners. Larrañaga, future manager, contacted Luis de Jaureguizar, general manager

of Quinta de Salud La Alianza hospital, to ensure that the project gained an important client as a partner.

START OF OPERATION

General Lab was officially established on July 5, 1991. This entailed multiple and ongoing management meetings oriented toward establishing values, objectives, criteria, and procedures to strengthen the strategy and culture of the new company.

A new, large clinical laboratory was built—more than 1,600 square feet in dimension—on the premises of the Hospital Universitario Sagrat Cor de Barcelona, owned by the Quinta de Salud La Alianza. Operations officially began on December 2, 1991.

From the beginning, General Lab received support and cooperation from suppliers, which allowed them to pay their debts in 180 days instead of 90 to 120 days—the standard in the industry at that time.

A MULTIDISCIPLINARY SHAREHOLDING

One of General Lab's unique features was a shareholding that integrated executives (23%), clients (26%), and business and financial shareholders (51%). The initial capital of €600,000 was distributed among various shareholders (see Table 1).

This shareholding had placed more priority on growth targets and creating long-term value than receiving dividends in the short term.

Table 1 General Lab Initial Shareholding	
Quinta de Salud La Alianza	18.0 %
Carles Sumarroca Coixet	14.0 %
Josep Ignasi Hornos Vila	14.0 %
Joaquim Sumarroca Coixet	10.0 %
Tirce, S.A.	8.0 %
Mercè Fulquet Azustench	7.0 %
Pere Sumarroca Coixet	7.0 %
Lluís Coll Huguet	5.0 %
Remei Cirera Rafanell	5.0 %
Proelec, S.A.	5.0 %
Jesús Mª Martínez Larrañaga	4.0 %
Joan Torres Picamal	1.5 %
Jordi Escribà Nadal	1.5 %
Total	00.0 %

A RELEVANT INDUSTRY WITH A HIGH LEVEL OF COMPETENCE

In the United States, the economic cost of clinical laboratories represents 4% of total public health, but it influences and is directly related to 70% of all medical decisions. The work of the clinical laboratory has three distinct phases (see Figure 1). Of all these phases, the analytical has been, up to the present day, the principle task. In many cases, it's the only one in the vast majority of clinical laboratories. Currently, the analytical process is increasingly likely to be not only automated but also robotic. Preanalytical and postanalytical phases are the true indicators of quality in clinical laboratories and will be increasingly so in the future.

Unfortunately, many clinical laboratories worldwide hold principles that aren't up-to-date—they meet the conditions of the industrial age from 100 years ago: a division of labor, division of management, separation of doing and thinking, reward for work, and so on. In many clinical laboratories, 21st Century technology is in the hands of a late 19th to early 20th Century management style.

The net revenue of private sector clinical laboratories in Spain is about €700 million a year. It's a highly competitive industry in price and quality. Unlike other European countries, Spain has no price regulation or official price rate. Often, companies within the industry have to operate at near-impossible prices, as some patients require free analysis or services.

GENERAL LAB'S STRATEGY AND BUSINESS MODEL

MISSION, VISION, AND VALUES
General Lab has a clear orientation toward business. Its main goal is to be a business leader, and it's essential for the motivation of its team to be able to carry out a large number of tests with high quality assurance in minimum periods of time and at low costs. Table 2 presents General Lab's mission, vision, and values.

Figure 1
Operational Phases of a Clinical Laboratory

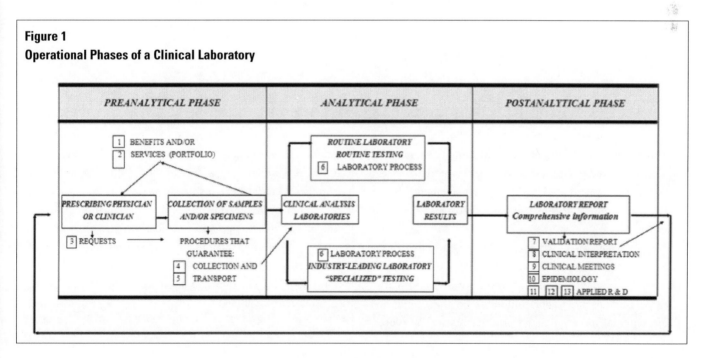

Table 2
General Lab's Mission, Vision and Values

WHAT DO WE WANT TO DO?

MISSION

TO OFFER THE BEST DIAGNOSTIC SERVICE WITH MAXIMUM TECHNICAL AND HUMAN QUALITY AND WITH ECONOMIC EFFICIENCY

WHAT DO WE DO?

VISION

GENERAL LAB IS A PROVIDER OF OPTIMAL AND EFFICIENT, CLIENT-ORIENTED SERVICES WITH THE AIM OF CONTINUOUSLY IMPROVING:

- Our organization and its expansion (be the industry leader)
- Our proximity to patients
- Our level of innovation and competitive differentiation
- Our overall quality of personalized service for each patient

OUR VALUES

- WE ARE MANAGERS AND COLLABORATIVE PARTNERS OF THE HEALTH LABORATORY
- WE ARE A TEAM OF EXPERTS IN ALL ASPECTS: TECHNICAL, MANAGERIAL, INFORMATION SYSTEMS, CUSTOMER SERVICE, AND BUSINESS
- WE OFFER PERSONALIZED SERVICE TO EACH PATIENT
- WE INNOVATE AT ALL LEVELS: MANAGEMENT, TECHNICAL, INFORMATION SYSTEMS, ETC.
- WE ARE LED BY INDUSTRY PROFESSIONALS AND NOT BY FINANCIAL GROUPS

STRATEGY

The clinical laboratory as an organization is a service company that is included in what are called "new technologies." Currently, the environment of these emerging technologies is defined by three realities: the globalization of markets, media technology, and total quality as a management culture. These three realities are subject to many changes, such as society itself.

As a service company, it's essential that a clinical laboratory is fully oriented toward the client. That is, the client should be the focus of the company strategy. Also, it's necessary to know and understand the two distinct types of clients: external and internal. External clients are considered prescribing physicians, patients, insurance companies, hospitals, mutual accident insurance and prevention services companies for large companies, pharmaceutical companies, public sector companies, and other clinical laboratories. Internal clients are employees of the company, shareholders, suppliers, and financial institutions.

General Lab's strategy is comprehensive and it covers the management of people, new technologies, the most efficient processes, total quality, and continuous innovation. Vila explains, "All activities involve costs, not all add value. Only some involve differentiation, and very few provide a competitive advantage."

This strategy allows General Lab to formulate annual goals related to:

- EBITDA (earnings before interests, taxes, depreciation, and amortization) increases in relation to sales.
- Reduction of operating costs, such as salaries, transportation, and consumables.
- Absenteeism reduction (not including maternal/paternal or long leaves).
- Increasing training hours.
- Reducing incidences.
- Meet inventory targets and delivery commitments.
- Increasing publications, conferences, and scientific articles written by employees.

HUMAN RESOURCES

Given the need to diagnose, satisfy, and retain different types of patients, managing people is a key strategic element in achieving the objectives of a clinical laboratory. As with any service provider in a clinical laboratory whose essential product is to provide a service that protects the health of others, people are the most valuable resource of the organization. It requires managing with a comprehensive vision of the laboratory and leadership capable of developing and integrating work teams and guiding them toward achieving the company's objectives.

General Lab's human resources policy is based on several pillars:

- A network organization (horizontal and decentralized) whose decisions are made close to where the service is provided. Thus, the continuous improvement and involvement of all employees is promoted, which maintains ongoing innovation.
- Training efforts: General Lab is the most active laboratory in all forums (business, technical, and scientific).
- Placing importance on motivation.
- A compensation policy that has a variable component based on goals and metrics; variable compensation considers what people do, rather than his or her academic status. Table 3 shows an example of how General Lab computes the incentive to be received by the head of a technical department. The incentive depends on the achievements of various targets based on cost, productivity, and quality indicators.
- Consensus with union representatives considering that General Lab has had a workers committee since its inception.

TOTAL QUALITY

Total Quality means obtaining internal and external client satisfaction with economic efficiency. Total Quality encompasses all services, processes, data analysis, and reports performed by the clinical laboratory, and it's based on several pillars: people, technology, quality management, client proximity, and economic efficiency (see Table 4).

Table 3
Example of Annual Incentive Based on the Achievement of Objectives

	Indicator	Objective	Metrics	Starting Point	Period Indicator	Maximum Incentive	Objective Achieved	Incentive per Indicator
1	Direct cost	5% reduction in relation to last year	Direct costs/No. of determinations	4.63	3.57	€750	Yes	€750
2	Productivity	5% increase in relation to last year	No. of determinations/ No. of full working days	11.734	15.757	€750	Yes	€750
3	Consumable ratios	Don't exceed preestablished limits	No. of determinations consumed/ No. of informed determinations	Hemo = 1.17 / Coag = 1.68 / Bioq = 1.17	Hemo = 1.2 / Coag = 1.43 / Bioq = 1.12	€750	Hemo not Only 66.7%	€500
4	External quality control	Keep unacceptable results under General Lab's average	% unacceptable results	5.13	3.9	€750	Yes	€750

Table 4
Pillars of Total Quality at General Lab

1. **HUMAN CAPITAL (professional and constantly motivated)**
   - NETWORK ORGANIZATION
   - TRAINING
   - INFORMATION (COMMUNICATION)
   - RESEARCH AND DEVELOPMENT
   - INCENTIVES

2. **AVAILABILITY OF CUTTING-EDGE TECHNOLOGY**
   - SET OF INSTRUMENTS
   - ROBOTICS
   - COMPUTER SCIENCE AND TELECOMMUNICATIONS

3. **QUALITY AND OPTIMAL SERVICE DELIVERY**
   - CERTIFICATIONS AND ACCREDITATIONS
   - QUALITY MANAGEMENT AND INSPECTION UNIT
   - TOTAL QUALITY CONTROL UNIT
   - INDICATORS OF QUALITY (CLIENT PERCEPTION)

4. **PROXIMITY TO THE CLIENT**
   - EXTERNAL (CLIENTS, PHYSICIANS, HOSPITALS, ADMINISTRATIONS, CENTERS, AND INSTITUTIONS)
   - INTERNAL (WORKERS AND ORGANIZATIONS)
   - PREDICT AND MEET THEIR EXPECTATIONS

5. **ECONOMIC EFFICIENCY**
   - BEARABLE COST, NOT THE LOWEST COST
   - QUALITY/SERVICE/PRICE BALANCE
   - BUDGETS AND COST ACCOUNTING
   - ANALYSIS OF NONQUALITY COSTS

To achieve these objectives, it's necessary that all members of the laboratory are quality managers. All people have the responsibility of quality management (prevention, self-control, continuous improvement, and to perceive everything from the perspective of a demanding client).

Total Quality policy is one that favors a balance between the objectives of quality, price, and service to be achieved globally but also at the level of each employee since each is like a small business. Competitiveness requires economic efficiency (bearable cost) that must be balanced with the quality of services provided. These objectives depend on very distinct issues:

- Quality largely depends on the professionalism of the members of the laboratory.
- Service depends on the expectations of the internal and external client. A key aspect of the company is managing complaints, as it has been found that a well-solved complaint means that the client becomes five times more loyal to the company.
- Price acquires its value and measurement when compared to laboratory competitors.

The challenge for the company is to find an appropriate balance between these three objectives.

General Lab was the first hospital clinical laboratory in Spain to receive ISO 9002:1994 certification in 1997 and ISO 9001:2000 in 2001. The latter is a comprehensive management system certification that promotes continuous improvement of all processes and seeks maximum client satisfaction with economic efficiency. For this purpose, the company measures client satisfaction. Periodically, internal management would conduct audits, and the official certifying body would conduct an annual audit.

INFORMATION SYSTEMS

General Lab is committed to pioneering innovative information systems. It began its operations with a powerful computer system that had its own new program called "WinLab," which was designed according to Vila's instructions and specifications and provided various innovations:

- Double coding per patient (a code per patient and another code for extraction or sampling).
- Barcode labels for positive identification of all biological samples and all analytical requests.
- Optical answer sheets for analytical requests.
- A display screen and barcode reader in each extraction or sampling room.
- Preanalytical incident control and daily reporting thereof to all sending centers as the best instrument for continuous improvement.
- Full validation levels (technical, departmental, and patient).
- Varied printed results with a cumulative report of the history of the last six requested analytical results.
- Cumulative reports from the patient.
- Analytical and statistical reports for large clients.
- Attendance monitoring for staff.
- Inventory program.

The complete computerization of information permits the tracking of all processes and people involved for all analysis requests. This combined with the streamlining of those processes enables General Lab to achieve cost leadership, which is essential in an industry where prices are very tight, and meet excellent delivery deadlines.

The company controls each key performance indicator (KPI) for various laboratories on monthly bases, including:

- The measurement of the activity; number of determinations (analysis) and requests or orders (patient).
- The average of determinations by petition.
- Costs per determination (raw material, production personnel, maintenance, and depreciation).
- Productivity (number of tests per full-time production employee).
- Absenteeism (hours not worked/contracted hours).
- The distribution of productive staff by category (physicians, nurses, technicians, administrative, and other).

TECHNICAL INNOVATION

Besides management innovation, General Lab also prioritizes technical innovation. This translates into significant advances in various types of analysis—for example, amniotic fluid QF-PCR (prenatal diagnosis), breath test (Helicobacter pylori), human papilloma virus detection, industrial toxicology (biological control), and drug abuse testing detected through saliva and sweat.

IMAGE

From its inception, General Lab established a powerful image, especially in its logo (Figure 2); a test tube shaped like the letter "g" in a tiny blue box, which was developed through a major marketing effort. This image and logo are present throughout the company.

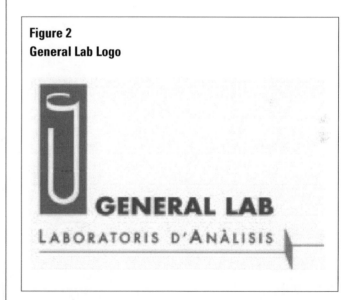

Figure 2
General Lab Logo

EXPANSION

General Lab has experienced exponential growth since its early years, which is consistent with the goal that inspired the company's strategy.

GROWTH STRATEGY

To grow, rather than competing with other companies, General Lab opted for integration (outsourcing) with existing clinical laboratories. Thus, it obtained large volumes of analytics, achieving scale economies, and making available a complete network of laboratories and collection centers that would be able to offer services to large clients globally while optimizing their level of quality and client service.

Therefore, General Lab's main path to growth and expansion has been the outsourcing of clinical laboratories in hospitals, mutual accident insurance companies, and other laboratories (eventually 40 in total). It has always had the support and consensus of workers committees and unions, and by outsourcing, it has successfully integrated all of the center's staff.

Growth Strategy Phase 1:
Incorporation of the Shareholders' Laboratories
In its early years, General Lab incorporated different shareholders' hospital laboratories with their corresponding personnel:

> Hospital Central L'Aliança – Barcelona, 1992
>> C.E.T.I.R. Laboratorio de RIA – Barcelona, 1992
>> Clínica Quirúrgica Onyar – Girona, 1992
>> Clínica de Ponent – Lleida, 1993
>> Clínica L'Aliança – Vic, 1993
>> Clínica L'Aliança – Sabadell, 1993

In these centers, General Lab installed emergency rooms with their own computer system and connected them to the central laboratory in Barcelona, thus providing continuous service 24 hours a day, 365 days a year.

Growth Strategy Phase 2:
Integration of Other Laboratories
Subsequently, after General Lab incorporated the shareholders' hospital laboratories, the technical position of the laboratory was stabilized. In 1993, it gained major clients including ONCE Catalunya, Servicios Penitenciarios del Departament de Justicia de la Generalitat de Catalunya, Telefónica Catalunya, and Mutua Metalúrgica de Accidentes y Enfermedades Profesionales. Agreements were established with private labs for them to work as state-assisted centers in Vic, Girona, Lleida, Sabadell, and Mataró.

In addition, they began to integrate personnel and the analytical operations of other clinical laboratories:

> MIDAT, Mutua Metalúrgica Barcelona –1993
> S.E.A.T. Factoría Zona Franca, Barcelona –1994
> General Lab – Dr. Euras – Vic, 1994
> General Lab – Dr. Vidal – Tarragona, 1994
> General Lab – Dr. Esteve – Girona, 1994
> General Lab – Dr. Colldeforn – Mataró, 1995
> General Lab – Dr. Olivé – Sabadell, 1995

Simultaneously, General Lab expanded into medical centers, healthcare companies, businesses, mutual accident insurance companies, and public agencies. In 1993, expansion also began in the rest of Spain, initiating operations in Valencia and Santander where the association of General Lab Cantabria was established.

GENERAL LAB GROUP

Since 1994, the General Lab Group has been comprised of three types of clinical laboratories:

- Owned laboratories- General Lab holds 100% of the property.
- Participating laboratories- those in which there isn't total shareholder participation. In the majority of cases, the participation exceeds 50% of the shares.
- Collaborating laboratories – those in which there is no shareholding. In this case, a cooperation agreement is signed where General Lab benefits from the healthcare network of the collaborating laboratory, and the latter benefits from General Lab's services (central purchasing, association with an industry-leading laboratory, and financing).

EXPANSION IN SPAIN

In September 1998, the facilities of the Central Laboratory of Madrid were established thanks to the integration of clinical laboratories and assigned personnel from Fraternidad and Museba Ivesbico; both societies were mutual accident and occupational disease insurance companies. From that moment on, contracts were signed. The vast majority of them with total statewide coverage and prevention services for large companies—Telefónica, ONCE, Correos, Iberia, Adif, National Police, Instituto Social de la Marina, Ministry of Internal Affairs, Metro de Madrid, Gas Natural Fenosa— and other mutual accident insurance companies, such as Mutual Cyclops, Ibermutuamur, and Umivale.

The territorial expansion of General Lab in Spain was consolidated with the incorporation of the Quirón Hospital Group in 1999, the progressive incorporation of emergency labs in five of their hospitals, and the U.S.P. Hospital Group in 2001, integrating 14 hospital emergency labs.

EXPANSION IN PORTUGAL

In the summer of 2006, General Lab Portugal established a modern clinical laboratory building in Lisbon. It quickly expanded an important network of emergency labs in Lisbon (Hospital da Luz, Hospital Lusíadas) and Porto (Hospital DaBoavista). It also integrated Germilab, a clinical laboratory site in Cascais. Thus, a large group of leading laboratories was consolidated in the Iberian Peninsula.

Table 5 shows the main data from 2007 when General Lab was already the leading clinical laboratory in Spain in services, information, management, and execution of laboratory diagnostic tests. Nearly 85% of its activity was carried out in Spain and the rest in Portugal.

Table 5
Main Data for General Lab in Spain and Portugal (2007)

Owned clinical laboratories	50
Shareholding laboratories/companies	17
Collaborating laboratories	27
Employees (150 licensed/doctors)	790
Annual analysis requests	2,462,230
Analysis requests per day	11,000
Annual tests or analyses	24,021,744
Tests or analyses per day	105,000
Estimated aggregate net revenue for the fiscal year 2007	€53,934,000

Note: These numbers do not include collaborating laboratories, only owned and participanting shareholders.

MERGER WITH LABCO AND ENTRY OF 3I CAPITAL

In December 2007, General Lab merged with Labco, the French leader in clinical laboratories, which at that time had 115 laboratories in France, Belgium, Italy, and Germany and has nearly 3,000 employees. Labco was founded in 2003 through the merger of several laboratories. Because of this, Labco managed to have a presence in Spain and Portugal. The merger was made by exchanging shares with Labco, and thereafter, General Lab continued to operate as a subsidiary of Labco, as did all other integrated laboratories from other countries. After the transaction, all General Lab shareholders acquired 14% of Labco's shares.

The merger of General Lab and Labco set a framework around the idea that the diagnostic industry has a tendency toward consolidation, and by this framework, they have aspired to create a great European group. In addition, it aimed to generate economies of scale to achieve cost and revenue synergies and has an advantage in that the two groups have a very similar philosophy for growth. The growth model of Labco is similar to that of General Lab because it consists of incorporating leading local and regional clinical laboratories in its network and allows those responsible for these laboratories to become partners of the group. In fact, Labco acts as a holding company, and all laboratories are subsidiaries of such holding. This model is valid for owners (more than 60% of the capital belongs to the clinical laboratories' directors) and management teams, which are usually teams from their own country. Thus after having joined the network, the management teams of different laboratories continue to work with a high degree of autonomy, ensuring the best service for their patients and prescribing physicians. This functional structure allows Labco to maintain management teams with deep knowledge of their local and regional markets and, at the same time, achieve economies of scale.

Subsequently, in July 2008, the venture capital group 3i joined Labco Capital with an investment of €130 million. Today 3i and other venture capital firms control 42% of Labco (TCR Capital, Natixis Investment Partners, and CIC Finance).

CURRENT SITUATION

Currently, General Lab serves in both the out-patient and in-patient scopes, in the private and public sectors, in all matters relating to emergency clinical analysis, and of routine diagnostics, specialists, and pathological anatomy. It also has shareholdings in companies focused in specific topics, such as medical centers.

Along with this group of interests, General Lab is open to all industries (hospitals, mutual accident insurance companies and prevention services, insurance companies, pharmaceutical laboratories, public administration, and other clinical laboratories). It's also open to all disciplines of study: pathology, radio-immuno analysis, molecular genetics, molecular biology, industrial toxicology, blood transfusion services, anti-aging, nutrition and functional medicine, and personalized preventive medicine, among others.

Albert Sumarroca is the current CEO of General Lab and general manager of Labco Iberia, which manages Labco Spain and Portugal. Vila is currently the general manager of General Lab.

Since 3i joined the capital group, Labco has acquired more than 80 laboratories throughout Europe. In Spain, they have acquired the Luso-Hispanic group Sample Test in July 2008 for €210 million and acquired other laboratories smaller in size. When Sample Test was bought, the Labco Iberia brand was created for all the Labco subsidiary laboratories in Spain and Portugal. Most laboratories continue to operate under their own brand name and with the Labco logo.

In 2012, Labco issued €500 million in bonds for individuals to finance its growth. Figure 3 and appendices A through F include financial information for General Lab and its main competitor, Laboratorios Dr. F. Echevarne.

Labco, headquartered in Paris, France, billed almost €600 million in 2012 (including Labco Iberia). It operates in seven countries, has 4,820 workers, and performs clinical analysis for nearly 20 million patients a year. It intends to continue to grow and enter the stock market; therefore, it doesn't distribute dividends. General Lab, by volume and history, continues to be Labco's most structured subsidiary model, and consequently, continues to maintain its management model. Apart from continuing to grow and consolidate its leadership in Spain and Portugal, its challenge is to succeed in not letting the continuous price declines caused by the economic recession to affect its quality of service. At this point, remember that Portugal and Spain are among the countries, with Greece, that had more economic troubles from 2008-2012. Table 6 provides various data from General Lab and Labco Iberia.

In 2013, 3i and the rest of Labco's shareholders stakes[1] went on sale, valuing the company around €1,000 million. According to Reuters, the potential buyers are private equity firms, including Bain Capital, Blackstone, EQT, and PAI—all of them with interests in the European healthcare industry.

ISSUES FOR DISCUSSION

1. Perform a diagnostic Strengths, Weaknesses, Opporunities, and Threats (SWOT) analysis on the basis of the financial statements and the qualitative information from General Lab.
2. Evaluate General Lab's key success factors.
3. Assess General Lab's growth policy, distinguishing between the initial phase (until 2007) and the current phase (after 2007).
4. Make recommendations on how General Lab can continue to grow based on your analysis.

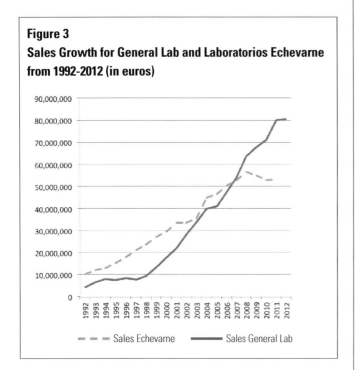

Figure 3
Sales Growth for General Lab and Laboratorios Echevarne from 1992-2012 (in euros)

- - - Sales Echevarne   ——— Sales General Lab

Table 6
Main Data from 2012 for General Lab and Labco Iberia

	General Lab (Spain & Portugal)	Labco Iberia (includes General Lab)
Owned clinical laboratories	64	144
Shareholding laboratories/companies	17	19
Collaborating laboratories	27	27
Employees (more than 200 licensed/doctors)	890*	1,695
Annual analysis requests (fiscal year 2012)	4,512,851	6,585,000
Analysis requests per day	19,600*	28,600
Annual tests or analyses (fiscal year 2012)	46,188,800*	60,000,000
Tests or analyses per day	200,000*	260,000
Estimated aggregate net revenue for fiscal year 2012	€80,518,000*	€148,000,000*

* Does not include collaborating laboratories, only owned and participating shareholders.

Appendix A
General Lab Balance Sheets from December 31, 2005, to December 31, 2011 (2009-2011 nonconsolidated data)

	12/31/2011	%	12/31/2010	%	12/31/2009	%	12/31/2008	%	12/31/2007	%	12/31/2006	%	12/31/2005	%
Non Current Assets	**21,087,000**	**40%**	**9,818,000**	**31%**	**11,046,956**	**33%**	**11,948,034**	**33%**	**11,938,000**	**36%**	**10,161,000**	**38%**	**5,900,000**	**34%**
Intangible assets	10,887,000	21%	1,082,000	3%	1,303,605	4%	1,232,736	3%	578,000	2%	671,000	2%	904,000	7%
Tangible assets	5,106,000	10%	4,182,000	13%	5,115,538	15%	5,835,584	16%	7,449,000	23%	5,354,000	20%	2,495,000	13%
Other nontangible assets	5,094,000	10%	4,554,000	14%	4,627,813	14%	4,879,714	13%	3,911,000	12%	4,136,000	15%	2,501,000	14%
Current Assets	**31,604,000**	**60%**	**22,217,000**	**69%**	**22,723,100**	**67%**	**24,281,701**	**67%**	**20,896,000**	**64%**	**16,723,000**	**62%**	**14,894,000**	**66%**
Stocks	1,562,000	3%	929,000	3%	1,000,946	3%	1,437,751	4%	1,295,000	4%	1,054,000	4%	843,000	4%
Debtors	27,692,000	53%	20,530,000	64%	20,189,587	60%	20,251,160	56%	18,058,000	55%	12,880,000	48%	12,909,000	60%
Cash	2,350,000	4%	758,000	2%	1,532,567	5%	2,592,790	7%	1,543,000	5%	2,789,000	10%	1,142,000	2%
Total Assets	**52,691,000**	**100%**	**32,035,000**	**100%**	**33,770,056**	**100%**	**36,229,735**	**100%**	**32,834,000**	**100%**	**26,884,000**	**100%**	**20,794,000**	**100%**
Owner's Equity	**24,808,000**	**47%**	**14,537,000**	**45%**	**11,266,118**	**33%**	**13,030,876**	**36%**	**8,886,000**	**27%**	**8,553,000**	**32%**	**6,567,000**	**41%**
Capital	1,880,000	4%	1,880,000	6%	1,880,000	6%	1,880,000	5%	1,880,000	6%	2,400,000	9%	2,400,000	17%
Other Owner's Equity	22,928,000	44%	12,657,000	40%	9,386,118	28%	11,150,876	31%	7,006,000	21%	6,153,000	23%	4,167,000	24%
Non Current Liabilities		**0%**		**0%**		**0%**		**0%**	99,000	**0%**	169,000	**1%**	69,000	**1%**
Current Liabilities	**27,883,000**	**53%**	**17,498,000**	**55%**	**22,503,938**	**67%**	**23,198,859**	**64%**	**23,849,000**	**73%**	**18,162,000**	**68%**	**14,158,000**	**59%**
Financial debts	543,000	1%	1,894,000	6%	4,343,894	13%	7,427,400	21%	9,396,000	29%	7,315,000	27%	5,269,000	17%
Suppliers	9,057,000	17%	6,573,000	21%	7,347,062	22%	9,878,704	27%	10,728,000	33%	8,283,000	31%	6,388,000	32%
Other current liabilities	18,283,000	35%	9,031,000	28%	10,812,982	32%	5,892,755	16%	3,725,000	11%	2,564,000	10%	2,501,000	10%
Total Owner's Equity and Liabilities	**52,691,000**	**100%**	**32,035,000**	**100%**	**33,770,056**	**100%**	**36,229,735**	**100%**	**32,834,000**	**100%**	**26,884,000**	**100%**	**20,794,000**	**100%**

Note: All monetary amounts in euros.

Appendix B
Laboratorios Echevarne Balance Sheets from December 31, 2005, to December 31, 2011

	12/31/2011	%	12/31/2010	%	12/31/2009	%	12/31/2008	%	12/31/2007	%	12/31/2006	%	12/31/2005	%
Non Current Assets	**25,223,405**	**51%**	**24,225,153**	**50%**	**24,191,320**	**51%**	**22,694,329**	**49%**	**21,229,136**	**50%**	**14,850,264**	**41%**	**14,014,086**	**43%**
Intangible assets	4,216,966	9%	4,437,275	9%	4,564,734	10%	1,831,832	4%	3,406,164	8%	3,950,618	11%	3,845,030	12%
Tangible assets	13,965,035	28%	14,614,814	30%	14,675,490	31%	13,710,666	30%	12,078,298	28%	8,443,345	24%	7,805,552	24%
Other nontangible assets	7,041,404	14%	5,173,065	11%	4,951,095	10%	7,151,831	16%	5,744,675	14%	2,456,301	7%	2,363,504	7%
Current Assets	**24,152,829**	**49%**	**23,867,448**	**50%**	**23,558,175**	**49%**	**23,204,564**	**51%**	**21,166,399**	**50%**	**20,974,564**	**59%**	**18,584,171**	**57%**
Stocks	409,482	1%	318,916	1%	NA		NA		NA		0	0%	NA	
Debtors	16,854,622	34%	19,682,229	41%	19,285,101	40%	19,989,167	44%	17,641,370	42%	17,267,617	48%	15,370,706	47%
Cash	6,888,724	14%	3,866,302	8%	4,273,074	9%	3,215,397	7%	3,525,029	8%	3,706,947	10%	3,213,465	10%
Total Assets	**49,376,234**	**100%**	**48,092,601**	**100%**	**47,749,495**	**100%**	**45,898,893**	**100%**	**42,395,535**	**100%**	**35,824,828**	**100%**	**32,598,257**	**100%**
Owner's Equity	**37,732,132**	**76%**	**35,887,918**	**75%**	**33,577,785**	**70%**	**30,566,538**	**67%**	**26,456,192**	**62%**	**23,133,504**	**65%**	**20,293,044**	**62%**
Capital	450,750	1%	450,750	1%	450,750	1%	450,750	1%	450,750	1%	450,750	1%	450,750	1%
Other Owner's Equity	37,281,382	76%	35,437,168	74%	33,127,035	69%	30,115,788	66%	26,005,442	61%	22,682,754	63%	19,842,294	61%
Non Current Liabilities	**2,981,003**	**6%**	**3,283,832**	**7%**	**3,863,906**	**8%**	**4,041,679**	**9%**	**4,600,088**	**11%**	**1,834,099**	**5%**	**2,160,422**	**7%**
Long term suppliers	2,054,379	4%	2,635,514	5%	3,230,541	7%	3,462,563	8%	4,600,088	11%	1,834,099	5%	2,160,422	7%
Other fixed liabilities	926,624	2%	648,318	1%	633,365	1%	579,116	1%	NA		0	0%	0	0%
Current liabilities	**8,663,100**	**18%**	**8,920,851**	**19%**	**10,307,804**	**22%**	**11,290,676**	**25%**	**11,339,255**	**27%**	**10,857,225**	**30%**	**10,144,791**	**31%**
Financial debts	642,303	1%	634,174	1%	1,282,745	3%	1,389,385	3%	1,957,500	5%	1,436,679	4%	1,129,708	3%
Suppliers	5,910,125	37%	5,836,731	37%	5,750,258	37%	6,038,663	37%	6,231,158	40%	6,037,298	39%	5,846,349	40%
Other current liabilities	2,110,672	4%	2,449,946	5%	3,274,801	7%	3,862,628	8%	3,150,597	7%	3,383,248	9%	3,168,734	10%
Total Owner's Equity and Liabilities	**49,376,234**	**100%**	**48,092,601**	**100%**	**47,749,495**	**100%**	**45,898,893**	**100%**	**42,395,535**	**100%**	**35,824,828**	**100%**	**32,598,257**	**100%**

Note: All monetary amounts in euros. NS = not available.

General Lab Income Statement for 2005-2011 (2009-2011 nonconsolidated data)

	12/31/2011	%	12/31/2010	%	12/31/2009	%	12/31/2008	%	12/31/2007	%	12/31/2006	%	12/31/2005	%
Total Revenue	**63,724,000**	**100%**	**53,375,000**	**100%**	**50,634,208**	**100%**	**50,578,926**	**100%**	**46,427,000**	**100%**	**39,615,000**	**100%**	**36,677,000**	**100%**
Materials	-23,459,000	-37%	-19,789,000	-37%	-17,944,574	-35%	-18,471,423	-37%	-15,280,000	-33%	-14,292,000	-36%	-13,532,000	-37%
Wages and salaries	-24,567,000	-39%	-20,053,000	-38%	-18,653,252	-37%	-17,044,927	-34%	-16,382,000	-35%	-13,294,000	-34%	-12,661,000	-35%
Depreciations	-1,956,000	-3%	-1,632,000	-3%	-1,536,621	-3%	-1,445,352	-3%	-1,642,000	-4%	-1,446,000	-4%	-1,127,000	-3%
Other operating expenses	-9,819,000	-15%	-7,438,000	-14%	-7,281,195	-14%	-6,074,380	-12%	-6,790,000	-15%	-6,087,000	-15%	-5,377,000	-15%
Earnings before interests and taxes (EBIT)	**3,923,000**	**6%**	**4,463,000**	**8%**	**5,218,566**	**10%**	**7,542,844**	**15%**	**6,333,000**	**14%**	**4,496,000**	**11%**	**3,980,000**	**11%**
Financial results	-111,000	0%	12,000	0%	-266,687	-1%	-169,152	0%	-603,000	-1%	-180,000	0%	-2,000	0%
Earnings before taxes (EBT)	**3,812,000**	**6%**	**4,475,000**	**8%**	**4,951,879**	**10%**	**7,373,692**	**15%**	**5,730,000**	**12%**	**4,316,000**	**11%**	**3,978,000**	**11%**
Income tax	-1,056,000	-2%	-1,238,000	-2%	-1,452,261	-3%	-2,174,746	-4%	-1,961,000	-4%	-1,515,000	-4%	-1,389,000	-4%
Earnings from continuing operations	**2,756,000**	**4%**	**3,237,000**	**6%**	**3,499,618**	**7%**	**5,198,946**	**10%**	**3,769,000**	**8%**	**2,801,000**	**7%**	**2,589,000**	**7%**
Earnings from discontinued operations		0%		0%		0%		0%	-94,000	0%	432,000	1%	-32,000	0%
Net Result	**2,756,000**	**4%**	**3,237,000**	**6%**	**3,499,618**	**7%**	**5,198,946**	**10%**	**3,675,000**	**8%**	**3,233,000**	**8%**	**2,557,000**	**7%**
Number of employees	**769**		**777**		**569**		**545**		**506**		**411**		**332**	

Note: All monetary amounts in euros.

Appendix D
Laboratorios Echevarne Income Statement for 2005-2011

	12/31/2011	%	12/31/2010	%	12/31/2009	%	12/31/2008	%	12/31/2007	%	12/31/2006	%	12/31/2005	%
Total Revenue	52,748,681	100%	52,711,046	100%	54,737,018	100%	56,164,482	100%	52,102,376	100%	50,135,636	100%	46,237,364	100%
Materials	-15,914,876	30%	-15,721,580	30%	-15,536,763	28%	-16,528,639	29%	-15,655,557	30%	-15,547,415	31%	-14,597,627	32%
Wages and salaries	-24,016,759	46%	-24,538,081	47%	-24,345,712	44%	-23,737,141	42%	-22,377,664	43%	-21,580,237	43%	-18,933,932	41%
Depreciations	-1,724,539	3%	-1,782,539	3%	-1,894,915	3%	-2,073,978	4%	-1,984,273	4%	-1,779,216	4%	-1,783,555	4%
Other operating expenses	-7,705,522	15%	-7,437,949	14%	-7,976,999	15%	-7,788,345	14%	-7,362,896	14%	-6,920,660	14%	-6,617,417	14%
Earnings before interests and taxes (EBIT)	3,386,985	6%	3,230,897	6%	4,982,629	9%	6,036,379	11%	4,721,986	9%	4,308,108	9%	4,304,833	9%
Financial results	-781,481	-1%	-92,518	0%	20,190	0%	-98,363	0%	62,049	0%	100,642	0%	94,798	0%
Earnings before taxes (EBT)	2,605,504	5%	3,138,378	6%	5,002,818	9%	5,938,017	11%	4,784,035	9%	4,408,751	9%	4,399,630	10%
Income tax	-725,913	1%	-870,185	2%	-1,410,758	3%	-1,673,239	3%	-1,461,348	3%	-1,305,812	3%	-1,261,557	3%
Earnings from continuing operations	1,879,592	4%	2,268,193	4%	3,592,059	7%	4,264,777	8%	3,322,688	6%	3,102,939	6%	3,138,073	7%
Earnings from discontinued operations											-262,477	-1%	-417,401	-1%
Net Result	1,879,592	4%	2,268,193	4%	3,592,059	7%	4,264,777	8%	3,322,688	6%	2,840,460	6%	2,720,671	6%
Number of employees	681		804		805		796		798		722		722	

Note: All monetary amounts in euros.

Appendix E
General Lab Financial Ratios for 2005-2011 (2009-2011 nonconsolidated data)

	2011	2010	2009	2008	2007	2006	2005
Liquidity:							
Liquidity (Current Assets/ Current Liabilities)	1.13	1.27	1.01	1.05	0.88	0.92	1.05
Acid Test Ratio ((Cash + Debtors) / Current Liabilities)	1.08	1.22	0.97	0.98	0.82	0.86	0.99
Debt:							
Debt-Equity Ratio (Total Liabilities / Equity)	1.12	1.20	1.99	1.78	2.70	2.14	2.17
Debt (Total Liabilities / Assets)	0.53	0.55	0.67	0.64	0.73	0.68	0.68
Debt Quality (Current Liabilities / Total Liabilities)	1.00	1.00	1.00	1.00	1.00	0.99	1.00
Asset Turnover:							
Asset Turnover (Total Revenues / Assets)	1.21	1.67	1.50	1.40	1.41	1.47	1.76
Non Current Assets Turnover (Total Revenues / Non Current Assets)	3.02	5.44	4.58	4.23	3.89	3.90	6.22
Current Assets Turnover (Total Revenues / Current Assets)	2.02	2.40	2.23	2.08	2.22	2.37	2.46
Stock Turnover (Total Revenues / Stocks)	40.80	57.45	50.59	35.18	35.85	37.59	43.51
Periods:							
Stock Period (Stocks /Materials) x 365	24	17	20	28	31	27	23
Collection Period (Debtors / Total Revenues) x 365	159	140	146	146	142	119	128
Payment Period (Suppliers / Materials) x 365	141	121	149	195	256	212	172
Suppliers / Debtors	0.33	0.32	0.36	0.49	0.59	0.64	0.49
Return:							
ROI (EBIT / Total Assets)	7.45%	13.93%	15.45%	20.82%	19.29%	16.72%	19.14%
ROE (Net Result / Owner's Equity)	11.11%	22.27%	31.06%	39.90%	41.36%	37.80%	38.94%

Note: All monetary amounts in euros.

Laboratorios Echevarne Financial Ratios for 2005-2011

	2011	2010	2009	2008	2007	2006	2005
Liquidity:							
Liquidity (Current Assets/ Current Liabilities)	2.79	2.68	2.29	2.06	1.87	1.93	1.83
Acid Test Ratio ((Cash + Debtors) / Current Liabilities)	2.74	2.64	2.29	2.06	1.87	1.93	1.83
Debt:							
Debt-Equity Ratio (Total Liabilities / Equity)	0.31	0.34	0.42	0.50	0.60	0.55	0.61
Debt (Total Liabilities / Assets)	0.24	0.25	0.30	0.33	0.38	0.35	0.38
Debt Quality (Current Liabilities / Total Liabilities)	0.74	0.73	0.73	0.74	0.71	0.86	0.82
Asset Turnover:							
Asset Turnover (Total Revenues / Assets)	1.07	1.10	1.15	1.22	1.23	1.40	1.42
Non Current Assets Turnover (Total Revenues / Non Current Assets)	2.09	2.18	2.26	2.47	2.45	3.38	3.30
Current Assets Turnover (Total Revenues / Current Assets)	2.18	2.21	2.32	2.42	2.46	2.39	2.49
Stock Turnover (Total Revenues / Stocks)	128.82	165.28	NA	NA	NA	NA	NA
Periods:							
Stock Period (Stocks /Materials) x 365	9	7	NA	NA	NA	NA	NA
Collection Period (Debtors / Total Revenues) x 365	117	136	129	130	124	126	121
Payment Period (Suppliers / Materials) x 365	136	136	135	133	145	142	146
Suppliers / Debtors	0.35	0.30	0.30	0.30	0.35	0.35	0.38
Return:							
ROI (EBIT / Total Assets)	6.86%	6.72%	10.43%	13.15%	11.14%	12.03%	13.21%
ROE (Net Result / Owner's Equity)	4.98%	6.32%	10.70%	13.95%	12.56%	12.28%	13.41%

Note: All monetary amounts in euros. NS = not available.

Autoliv, Inc.: Using Lean Practices to Improve the A/P Reconciliation Process

Rosemary Fullerton, Utah State University; Staci F. Gunnell, ThermoFisher Scientific; and
R. Chance Murray, Utah State University

THIS CASE DESCRIBES A PROCESS IMPROVEMENT PROJECT that occurred in collaboration between the finance department at an Autoliv, Inc. facility and a graduate cost accounting class. The graduate students were asked to use their understanding of lean concepts to help identify and eliminate waste in the AP reconciliation process at Autoliv. Students were assigned to small groups, and the group with the solution that best fit the customer needs was chosen by the Autoliv finance team. The new process was implemented at Autoliv by the student team leader. The case study duplicates this collaborative experience and provides a real-world example for using problem-solving skills, accounting knowledge, Excel experience, lean practices, and creative thinking to prepare a feasible, simple, and sustainable improved process. There is no right answer to the case study, but the process to come up with a solution can be used for many different types of applications.

This case was designed for an advanced or graduate cost accounting class with a focus on strategic management and process improvement. The case study would also work in an upper division cost accounting class, an upper division accounting information systems class, or an MBA class. It is best assigned as a small group project to students who have been introduced to lean concepts and have a basic knowledge of Excel.

Keywords: process improvement, lean practices, Excel data manipulations, cost accounting.

Autoliv Inc.: Using Lean Practices to Improve the AP Reconciliation Process

Rosemary Fullerton
Utah State University

Staci F. Gunnell
ThermoFisher Scientific

R. Chance Murray
Utah State University

INTRODUCTION TO AUTOLIV AND THE LEAN CULTURE

Autoliv Inc. was created in 1997 when Europe's leading automotive safety company, Autoliv AB of Sweden, merged with North America and Asia's leading airbag manufacturer, Morton Automotive Safety Products. Autoliv AB pioneered seatbelt technology in 1956, while Morton ASP was a leader in airbag development, launching the first commercially successful airbag system in 1980. Today, Autoliv is a worldwide leader in technology and automotive safety, having the widest product offerings for automotive safety. Autoliv supplies all major and most other vehicle manufacturers in the world. The company is often a partner with car manufacturers in the development of new vehicle models, a process that can take several years. Based in Sweden and headquartered in Delaware, Autoliv is composed of 80 facilities in 29 countries, 21 crash test tracks in 11 countries, and has more than 50,000 employees.

Autoliv realized in the late 1980s that the fundamental goal of any business is to produce the highest value products and services with the least amount of time, effort, and cost. This led to its interest in the lean philosophy. While mentoring Toyota, Autoliv began implementing lean practices in the production arena as early as 1990. The Autoliv Production System (APS) patterned after the Toyota Production System escalated into a system-wide culture that encompassed all areas of the business. Support personnel were trained in lean concepts and began to use them to improve their processes as well. The facility-wide successes achieved from adopting a lean culture throughout Autoliv led to multiple Shingo Prizes—internationally recognized awards for outstanding achievement in operational excellence.

This case study focuses on applying lean concepts in the accounting area. It represents an example of how to apply APS lean tools to improve the accounts payable (AP) process in the finance department of a North American Autoliv division. For more information on the company, visit its website at www.autoliv.com.

INTRODUCTION TO ACCOUNTS PAYABLE (AP) RECONCILIATION PROCESS AT AUTOLIV

The AP group for Autoliv is a centralized function for North America. The group consists of one supervisor and four accounting clerks. At the end of each month, Emily, an AP clerk, prepares the AP balance sheet reconciliation for 30 facilities within North America. Two accounts for each facility are reconciled: the AP Open account and the Material Clearing (MC) account. Emily follows the process that was previously developed and performed by Anne, an individual who is no longer employed at Autoliv.

After Anne left Autoliv, several problems with the current AP reconciliation process were exposed:

1. There weren't any documented standard work instructions, and no other employees were cross-trained to perform this process.
2. Several intercompany transactions had to be hand manipulated because of the way the reports were created and the legal taxing issues for operations in Mexico and Canada.
3. Some unnecessary data continued to be added to the report primarily because the previous employee had included it.
4. Due to the size of Autoliv operations and the transactions in the reports, the downloaded subsidiary report for the AP detail account was over 200,000 lines in Excel, which populated several different Excel worksheets. In addition, the downloaded subsidiary report for the MC account was approximately 28,000 lines in Excel.
5. Due to Emily's lack of proficiency in Excel and the manual interaction required in reviewing 228,000 individual lines of data, the total process for all facilities took in excess of two days to complete.

Upon review of the situation, it was evident that there was much room for process improvement.

Autoliv applies the SMART objective to its improvement initiatives, which stands for Specific, Measurable, Ambitious, Relevant, and Time-based goals: Specific—goals are clear enough to know exactly what needs to be done to achieve the objective; Measureable—the successful completion of a goal should have tangible evidence of completion; Ambitious—goals should be attainable through stretching capabilities; Relevant—goals should be aligned with higher corporate strategies; and Time-based—goals should have a specified completion date. Emily's supervisor has asked her to improve the reconciliation process. Her SMART objective is to decrease the average process time in AP reconciliation preparation by 60%, from an average of 35 minutes per facility to 14 minutes for Account 710 (A710) by the end of April. Emily has asked for your help in achieving this SMART objective. She will walk you through the current state of the reconciliation process in detail.[1]

CURRENT STATE OF THE AP RECONCILIATION PROCESS

The Saturday before the monthly close, staff accountant Amanda is responsible for preparing two AP reports for each of the Autoliv facilities. First she checks with the IT department to make certain that the monthly information has been posted. Then she runs the two reports in Autoliv's system software, Crystal: one report is for MC, which represents those items that have been received but not paid for; and one is for AP Open items, which are items that have been processed for payment. These two reports contain data for all 30 Autoliv facilities. This process takes approximately 10 minutes of Amanda's time in preparation and 360 minutes of computer time. Amanda is able to do the work during the computer processing time. On Monday morning, the first day of close, Emily opens the two Crystal reports Amanda prepared on Saturday and exports the reports to two excel files: MC_AL and AP OPEN_AL. This takes about 10 minutes of Emily's time and populates the two files with data for all 30 facilities.[2] Emily is now ready to work on reports that facilitate the AP reconciliation process for each of the Autoliv facilities. The tasks and time commitment for preparing the AP reconciling numbers for a single facility are described below.

Current process for AP reconciliation for Open items:

- Emily opens the Excel AP_MC Template_AL file that has two worksheets prepared: One is a template for the accounts payable MC by supplier data file, and the other is a template for the AP Open items data file.[3] The template file contains the correct "if" statements for establishing the AP aging. Emily first opens the AP Template worksheet for the AP Open items from the AP_MC Template_AL file and copies the first two rows. These rows are then pasted over the original two rows of the AP Open_AL data file.[4] The purpose of row 2 is to facilitate copying the "if" statements on the report. Emily highlights row 2 to remind her that this is not actual data. This procedure takes Emily approximately two minutes for each facility's report.

- Emily then puts the last day of the month (12/31/2011) in cell S1 and the first day of the following month (01/01/2012) in cell T1. In order to establish the aging schedule, Emily removes the highlights from cells O2, P2, Q2, and R2 and copies the formulas in these four cells through to the bottom of the file. For Autoliv, this usually represents upwards of 200,000 data items and takes Emily about three minutes to complete this stage of the process.[5] Emily then deletes the highlighted row 2 since this data is not real data.

- The next step in the process identifies the internal and external vendor amounts. If the mailing name in column E contains "Autoliv," then "INT" (for internal vendor) should be put in column B (User Code). If there is no reference to Autoliv in the vendor name, then "EXT" (for external vendor) should be input into column B. These tasks take Emily about four minutes for each division.
- The next step in the process establishes the remittance method. Automatic clearing house payments (ACH) should be put into all the blank cells in column C. Looking for the blank cells is a tedious process that takes Emily about six minutes to complete.
- Emily then creates a pivot table in the AP Open_AL Excel data file in which she is working.[6] She uses all of the data in columns A through T and defines the aging schedule (Sum of 0-45, Sum of 46-90, Sum of 90+, and Sum of Overdue) by "EXT" or "INT." Creation of the pivot table takes Emily approximately two minutes. This completes Emily's process for developing the AP reconciliation information for the Open items by company.

Current process for AP reconciliation by supplier:

- Then Emily does approximately the same routine with the AP MC by Supplier Excel data file.[7] She opens this file and inserts a column before column B to initially prep it for the reconciliation schedule. Then she returns to the AP_MC Template_AL file and opens the MC Template worksheet. She copies the first two rows of this file to transfer the correct "if" statements to the supplier data file for establishing the AP aging schedule. The copied rows from the template are pasted over the first two rows in the MC_AL file. Emily again highlights row 2 of the edited file to remind her that this row will be deleted as soon as the aging formulas are copied to the data fields. This takes Emily about one minute to complete.
- Emily then puts the last day of the month (12/31/2011) into cell U1 and the first day of the following month (01/01/2012) into cell V1. After removing the highlights from cells Q2, R2, S2, and T2, the formulas in these four cells are copied down the columns to the end of the data.[8] Emily deletes row 2 to eliminate the false data from the template. It takes Emily approximately two minutes to set up this aging schedule.
- Emily then sorts the data by vendor number (column C) from low to high. All intercompany vendor entries should be eliminated. Intercompany vendors are those that have a vendor number less than 20. Identification and elimination of these entries take Emily approximately two minutes.

- Column B that was inserted when this data file was first opened needs to differentiate between internal and external suppliers. The internal vendors that were just deleted with numbers less than 20 were "legal entity intercompany vendors," where actual cash transactions are not exchanged. Vendors with numbers from 20 to 100 represent internal, intercompany vendors. These must be tracked separately because there is a central treasury, and no actual cash transactions occur between legal taxing entity facilities. For vendors in this range, Emily puts "INT" in column B. For all other vendors (those with numbers greater than 100), Emily puts "EXT" in column B. This is a simple process that only takes about one minute.
- Emily is then ready to create the AP MC aging pivot table. The pivot table for the MC_AL file is the same format as for the AP Open_AL file, as described above. The data in columns A through T is used, and the aging schedule is defined by "EXT" or "INT." Emily spends approximately two minutes creating this pivot table.

AP aging reconciliation reports:

- Emily is now ready to complete the AP aging reconciliation reports. She opens the AP Recon_AL Excel file.[9] There are three tabs in this file: Subsidiary Info, GL (General Ledger), and REC (Reconciliation). She first goes to the Subsidiary Info tab and fills in the aging amounts determined from her two pivot tables. She copies the appropriate "EXT" or "INT" aging amounts from the AP Open_AL file into cells (E5: E12). She copies the appropriate "EXT" or "INT" aging amounts from the MC_AL file into cells (E22: E29). This takes approximately five minutes.
- Emily then copies the general ledger balances from her trial balance onto the GL tab. This task requires approximately three minutes.[10]
- The only account that Autoliv requires Emily to reconcile is A710 which is the control account for all AP on the balance sheet. Within A710, there are only two accounts that have subsidiary accounts and require reconciliation. These are the MC account and the AP Open account. Emily is now ready to review the results and determine if reconciliation for AP is necessary. She examines the REC worksheet in the AP Recon_AL file. This worksheet is automatically updated from the information in the Subsidiary and GL worksheets. Cells (H7: K7) are populated for the AP Open subsidiary account and cells (H9: K9) are populated for the MC subsidiary account. Column B amounts are populated automatically from the GL information. Formulas are built into the reconciliation

report to determine variances between the general ledger balances and the supporting aging schedules. If the ending month-end variance (highlighted in yellow) is greater than $200,000, reconciliation must be performed.[11] If there is a quarter-end variance that is material, Emily will proceed with the reconciliation. If it is considered immaterial, the difference is booked.[12] The review of the variances and determination of whether reconciliation needs to be performed takes Emily approximately two minutes.

IMPROVEMENT OBJECTIVE

Emily recognizes that there is a lot of waste built into the AP reconciliation process and is looking for ways to eliminate some of her time in preparing the AP reconciliation reports. Currently, she is not concerned about ways to change the 20 minutes of setup and preparation time that she and Amanda incur while transferring information from Crystal files to Excel files. That will be a future Kaizen opportunity. Emily's most immediate objective is to reduce some of the non-value added activities that occur after the transfer of data to the Excel files. She is asking for your "fresh set of eyes" to help her improvement efforts in meeting her SMART objective.

ASSIGNMENT

1. Prepare a 5-10 minute oral presentation demonstrating your process improvements for the Autoliv AP reconciliation process.
2. Prepare and submit the Excel files that Emily can use to achieve her SMART objective.
3. Turn in a written report that:
   a. Explains how your new process satisfies Autoliv's SMART objectives.
   b. Identifies and explains which of the seven wastes are found in this current process.
   c. Explains the "lean lessons" learned from this case study.

4. Write the standard work instructions for the current and new reconciliation processes.
5. Prepare a process map for the current and future state. Identify any Kaizen bursts for a future ideal state.

APPENDIX A

Instructions for Building a Pivot Table

Step 1: Click Insert then PivotTable. A dialog box will pop up where you can select which data you want to be included.

Step 2: Select the data range you would like to include in the pivot table. For this case, it should be the whole worksheet. (This should be done for you automatically.) Make sure New Worksheet is selected in the bottom half of the box under "PivotTable report to be placed." Click OK.

Step 3: From the PivotTable Field List on the right, drag "User Code" ("IC" for MC) and "Co" ("Company" for MC) down to the box labeled Row Labels. Drag "0-45," "46-90," "90+," and "overdue" down to the box labeled Values.

Step 4: A drop-down menu titled $\sum$ Values should appear in the box labeled Column Labels. Drag this into the Row Labels box.

Step 5: Ensure that values are presented as SUM (not COUNT). To change this, click on each value individually (i.e., 0-45, 46-90, 90+, or overdue). In the drop-down menu, select Value Field Settings, then change COUNT to SUM, then click OK. Repeat this step for each value displayed.

The information now displayed in the worksheet is formatted according to the needs of this case study.

ENDNOTES

[1] Sample data files (Excel program needed) for one major Autoliv facility that will be used for this case study are located at the following URLs: http://huntsman.usu.edu/files/uploads/Fullerton/AP_MC Template_AL.xlsx, http://huntsman.usu.edu/files/uploads/Fullerton/AP Open_AL.xlsx, http://huntsman.usu.edu/files/uploads/Fullerton/MC_AL.xlsx, and http://huntsman.usu.edu/files/uploads/Fullerton/AP Recon_AL.xlsx.

[2] These data files for one facility are already prepared for you. Refer to first endnote for URLs.

[3] http://huntsman.usu.edu/files/uploads/Fullerton/AP_MC Template_AL.xlsx

[4] http://huntsman.usu.edu/files/uploads/Fullerton/AP Open_AL.xlsx

[5] Note that the sample data for this case study is about one fourth of the actual Autoliv data file.

[6] If you are not familiar with creating pivot tables in Excel, simple instructions are provided in Appendix A.

[7] http://huntsman.usu.edu/files/uploads/Fullerton/MC_AL.xlsx

[8] You will be copying over unnecessary data in columns Q, R, and S. Autoliv generally has in excess of 28,000 line items in this file, but your sample file is about one fourth of the actual Autoliv file.

[9] http://huntsman.usu.edu/files/uploads/Fullerton/AP Recon_AL.xlsx

[10] The general ledger numbers have been copied for you and are in the AP Recon_AL file on the GL worksheet.

[11] The reconciliation schedule indicates that the variance "must be zero." This is the visual cue that Autoliv provided to indicate that a reconciliation entry needed to be made if there is a variance. However, this is only for year-end, not monthly reconciliation, where in this case the reconciliation is made only if the variance is over $200,000.

[12] The "overdue" amounts are included in the 0-46, 46-90, and 90+ days outstanding figures.

Sometimes Accountants Fail to Budget

Gail Hoover King, Purdue University Calumet; Jane Saly, University of St. Thomas

THE CASE IS BASED ON THE ACTUAL EVENTS within a nonprofit organization. Students are required to analyze the information given in the case to determine what information is relevant for analyzing variances, determine the reason for variances, and provide suggestions to avoid further losses. In addition, the case simulates a real-world situation where all relevant information is not available or not in a format that allows for detailed analysis.

The case can be used in both an undergraduate intermediate managerial accounting/cost courses and graduate-level cost accounting courses. It is helpful if students have studied profit planning, budgeting, and basic variance analysis.

Keywords: budgeting, variance analysis, not-for-profit, and volunteer board's responsibility.

The Association of
Accountants and
Financial Professionals
in Business

Sometimes Accountants Fail to Budget

Gail Hoover King
Purdue University Calumet

Jane Saly
University of St. Thomas

*Budgeting is important in all organizations, but it is especially in
nonprofit organizations where revenue sources are often inconsistent
from year to year. Nonprofit leadership has a fiscal responsibility to
monitor the variances between actual revenues and cost and make
operating decisions to ensure the organization's viability and success.*

INTRODUCTION

In August 2003, the Steering Committee of the American
Accounting Association Midwest Region (AAA-MW)
discovered that its 2003 annual meeting had a net loss of
$24,232, leaving a net account balance at less than $50,000.
This was on top of a loss of $13,264 the previous year.
Concerned about a possible trend, the board created a
treasurer position and asked the treasurer to investigate
these losses.

THE ORGANIZATION

The steering committee is an entirely volunteer board
whose task is to organize and run an annual conference
targeting members of the American Accounting
Association who reside in the states of Illinois, Indiana,
Iowa, Kansas, Michigan, Minnesota, Missouri, North
Dakota, South Dakota, Nebraska, and Wisconsin. The
American Accounting Association (AAA) is a not-for-profit
organization whose members are primarily accounting
academics. The organization "promotes worldwide
excellence in accounting education, research and practice.
Founded in 1916 as the American Association of University

Instructors in Accounting, its present name was adopted
in 1936. The Association brings together the academic
community to further accounting education and to advance
the discipline and profession of accounting." *(American
Accounting Association Our Shared Vision, http://aaahq.org/about/
AAAShareVisionDocumentJan08fnl_4_.pdf, 2008, p 6)*

The steering committee meets twice a year; every spring
at the annual AAA-MW Region meeting and in August at the
national meeting of the American Accounting Association.
The typical process for organizing the AAA-MW annual
meeting was as follows:

1. Eighteen months prior to the meeting (usually at the
   August AAA national meeting), the steering committee
   determines in which city within the Midwest region
   to hold the meeting and submits a meeting site search
   request to the AAA national office.
2. The program chair for the meeting is a volunteer of the
   steering committee and is a different (and new) person
   each year.
3. The event coordinator (a third party hired by the AAA
   national office) contacts hotels in the chosen city and
   provides the AAA-MW steering committee with a list of
   hotels, room rates, and parking rates.
4. At the spring AAA-MW regional meeting, one year prior to
   the next meeting, the steering committee chooses a hotel
   based on its location in the city and room rates offered.
5. The event coordinator negotiates the final contract, it is
   signed by the AAA executive director, and a copy is kept
   in the AAA headquarter files.

6. The new AAA-MW regional meeting program chair is then responsible for organizing the meeting.

There was little in the way of a formal process, so each program chair would determine how he/she wanted to run the meeting. There was a tradition of charging a registration fee that covered food, audiovisual needs, and meeting rooms. The program chair, working with a few other volunteers, would organize the call for papers, review of papers, program speakers, receptions, and communication with members within the region. Typically, the meeting had multiple continuing professional education (CPE) sessions, offered breakfast on Friday and Saturday, lunch on Friday, snack breaks on Friday and Saturday morning and Friday afternoon, and evening receptions on both Thursday and Friday. All of this planning was a significant amount of effort and generally consumed the program chair's attention. All cash inflows and outflows were handled by the AAA staff members. They collected registration fees, paid the hotel bills, etc., charging or crediting the region's accounts. The AAA-MW steering committee president would receive periodic account activity reports. Prior to 2002, the AAA-MW meetings had generally resulted in an increase in cash flow and the steering committee had little need to worry about finances.

BACKGROUND

At the August 2002 meeting of the AAA-MW steering committee, the committee learned that the spring 2002 regional meeting showed a loss of $14,389.13. The comparison of 2001 and 2002 is shown in Exhibit 1. The 2002 AAA-MW regional meeting had been held in Milwaukee in March and the attendance at that meeting was 170. This was a 30.6 percent drop from the previous year's meeting held in St. Louis, and one of the few times in the region's recent history that the meeting attendance was below 200 attendees. The committee believed the main reason for the low attendance was reluctance to fly (travel) so soon after the after the 9/11 terrorist attack. In addition, the committee believed the location (Milwaukee, Wisconsin) in early spring was difficult to travel to and may not have been appealing. Therefore, the committee was satisfied that the net cash outflow for the 2002 meeting was an anomaly and there was no need for more investigation. As such, the committee proceeded to discuss the plans for the 2003 AAA-MW annual meeting, which was to be held the following spring at the Millennium Hotel in St. Louis. The Midwest region had the policy of holding the annual meeting in St. Louis every other year and, because of the central location

and more favorable spring weather, the St. Louis meetings had always been well attended. For that reason, the committee was not concerned that the 2003 meeting might result in a loss.

Exhibit 1
Comparison of 2001 and 2002

Financial Report
AAA Midwest Region
For years ending September 30, 2001, and September 30, 2002

	09/01-08/02	09/00-08/01
Attendance	170	245
INFLOWS		
Mid-year Meeting		
Registration	$ 14,835.00	$ 20,125.00
Contributions	0.00	1,990.00
Exhibitor Fees	4,200.00	4,500.00
CPE	2,400.00	3,270.00
Total Meeting	$ 21,435.00	$ 29,885.00
Interest	1,313.29	4,312.20
Total Inflows	$ 22,748.29	$ 34,197.20
OUTFLOWS		
Mid-year Meeting		
Printing	$ 2,890.55	$ 2,425.52
Mailing	752.35	470.17
Exhibitor Expense	354.82	460.00
Food/Bev	28,527.36	18,490.63
Audio Visual	0.00	2,965.85
Speakers	469.76	1,477.92
Mtg Coord	2,231.05	0.00
Postage	55.97	0.00
Travel	0.00	184.79
AAA Staff	154.00	105.00
CPE travel	350.00	1,990.00
Total Meeting	$ 35,785.86	$ 28,569.88
G&A	1,351.61	1,590.02
Total Outflows	$ 37,137.47	$ 30,159.90
Net change in assets	$(14,389.18)	$ 4,037.30
Beginning Cash	88,783.55	84,746.25
Ending Cash	$ 74,394.37	$ 88,783.55

The March 2003, AAA-MW meeting was held and followed the typical two-and-a-half-day format, with participants attending a number of CPE sessions and other activities included in their registration fee. The schedule of events for the 2003 AAA-MW annual meeting is shown in Exhibit 2.

Immediately after the meeting, during the Saturday steering committee luncheon meeting, the new AAA-MW president (the 2003 program chair) presided over the meeting. As normal, the event coordinator attended and reported the final attendance numbers. The attendance was 185, which was higher than the previous year's attendance of 170, but still lower than the 200 or more expected. The steering committee, not yet having any financial figures from the meeting, did not consider that the low attendance might result in a loss. Therefore, the remainder of the meeting was spent discussing the plans for the 2004 meeting in Kansas City and the plan for the 2005 meeting, which would be back in St. Louis.

The steering committee met again in August 2003 at the AAA national meeting and received from AAA headquarters' staff the financial information about the March 2003 meeting. (See Exhibit 3.) The committee was shocked to find that the spring meeting had resulted in a loss that was almost twice the loss incurred in 2002. If this pattern continued, the Midwest region would be bankrupt within a couple of years. Concerned, the committee decided to appoint a treasurer. The official duties of the treasurer would be to receive monthly financial reports of the AAA-MW from the AAA and report on the AAA-MW region's financial situation at steering committee meetings and the annual meeting. First, however, the treasurer would need to investigate the 2003 loss.

REQUIRED

1. As treasurer, determine what additional information you would like.
2. Analyze the information and prepare a report for the steering committee explaining the losses.
3. Provide suggestions to the steering committee on how to avoid future meeting losses.

Exhibit 2

Midwest Region of the American Accounting Association 2003 Meeting Program

Day	Time	Participant Events	Steering Committee Activities
Thursday	Afternoon	Tour of Cardinals Baseball Stadium	
	Evening	Welcome reception with appetizers and open bar. Reception was sponsored in part by the textbook publishers	
Friday	7:00 pm	Buffet breakfast: continental rolls, cereal, toast, yogurt, fruit, coffee, milk, tea	Steering committee breakfast meeting to receive information on meeting attendance and issues that needed to be addressed and finalize location or other details not yet decided for next year's event.
	8:30 -10 am	5 concurrent CPE sessions	
	10-10:30 pm	Morning reception with food and drink (coffee, bottled water, and juice)	
	10:30 – noon	7 concurrent CPE sessions	
	Noon – 1:30 pm	Luncheon with speaker	Awards for papers and lifetime members
	1:45-3:15 pm	7 concurrent CPE sessions	
	3:15– 3:45 pm	Afternoon refreshment break with coffee/soda and snack	
	3:45-5:15 pm	7 concurrent CPE sessions	
	6-7:30 pm	Reception with hot and cold hors d'oeuvres including two carving stations (roast beef and turkey) as well as vegetables, egg rolls, chips and dips…and an open bar	
	7:30-9:00 pm	Ice cream social sponsored by the Teaching and Curriculum Section of the AAA*	
Saturday	7:30-9:00 am	AAA-MW business meeting	President and program chair preside over the meeting; Nominate and vote on new steering committee members
	9- 10:30	FASB update and 2 other concurrent CPE sessions	
	10.30-11.00 am	Morning break with coffee and snacks	
	11 - 12.30 pm	5 concurrent CPE sessions	
	12.30–2:00 pm Steering Committee Meeting	No events; conference has ended	Steering committee luncheon and meeting; the program chair becomes the president and presides over the meeting

* AAA stands for American Accounting Association

Exhibit 3
AAA-MW Financial Information Provided to Steering Committee for 2002-2003

	Sep-02	Oct-02	Nov-02	Dec-02	Jan-03	Feb-03	Mar-03	Apr-03	May-03	Jun-03	Jul-03	Aug-03	TOTAL	Prior Year Totals
Beginning Cash Balance	74394.37	75500.56	75568.03	74529.07	74562.27	76392.44	79251.84	92040.53	91981.19	53269.27				
INFLOW MID-YEAR MEETING														
Advertising													0.00	0.00
Registration Fees						1032.00	12477.00	2919.00					16428.00	14835.00
Contributions													0.00	0.00
Exhibitor Fees					1800.00	1800.00	600.00						4200.00	4200.00
CPE													0.00	2400.00
Registration Fees								-		-			0.00	0.00
Total Mid-year Meeting	0.00	0.00	0.00	0.00	1800.00	2832.00	13077.00	2919.00	0.00	0.00			20628.00	21435.00
OTHER INCOME														
Contributions													-	-
Interest Income		67.47	67.83	33.80	30.77	30.59	26.53	33.73	28.76	13.36			332.84	1313.29
Total Inflow	0.00	67.47	67.83	33.80	1830.77	2862.59	13103.53	2952.73	28.76	13.36			20960.84	22748.29
OUTFLOW MID-YEAR MEETING														
Printing								2716.25					2716.25	2890.55
Copying													0.00	0.00
Mailing													0.00	752.35
Registration Expense													0.00	0.00
Exhibitor Expense													0.00	354.82
Hotel-Rooms/Food/Bev									34010.36	(40.00)			33970.36	28527.36
Hotel-Audio Visuals									3983.40				3983.40	-
Mtg. Entertainment									84.00				84.00	-
Speakers									662.32	507.35			1169.68	469.76
Mtg. Coord.-Exp.	(1106.19)		1106.19							1244.59			1244.59	2231.05
Postage													0.00	55.97
Supplies								105.00					105.00	-
Telephone													0.00	-
Travel													0.00	-
AAA Staff Support													0.00	350.00
Misc.													0.00	154.00
CPE													0.00	-
Hotel-Rooms/Food/Bev														
Hotel-Audio Visuals														
Misc.														
Speakers														
Travel														
Total Meeting	(1106.19)	0.00	1106.19	0.00	0.00	0.00	0.00	2821.25	38740.08	1711.94	0.00	0.00	43273.28	35785.86
GENERAL/ADMIN.														
Postage		0.60	0.60	0.60	0.60	3.19	58.04	78.32	0.60	0.60			142.55	86.11
Misc.													0.00	-
Council Fee													0.00	1000.00
Awards							256.80	112.50					369.30	265.50
Total General		0.60	0.60	0.60	0.60	3.19	314.84	190.82	0.60	0.60			511.85	1351.61
COMMITTEES/OFFICERS														
Hotel-Rooms/Food/Bev														
Travel														
Misc.														
Total Committee/Officers														
Total Outflow	(1106.19)	0.00	1106.79	0.60	0.60	3.19	314.84	3012.07	38740.68	1712.54	-	-	43785.13	37137.47
Ending Cash Balance	75500.56	75568.03	74529.07	74562.27	76392.44	79251.84	92040.53	91981.19	53269.27	51570.09	-	-	-	-

Tri-Cities Community Bank: A Balanced Scorecard Case

Tom Albright, University of Alabama; Stan Davis, University of Tennessee at Chattanooga; and
Aleecia R. Hibbets, University of Louisiana at Monroe

THE TRI-CITIES COMMUNITY BANK CASE IS BASED ON A TWO-YEAR BALANCED SCORECARD IMPLEMENTATION at a medium-sized regional bank. The time horizon, scorecard measures, financial data, and branch interviews closely parallel the actual implementation. The case requires students to develop scorecard relationships, analyze outcomes, and make recommendations for successful scorecard implementations. The case can promote a rich class discussion because students may develop many acceptable causal chains. The data analysis, however, should lead students to the same conclusion about the success of the implementation.

This case introduces fundamental scorecard concepts at an introductory level. But, the case can be taught at a higher level by integrating other core business school materials taught in management and statistics.

Keywords: balanced scorecard, cause-and-effect chain, financial perspective, customer perspective, internal business perspective, learning and growth perspective, and lead and lag indicators.

The Association of
Accountants and
Financial Professionals
in Business

Tri-Cities Community Bank: A Balanced Scorecard Case

Tom Albright
University of Alabama

Stan Davis
University of Tennessee
at Chattanooga

Aleecia R. Hibbets
University of Louisiana
at Monroe

CASE A: BSC DEVELOPMENT

Tri-Cities Community Bank (TCCB) is located in the Midwest US and has a total of 10 branches grouped into two divisions, the southern division (SD) and the northern division (ND). Each division consists of five branches; each branch employs a branch president, branch vice-president/ chief loan officer, customer service representatives, loan representatives, mortgage loan originators, head tellers, tellers, and administrative assistants. All branches are located within a 60-mile radius.

TCCB has enjoyed strong financial success over the past few years but continues to look for ways to improve its performance. The strategic direction of the bank is reviewed annually at a meeting of top bank officials and outside consultants. The purpose of the meeting is to outline the vision and mission of the bank and to ensure all top managers understand and agree on the direction of the organization. In 2004, TCCB management adopted the master strategy of balancing profits with growth to ensure the bank remains an independent entity existing to provide quality service and products to an increasingly diverse customer base.

Chris Billings recently was promoted from marketing director to SD president. The promotion came just as Chris finished her evening Masters of Business Administration degree in December 2006. As part of her graduate studies, she was introduced to the balanced scorecard (BSC), a performance measurement system that directs decision-makers toward long-term value creating activities. Chris thought the BSC could be used to improve the financial performance of TCCB. In late December 2006, she approached the chief executive officer (CEO) and requested permission to implement the new program.

TCCB's CEO was apprehensive about the new program. His reluctance stemmed from his own unfamiliarity with the BSC and Chris's short tenure as SD president. The CEO also was concerned about whether Chris's ideas would be accepted by the ND president and ND branch employees. Finally he was uncertain about the BSC's benefits. At the same time, the CEO did not want to respond negatively to Chris's first efforts as SD president. To appease Chris without totally committing the bank to implement the BSC, the CEO agreed to allow Chris to begin the process of developing the BSC in the five branches of her division. In turn, Chris agreed to make a presentation to the CEO and the bank's Board of Directors in three months. In this meeting, Chris would present BSC concepts and how she planned to use the program to improve the financial performance of her branches. Given the short period of time to design a pilot study, Chris wondered how she could convince the Board of Directors to give her permission to implement the BSC. She knew she must convince the SD branch presidents of its value.

On January 7th, 2007, Chris met with her branch presidents to discuss the BSC program and enlist their help in developing balanced scorecards for their branches. She began the meeting by distributing a handout (Exhibit A1) highlighting the key objectives of the BSC. She used the handout to inform the branch presidents of the four business "perspectives" (categories of measures to be included on the BSC). The example measures she included on the handout are from a hospital that had implemented the BSC. Since she did not have example measures from a bank using the BSC, she wanted to show the branch presidents measures from another service industry for them to consider. As the handout shows, the hospital uses operating margin and cost per case as their primary financial measures, recommendation ratings from outgoing patients and discharge timeliness information as customer measures, length of stay and readmission rate (patients being admitted again for the same injury or illness) for the internal business measures, and employee training and retention measures in the learning and growth perspective. She then instructed the branch presidents to work together to develop meaningful measures to be included on branch BSCs. While each branch would eventually develop a branch-specific scorecard, she believed the branches were similar enough to allow branch presidents to work together initially. The group was to meet again in six weeks to discuss their progress in developing branch BSCs.

The group meeting on February 25th did not go as well as Chris had hoped. While the branch presidents had done a good job of identifying areas that needed attention within each branch, the information presented could, at best, only be considered as raw materials necessary to build a BSC program. Much work was needed prior to implementing the program.

With time running out, Chris grew concerned about the scheduled meeting with the Board of Directors on March 31st. She had nothing concrete to present at the meeting and worried she might not receive permission to pursue the program if she did not make a solid presentation to the board. Chris's goal is to present a group of quantifiable measures that are linked through causal relationships and lead to improvement of key financial measures.

One of the primary benefits of the BSC comes through mapping the causal relationships from nonfinancial performance measures to the three primary financial measures the bank monitors. Nonfinancial measures are categorized into three perspectives: Learning and Growth, Internal Business Processes, and Customer Focus. The cause and effect linkages in the BSC will occur in the following manner: if learning improves, then internal processes will improve. If internal processes improve, then customer value will increase. If customer value increases, financial performance will improve. Financial performance is the ultimate evaluation of a firm's strategy. If financial performance improves significantly, the firm's strategy is successful. Thus, if the strategy is good,

the measures of the nonfinancial perspectives will be lead indicators of increasing value that will ultimately be proven by improved financial measures.

Exhibit A2 provides a list of performance measures developed by the branch presidents and notes Chris took during meetings with them. Exhibit A3 illustrates a sample cause-and-effect chain. For example, as shown in Exhibit A3, if employees receive training in sales effectiveness, customer service, product profitability, and local bank knowledge, they will be better equipped to provide customers with higher quality service. TCCB measures the effectiveness of its training programs by having employees take in-house tests on various training topics. By increasing employee knowledge and skills, higher quality referrals and cross-sell proposals will take place, leading to higher customer satisfaction and greater customer retention. Maintaining the current customer base provides the basis for growth in deposit and loan balances, while a greater number of successful referrals and cross-sells increase non-interest income.

Chris wants to prepare a series of cause-and-effect chains to illustrate to the Board of Directors how the BSC can be used to improve performance on three key financial measures: loan balances, deposit balances, and non-interest income. She knows that any program emphasizing improvement in these three measures has a strong chance of receiving approval.

REQUIRED:

Prepare a report to the Board of Directors that explains how the BSC may be used to help TCCB achieve its strategic goals. Include the following in your report:

1) A table that categorizes each of the measures in Exhibit A2 into one of the four BSC perspectives. State why you placed a measure in a particular perspective.

2) Two cause-and-effect chains similar to the one shown in Exhibit A3. Use the measures listed in Exhibit A2 or suggest other measures you feel are appropriate. Be sure to include a causal chain explanation with your answer.

CASE B: ASSESSING FINANCIAL IMPROVEMENT

The presentation to the Board of Directors was well received and Chris secured permission for a pilot study of the BSC in the five SD branches. She had one year to convince the CEO and Board of Directors of the BSC's ability to improve branch performance. During the year, all five SD branches implemented the BSC. However, each manager brought his or her individual style to the implementation process.

Now, the one-year trial period is over and Chris has collected data to determine whether the program was successful. Because no unusual business situations occurred during the year, Chris believes any changes in performance among the adopting branches can be attributed to the BSC. Exhibit B1 reports financial data on loan balances, deposit balances, and non-interest income for the periods ended June 30, 2008 and June 30, 2007, respectively. The SD branches, Branches A-E in Exhibit B1, began their BSC programs on July 1, 2007.

As part of her program assessment, Chris interviewed several employees at each branch . The interviews are summarized below:

BRANCH A:

Customer service representative - Mary Richards
One reason for implementing the BSC is to help us reach our branch goals. Everyone understands that our strategy is to balance loans, deposits, and Certificates of Deposit with growth. For example, to create greater loan volume, we are willing to accept a lower profit margin on each loan. The BSC helps clarify our strategy.

Loan representative - Mike Moore
We have to work at our scorecard measures. They're not easy, but they are realistic. The process seems fair because my measures are just as hard as the other scorecards I have seen. Of course, the measures on my co-workers' scorecards may be different from mine, but everyone has to work hard.

Head teller - Paul Franks
If we meet or exceed our targets, we are eligible to earn cash bonuses. Each month the top performers are recognized and rewarded. There's also a $1,000 reward per quarter to the individual who performs the best on his or her scorecard.

BRANCH B:

Loan representative - Pamela Wise
As I understand it, the BSC is a tool to measure our progress in achieving the goals established by management. In our case, we want to meet the financial needs of a growing community, yet keep a small-town feeling to our services.

Teller - Glenda Smalley
Some of my scorecard measures are challenging, but no more so than the other scorecards I have seen. The measures are difficult, but not unattainable. I think the BSC is being used to encourage us to do better. We are rewarded when we improve. For example, our performance on the BSC helps to determine our year-end bonuses, as well as promotions and raises.

BRANCH C:

Customer service representative - Bill Sorensen
Sure, I understand why we implemented the balanced scorecard. It's purpose is to promote teamwork among tellers, loan officers, and customer service representatives. Also, it helps everyone understand our goals and how to reach them.

Mortgage loan originator - Debbie Hansen
The scorecard taught us how everyone has a part in achieving branch goals by selling, cross-selling, serving as a communication port, and making customers feel welcome. Management wanted a lot of employee feedback when we were deciding to start the BSC. They wanted to be sure we knew about the program.

Administrative assistant - Lou Martin
When we reach our BSC goals as a branch on a quarterly basis, we throw a big party. Individually, we can earn time off, up to a day every two months, if we do well on the BSC. Unfortunately, some of my scorecard measures are next to impossible to achieve.

BRANCH D:

Loan representative - Gary Smith
As I understand it, the BSC is for charting growth. We had to determine which measures were important to the company. Thus, our branch manager asked a few questions when we were deciding which measures to include on the scorecards. I think she helped focus our ideas.

Customer service representative – Al Taylor
My scorecard measures are not impossible; they are fair. All of our measures are probably about the same difficulty. There are some incentives to achieve our goals. For example, we can earn $50 each month if we meet our individual BSC goals. Our branch president is always looking for better ways to reward us for good BSC performance.

BRANCH E:

Loan representative – Ann Stone

In our branch, the BSC is to keep track of what we're doing and to compare our performance with others. I don't see it as a big deal. I reached all of my goals within two months of starting the program.

Teller – Pete Jones

I think the scorecard is used just to keep up with people's activities. I'm not sure any tangible rewards are associated with my performance on the BSC. If I do poorly, I'll probably be fired, however. On the other hand, keeping my job may be considered a tangible reward.

Administrative assistant – Daniel Hughes

We didn't get to participate very much in developing our scorecards. Management just came in one day and told us about the new performance measurement system.

Loan representative – Tim Vines

I've read that the scorecard is supposed to help companies with their strategy. It's difficult to get an idea of our strategy from management. Maybe what I do helps (or does not help) us achieve our strategic goals.

Chris believed the BSC had been a success. She expressed her confidence to the CEO about winning board approval for her plan to expand the BSC to all branches. However, she understood the board would require hard evidence before approving a plan. Chris also understood she must be prepared to answer questions about what went right and what went wrong during the pilot study in the SD branches.

REQUIRED:

1) Prepare an analysis to determine whether the BSC appears to have had an effect.

2) Summarize your results in a report appropriate for the Board of Directors.

3) Identify differences in implementation quality that may explain variation in performance among branches A-E. What implementation recommendations would you make to ND managers who are considering adopting the balanced scorecard?

Exhibit A1

Key Business Perspectives and Lead/Lag Indicators*

KEY BUSINESS PERSPECTIVES:

Financial Perspective – How do we look to our shareholders?

• The financial objectives of the organization serve as the focus of all activities. Every measure selected for a balanced scorecard should be part of a causal chain that results in improved performance on financial objectives.

• Some examples of financial perspective objectives in the hospital industry include operating margins, cost per case, and capital fund-raising.

Customer Perspective – How do customers view us?

• In the customer perspective, organizations must identify key customers and market segments. Organizations must also determine how they add value for customers and seek to deliver better products and services that are tailored to specific customer needs.

• Some examples of customer perspective objectives in the hospital industry include improved recommendation ratings and discharge timeliness.

Internal Business Perspective – At what must we excel?

• For the internal business perspective, organizations identify those processes that must be improved or created in order to reach the objectives of the customer and financial perspectives.

• Some examples of internal business perspective objectives in the hospital industry include reducing the readmission rate (for the same medical condition) and increasing the doctor-to-patient contact time.

Learning and Growth Perspective – How do we continue to improve and create value?

• To achieve the lofty standards set in the previous three objectives, organizations must invest in their people and infrastructure. For this perspective, organizations identify where resources are needed and craft a plan to enable its employees to achieve the objectives of the other perspectives.

• Some examples of learning and growth perspective objectives in the hospital industry include increased employee training and retention, improved information technology systems, and adequate staffing for all shifts.

LEAD AND LAG INDICATORS:

Nonfinancial measures (NFMs) selected in the customer, internal business process, and learning and growth perspectives serve as lead indicators of improvement in financial objectives because improvement in these NFMs often "lead" or precede the improvement observed in financial measures. Likewise, the financial measures selected in the financial perspective are often called lag indicators because improvement in these financial measures often "lags" or comes after the improvement in the NFMs.

*Adapted from Kaplan and Norton's 1996 *Translating Strategy into Action: The Balanced Scorecard* (1996) and *The Strategy-Focused Organization* (2001).

Exhibit A2

Performance Measures for TCCB Balanced Scorecards

- Outstanding Loan Balances

- Deposit Balances

- Number of Products per Customer

- Number of New Customers

- Non-Interest Income-income earned from fees on services and products provided by the bank. NII includes fees associated with CDs, ATM cards, insurance policies, lock boxes, annuities, brokerage accounts, checking accounts, and travelers' checks.

- New Loans Created

- New Accounts

- New Products Introduced

- Employee Training Hours

- Customer Satisfaction

- Customer Retention

- Employee Satisfaction

- Sales Calls to Potential Customers

- Thank-You Calls/Cards to New & Existing Customers

- Employee Turnover

- Referrals-referrals occur when an employee suggests a customer see another branch employee for more information about a product

- Cross-Sells-selling multiple products to a customer when the customer comes in for only one product

Notes from Branch Presidents' Meetings

The most important financial measures are loan balances, deposit balances, and non-interest income. Everything we do should be aimed toward improving these three financial measures.

Customer satisfaction must be improved. Because we are a small community bank, we rely on delivering quality services with a "hometown" feel. We rely on word-of-mouth advertising as much as we do radio and newspaper ads.

Our employees must have training in several different areas, including sales techniques, customer service, and product knowledge/profitability. This type of training would improve the interactions between our employees and customers, allowing tellers and customer sales representatives to recognize customer needs and make more effective referrals and new product offerings.

Exhibit A3

Cause-and-Effect Chain Illustration for TCCB

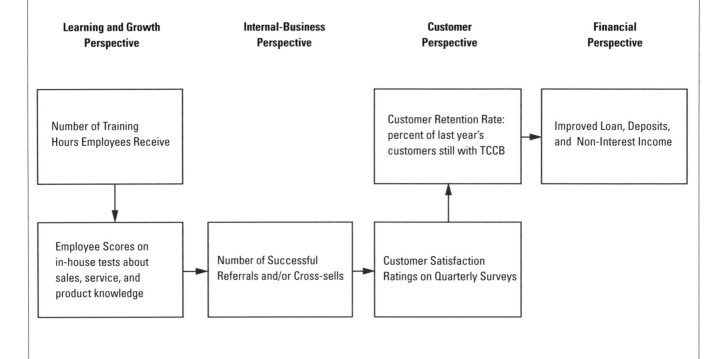

Causal Chain Explanation:

If employees receive training in sales effectiveness, customer service, product profitability, and local bank knowledge, then they can provide better customer service and higher quality interactions with existing clients can take place. TCCB employees will be better able to ascertain the needs of customers, thereby making higher quality referrals and cross-sell proposals to customers, and customers will be more satisfied and choose to continue banking with TCCB. Increased referrals or cross-sales increases non-interest income and provides the basis for growth in deposit and loan balances.

Exhibit B1

Branch performance on key financial indicators

	As of June 30, 2008			As of June 30, 2007		
Branch	Loan Balance (Million $)	Deposit Balance (Million $)	Non-Interest Income (Thousand $)	Loan Balance (Million $)	Deposit Balance (Million $)	Non-Interest Income (Thousand $)
A	39.3	85.1	476.0	35.9	77.0	411.0
B	58.1	104.5	428.0	49.7	101.4	399.0
C	63.7	136.3	529.0	56.1	124.0	474.0
D	46.7	93.1	291.0	45.1	86.7	276.0
E	54.4	109.3	343.0	53.9	108.2	344.0
F	42.9	87.5	345.0	41.9	88.5	335.0
G	64.5	115.2	498.0	64.5	114.8	477.0
H	33.2	78.2	230.0	32.7	77.8	233.0
I	51.1	93.7	293.0	50.8	91.6	280.0
J	71.2	150.8	589.0	68.0	145.0	571.0

Creating a Lean Enterprise: The Case of the Lebanon Gasket Company

Peter Brewer, Miami University; Frances Kennedy, Clemson University

THIS CASE TELLS THE STORY OF THE TRANSITION OF A TRADITIONALLY MANAGED MANUFACTURING FACILITY to a lean facility. It describes the difficulties using volume-based standard costing methods to manage a plant that is trying not to produce excess volume. The case prompts discussion on traditional income statement reporting versus value stream costing, product-related decisions, capacity analysis, and performance measurement alignment with strategy.

This case is appropriate for upper-level undergraduate and MBA/graduate courses. It provides students an opportunity to contemplate the role of accounting within a lean organization. Students will be able to engage in rigorous quantitative and qualitative analyses based on the facts in the case. Furthermore, the case provides an excellent platform for students to enrich their presentations through outside research into the principles of lean production and lean accounting.

Keywords: lean manufacturing; lean accounting; performance measurement; strategic alignment.

Creating a Lean Enterprise:
The Case of the Lebanon Gasket Company

Peter Brewer
Miami University

Frances Kennedy
Clemson University

INTRODUCTION

The Lebanon Gasket Company (LGC) hired Tom Walsh as the plant manager of its Topeka, Kansas, facility in January 2004. LGC was impressed by Walsh's 20 years of experience as a manufacturing engineer, including four years of employment as a manager in Toyota's Georgetown, Kentucky, facility. Walsh's charge at Topeka was to turn around a plant that had been suffering from declining profits and margins, excessive waste and inventory levels, unsatisfactory on-time customer delivery performance, and shrinking market share. His game plan for overcoming these problems was to focus on one core strategy – operational excellence. He intended to abandon the mass production mindset that had guided the Topeka plant since its inception in 1979 in favor of the lean thinking approach that he had seen work effectively at Toyota.

After 18 months on the job, Walsh and his co-workers had accomplished many goals related to the plant's lean transition. Two value streams and four manufacturing cells were up and running. The lean training program was proceeding on schedule. The production, engineering, and maintenance employees had started to buy in to lean thinking. Customer order-to-delivery cycle time had drastically improved, which in turn was growing sales. Nonetheless, the financial results were disappointing. The absorption income statements shown in Exhibit 1 indicated that the plant's net operating income and return on sales had continued to decline from the 11.5% that was reported for the fourth quarter of 2004. To make matters worse, organizational in-fighting was at an all-time high – the Finance Department was blaming the Production Department for the plant's declining performance, and vice versa.

Exhibit 1
LGC Absorption Income Statements
For the quarters ended March 31 and June 30, 2005

	Quarter ended 3/31/2005	Quarter ended 6/30/2005
Sales	$4,022,755	$4,182,214
Cost of Goods Sold	2,909,477	3,049,357
Gross Profit @ Standard	1,113,278	1,132,856
Adjustments:		
Direct Material Variance	24,485	28,065
Direct Labor Variance	31,380	37,562
Overhead Variance	64,527	88,880
Scrap	34,392	26,782
Total Variances	154,784	181,289
Gross Operating Margin	958,494	951,568
Operating Expenses		
Selling Expenses	96,006	97,670
Shipping*	429,797	432,047
Total Operating Expenses	525,803	529,717
Net Operating Income	$ 432,691	$ 421,851
Return on Sales	10.8%	10.1%

*Shipping expenses include salaries, occupancy cost, and supplies.

As Walsh stared at his plant's 2005 quarterly income statements and reflected on his stressful refereeing duties between Finance and Production, he wondered aloud, "Where do I go from here?" Perhaps it was time to have a conversation with his Finance Manager to explore the role accounting should play in a lean enterprise.

THE PLANT AND ITS PRODUCTS

Topeka's headcount had held steady in recent years at about 109 employees (see Exhibit 2 for an organization chart as of January 2004). The plant relies on two main manufacturing processes – injection molding and extrusion molding – to produce a variety of rubber sealing systems for automotive, healthcare, plumbing, and telecommunications applications. Three main product families – OS1, TX4, and KC13 – are produced in the injection molding process. More than 100 product models are produced across these three product families. Two main product families – LX22 and KB8 – are produced in the extrusion molding process. More than 75 product models are produced across these two product families.

In the injection molding process, small resin pellets are fed into a machine where they travel down a large screw that carries them to the molding cavity. As they move down the screw, the pellets are melted to form a liquid compound that is injected into a mold. While in the mold, the liquid is cooled using a combination of water and air. The mold eventually opens and the completed part drops onto a conveyor belt where it continues to cool until it reaches a machine operator. The injection molding machines are expensive pieces of equipment that constrain the pace of production within this process.

In the extrusion molding process, small pellets are heated and transformed into a liquid compound. However, instead of shooting a predetermined amount of compound into a mold to form a completed part, the liquid compound flows in a continuous stream through a shaping mold. The resulting tubular product is then heated treated and either cut to a specific length or spliced into hollow circular seals to meet the customer's requirements. The heat treating activity constrains the level of output from this process.

Exhibit 2
Lebanon Gasket Company Organizational Chart Prior to Lean Reorganization
(Total headcount = 109 employees)

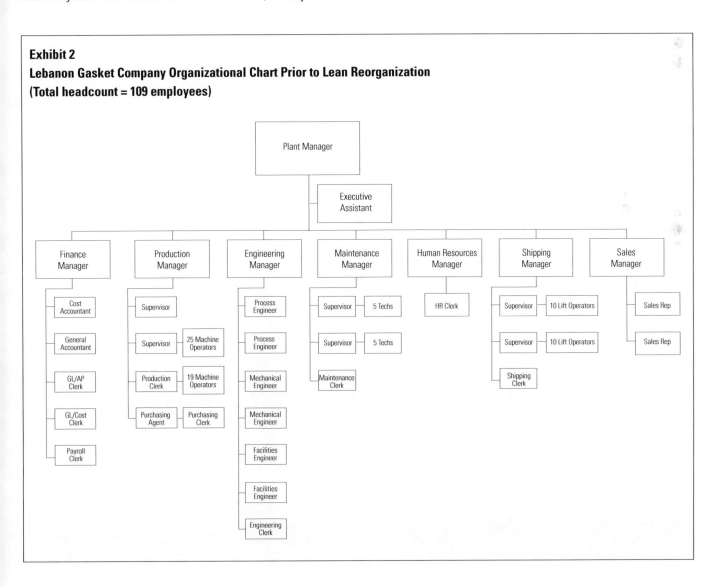

THE LEAN ORGANIZATION

Exhibit 3 shows a Topeka plant organization chart as of June 2005. A total of 109 employees are shown in this chart, which corresponds to the total number of employees shown in Exhibit 2.[1] The fact that these two numbers correspond is not an accident because Walsh had made a conscious effort to retain all employees when transitioning to lean production, based on the belief that layoffs would lower employee morale and decrease the likelihood of a successful lean implementation.

As Exhibit 3 indicates, Topeka's lean plant layout contains two value streams—one for the injection molding process and one for the extrusion molding process. Each value stream team is represented by one value stream manager. Although the value stream manager can be chosen from any of the functions represented on the value stream core team, the individual selected should have substantial manufacturing process knowledge and strong leadership skills. Both value stream teams report directly to the Production Manager and have cross-functional representation from every department within the plant except the Human Resources Department.[2] Each value stream contains two manufacturing cells as

Exhibit 3
Lebanon Gasket Company Lean Organization Chart
(Total headcount = 109 employees)

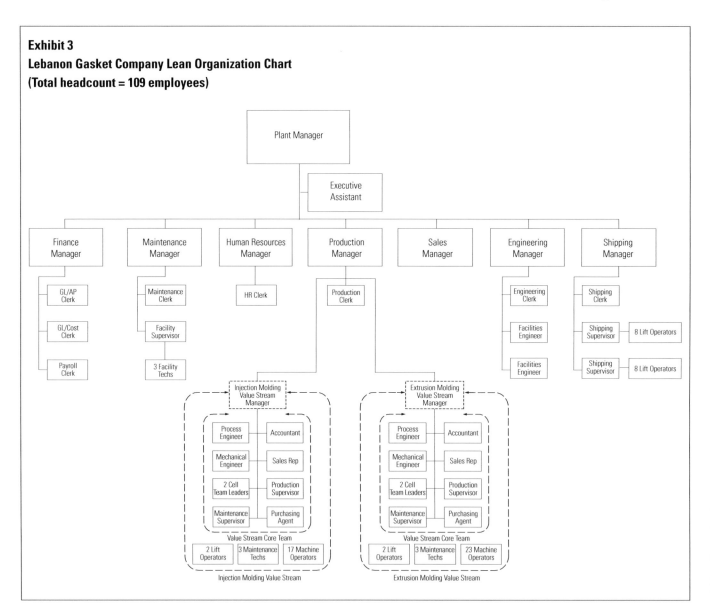

---

1 The value stream managers depicted in the dotted line boxes shown in Exhibit 3 are chosen from the members of the value stream core team. Therefore, it would be redundant to count the value stream manager boxes when tabulating the headcount of 109 employees.

2 Each employee on the value stream teams maintains dotted-line accountability (which is secondary in importance to their primary accountability to the Production Manager) to their respective functional manager.

---

indicated by the fact that there are two cell team leaders on each value stream team.[3]

MASS VERSUS LEAN PRODUCTION

Implementing the lean approach dramatically changed the goal of the Topeka plant's manufacturing processes and the routings for all of its products. Previously, the goal of the plant's mass production process was to achieve the lowest possible cost per unit by maximizing employee and equipment productivity. Exhibit 4 shows the plant layout that was used to achieve this goal. (The arrows in the exhibit depict the routing for products made in the extrusion molding process.) Notice that all of the plant's resources were organized functionally. In other words, its heat treating, assembly and pack, cutting and splicing, injection molding, and extrusion molding resources were maintained in physically separated and autonomously managed departments. Units of production were scheduled based on a forecast of expected customer demand and then processed in large batches

to minimize changeover costs. Work-in-process inventory was stored as needed in between work stations. Supervisors administered strong oversight to ensure that front-line workers met productivity standards. The purchasing agent frequently pitted numerous suppliers against one another in a bidding war to drive down raw material costs.

As a point of contrast, Exhibit 5 shows one of the two manufacturing cells within the Topeka plant's extrusion molding value stream. The goal of the plant's cellular-oriented lean approach is to deliver customer-driven value. Resources are organized in a manner that mirrors the linked set of activities that deliver products to customers. Units of production are pulled through manufacturing cells in a one-piece flow in response to actual customer orders. Cross-trained cell workers are empowered to collaborate with one another to continuously improve performance within the cell. Raw materials are frequently replenished by a limited number of long-term suppliers through the use of visual cues called kanban cards.

Exhibit 4
Topeka Plant: Functional Plant Layout
(arrows depict extrusion molding product routing)

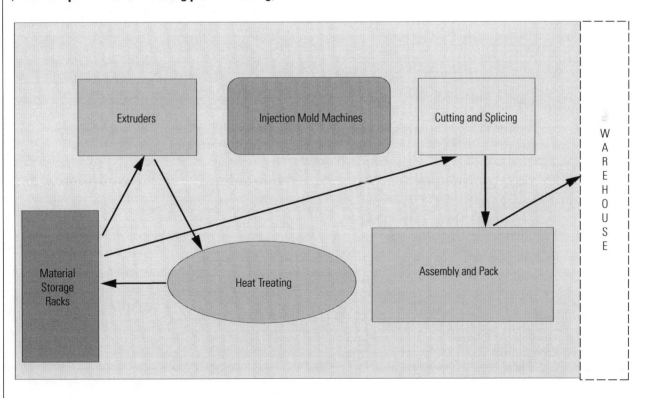

*The product routing depicted above covers approximately 300 yards.

---

[3]The cell team leaders are shown as machine operators in Exhibit 2.

Exhibit 5

Topeka Plant: Extrusion Molding Manufacturing Cell
(arrows depict extrusion molding product routing)

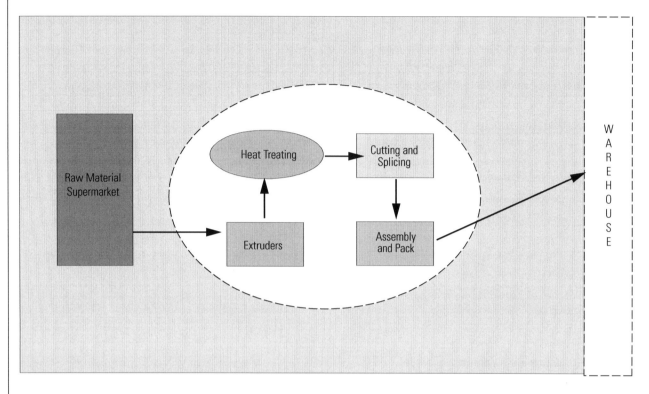

*The product routing depicted above covers approximately 140 yards.

THE FINANCE FUNCTION

Tom Walsh was an engineer, not an accountant. He always believed that if he properly managed the manufacturing floor, the financial results would take care of themselves. Yet, after his first 18 months at the Topeka plant, his rule of thumb had not held true. In an effort to understand the plant's unsettling financial performance, Walsh decided it was time to truly acquaint himself with the role of the finance function within his plant. He set up a meeting with his Finance Manager, Mike Dwyer, and asked him to provide an explanation for the plant's shrinking return on sales.

Dwyer focused his comments on defining the attributes of the plant's standard costing system. He explained that the standard costing system provides the foundation for the plant's: (1) cost-plus pricing system that is used by the sales staff to bid on new business opportunities, (2) monthly variances analysis reports that are used to facilitate operational control on the manufacturing floor, and (3) incentive system that is used to evaluate and reward the performance of employees within each department. Dwyer argued that the plant's poor performance was due to three operational inefficiencies. First, the purchasing agents were paying too much money for raw material inputs as indicated by the unfavorable direct materials variance on the income statements shown in Exhibit 1. Second, direct labor inefficiency was at an all-time high as indicated by the unfavorable direct labor variance on the income statements. Dwyer suggested that the low labor inefficiency highlighted a cost-cutting opportunity that could be realized by laying off a few laborers. Finally, the plant's equipment utilization and overhead cost recovery were nose-diving as highlighted by the unfavorable overhead variance on the income statement.

After Walsh's meeting with Dwyer, four things became very clear. First, Walsh was confused by the language of accounting. Terms such as variances and overhead absorption were difficult for him to understand, to say the least. Second, Walsh was not comfortable with the thought of laying off employees. He felt that his employees were intellectual assets that should be optimized to grow sales, not an expense that should be minimized whenever possible. Third, Walsh had a "gut feel" that something was not quite right with the standard costing approach. The accounting conventions that Dwyer described had been in place since 1979 when he was hired as the plant's Finance Manager. It seemed to Walsh that if the production process had been changed dramatically, the finance function ought to adapt accordingly. Fourth, it was obvious that Dwyer was disinterested in the whole lean concept. He had more than 30 years of experience with standard costing and it defined his view of how to run a manufacturing facility. Furthermore, Dwyer was planning to retire in the near future and didn't have an interest in critically reviewing his department's procedures and reporting practices.

Walsh decided he needed a fresh perspective on the role accounting should play within his plant. Although he tended to have an adverse reaction to the word "consultant," he realized that consulting advice was exactly what he needed. After reviewing proposals from three consulting firms, Walsh hired Lean Enterprise Development from Chicago, Illinois. He asked the consulting firm to help him answer three questions:

1. Do the traditional accounting practices that the Topeka plant adopted in 1979 to support its mass production process have value in a lean environment? Explain the specific reasons that support your answer.

Exhibit 6
Lebanon Gasket Company Product Family Information
(unit cost information is averaged across all product models)

		Injection Molding			Extrusion Molding	
		OS1	TX4	KC13	LX22	KB8
Unit Cost						
Material		$ 0.093	$ 0.148	$ 0.129	$ 0.587	$ 1.101
Labor		$ 0.046	$ 0.069	$ 0.050	$ 0.261	$ 0.289
OH		$ 0.086	$ 0.148	$ 0.148	$ 1.650	$ 1.400
Total Unit Cost		$ 0.225	$ 0.365	$ 0.327	$ 2.498	$ 2.790
Sales Dollars	March	$ 195,118	$ 399,642	$ 432,003	$ 1,227,003	$ 1,768,988
	June	$ 187,599	$ 375,366	$ 414,282	$ 1,323,012	$ 1,881,954
Units Sold	March	542,960	684,319	825,694	350,853	452,890
	June	556,900	685,600	844,612	365,261	465,247
Units Produced	March	534,290	662,498	808,723	354,972	442,099
	June	550,900	650,430	885,900	360,890	450,890
Units Processed per Hour						
Extrusion		n/a	n/a	n/a	1,080	1,110
Injection		2,040	1,650	2,050	n/a	n/a
Heat Treating		n/a	n/a	n/a	970	920
Cutting and Splicing		n/a	n/a	n/a	1,250	1,280
Assembly and Pack		2,760	2,600	2,400	1,100	1,150

Facility Information	March 2005	June 2005
Occupancy Costs		
Utilities, Insurance, Property, Taxes, Insurance, etc.	$ 372,000	$ 396,000
Janitorial, Security, and Grounds Maintenance*	$ 62,000	$ 54,000
Facility Maintenance Personnel	$ 87,835	$ 95,835
Corporate Allocation	$ 84,874	$ 97,670

*These services are performed by outside contractors.

Exhibit 7

Lebanon Gasket Company Value Stream Information

Stream		Injection Value Stream	Extrusion Value
Raw Material Inventory			
Beginning Inventory	March	$ 156,920	$ 372,690
	June	$ 142,450	$ 368,759
Ending Inventory	June	$ 112,461	$ 333,048
Material Purchases	March	$ 237,594	$ 691,189
	June	$ 231,789	$ 672,426
In-Process Inventory			
Beginning Inventory	March	$ 79,850	$ 156,980
	June	$ 56,750	$ 102,578
Ending Inventory	June	$ 32,698	$ 34,890
Finished Goods			
Beginning Inventory	March	$ 120,568	$ 230,890
	June	$ 78,493	$ 187,432
Ending Inventory	June	$ 60,361	$ 58,126
Equipment Related Costs	March	$ 139,098	$ 357,826
(repairs, depreciation, parts, etc.)	June	$ 106,699	$ 384,116
Other Costs	March	$ 8,407	$ 14,799
(selling supplies, travel, etc.)	June	$ 9,840	$ 15,030
Square Footage**	March	57,500 s.f.	112,500 s.f.
	June	47,500 s.f.	105,000 s.f.

** There is 250,000 square feet in the facility, 62,500 feet of which is in the warehouse. The remainder is shared office space and unused production space.

AVERAGE ANNUAL SALARIES*

Position	Salary Amount
Plant Manager	$ 125,000
Executive Assistant	$ 33,000
Sales Representative	$ 72,000
Clerks	$ 27,500
Accountant	$ 52,000
Engineer	$ 65,000
All Managers	$ 80,000
All Supervisors	$ 45,000
Technicians	$ 36,000
Forklift Operators	$ 32,000
Machine Operator	$ 26,000

*Salary amounts do not include 30% fringe (e.g., insurance, payroll taxes).

2. How can the accounting function better serve our senior management team's strategic planning, control, and decision-making efforts within its current lean environment? Specifically, address issues related to capacity planning, aligning employee incentives with lean goals, and product mix decision making.

3. How can the accounting function better serve the needs of our value stream teams and manufacturing cells in their efforts to optimize performance? Specifically address issues related to value stream profitability analysis, linking strategic goals to operational performance measures, and eliminating non-value-added transactions and activities.

In an effort to answer these questions, the consulting firm reviewed the Topeka plant's operations and accounting practices for two weeks and gathered the data shown in Exhibits 6 and 7. Walsh anxiously awaited the answers to his questions as well as the firm's overall recommendations.

THE ASSIGNMENT

Assume that you are employed by Lean Enterprise Development. The principal in charge of this engagement has asked you to create a draft of the presentation that answers Walsh's questions.

SUPPLEMENTAL RESOURCES

B. Maskell and B. Baggaley, *Practical Lean Accounting*, Productivity Press, New York, 2004.

K.M. Kroll, "The Lowdown on Lean Accounting: A New Way of Looking at the Numbers," *Journal of Accountancy*, July 2004, pp. 69-76.

III. Planning and Decision Making

Hula Island: Strategic Decisions Involving Costs and Benefits of Internet Advertising Programs

Stephen C. Hansen and Tom Albright, Naval Postgraduate School

HULA ISLAND IS A BOUTIQUE INTERNET SHOP THAT specializes in hand-painted glassware and Hawaiian-themed products. The company is a pure Internet shop without any brick-and-mortar stores. Internet advertising services offer Hula a variety of options, each with different pricing structures and outcomes. Management must use its resources wisely to generate sales, earnings, and cash flow. Students use their knowledge of Cost-Volume-Profit (CVP) relationships to make advertising decisions that impact short- and long-run profitability. Students then prepare cash budgets to support the timing of their advertising decisions.

The case is suitable for an introductory managerial accounting course at both the undergraduate and graduate levels. You can introduce this case early in each course. The case is applicable to use as an extension of Cost-Volume-Profit (CVP) analysis, as an example of customer profitability analysis, and to introduce the difference between ranking using total profits and profit ratios. This case can also be used to describe the differences between a cash flow and accrual approach or to start a discussion about matching advertising campaigns to available cash flow.

Keywords: cash flow, cash budget, breakeven, conversion, pay-per-click, search engine advertising auction.

Hula Island: Strategic Decisions Involving Costs and Benefits of Internet Advertising Programs

Stephen C. Hansen
Associate Professor
Naval Postgraduate School
Monterey, CA

Tom Albright
Professor and Area Chair Financial Management
Naval Postgraduate School
Monterey, CA

Authors note: The views expressed in this document are those of the authors and do not reflect the official policy or position of the Department of Defense or the U.S. Government.

INTRODUCTION

Hula Island is a boutique Internet shop, not a brick-and-mortar store, specializing in hand-painted glassware and Hawaiian-themed products.[1] Its customers are primarily women between the ages of 30 and 50 whose household earnings are above the national average. Hula Island caters to a unique niche market, providing its customers with a combination of artsy products, custom glassware, and vivid pictures at comparatively low prices. They also offer a generous return policy. To encourage impulse purchases, most items are priced between $15 and $30 with a very small markup. An extensive analysis of the company's customer list shows that, on average, each new customer will generate approximately $3.50 in immediate profits and $25 in lifetime profits (the lifetime profits include the immediate profits).

The owner, who refers to himself as the Chief Coconut of Hula Island, has strong industry contacts and can usually obtain inventory items a month or so before the company's competitors. As a result, Hula has a comparatively loyal customer base. Most customers consider the company's hand-painted glassware products as collectible art objects. For instance, many customers collect the annual Lolita® Wicked Witch wine glass.[2] Hula's best customers collect and display sets of specialty glasses—the "Sister Wife," glass for

example—along with holiday-themed glasses for Halloween and Christmas. The wine glass shown in Figure 1 is one of its best-selling products.

> **Figure 1: An example of a Hula Island product, the "Rich Witch, Too" Wine Glass by Lolita.**
>
>

Hula is a small business with approximately $300,000 in annual sales and roughly $48,000 in annual profits. Table 1 presents a simplified version of Hula's monthly income statements for the fiscal year ended May 31. The monthly sales numbers show a moderate degree of seasonality: 38% of annual sales occur in November, December, and January. But above-average sales also occur in September (end of summer) and April (Halloween and Christmas preorders). It may appear surprising that customers will preorder Halloween and Christmas products in April, but many customers are avid collectors and know that Hula will ship the preordered items a month earlier than competing companies.

The company has no long-term debt, and the owner—the Chief Coconut—will not consider taking on debt to fund advertising campaigns. One important element is that the owner relies on company profits to pay his own rent. Every month, he takes $2,000 as a personal distribution knowing it will restrict the company's ability to expand or to advertise. After the $2,000 monthly distribution, Hula is close to breakeven in most months. A comparatively small miss in sales can lead to a monthly loss.

INTERNET ADVERTISING CAMPAIGNS

Figure 2 shows the steps leading to an Internet purchase on HulaIsland.com. The initial stage of an Internet advertising campaign is to place an advertisement or send an e-mail that attracts a customer's attention. A well-placed advertisement will generate customers who click on the advertisement leading them to the company's website. Tracking the number of clicks captures the essence of advertising. The advertisement is supposed to generate clicks, which also means eyeballs that look at the company's website. Once eyes are on the website, the company is responsible for enticing the customer to purchase its products. Thus, one measure of success for an advertising campaign is the number of clicks generated.

Once customers are on the website, they may identify products or categories they find interesting and look at multiple pages. Customers who are well-matched to the site will look at many pages. The average number of page views per visitor is another measure of campaign success because a large number of page views indicates that a good customer match has occurred.

Table 2: Costs and Predicted Outcomes for each Advertising Option

Costs	Option 1 Monthly Online Magazine	Option 2 Affiliated Retail Store	Option 3 Search Engine Auction
Variable	$0.00	$0.25/click	$0.005/click
Fixed	$500	$50	Auction
Outcomes			
Expected Clicks	1,550	5,780	84,000
Average Page views	20	5	1.5
Percentage of Clicks Converted	7.00%	3.00%	0.14%

The final and most important measure of success is the number of customers who purchase a product. This is known as converting. For purposes of this case, consider conversion as a purchase by a new customer. An advertising campaign is only going to be successful if Hula can generate enough profits (short- or long-run profits) from the converted customers to cover the advertising cost. Conversion is measured in several ways, including advertising cost per conversion and conversions as a percentage of clicks.

INTERNET ADVERTISING OPTIONS

Hula has extensive, successful advertising campaigns directed at its existing customers. Customers routinely receive coupons and notifications of new products and sales from the Chief Coconut. He feels that he has the correct mix of advertising to retain his current customers. But now the Chief Coconut is interested in growing the customer base by attracting new customers. Increasing the number of collectors will provide a greater revenue cushion and move the company away from breakeven in most months.

The Chief Coconut has successfully run Internet advertising campaigns in the past. In May 2015, he was

Figure 2: Steps Leading to an Internet Purchase

Attract Customers ➔ Click on Site ➔ Browse Site ➔ Purchase Product (Convert)

considering three different approaches that have worked for him previously: (1) purchase an advertisement in a monthly online magazine, (2) purchase a pay-per-click advertisement on an affiliated retail store's website, and (3) purchase a search engine advertisement in an auction. Table 2 summarizes the costs and predicted outcomes for each approach. The conversion percentages shown in Table 2 reflect expected conversions by new customers. While the cost of each option is known once the contract is signed, the number of clicks, number of page views, and conversion rates are only estimates. As with all advertising, there is substantial uncertainty about the outcome of each campaign. Each campaign will almost surely generate different actual numbers.

1. **Purchase an advertisement in a monthly online magazine.**
   The first option is an Internet version of a classic advertising technique. Hula could purchase an advertisement in a monthly online magazine. Two possibilities would be *Hawai'i Magazine*® or *Everyday Party*® Magazine. Online magazine advertisements require a fixed cost of $500 and have no click-through costs. Each advertisement yields a fairly low rate of 1,550 monthly clicks, though potential customers are well-matched to the site, as shown by the high number of page views (20) and the highest conversion rate of the three options (7%) (See Table 2).

2. **Purchase a pay-per-click advertisement on an affiliated retail store's website.**
   The second option is to purchase an advertisement on the website of a very large online store. The website would likely generate a very large amount of traffic that could possibly be attracted to Hula's product offerings. For instance, the retail store may have generic wine glasses; Hula Island could purchase an ad that would offer Hawaiian-themed wine glasses.

   The hard part for these campaigns is to find the right search level for the advertisement. Customers usually start on a retailer's website at the homepage and progressively narrow their search results through a "search tree." For instance, a customer might click on the homepage; then patio, lawn, and garden; then outdoor décor; and finally tiki torches. If the advertisement level is too high in the search tree (i.e., patio, lawn, and garden) the ad will not generate much interest. Conversely, if the advertisement level is too low in the tree (i.e., tiki torches) it will not have much traffic. Therefore, Hula places its advertisements at an intermediate product category level (i.e., outdoor décor or party supplies).

   A pay-per-click advertisement that runs for a month on an affiliated retail store has a small fixed cost of $50, and Hula

pays $0.25 for each click. The typical advertisement generates 5,780 monthly clicks. Customers have a moderate number of page views (5) and a moderate conversion rate (3%) (See Table 2).

3. **Purchase a search engine advertisement in an auction.**
   The final option is to participate in a search engine advertising auction. Many high-traffic Web search engines hold auctions where they sell the right to place an ad next to the outcomes of search terms (e.g., Google Adwords). For instance, they could auction off the right to place an advertisement on the outcome page when a user types in "Hawaiian vacation." In order to make this option comparable to the others, we assume the auction provides one month of advertising next to the outcomes of search terms.[3] Selecting the search term item is difficult. At one extreme, Hula is the number one search outcome when "tropical glassware" is typed into most major search engines. It would not make sense to purchase an ad if you are already on the outcome of the search. At the other extreme, bidding on "Hawaiian vacation" would be fruitless since major travel agencies are going to bid large amounts for the ad, and Hula does not have much to do with vacations. After experimenting, management found that the search term "Hawaiian souvenir" is usually within Hula's price range and provides an acceptable amount of traffic.

   In addition to paying the final auction price, Hula must pay $0.005 for each click-through. Showing up on a search engine search generates a large number of monthly click-throughs (84,000). Yet few customers are well-matched— as evidenced by the low number of page views (1.5) and the low conversion rate (0.14%) (See Table 2).

   The Chief Coconut is considering his options for increasing Hula's customer base. Interesting challenges include forecasting costs, revenues, profits, and return on invested resources associated with Internet advertising. Further, the company does not have unlimited cash with which to invest in advertising, and the cash flow throughout the year is inconsistent from month to month.

SUGGESTED DISCUSSION QUESTIONS

Prepare a report to the Chief Coconut of Hula Island that discusses the following:

1. Recall that Hula's management believes that each customer generates $3.50 in short-run profit and $25 in lifetime profit. Calculate the advertising cost per conversion for Internet advertising Options 1 (Monthly Online Magazine) and 2 (Affiliated Retail Store). Calculate

the total expected profit from each option (short-run and lifetime), as well as the ratio of total profit to advertising cost (short-run and lifetime). To determine the benefits of an advertising campaign, should Hula Island use the profit on the first sale or the expected lifetime profits? To choose between advertising campaigns, should Hula Island use the total expected profits or the ratio of total expected profits to advertising costs?

2. Using your answer from Question 1 (either short-run or lifetime, total expected profits, or the ratio of total expected profits to advertising costs), determine the winner of the comparison between Options 1 and 2. Advertising Option 3 is different from the other two options in that the auction determines the fixed advertising cost. Assume Hula wins the search engine auction with a bid of $105. Which advertising option (1, 2, or 3) would you recommend to management?

3. Prepare a cash budget for Hula Island on a monthly basis for the period June 2014 through May 2015. Perform the calculations on an incremental basis (i.e., determine the increase or decrease in cash for each month). The following information will allow you to structure the cash budget: The cash coming in each month is approximately one-half of the current month's sales and one-half of the previous month's sales. The cash out for each month has several parts. Each month Hula pays cash for invoices approximately equal to the cost of products sold in the prior month. Rent of $2,000 is a fixed cost paid during the same month it is incurred. Variable costs are paid each month. They consist of part-time labor costs that average $1.25 per order and shipping and taxes that average $4.10 per order. Finally, the owner takes $2,000 a month as a personal distribution.

4. Although Hula Island is profitable on an annual basis, the company has a very tight budget and a small margin for error. The owner is always concerned about being able to pay his monthly bills. Should the focus of the analysis be accrual accounting, or should it shift to cash accounting?

5. Hula Island will only pay for an advertising campaign out of current cash. Given your understanding of Hula's market, when would be the best time to conduct a single advertising campaign? Why?

6. Should Hula Island run multiple advertising campaigns of potentially different types over the course of a year? Why or why not?

ENDNOTES

[1] Hula Island is a real company that can be found at www.hulaisland.com. The qualitative features of this case reflect Hula Island's business environment, but the numbers are modified to preserve confidentiality.

[2] The current glass is "Wicked Witch, Too," the seventh wine glass by Lolita.

[3] Search engines also auction advertisements with prices that vary by season, day of week, and time of day.

Table 1: Hula Island Income Statement—Entire Year Ended May 2015

Unit Sales	13,926
Revenues	$292,446
Less:	
Rent	24,000
COGS	146,227
Labor	17,408
Shipping and Taxes	57,097
Profits	$47,714
Average profit/order	$3.43

Hula Island Income Statement—By Month

	June*	July	Aug	Sept	Oct	Nov	Dec	Jan	Feb	Mar	Apr	May
Unit Sales	731	981	973	1,301	959	1,245	2,359	1,700	850	769	1,218	840
Revenues	$15,351	$20,601	$20,433	$27,321	$20,139	$26,145	$49,539	$35,700	$17,850	$16,149	$25,578	$17,640
Less:												
Rent	2,000	2,000	2,000	2,000	2,000	2,000	2,000	2,000	2,000	2,000	2,000	2,000
COGS	7,676	10,301	10,217	13,661	10,070	13,073	24,770	17,850	8,925	8,075	12,789	8,820
Labor	914	1,226	1,216	1,626	1,199	1,556	2,949	2,125	1,063	961	1,523	1,050
Ship/Taxes	2,997	4,022	3,989	5,334	3,932	5,105	9,672	6,970	3,485	3,153	4,994	3,444
Profits	$1,764	$3,052	$3,011	$4,700	$2,938	$4,411	$10,148	$6,755	$2,377	$1,960	$4,272	$2,326

XYZ Company: An Integrated Capital Budgeting Instructional Case

David E. Stout, Raymond J. Shaffer, and Jeremy T. Schwartz, Youngstown State University

THIS FICTIONAL U.S.-BASED CASE REQUIRES STUDENTS TO evaluate an asset-replacement decision in relation to whether a company should keep an asset it purchased and put into operation two years ago or whether it should replace that asset with a newer, more efficient model. Increasingly, accountants are being called upon to be "value integrators," that is, to integrate knowledge and skills from across a variety of disciplines. To complete the XYZ case successfully, students will need to draw upon and integrate concepts from accounting (determining relevant cash flows), finance (modeling-related issues associated with the analysis of a capital budgeting decision), and tax (various real-world considerations). In addition, students are asked to complement their financial analysis with strategic and/or qualitative considerations associated with the capital investment proposal under consideration. A final requirement of the case is to prepare an effective document (or table) that summarizes the various analyses students conduct in conjunction with the present case analysis.

The case could be used in an undergraduate cost accounting course or in an MBA managerial accounting course that includes capital budgeting. It is most appropriate for use in undergraduate curricula where the pedagogy is integrative in nature (e.g., in a capstone undergraduate accounting course, in a strategic cost management course, or a similar course in a graduate accounting program). Extensive use of Microsoft Excel is required to complete the case, including the use of Excel to deal with the issue of uncertainty.

Keywords: capital budgeting, curricular integration, discounted cash-flow (DCF) analysis, tax, decision making, qualitative/ strategic considerations.

The Association of
Accountants and
Financial Professionals
in Business

XYZ Company: An Integrated Capital Budgeting Instructional Case

David E. Stout
Andrews Chair in Accounting
Lariccia School of
  Accounting & Finance
Williamson College of
  Business Administration
Youngstown State University
destout@ysu.edu

Raymond J. Shaffer
Lariccia School of
  Accounting & Finance
Williamson College of
  Business Administration
Youngstown State University
rjshaffer@ysu.edu

Jeremy T. Schwartz
Lariccia School of
  Accounting & Finance
Williamson College of
  Business Administration
Youngstown State University
jtschwartz@ysu.edu

THE COMPANY

XYZ Company was formed in the United States seven years ago by Jim Smith, Marsha Chang, and Earl Watson, who together purchased a commercial machine shop that had been in business for more than 40 years but, at the time of the acquisition, was feeling pressure from a variety of new entrants into the markets in which the machine shop competed. Smith had a distinguished military career and felt he could use the skills he acquired in the military to help this business return to its previously highly profitable state. Smith currently serves as the president and CEO of the company.

XYZ produces three primary product lines, all of which are made of brass and are water-related: flow controllers, valves, and pumps. Marsha Chang, a long-time friend of Smith and his family, and a practicing CPA (Certified Public Accountant) and CMA® (Certified Management Accountant), joined the company as its CFO shortly before the formation of XYZ. Earl Watson, a high school friend of Smith, had worked as the manufacturing supervisor at the company for the past 10 years and, at the request of Smith, decided to stay onboard after the formation of XYZ. Over the past several years, Watson had

toyed with the idea of introducing more technologically up-to-date equipment that, he thought, could help ameliorate the competitive position of the company.

Recently, Chang instituted an activity-based costing (ABC) system and a "bare-bones" Enterprise Resource Planning (ERP) system that, among other things, helped the company assess customer profitability and price its products more competitively. A new marketing manager, Maria Sanchez, was hired last year to develop and implement an aggressive product-promotion plan.

These combined changes helped turn the company around. Two years ago, to raise capital needed for an expansion of the plant and the modernization of certain equipment key to the manufacturing process, the company went public. The company was enjoying a renewed reputation as a producer of high-quality brass products, sold principally in the southeast region of the U.S. XYZ was, in fact, profitable in each of the past four years.[1] At the end of the most recent year, total assets were approximately $10 million. Over the past two years, sales for the company amounted to approximately $25 million per year. The company's fiscal year corresponds to the calendar year.

THE PROPOSED INVESTMENT: AN ASSET-REPLACEMENT DECISION

Assume that it is sometime in the fourth quarter of 2014. Watson has presented to Smith and Chang a proposal to purchase a replacement to a machine used to manufacture one of the three products. The existing machine was purchased on January 1, 2013. Assume that the asset replacement, if it occurs, will take place on January 1, 2015. Thus, the issue before Smith, Chang, and Watson is whether to keep the existing machine or to replace it with a new, more technologically advanced machine.[2]

ADDITIONAL ASSUMPTIONS REGARDING THE CAPITAL BUDGETING DECISION

XYZ uses two discounted cash flow (DCF) models—net present value (NPV) and internal rate of return (IRR)—to assess capital investment proposals, including the current asset-replacement decision. Because XYZ has been a listed company for only a short period of time and is thinly traded, Chang has recommended that, for discounting purposes, the company should use 10% (an estimate of XYZ's after-tax weighted average cost of capital [WACC]). In conjunction with your evaluation of the investment proposal at hand, you can assume the following additional facts:

- The tax law that governs this decision is the U.S. income tax law that is (or was) in effect for 2015.
- The proposed acquisition date is January 1, 2015, which can therefore be considered "time period 0" for purposes of your DCF analysis.
- Depreciation on the proposed investment for tax purposes will be calculated using the appropriate rates (to be determined by you) under MACRS half-year convention. As previously noted (see Endnote #2), this means that a half-year's worth of depreciation is taken in the year of asset disposal, regardless of the date of sale within the year. For financial reporting purposes, the straight-line (S/L) method is used to record depreciation charges.
- Over the past two years, the marginal income tax rates paid by XYZ are: local 5%, state 10%, and federal 25%. For analysis purposes, assume that marginal tax rates for XYZ will, during the years covered by this case, remain constant and equal to the preceding amounts.
- Unless otherwise noted, assume that the company does NOT elect to take advantage of write-offs (if any) allowed by Internal Revenue Code (IRC) §179, "Election to expense certain depreciable business

assets," but DOES decline to take "bonus depreciation" (if applicable, and as outlined in IRC §179).
- Prior to considering the capital budgeting decision at hand, the company has already committed to $2 million of other capital expenditures for 2015.
- For simplicity, the timing convention for discounting estimated after-tax cash flows to present value is:
  - All pre-tax operating cash flows, taxes on pre-tax cash flows, and income tax effects from depreciation deductions occur *at the end of each year.* For example, time-period-1 operating cash flows are assumed to be received by XYZ on December 31, 2015. Likewise, taxes on these cash flows as well as time-period-1 tax savings due to MACRS-based depreciation deductions are assumed to occur on December 31, 2015.
  - Opportunity costs (if any) associated with the decision to replace the existing asset are assumed to occur at the end of year 1 (that is, on December 31, 2015).
  - If the old asset is sold, the pre-tax cash inflow from this sale is assumed to occur at the point of sale (at time period zero, January 1, 2015). By contrast, tax savings associated with the half-year depreciation deduction on the old asset under MACRS are assumed to occur at the end of the year, December 31, 2015.

BASE-CASE ANALYSIS: KEEP OR REPLACE THE EXISTING MACHINE?

The current machine, which is being considered for replacement, was purchased on January 1, 2013, for $120,000 with an estimated useful life of 12 years and zero salvage value for financial reporting purposes.[3] The estimated disposal value of this machine on January 1, 2015, is $36,000. If not disposed of (i.e., if not sold outright), it is estimated that the current machine could be used for another 10 years (i.e., the same total number of years as its original estimated useful life).

The base purchase price for the replacement machine is $170,000.[4] Delivery cost for the machine, to be born separately by XYZ, is estimated as $5,000. Installation and testing costs for the new machine are estimated to be $25,000. In the past, XYZ has "charged" each major investment project with an administrative fee equal to 10% of the purchase price of the asset (investment). This imputed fee represents an allocation of corporate headquarters' (i.e., "overhead") expense.

During the discussion of the proposed investment, Watson pointed out that if the company purchases the replacement machine, it is likely to lose some business during the time the old machine is being removed and the replacement machine is installed (and tested). His best guess—and it is only a guess—is that the contribution margin lost during this time would be $5,000 (pre-tax).[5]

If the replacement asset is purchased, pre-tax operating cash flows are expected to increase by $35,000 per year.[6] The new machine is technologically advanced, which is expected to provide two benefits: (1) a reduction in annual cash operating expenses and (2) an increase in sales volume. The latter is attributable to the greater output capacity of the replacement machine. The new machine has an expected useful life of 10 years.[7]

DEALING WITH UNCERTAINTY: SENSITIVITY ANALYSIS

The decision team is aware that many assumptions will be going into the DCF analysis of the present asset-replacement decision.[8] Team members are therefore curious as to how sensitive the replacement decision is with respect to each of the following issues or considerations:

- The discount rate (WACC) used to estimate the present value of after-tax cash flows;
- The amount of annual after-tax operating cash inflow associated with each investment alternative (keep vs. replace);
- The estimated useful life of each of the two assets (i.e., these lives may be different); and
- The possible need to account for an additional investment in (net) working capital should the company purchase the replacement machine.

In terms of the assumed discount rate, Watson offered the following observations at a recent business meeting with Smith and Chang: "OK, we see that on the basis of our DCF analysis one decision option is preferable (in a present-value sense). This analysis assumed an after-tax discount rate (i.e., a WACC) of 10%. Is this the correct amount? Does the rate we use 'matter' in terms of our assessment of the present investment proposal? Over the weekend, I came across a *Harvard Business Review* article that suggested we might have to give more thought to this issue.[9] What do you folks think?"

At the next planning meeting, Watson raised another sensitivity-analysis issue: "Well, we addressed the issue of how sensitive our recommended course of action would be in terms of the assumption regarding the discount rate used in our DCF decision models. It seems to me, however, that there are other areas of concern regarding the numbers we used in our base-case analysis. Key concerns among these might be the 'guestimates' we are making—and up to 10 years out!—regarding the annual pre-tax operating cash

inflows associated with each decision alternative. I think we have a pretty good handle on the operating cash flows associated with the existing asset. After all, we've been using that machine now for two years. The operating cash flow estimate associated with the replacement asset, on the other hand, was determined in conjunction with the discussions we had with the sales agent for the new machine, which suggests to me the possibility that those estimates could be, well, overly optimistic. I know we are dealing with a lot of assumptions here. To keep the analysis manageable, let's go with the discount rate we used in our base-case analysis, 10% (after-tax), and let's assume the use of NPV as our decision model. I'm curious as to how sensitive our recommendation is with respect to the assumption we are making regarding the amount of annual pre-tax operating cash inflows associated with the replacement asset. Perhaps we can rely on Excel to help us explore this issue."

At that point, Watson said: "Two-plus years ago I was involved in the decision to purchase the existing asset. At the time, I remember we factored into the decision the amount of 'net working capital' we thought necessary to support the increased sales volume associated with our investment. I also remember that the amount was something like $20,000. I'm not really sure what this is all about, but I'm thinking that we should at least address this issue. At a minimum, I think we should answer some questions: (1) Conceptually, do we need to amend our base-case analysis to incorporate this information? Why or why not? (2) Assuming we replace the existing asset with the new machine, we would have to commit another $20,000 of (net) working capital to support the anticipated increase in sales. Would this affect our recommended course of action?"

Before the meeting concluded, Smith commented: "Since we're on the subject, does anyone here think it's strange that we're assuming, in our base-case analysis, that the useful life of each asset—both the existing asset and the replacement asset—are equal, that is, 10 years? I would agree that the existing asset is likely to last another 10 years. But I'm not so sure about the replacement asset. Yes, it's supposed to be more efficient, and it's supposed to increase our sales volume—hence the additional projected pre-tax operating cash inflows each year. But I did some research on my own recently, and, on the basis of this research, I feel that a more conservative estimate of the useful life of the replacement asset may be eight rather than 10 years. So, if this is true, we're now left with the unfortunate situation of having to compare two assets of unequal lives. How do we do this analytically?"

The meeting then concluded. All three team members felt comfortable that the team had identified the primary sources of uncertainty regarding the NPV analyses they were about to conduct. At the request of Chang, the next team meeting would be devoted to raising tax-related questions regarding the proposed acquisition.

ADDITIONAL TAX CONSIDERATIONS

At the end of the following week, the team reconvened to discuss three tax-related issues that arose from their informal conversations during the week: (1) the issue of "like-kind exchanges," (2) the possibility of taking an accelerated write-off, and (3) the possible use of a "STARKER escrow" for the sale of the existing machine (if the decision were made to replace that machine).

Smith began the meeting by saying: "Well, we've covered a lot of ground here so far, but I wonder whether we're missing something important from a tax standpoint. For example, our baseline DCF analysis assumes that we're going to sell the existing asset outright in the open market. In fact, we have a firm offer from a reputable buyer for the existing machine. But I wonder: (1) Would there be any tax advantage to *trading in (rather than selling outright) the old asset*, under the assumption that the trade-in amount would be equal to, say, the agreed-upon external sales price, $36,000? (2) If we were to negotiate a trade-in value, what would the breakeven value be? That is, can we come up with the trade-in value that would make us indifferent between keeping and replacing the existing asset? To make the analysis tractable, let's assume data associated with our base-case scenario and the use of NPV analysis to address this question." Chang agreed that Smith's point was interesting and worth exploring. She pointed out that the relevant tax law pertaining to this issue is covered in IRC §1031, "Exchange of property held for productive use or investment."

Smith continued, "I also recall that two years ago, when we purchased the existing machine, we talked about expensing the machine immediately, under (I think) IRC §179. I don't remember the details, but I do remember someone making the point that this election could have saved us more than a trifling amount in terms of our tax bill. I really can't remember why we chose not to go that route. Chang, in your opinion, is this option available this year? Would it benefit us? Why or why not? I think we need to address these questions as we evaluate the present investment opportunity." Chang replied, "I remember an article from a couple of years ago that dealt with these very issues.[10] I'll retrieve and reread it—it may be relevant to the present decision analysis."

Chang continued, "Speaking of additional tax-related issues, I recently read something—in the *Bozeman Daily Chronicle* of all places!—that might apply to our situation: using a so-called STARKER escrow in conjunction with a possible disposal of our existing asset. I never heard of such a thing, but I'm intrigued about this possible tax-related option. I wonder whether this STARKER thing would apply to our situation."

STRATEGIC/QUALITATIVE CONSIDERATIONS: BEYOND THE "NUMBERS"

Then, Smith commented: "I think we've done a pretty good job covering all of the financial dimensions of the present decision, including some interesting income tax considerations. As agreed to in our earlier meetings, our base-case analysis will be supplemented with various sensitivity analyses. At this point, I think we should ask ourselves whether we've covered all relevant aspects of the proposed decision. Why don't we call in Mark Callaway to see whether we are missing something here—something that goes beyond the 'numbers'? I'm concerned, for example, about whether we have properly considered any pertinent strategic or qualitative considerations."

Smith knows that, at a minimum, it will be prudent to consult with Mark Callaway, director of Investor Relations for XYZ. After hearing the back story for the proposal and examining the underlying data discussed thus far by the team, Callaway skeptically responds, "We have been profitable the past two years with the current machine. What you are proposing is giving me a public relations headache—if we sell the old machine, we could very well take a hit on our published financial statements for the first quarter of 2015 and perhaps beyond."

Smith interjects, "On paper, Callaway. The sale of the existing machine would actually provide a tax *benefit*."

Callaway responds, "Yes, we record a loss for financial reporting purposes, but it's truly a loss since we paid $120,000 for the machine, used it for only two years, and now will receive only $36,000 for it. That's quite a rental fee!"

Smith concedes, "You have a point there."

Callaway continues, "We are also pushing aside business during the transition period."

Watson speaks up. "Temporarily, this should only be a minor delay."

Callaway retorts, "So you say. Forgive me for my skepticism, but I would be concerned about how long this 'minor' delay will be. You were the one who promoted the current machine, which is supposed to last another decade but now isn't good enough? Two years ago we raised capital in part by promising profits through use of the current machine, which profits you have delivered thus far. Now, you're asking the company to cough up even more money for a replacement machine, which may or may not be more profitable. As well, you're telling me that the new machine may actually have a shorter useful life than the existing machine it's supposed to replace."

Watson rejoins, "It *will* be more profitable. As noted in the DCF analysis we performed, we anticipate having both operational cost savings and increased sales volume due to increased capacity of the new machine."

Callaway shakes his head, saying, "Look, I think it's great that you're looking for ways to increase the value the company and our bottom line. I'm concerned, however, that you're being overly optimistic. Do you have a handle on how many more units we can sell? Will the cost savings allow us to reduce price to the point where we maintain margins? Best-case scenario, we take a step back only in the next quarter, entirely due to changing the machines. Worst-case, the new machine enables us to produce much more than we can sell, and we're stuck squeezing margins to move our products."

Smith intercedes, "But, we have a real opportunity for growth with the new equipment."

Callaway responds, "Yes, but is bigger really better? I'm leery of making this proposed financial commitment. So much has to go right for us. Let's assume that Watson is right about the cost savings from using the new machine. That would be great, but for what production range will that be valid? Will we really be able to sell enough to make it worthwhile?"

Watson remains emboldened, "I guarantee that the replacement machine will be worth it. You're focusing too narrowly on the short-term adjustment period."

Callaway replies, "Yeah, but how do I know that you won't come back again in two years asking the shareholders to buy another toy that you say will last 10 years?"

Smith brings the matter to a close. "Callaway, we'll take your concerns under advisement. I'm confident that you'll be effective in explaining to our investors any short-term hiccups in profits. But we're putting the cart before the horse here. I think that Watson, Chang, and I need to run the numbers to assess the short-term financial-reporting effect of our decision."

As Callaway walks off, Smith turns to Chang and Watson: "Our earlier discussion with Callaway has made me step back a bit and think more broadly about the decision we're facing. My sense is that it would be worthwhile for us to supplement our financial analysis with a listing of strategic and/or qualitative factors that are associated with this decision. I guess my concern is whether 'the numbers' capture all pertinent aspects of this decision. What do you think? At a minimum, I suggest we address the following questions: (1) Are there important strategic considerations associated with each decision alternative? If so, what are they? (2) If the answer is 'yes,' have we already captured the effect of these factors in our financial analysis? If not, what exactly do we do with this information? That is, is there a way for us to incorporate both financial and nonfinancial information formally into our decision process?" Chang and Watson agreed that these were legitimate questions to address in conjunction with the proposed acquisition.

PROJECT EVALUATION SUMMARY

At the conclusion of the meeting, Watson said: "We've really covered a lot of territory here, to the point that we now have what might be viewed as a bewildering array of facts, figures, and calculations. Can we put our heads together and craft a useful summary of our analyses—perhaps in the form of a table? I know I'd find this very helpful. I think this would be a nice way to prepare for the final meeting, at which time we'll make a decision regarding the asset replacement." Smith and Watson agreed to work with Chang over the next few days to prepare a project evaluation summary report that could be used to guide the discussion scheduled for the following week.

CASE REQUIREMENTS

1. **Base-case analysis:**[11] Should the replacement asset be purchased? That is, does it make economic (financial) sense for XYZ to replace the existing machine? Support your answer by clearly showing the tax basis of the replacement asset (if purchased and under the assumption that the existing asset would be sold outright rather than traded in) and the annual after-tax cash flows associated with both decision options. Remember to record appropriate depreciation expense under MACRS for the existing asset, assuming it is sold January 1, 2015. Recall that the pre-tax cash flow from the disposal of the existing asset is assumed to occur on January 1, 2015, while the tax savings due to depreciation deductions under MACRS, as well as tax-related effects of the disposal (if any), are assumed to be realized at the end of 2015. Base your recommendation on both an NPV analysis and a comparison of the IRR associated with each of the two investment alternatives (keep vs. replace). Comment on your comparative results. Round all calculations, including intermediate calculations, to whole numbers (i.e., to zero decimal points).

2. **Dealing with Uncertainty/Sensitivity Analysis:**

   a. **Issues related to the discount rate:** How (conceptually) is the discount rate for capital budgeting purposes defined and calculated? Is this number appropriate for analyzing the asset-replacement decision at hand? Why or why not? What impact, if any, would a rate below or above 10% have on the recommended course of action for XYZ Company? To address this issue, first prepare a schedule in Excel showing what the NPV results of the base-case analysis would be after letting the WACC vary from a low of 8% to a high of 13%, in increments of 1%. For each discount rate, recalculate the difference in NPV of the two investment alternatives. Next, use the Data Table option in Excel to perform and present the results of this sensitivity analysis. Finally, using the Goal Seek option in Excel, determine the "breakeven" discount rate, that is, the rate that would make XYZ indifferent between the two decision options (based on an NPV analysis of the base-case facts).

   b. **Estimates of annual pre-tax cash inflows of the replacement machine:** Use the Goal Seek option in Excel to determine the breakeven operating pre-tax cash inflow associated with the replacement asset (i.e., the annual pre-tax cash inflow for the replacement machine that would make XYZ indifferent between keeping vs. replacing the existing machine). What keen managerial insight is yielded from this analysis?

   c. **Addressing incremental investment in (net) working capital:** Respond to the two queries raised by Watson regarding the possible need to make an up-front commitment of additional (net) working capital if the replacement machine is purchased: (1) Does the base-case anºalysis need to be changed? Why or why not? (2) If the team replaces the machine, XYZ would have to commit to incremental (net) working capital of $20,000. Would this incremental investment affect the recommended course of action? (Show calculations.)

   d. **Unequal asset lives:** Under the assumption that the useful lives of the two assets differ, a possibility noted by Smith, and based on the use of the NPV decision model, provide a recommendation as to which asset XYZ should choose. Support your answer with appropriate calculations and citations to the literature.

3. **Additional Tax-Related Issues:**

   a. **Like-kind exchanges, IRC §1031:** Prepare a response with supporting calculations (if appropriate) to the two tax-related questions raised by Smith in conjunction with the possibility of trading in rather than selling the existing machine outright (if the new machine were purchased): (1) Would there be any tax advantage to trading in (rather than selling) the old asset? (2) What would the breakeven value of the trade in be? Note: When responding to Smith's second question, assume base-case data. For purposes of responding to this question, you can ignore the incremental investment in net working capital (if any) that would be required if the new asset is purchased.

   b. **Applicability of IRC §179:** Prepare a response, with appropriate authoritative support, to the two questions raised by Smith regarding the provisions of IRC §179, as it pertains to expensing of the cost of the replacement asset: Does XYZ have this option? What are the benefits of this option (if any)?

   c. **Use of a STARKER escrow in conjunction with the disposal of the existing asset:** Prepare a response, with authoritative support, to Chang's issue regarding the STARKER escrow: What is it and is it applicable to the present situation?

4. **Strategic and/or Qualitative Considerations/Multi-Criteria Decision Models:**

   a. **Incentive effects:** Calculate the book loss (i.e., the loss for financial reporting purposes) that Callaway references regarding the disposal (i.e., the outright sale) of the old machine. What effect should the book value have on the decision to purchase the new machine? How will external users, such as shareholders, likely react to this information? What incentive does Watson have in representing the length of time for retooling? How might the present decision affect customer relations? What general issue regarding incentive effects and the design of management accounting control systems is raised by this example?

   b. **Demand and pricing-related considerations:** Expand on Callaway's criticisms from a strategic perspective. For example, what does he mean by "squeezing margins"? What economic assumption regarding price elasticity of demand is XYZ making for its products? How does XYZ balance its desire to gain market share through cost efficiencies with the "commitment" it made to shareholders regarding the original machine?

c. Additional qualitative/strategic considerations and the use of multi-criteria decision models: Prepare a response to the two questions raised by Smith regarding strategic/qualitative considerations associated with the proposed investment: (1) What additional nonfinancial/strategic factors (beyond those discussed in 4(a) and 4(b)) might bear on the decision facing XYZ Company? (2) How could such factors (if any) be formally incorporated into a capital budgeting analysis? To the extent possible, support your position by offering several additional qualitative/strategic considerations and by referencing the appropriate literature (e.g., the literature pertaining to "multi-criteria decision making" models as applied to a capital budgeting context).

5. **Project Evaluation Summary:** Prepare a summary report (in the form of a table) that reflects the major issues addressed in the case. Each row in your table should deal with a separate issue you addressed. For each issue, provide a statement as to whether and why (or how) the issue at hand would affect the recommended decision as well as any additional information you think is pertinent. Assume that the document you prepare would be the type that could be used to guide the discussion at the decision team's final meeting (or the presentation of your report to a client) and that the project evaluation summary would be supported by the various analyses conducted in conjunction with answering previous case questions.

ENDNOTES

[1] As such, the company currently has no operating loss carryforwards for U.S. tax purposes.

[2] By the time of the investment decision (January 1, 2015), the machine in question would have recorded two years' worth of depreciation for financial reporting purposes and two and a half years' worth of MACRS-based depreciation for tax purposes. Under current MACRS rules, a half-year of depreciation is taken in the year of asset disposal. Since the proposed transaction is assumed to occur on the first day of the fiscal year, under MACRS (Modified Accelerated Cost Recovery System) XYZ would record a half-year of depreciation expense for the existing asset for tax purposes for 2015.

[3] Annual depreciation expense for financial reporting purposes = (Purchase price – Salvage Value) / Useful Life. In the present case, depreciation charges = ($120,000 – $0) / 12 years = $10,000 per year.

[4] Currently, there is no sales tax in the state in which XYZ is located.

[5] For simplicity (as noted above), assume that these effects occur at the end of year 1 (i.e., on December 31, 2015).

[6] Pre-tax operating cash inflows from using the new machine are estimated as $55,000 per year. Pre-tax operating cash inflows from using the existing machine are assumed to be $20,000 per year.

[7] Note that this can be different from the period over which depreciation on the asset is recorded under MACRS for U.S. income tax purposes.

[8] In structuring the DCF analysis of the present asset-replacement decision, you may want to consult a corporate finance or intermediate-level financial management textbook and/or the following article: Su-Jane Chen and Timothy R. Mayes, "A Note on Capital Budgeting: Treating a Replacement Project as Two Mutually Exclusive Projects," *Journal of Financial Education*, Spring/Summer 2012, pp. 56-66.

[9] Michael T. Jacobs and Anil Shivdasani, "Do You Know Your Cost of Capital?" *Harvard Business Review*, July 2012, pp. 118-124.

[10] Richard Mason, Sonja Pippin, and Anthony Curatola, "Expensing vs. Capitalizing Business Property in Light of ATRA," *Strategic Finance*, April 2013, pp. 8-12.

[11] Note that all tax-related questions and calculations in the case pertain to U.S. tax law in effect at the indicated date. This law may change over time (which suggests the need for accountants to maintain up-to-date knowledge in the area). Further, the tax laws in effect in countries other than the U.S. may produce different results from those based on U.S. tax law.

The Glenridge Retail Development

Regina M. Anctil, University of St. Thomas; Michael E. Borneman, Connolly, Inc.; and Theodore J. Long, 3M Company

THIS CASE FOLLOWS A WHOLESALE GROCERY DISTRIBUTOR PLANNING to develop newly acquired property into a large retail store. The wholesaler will build and finance the store for a given operator/buyer. At the time of the case, the buyer has not been identified nor has the type of retail grocery store been determined. Company management concurs that the site should either be developed into a conventional supermarket or a warehouse supermarket. The format determination will narrow the choice of potential buyers to either conventional store operators or warehouse store operators. Company management is under pressure to honor existing customer relationships and pursue a local warehouse store operator within their current customer base. But strategic considerations also motivate the company to pursue an external buyer of strategic importance. Internal analysts are given the task of projecting and analyzing master budgets, including income statements and balance sheets, to help assess which type of operation would be stronger in this site.

The case is designed to be used in an advanced undergraduate or graduate-level introductory or intermediate-level management accounting class. Students should be proficient in Excel and in financial accounting principles. The basic case assignment requires students to build and analyze their own budget instrument, providing extensive practice in financial modeling. If you want to examine the case problem without assigning the budget construction task, you can utilize the budget instrument accompanying this teaching note (Glenridge Teaching Note Interactive Budget) for in-class discussion.

Keywords: budgeting, budget analysis, merchandising industry.

The Association of
Accountants and
Financial Professionals
in Business

The Glenridge Retail Development

Regina M. Anctil
University of St. Thomas

Michael E. Borneman
Connolly, Inc.

Theodore J. Long
3M Company

INTRODUCTION

"As far as I'm concerned, a promise is a promise. This is exactly the opportunity Alex Krikorian has been waiting for. We need to offer it to him first," John Caliendo said before hanging up the phone. On the other end of the conversation, Pam Chambers thought about the news she had just received from her division president and the complications coming with it.

For six years, Chambers has been the Northwest Division Sales Manager at Allied Foods, Inc. Allied Foods is a national grocery distributor headquartered in Fort Worth, Texas. Allied Foods is organized into regional divisions, including the Northwest Division. Allied Foods owns and operates 32 corporate retail stores within the Northwest Division. In addition, the Northwest Division serves as wholesaler for 318 independent grocery stores—including single-store operators and multiple-store chains—throughout the Pacific Northwest with distribution warehouses in Tacoma, Wash., and Redding, Calif. Allied Foods operates and serves several different types of stores: conventional supermarkets, warehouse stores, and small neighborhood stores. Approximately 80% of all Allied Foods and its affiliate stores in the Northwest Division operate under one of three brand names, called "banners," representing alternative operating formats and marketing. Market Fare stores are conventional, full-line supermarkets. Value Fare stores are warehouse-type supermarkets. Coronet stores are neighborhood grocery stores.

Chambers has recently been helping Allied Foods negotiate the purchase of a retail site, the Glenridge Coronet store in Eugene, Ore., for development. Allied Foods will expand the existing retail site and redevelop it to the specifications of a particular retail operator, yet to be determined. Allied Foods plans to retain ownership of the land and building, leasing these out to the retail operator. The operator will purchase the fixtures, equipment, and initial inventory outright from Allied Foods, and potentially be a customer of Allied Foods' Northwest Division. Chambers believes the site represents an exceptional opportunity for the company to pursue a particular new customer.

Figure 1 summarizes the transaction Allied Foods will be undertaking with the Glenridge site's current owner and the potential transaction between Allied Foods and the future retail operator.

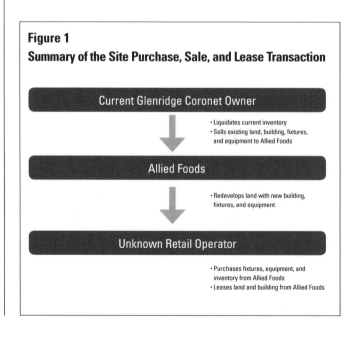

Figure 1
Summary of the Site Purchase, Sale, and Lease Transaction

Current Glenridge Coronet Owner
- Liquidates current inventory
- Sells existing land, building, fixtures, and equipment to Allied Foods

Allied Foods
- Redevelops land with new building, fixtures, and equipment

Unknown Retail Operator
- Purchases fixtures, equipment, and inventory from Allied Foods
- Leases land and building from Allied Foods

THE GLENRIDGE CORONET STORE

The development site is one of four existing McCormick's Coronet stores belonging to Jerry and Marie McCormick, longtime customers of the Northwest Division of Allied Foods. The McCormicks are unusual among retail operators because they own the land, buildings, fixtures, and inventory of their stores outright. Most retail operators lease their land and buildings from third parties. The McCormicks, now in their sixties, have decided to sell everything and retire. Three of the four Coronet sites are too small for a large-scale development project. These are expected to be offered for sale as Coronet stores. The fourth site, the Glenridge Coronet store, is on a large lot near two major intersections and other retail businesses. Chambers has long believed the Glenridge site to be a prime location for a large-scale Market Fare or Value Fare store. For years she has cultivated a close relationship with the McCormicks, trying to persuade them to carry out an expansion using capital from Allied Foods as leverage. But the owners have always resisted, shying away from the large debt burden it would require. They surprised Chambers on her last visit by announcing their retirement, saying, "We decided you should have the first chance to purchase Glenridge."

Chambers always thought that if the Glenridge location came under the control of the Northwest Division she might be able to use it to entice the Sorenson's Grocery chain to join Allied as a customer. Sorenson's is a 22-store conventional supermarket chain operating in northern California and southern Oregon and is currently a customer of the Fitch Foods Group, a California-based wholesaler. Sorenson's interest in a Eugene, Ore., location is well known in the industry, and Chambers expected that Sorenson's would eventually try to purchase the Glenridge site directly from the McCormicks. She would not have been surprised to find Allied Foods and Sorenson's competing for the site had the McCormicks not favored Allied Foods outright. Purchase of the real estate means Allied Foods, as lessor, would have considerable leverage with the store operator. Chambers was delighted to receive the call from her division president John Caliendo, who let her know that Allied had reached a final purchase agreement with the McCormicks. What surprised her in their conversation was Caliendo's negative reaction to her plan to use the location to pursue Sorenson's.

"This site would have to be a gold mine to get Sorenson's to switch suppliers," he said. "Even if we could win their business, we have a commitment. We promised to work with Alex Krikorian to develop a Eugene Value Fare store at the first opportunity. This is the opportunity. How is he going to react if we bring in a big competitor instead?"

Chambers knew about the informal agreement between her division president and Krikorian, who owns a Value Fare warehouse store in Springfield, Ore. He is considered one of the bright lights among the young store owners, having turned a rundown grocery store into a success. Caliendo had been the one to convince Krikorian to make the leap from store manager to owner and acted as Krikorian's mentor through the transformation of the Springfield store. Caliendo also encouraged Krikorian's ambition to open a second warehouse store in neighboring Eugene, promising to help Krikorian pursue any promising opportunity. While Chambers liked and respected Krikorian, she believed his success to be partly due to overworking himself. In her estimation, he did not have the resources or the management skill to own and operate a second, larger location.

Chambers and Caliendo would be meeting with the Allied Foods site development team the following month to discuss development of the Glenridge site. Top of their agenda would be Caliendo's decision on whom to approach as a potential buyer of the operations. The key to identifying the potential buyer is determining the more competitive operating format, conventional or warehouse, for the new site. While Caliendo and Chambers had conflicting views regarding the desired operator, a strong case for a given operating format would narrow the pool of potential operators. Chambers would be responsible for bringing together documentation, in the form of comparative operating budgets, to help determine if the Glenridge development would be more competitive as a warehouse store or a conventional store. Chambers knew if she had any hope of swaying her division president toward Sorenson's, she would have to give him a good reason to change his mind to favor the conventional format over the warehouse format.

Table 1 presents a summary of the internal and external environmental factors surrounding Allied Foods.

THE SORENSON'S CHAIN

Since the day Chambers joined Allied Foods as a retail pricing clerk, Sorenson's and its wholesale supplier, Fitch Foods Group, have been an issue. At that time, Sorenson's had 14 stores in northern California. Fitch, based in Los Angeles, serviced the Sorenson's stores from its northernmost warehouse in Sacramento. As California's largest grocery distributor, Fitch is also the biggest competitor on the west coast for Allied Foods. Fitch continues to hold onto Sorenson's business, even as the chain expands further north.

Table 1
Allied Foods Internal and External Environment

Internal Environment	External Environment

Corporate Headquarters: Fort Worth, Texas
 Structure: Organized by region into operating divisions
 	
 Allied Foods Northwest Division:
 	
     Controls distribution centers in Tacoma, Wash.; Redding, Calif.
 	
     Operates 32 corporate-owned Market Fare, Value Fare, and Coronet retail stores
 	
     Provides distribution services to 318 independently owned Market Fare, Value Fare, and Coronet retail stores
 	
 Northwest Division President: John Caliendo
 Northwest Division Sales Manager: Pam Chambers
	Suppliers:
	 Grocery and home goods producers and manufacturers
	
	 Retail customers:
	 Shoppers of the corporate-owned stores
	
	 Wholesale customers:
	 Independently owned Market Fare, Value Fare, Coronet, and other retail stores including:
	
	     McCormick's Coronet stores
	     Krikorian's Springfield Value Fare
	
	 Potential wholesale customer:
	 Sorenson's grocery chain
	
	 Distribution competitor:
	 Fitch Foods Group, current distributor for Sorenson's grocery chain

Much of Sorenson's growth has been in areas where economic conditions are tough. Sorenson's strategy has been to identify and acquire locations where owners have inadequate capital to weather economic fluctuations, meet debt obligations, and keep the store facility up to date. Sorenson's success combined tight working capital management and months of hands-on attention from the company's general management team for each new store. Sorenson's capital and management style gave each acquisition a fresh start.

There was a great deal of criticism of the Northwest Division management for not initially responding to Sorenson's expansion. Many in the Allied Foods management ranks voiced concern that the retailer's expansion would eventually lead Fitch to expand north as well. Criticism came to a head when Sorenson's took over two Market Fare stores in Oregon, giving that wholesale business to Fitch. At that time, Northwest Division management had some recourse to prevent the loss of the two stores. They could have stepped in with additional financing or financial restructuring for the owner, tried to purchase the sites, or tried to bring in another buyer. Barring those options, they could have made a pitch to win Sorenson's business from Fitch. Subsequently, the Northwest Division's sales manager left Allied Foods, and Caliendo became the new division sales manager, naming Chambers as assistant sales manager. Allied headquarters treated the management transition as the solution to the problem, but Chambers believed that the Northwest

Division's response to Sorenson's expansion strategy was only part of the issue. Also at issue was whether her own company had created Sorenson's opportunity by not intervening with the troubled stores sooner.

As the current division sales manager, Chambers believes Sorenson's northward expansion presents an opportunity for Allied Foods because the Oregon stores are farther away from Fitch's Sacramento warehouse and thus more costly to serve. Allied Foods could be in a position to offer Sorenson's greatly improved logistics for its stores through its Redding, Calif., warehouse, 160 miles to the north.

ALLIED FOODS AND THE WHOLESALE CUSTOMER

As a grocery distributor, Allied Foods offers its wholesale customers a full line of warehouse, distribution, and store support services. Below is a list of the supply chain and retail support services provided by the Northwest Division.

- **Warehouse and Distribution Management:** Allied Foods provides full procurement, warehousing, distribution, delivery, order input, and data transfer services to all retail stores. The biggest source of revenue for the Northwest Division and Allied Foods comes from these services.

- **Retail Management Support:** Allied Foods develops competitive strategies for product selection and placement, maintains and updates designs and schematics for various store formats, and manages each store's retail pricing database, which includes determining the retail price for each product under the particular store banner of the customer and taking into account product cost, promotional offers, individual store price adjustments, and competitors' prices. The pricing data file is transmitted electronically to each customer on a daily basis. Allied Foods plans marketing and weekly advertising for stores, producing and distributing advertising materials to households served by the store via newspaper, radio, television, and internet.

- **Other Management Support:** Allied Foods provides full-service payroll; accounts payable management; monthly, quarterly, and annual financial statements; and financial analysis. The purchase of these various accounting services is discretionary but required for all retailers using financing from Allied. Allied Foods also offers management consulting, including in-store operations analysis, management training, shrink control, cash management, human resource management, and safety.

- **Financial Support:** Most retail operators are unable to obtain conventional bank financing for the capital required to purchase and operate a retail store. Allied Foods provides financial leverage in the form of loans and leases to support new store purchases and store remodeling.

BINDING THE WHOLESALER-RETAILER RELATIONSHIP

The goal in any new store development for Allied Foods is to launch a profitable long-term supply relationship with the new store owner. But the level and stability of that revenue stream largely depends on the supply agreement between Allied Foods and the retail operator. Through its regional operating divisions, Allied Foods tries to contract a formal supply agreement with each retail store or chain, binding the store owner to a minimum percentage of total inventory purchases from Allied Foods.

A supply agreement does not specify what inventory must be purchased from the wholesaler, but the logistics of buying and receiving different types of merchandise lend themselves to agreements that effectively lock in the retailer for certain merchandise from the wholesaler. First, a significant percentage—typically 25% to 35%—of a store's purchases are Direct Store Delivery (DSD), which refers to merchandise stores must purchase directly from the manufacturer, bypassing the wholesaler. On top of that constraint, the wholesale supply agreement typically sets minimum purchases at 45% to 60%, leaving the stores with limited discretion to use alternative suppliers.

Figure 2 illustrates the constraint on the retailers' purchases imposed by DSD purchases and a wholesale supply agreement.

Figure 2
Potential Inventory Sourcing Constraints for the Retail Operator Under a Supply Agreement

Purchases only Available Through Direct Store Delivery (DSD) 25% - 35%

Purchases from Wholesale Distributor per Supply Agreement 45% - 60%

Purchases Allowed from Alternative Suppliers 5% - 30%

Retail Inventory Purchases

A 60% supply agreement would effectively make Allied Foods the primary source for almost all of the non-DSD products sold. A 60% supply agreement is very desirable for Allied Foods because of the volume and predictability of the purchasing. But, frequently, store owners opt for a supply agreement that leaves them more flexibility to select alternative suppliers. A 45% supply agreement is common, where the store uses the wholesaler as its primary source for grocery, deli, frozen, bakery, health, and household products and the secondary or contingent supplier of meat and produce. A 45% supply agreement is riskier for the wholesaler because of an unpredictable order flow for highly perishable products.

For the retail operator, a supply agreement is not as advantageous as it is for the wholesaler because the wholesaler uses short payment terms—typically payment is due within 10 days of the purchase. Short payment terms mitigate the working capital burden on the wholesaler and reduce collection loss. They are considered crucial to the wholesaler's viability and thus are rarely compromised. Alternative suppliers competing for sales offer much more generous terms—30 days or more.

Because a supply agreement can reduce the flexibility and liquidity of the retailer's operation, getting a customer to contract a supply agreement requires some additional inducement. A very powerful customer will demand a lower supply agreement or choose to operate without one. For others, a higher supply agreement might be part of the cost of retaining an Allied banner, with its associated marketing support and brand recognition. Most commonly, a customer borrowing development capital and leasing land and a building from Allied would negotiate a supply agreement as part of the terms of the financing contracts and might receive lower interest on a development loan, for example, in exchange for a 60% supply agreement.

ALTERNATIVE STORE FORMATS AND COST STRUCTURE

Whether Allied Foods pursues development of the Glenridge site with Sorenson's, Krikorian's, or another retail operator partly depends on which store format is expected to be more competitive in the geographical location. Most independent store owners specialize in a particular format. Conventional stores, such as Allied Foods' Market Fare and Sorenson's, differ from warehouse stores, such as Krikorian's Value Fare, in several respects. Operationally, two stores of the same size use very different layout, inventory, pricing, and service practices. Accordingly, volume and cost structure also differ. Although there is variability within each category, there are predictable differences, driven by the contrasting pricing and operating strategies. Table 2 presents a summary of key pricing, operational, and cost differences between the warehouse format and the conventional format.

At a warehouse, or "price-impact," store customers shop for everyday low prices and do not expect a high level of individual service or amenities. Sales volume needs to be higher than in a conventional retail store because of lower gross margin. Operations focus on purchasing, stocking, and handling efficiency to drive down costs. Operators receive and stock large lots, much like a wholesale warehouse, with little storage area. Shelves are stocked by cases rather than individual units. Cost savings from efficiency gains are continuously reflected in lower retail prices, resulting in consistently low gross margin.

A conventional, or "high-low," store provides greater variety and selection. Operators try to balance customers' price consciousness on basic groceries with higher-priced specialty items and prepared convenience food. Operators use less shelf space for each item. Shelves are stocked by hand and must be continuously maintained. Average prices are higher, and volume is lower than in a warehouse store, providing a larger gross margin percentage. But stores offer aggressive sale promotions and services to attract customers.

While the basic structure of the income statement is the same for warehouse- and conventional-format stores, the choice of format differentially affects some of the operating costs. Sales volume is the primary cost driver for both conventional and warehouse stores. Table 3 is a profit statement that describes the basic costs and cost behavior of a retail store.

Cost of goods sold as a percentage of sales is higher in warehouses than conventional stores because of their high-volume, low-price strategy. Conventional stores use a higher mark-up on average, so the gross margin percentage is higher. But conventional stores tend to experience higher-variable operating costs as a percentage of sales, particularly their labor, advertising, supplies, and repair and maintenance costs. These costs are higher because of the strategy of offering more customer service amenities and more food prepared and packaged on the premises. The conventional store format also requires more hands-on shelf stocking.

Table 2
Comparison of Warehouse and Conventional Operating Formats and their Impact on Profit

	Warehouse Store	Conventional Store
Pricing Strategy	Price impact: Everyday low prices	High-Low: Higher margin pricing with promotions
Inventory Offered	Basic grocery selection; limited brand representation	Broader selection and brand representation
Service Level	Basic services (restocking and checking)	More services (counter service, bagging, carry out); more food preparation on premises
Gross Margin Percent	Lower	Higher
Variable Operating Costs as a Percentage of Sales	Lower	Higher

Table 3
Profit Statement for a Retail Store

Account	Definition	Cost Behavior
Sales	Sales at retail price less markdowns	
Less: Cost of Goods Sold	Merchandise cost plus inbound freight cost	Variable
Gross Profit		
Less: Other Operating Costs		
Labor Cost	Gross salaries and wages for employees	Variable
Labor Benefits and Payroll Tax	Vacation pay, insurance, and employer's payroll tax	Variable
Advertising Cost	Store-level advertising costs, store coupons, and store promotion costs	Variable
Supplies Cost	Bags, packaging, cleaning and sanitary supplies, receipt tape, aprons, smocks, and towels	Variable
Repair and Maintenance Cost	Cleaning, repair, and maintenance of store fixtures and equipment including floors, washrooms, and offices	Variable
Utilities Cost	Energy costs of in-store heating, air conditioning, lighting, cooking, and refrigeration	Fixed
Rent Cost	Cost of leasing land and store buildings	Fixed
Common Area Maintenance	Costs of services provided by lessor for any property maintenance, including landscaping, insurance, and security	Fixed
Administrative Expense	Costs of accounting, tax, and other business services, operating fees and licenses, liability insurance, and owner's discretionary expenses	Fixed
Depreciation Expense	Periodic allocation of historical cost of purchased fixtures and equipment	Fixed
Operating Income		
Less: Interest Expense	Interest cost of long-term debt	
Income Before Tax		
Less: Tax Expense	Income tax accrued on current income before tax	
Net Income		

Most of the fixed costs of operations, including utilities, rent, common area maintenance, and administrative expenses do not depend on the store format. They are more of a function of a store's size, age, and location. But a conventional store usually requires more equipment and fixtures than a similar-sized warehouse store, which will drive up its depreciation.

Of the fixed costs, the administrative expense category is the least predictable because it includes many costs that are incurred at the owners' discretion. This category includes costs associated with business licensing, liability insurance, and administrative services such as accounting and inventory control. Discretionary expenditures include tax and estate planning, travel, and entertainment. Also discretionary is the amount of administrative work that is externally contracted vs. performed by the owner. If the owner leases any equipment or vehicles, the cost would be included here. The category also can include the owner's salary and salary paid to the owner's spouse. Finally, if the owner has more than one store, administrative costs might be allocated to each store, rather than recorded as incurred at a particular store.

FORECASTING THE OPERATIONS OF THE NEW GLENRIDGE SITE

As the sales manager of the Northwest Division of Allied Foods, Chambers is prepared to support the negotiation with the potential buyer as soon as Caliendo makes his decision, which will partly depend on the side-by-side comparison of a warehouse store development to a conventional store

Table 4

Contents of the Glenridge Analysts' Data Workbook

Worksheet	Tab Title	Contents
Site Survey Tab	Site survey – Glenridge	• Site description • Demographic profile for two-mile radius • List of competitors in two-mile radius by type • Main assumptions • Weekly sales forecast by store for Glenridge site and competitors (2012-2017)
Comparative Store Tabs	Ross Market Fare, Corvallis Estacada Market Fare, Estacada South East Value Fare, Medford Centennial Value Fare, Salem Capital Market Fare, Salem Krikorian's Value Fare, Springfield	• Store profile, size, opening date, format, affiliates, initial capital investment, Allied Foods supply agreement • Income statements 2007-2011 • Balance sheets for years ending 2007-2011 • Schedule of Allied Foods revenue earned from the store (2007-2011) • All data for Krikorian's Value Fare dates (2006-2011)

development. To facilitate this, Chambers has gathered a team of analysts to forecast cash budgets, income statements, and balance sheets for the Glenridge site. In addition to informing the decision, these documents will also be used in negotiation with the buyer.

Chambers provides her team with two inputs to perform their budgeting task. The first input is a summary of the Glenridge "site survey." The site survey is a study of the Glenridge location, including population demographics, household purchases, and local retail competition, resulting in a forecast of the expected store sales given the store size and format. This survey has been carried out by special staff from Allied Foods. The second input is historical accounting records, income statements, and balance sheets from stores deemed comparable to the planned Glenridge store. Comparable financial statements from these stores will guide the analysts in forecasting budgeted income statements and balance sheets for the Glenridge site, ensuring that key performance measures, such as gross profit percent, contribution margin percent, inventory turnover, accounts payable turnover, and other measures are in line with those achieved by stores of a similar format. Comparability is never perfect, and stores that offer a good comparison on some dimensions are poor on other dimensions. So Chambers has selected multiple comparable stores.

Chambers has compiled the two inputs into a spreadsheet titled "Glenridge Analysts' Data Workbook." Table 4 provides a summary of the content of the workbook.

THE GLENRIDGE SITE SURVEY

The site survey supports Chambers' belief that the site can support a 50,000-square-foot store development. The survey shows the site is located on a major intersection that carries outbound downtown and local university traffic to residential areas south and west of the city. The residential areas served range widely from blue collar and service workers to affluent two-income households. The surveyors compiled a list of the store's direct competitors, estimates of household purchases, and estimates of population growth and inflation to support projections of sales volume for the site over a five-year period. Table 5 summarizes the results of the survey, showing the forecast of weekly sales for a 50,000-square-foot store at the Glenridge site under both a warehouse and a conventional format.

Table 5

Glenridge Site Weekly Sales Forecast from Survey of the Glenridge Retail Site as of January 14, 2012*

	Warehouse Store	Conventional Store
2013	$413,623	$383,623
2014	435,686	404,756
2015	451,510	419,714
2016	467,100	434,414
2017	481,855	448,254

*The survey is based on a January 1, 2013, opening date for the developed store.

The survey is based on estimated total weekly household grocery purchases of $1,997,933 for 2012 in the two-mile area surrounding the Glenridge site. To obtain the total weekly purchases for each of the next five years—beginning in 2013, the year the newly developed Glenridge store is expected to open—the weekly household purchases number was allowed to grow each year by the forecast rate of population growth and inflation. The surveyors then estimated how much of that amount will be captured by each store in the two-mile radius. The survey also assumed a certain percentage of aggregate household purchases would "bleed" out to retailers outside of the two-mile radius. Major suburban power centers and warehouse stores that pull shoppers from a larger geographic area are the reason for the bleed. Figures 3 and 4 show how the 2013 forecast total weekly household purchases of $2,059,868 is expected to be captured by each store in the two-mile radius of the Glenridge site area, assuming the Glenridge location is a warehouse store (Figure 3) vs. a conventional store (Figure 4).

Figure 3
Total Weekly Household Purchases Forecast in 2013 Warehouse Format

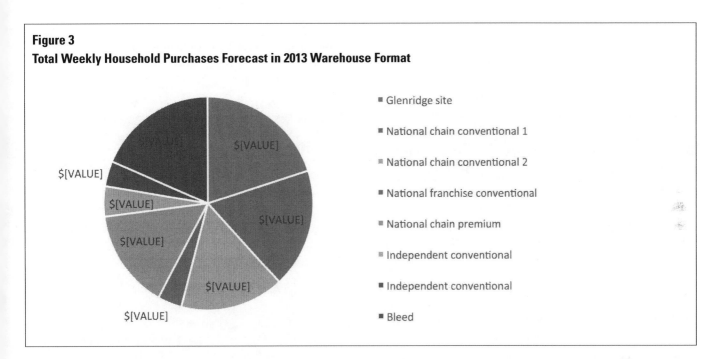

Figure 4
Total Weekly Household Purchases Forecast in 2013 Conventional Format

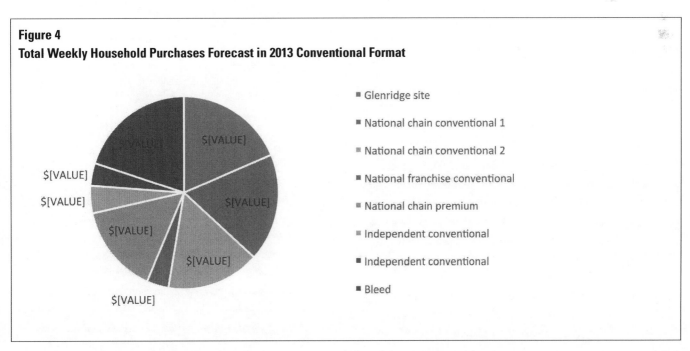

Creating a sales forecast using the survey tools is not an exact science. It reflects the experience and judgment of the surveyors. A new store initially pulls significant existing sales from competitors. Whether those sales remain with the new store depends on how aggressively the competitors respond. The Glenridge survey judged that the warehouse format will also capture significant sales from outside the listed group of competitors, resulting in lower bleed than under the conventional format.

STRUCTURING AN AGREEMENT WITH THE PROSPECTIVE BUYER

As described in the introduction, the retail operator's outright purchase will consist of the store's furnishings and equipment and its initial inventory. The store's land and building will be leased from Allied Foods. So the purchaser must come into the transaction with a cash contribution large enough to cover the purchase price of the inventory, fixtures, and equipment plus an adequate cash balance to lease and operate the store. This amount of cash can come from two basic sources. The purchaser's own resources will provide the owner's equity portion of the initial investment. The remaining cash needed will be provided by a loan from Allied Foods. In addition to negotiating these amounts, the contract with the buyer will also cover the terms of the loan repayment, the lease agreement, the wholesale supply agreement, and the wholesale support services contract. Allied Foods' negotiation will start with the budget projections for the store site provided by Chambers and her team of analysts.

CHAMBERS MEETS WITH THE ANALYSTS

With the purchase of the Glenridge Coronet nearly complete, Chambers begins work on the material she will need to present the site to a potential operator. She is convinced that pursuing Sorenson's is the best long-term strategy for her company and that the Glenridge site represents an opportunity that will not soon be repeated. She knows that if her team's work does not clearly show that the conventional format will perform better than the warehouse format, Caliendo will choose to approach Krikorian with the development opportunity.

Beyond the objections of her division president, Chambers knows that the prospect of winning a supply agreement with Sorenson's has enormous hurdles. The Sorenson's chain has a longstanding relationship with Fitch—all its existing systems would be tied to that supplier.

It would take a substantial inducement just to get the retailer to test the water with Allied Foods. Chambers decided to try, on her own, to compile the key selling points Allied Foods could offer the Sorenson's chain and hopes her analysts' work will back her up.

She calls a meeting of her analytical team and provides a list of schedules and measures that she will ask her team to compile for a side-by-side comparison of the conventional and warehouse formats for the Glenridge site. Table 6 shows the list she distributes.

Table 6
Glenridge Site Comparative Budgets and Analysis Requested Schedules and Measures

Master Budgets for 2013-2017

Cash Budget:
  Sales/collections budget
  Inventory purchases budget
  Inventory payments budget
  Cash operating expense budget
  Capital expenditures budget
  Summary cash budget including loan and financing costs

Financial Statements:
  Income statements including depreciation, interest, and tax expense
  Balance sheets

Financial Analysis

Ratio Analysis:
  Liquidity – cash conversion cycle
  Efficiency – asset turnover ratios (inventory, accounts payable, total assets)
  Profitability – gross margin, operating profit margin, return on assets, return on equity
  Solvency/risk – operating leverage, interest coverage ratio

Sensitivity Analysis:
  Sensitivity of earnings and cash flow to volume reduction
  Sensitivity of earnings and cash flow to gross margin reduction

---

She instructs the analysts as follows:

"The goal of your analysis is to determine how successful the Glenridge site will be for the potential operator. We will need to project five-year master budgets, including inventory purchases and payments budgets, cash budgets, income statements, and balance sheets for a warehouse store vs. a conventional store. Once you have the budgets, go over them with basic financial analysis tools: ratio analysis and sensitivity analysis.

The data file I'm giving you contains the five-year revenue forecasts for the Glenridge site from the Allied Foods site survey, assuming a January 2013 opening. Though we know these aren't firm numbers, they are a good start. The sensitivity analysis you perform will help us see how the store stands up under competitive pressure.

You also have the most recent historical financial statements for three Market Fare stores and three Value Fare stores, including Krikorian's Springfield store. These comparison stores should be helpful in guiding most of your operating cost projections as well as the store's inventory requirements and accounts payable levels. But some of the cost amounts will be negotiated between Allied Foods and the purchaser. I can give you some working assumptions to use.

The purchaser will be leasing the land and building from Allied Foods. The rent will be determined in the negotiation, but I think the starting price will be at least $500,000 per year and 10% for common area maintenance. Assume the store fixtures and equipment will be purchased and that a 50,000-square-foot warehouse store will require about $1.8 million in fixtures and equipment. That number will be about $2 million for a conventional store. Use an average life of seven years and straight-line depreciation on that.

All of the initial cash to buy the opening inventory, fixtures, and equipment and to operate the store will come from the buyer's equity contribution and a loan from Allied Foods. Those amounts will be part of our negotiation, but for now assume the entire initial cash contribution is 20% financed with owner's equity and 80% financed by Allied Foods at a 5% rate. With a sizable loan, Allied Foods will impose a minimum cash balance requirement, so assume the store needs to leave $50,000 minimum cash balance at the end of each year of operations. This will influence the initial cash contribution required. Allied Foods will refine the financing possibilities when we show them this work.

Finally, I want to stress that this site represents a major strategic opportunity for Allied Foods and our division. Since we control the lease in this site, any interested buyer has to work with us. You are all aware of how John Caliendo is thinking on this. Granted, we all respect what Alex Krikorian had been able to accomplish in his first store, but in our competitive environment we have to look at the big picture. Our job is to give John the numbers to do that. I know it's tempting to use Alex's current numbers to project the warehouse format's performance, but I want you to think hard about whether his performance is truly representative of a large-scale warehouse store. It is likely he is holding his labor and administrative costs down by overworking and underpaying himself. That is not going to be sustainable with two stores. Pay particular attention to the operating costs at Centennial Value Fare, which I have also included.

Make sure you document your estimates back to the source and that any assumptions are explicitly stated and justified. John will want to know where every number comes from before he is convinced, and so will I."

Cat & Joe's Pig Rig: Should We Stay or Should We Go?

Tony Bell, Thompson Rivers University; and Andrew Fergus, Thompson Rivers University

CATHY OBERTOWITCH AND JOE THOMPSON HAD JUST RECEIVED AN INVITATION TO bring their food truck, Cat & Joe's Pig Rig, to a rodeo event in a town 70 kilometers away. They weren't sure whether attending the special event would be worth their time, effort, and expense or if they would be better off not attending at all and continuing with business as usual.

This case encourages students to analyze the profitability and viability of attending the event and to examine both the financial and nonfinancial aspects of the decision. Students will be called upon to perform breakeven calculations, a target profit analysis, and a "what if?" analysis of the opportunity. This case represents a straightforward, real-world application of Cost-Volume-Profit (CVP) analysis.

This case was designed for use in the CVP module of an introductory management accounting course. It can be used at both the undergraduate and graduate levels.

Keywords: CVP analysis, breakeven analysis, food trucks, what-if analysis.

The Association of
Accountants and
Financial Professionals
in Business

Cat & Joe's Pig Rig: Should We Stay or Should We Go?

Tony Bell
Thompson Rivers University

Andrew Fergus
Thompson Rivers University

INTRODUCTION

When the invitation arrived, Joe Thompson and Cathy (Cat) Obertowitch were not sure what to do. The event looked promising, but the last time they agreed to attend a similar special event, they had barely broke even. They had left the event reminding themselves, "We don't need to say 'yes' to every opportunity."

Joe and Cat were an engaged couple who had been running their food truck, Cat & Joe's Pig Rig, for several months. Their truck specialized in pulled pork and southern-style barbecue. "Slow and low[1]" was the cooking philosophy of the food truck, which was based in Kamloops, British Columbia, Canada, a city of 100,000. Business had been brisk, the truck was outperforming projections, and their customer base was growing. They had also supplemented their day-to-day business by attending local events and doing catering jobs.

The couple had just received a request to bring their truck to an event called "Bullarama"—a rodeo held in the nearby town of Barriere, located 70 kilometers north of Kamloops (Exhibit 1). Bullarama looked great on paper: the promoters noted that 700 attendees were expected, Cat & Joe's Pig Rig would be the only food option, and rodeo fans would be a great market for the company's southern-style barbecue. Tempering their enthusiasm for the event were a few mitigating factors: (1) event promoters tended to be optimistic with promises and projections, (2) the 70-kilometer drive to Barriere added a number of costs that may be significant, and (3) perhaps most importantly, business was good in Kamloops, and if they did the Bullarama event, they would forgo one day's revenues in their home market. The couple couldn't be sure of what to do until they fully analyzed the opportunity.

CAT AND JOE

Cat and Joe came from the neighbouring towns of Smithers and Houston in northern British Columbia. They knew each other growing up but never connected beyond the level of acquaintances. Cat recalled their relationship as teens: "I was interested in Joe, and Joe was interested in hockey." The two lost touch, married other people, and started their own families. Cat had one daughter and two sons, while Joe had two sons of his own.

Cat went to school for nursing and referred to her career as that of a "gypsy nurse" working for a wide variety of organizations. Her most recent jobs included a role at a pregnancy outreach center and an instructional post in the nursing program at the local university in Kamloops. Joe's career had been more stable. After a short time as a cook in a restaurant, he found a permanent career behind the wheel of a logging truck, first in northern British Columbia then moving to the city of Merritt, 100 kilometers south of Kamloops.

Cat and Joe's marriages dissolved. Eventually, the newly single acquaintances reconnected on Facebook when the social media site suggested that they might know each other. The two began dating, and on one of their earliest dates, Joe cooked for Cat. On that night, Joe's pulled pork sandwich proved to be his way into Cat's heart. She was surprised to learn that one of Joe's hobbies was smoking meat. After high school, as soon as Joe could afford a smoker, he bought one, and in the two decades since, he had become an expert in the art of smoking and slow-cooking beef and pork. He also enjoyed making his own rubs and sauces.

As their relationship became more serious, Joe moved from Merritt to Kamloops to live with Cat. Joe's workplace was still based an hour away in Merritt, leaving him little time for family after the commute and his long days driving the logging truck. Neither Joe nor Cat was happy with this arrangement, with Joe spending a lot more time on the road than at home. Something had to give, so Joe began to look for new opportunities closer to Kamloops.

It was at a potluck dinner that Cat and Joe got the inspiration for their business. Joe brought a dish from his smoker, and it was a hit. Two of their friends who attended the party, Cye Delaney and Denise Leigh, were owner-operators of a popular local tattoo parlour. These experienced entrepreneurs suggested that Joe's pork was so good that he and Cat had a legitimate business opportunity. They agreed to give Cat and Joe advice if needed and put the couple in touch with an angel investor.

When it came time to meet the potential investor, both Cat and Joe were nervous. They wanted the opportunity badly, but it was one thing to impress friends at a potluck and another thing entirely to impress a stranger—and to impress him so much that he would be willing to invest tens of thousands of dollars in a business concept proposed by two inexperienced entrepreneurs. Joe and Cat brought the possible investor a sample of the items they planned to include on the menu, and perhaps more importantly, they also brought a conservative, but thorough, business plan. The angel investor was so excited by the food and the business plan that he wrote them a check on the spot. With that meeting, Cat & Joe's Pig Rig was born.

FOOD TRUCKS

During this time, food trucks were an emerging culinary trend in Canada and around the world. While mobile concessions and canteens had existed for decades, there was a new wave of food trucks, which focused on bringing higher-end fare to the marketplace. The old model for food trucks often involved selling frozen or nonperishable products, whereas the new model relied on technological improvements to miniaturize and mobilize full, gourmet kitchens, enabling vendors to offer a much broader array of dishes.

As of 2014, Vancouver, British Columbia, had more than 100 active food trucks selling all types of dishes, including Indian, Korean, Japanese, seafood, Mexican, barbecue, crepes, Ukrainian, and more.[2]

Cat and Joe's pulled pork concept would be the first food truck attempted in the city of Kamloops. After meeting with local politicians and agreeing to some limitations[3], Cat & Joe's Pig Rig was given the city's blessing to begin operating. They purchased and outfitted their truck and opened for business (Exhibit 2).

THE BUSINESS

Cat & Joe's Pig Rig saw immediate success. In the early months, the business outperformed its revenue and profit projections. But Cat and Joe did not wish to rest on their laurels. They knew that they were enjoying early success not only because they offered a good product but also because the food truck was a novelty in Kamloops. They were pleased to have a first-mover advantage, but they knew it would not last forever. They needed to continue to develop a loyal customer base and were also working hard to expand the event and private catering side of their business.

The food truck's signature dish was its "Ripped Pig" pulled pork sandwich.[4] The sandwich came in a combo with coleslaw, baked beans, and French fries and was priced at $12. The company had variable costs, which included the cost of the food, clamshell packaging, and variable overhead. Variable costs were 40% of the company's revenues. There was no labor cost as neither Joe nor Cat drew a wage or salary.

Fixed costs included items such as gas for the generator, maintenance, business licenses, and truck depreciation. These costs totaled $10,000 per year. The operational year for the food druck was 180 days. Corporate income tax rates for small businesses in British Columbia were approximately 20% around that time.

The pork needed to be put in the smoker at least 12 hours in advance of service, which created two challenges for Joe. First, it meant that he worked virtually 24 hours a day. Operating the truck meant setting up, serving, and cleaning up from 10 a.m. to 7 p.m. But when service was over, Joe's day was not done. He needed to smoke the pork overnight—which involved putting the pork in the smoker late in the evening (with just the right blend of wood chips), and waking up to tend to the meat in two-hour intervals throughout the night, spraying the meat to ensure it would have the right consistency and tender quality when it was served the next day. Although it was exhausting work, Joe was willing; he had a great work ethic, he was his own boss, and smoking meat was one of his passions.

The second challenge presented by the 12-hour cooking requirement was determining how much pork to smoke—too much or too little could be a disaster. If Joe did not prepare enough meat the night before, he could not simply go out and buy more if they were having an unusually busy day. Failure to project high demand meant the Pig Rig would be sold out for the day, and Joe and Cat would need to close the truck early, leaving customers unsatisfied. If Joe prepared too much meat, and they didn't sell out, the extra meat would be donated to a local soup kitchen. While Cat and Joe felt good about doing something generous in their community, donating pork meant inefficiency and significantly reduced their profits.

Forecasting poorly was a huge risk for their business, and mistakes were costly. Fortunately, experience meant that Cat and Joe were getting better at predicting how many customers they could expect in a day. On a typical day, Cat and Joe served between 75 and 125 patrons, with an average of 100. The amount varied based on the weather, the day of the week, and other factors such as nearby local events. Joe also had a formula for when the truck was invited to special events: He expected 35% of attendees would purchase food, not necessarily from him, but from one of the food vendors at the event. He would use this ratio to estimate the number of potential customers. He would then divide his estimate for potential customers by the number of vendors serving the event. If he was the only vendor, he would get all of the potential customers, if there were two vendors, he expected to get 50% of the food-buying customers. This number would serve as his guideline for how many pounds of meat he would need to smoke the night before. It had proven to be accurate in the past, and Joe intended to use this formula for any special events going in the future.

A crucial aspect of the company's success was its marketing strategy, which focused on social media. Because their food truck changed locations frequently, Cat and Joe wanted to ensure that customers knew where to find them, and the best way to do this was online. They were very active on Facebook, Instagram, and Twitter[5] and, as of 2014, had not spent any money on traditional marketing. They had the largest social media presence of any restaurant or food truck in Kamloops. And it was through social media that the organizers of Bullarama contacted Cat and Joe.

THE BULLARAMA DILEMMA

The invitation was succinct. It explained that Cat & Joe's Pig Rig would be welcomed at Bullarama in Barriere, British Columbia. Bullarama was a charity rodeo event, where novice, junior, senior, and professional riders would compete. A handicapping system would be used to ensure all riders could expect competitive scores. According to event organizers, 700 tickets had been sold.

When Joe and Cat brought their truck to special events they did not serve their usual pulled pork sandwich combo. They served only the sandwich, with no beans, coleslaw, or French fries. This enabled them to serve customers much more quickly and to reduce their price to $9 per serving. It also let them replace their expensive clamshell packaging with a much cheaper foil wrapping. With fewer side dishes and less expensive packaging, variable costs would be reduced by $1.90 per customer when compared to their normal menu.

There were several other cost considerations related to the Bullarama event. First, the event organizers suggested a donation of $100.[6] Second, their food truck ran on propane, and the 140 kilometer round trip to Barriere would add $100 to their typical fuel costs. Finally, in order to maximize space for the mobile cooking equipment, the truck only had one seat (for the driver), so if Joe drove the food truck, Cat would need to drive her car separately, with an expected extra gas cost of $30. All of these costs would be avoided if they stayed home in Kamloops.

The couple had one other concern. The organizers promised that Cat & Joe's Pig Rig would be the only food option available to event attendees, but the entrepreneurs had heard such promises before and found they were not always reliable. While they trusted the event organizers, they were worried about the potential for other onsite competitors. They planned to do calculations for multiple scenarios.

The couple reminded themselves that business was good in Kamloops, but this represented an opportunity to expose their product to a new, potentially lucrative market. As Joe opened the calculator app on his smartphone, he reminded himself that numbers were important, but this decision would not be based on numbers alone. There were a lot of other factors to consider.

ASSIGNMENT

1. List and briefly describe the advantages and disadvantages inherent to the food truck business model as compared to traditional restaurants.
2a. On a typical day in Kamloops, how many "Ripped Pig" sandwiches must be sold in order to break even?
2b. Comment on Cat and Joe's breakeven point (calculated in Part a). Should this number be relevant to the entrepreneurs?
2c. If Cat and Joe wish to make a $100,000 profit for the year (after tax), how many pulled pork sandwiches must the Pig Rig sell each day? Assume all days are in Kamloops at regular prices.
3. Prepare a contribution-format income statement for one day's business at the Pig Rig based on optimistic, realistic, and pessimistic projections for a regular, non-event day in Kamloops.
4. Prepare a contribution-format income statement for the Bullarama event based on an optimistic projection (no onsite competitors), a conservative projection (one onsite competitor), and a pessimistic projection (two onsite competitors).
5. What are the nonfinancial advantages and disadvantages of attending Bullarama?
6. Assume Cat and Joe were told that they should expect one onsite competitor. Would you recommend they stay in Kamloops for the day or go to Bullarama? Justify your answer with both financial and nonfinancial data.

ENDNOTES

[1] Slow and low is a cooking style synonymous with southern-style barbecue. It refers to the fact that meat is cooked slowly at a low temperature to achieve an extremely tender texture.

[2] A full list of active food trucks in Vancouver can be found at http://vancouver.ca/people-programs/street-food-vending.aspx.

[3] Limitations included meeting all health-code standards that apply to restaurants and adhering to operating boundaries to prevent the food truck from poaching customers from established restaurants.

[4] Although there were other items on the menu, they had very similar prices and costs (margins were virtually identical). For the purposes of calculations in this case, assume there was only one item on the menu: the Ripped Pig sandwich.

[5] Cat & Joe's Pig Rig had more than 1,700 "Likes" on Facebook, more than 600 Twitter followers, and nearly 200 followers on Instagram.

[6] It was not unusual for charity events to request its vendors to make a donation, and although the donation was "suggested," it was realistically a requirement if Cat and Joe wished to attend the event.

Exhibit 1. British Columbia Map

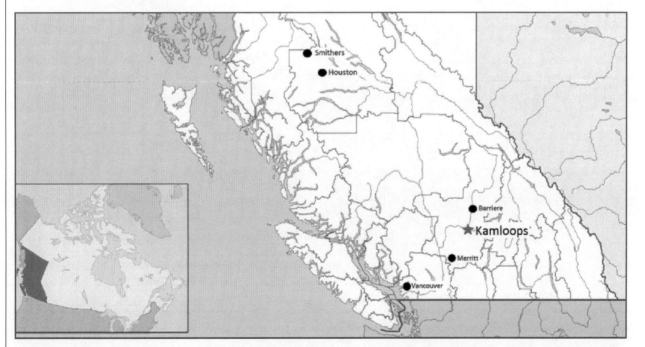

Note: This image was used under Creative Commons Attribution-Share Alike 3.0 licensing. The original image has been adapted to include the six labeled locations. The original image and licensing information can be found at http://en.wikipedia.org/wiki/Rogers_Pass_(British_Columbia)#mediaviewer/File:Canada_British_Columbia_location_map_2.svg.

Exhibit 2. Cat & Joe's Pig Rig
Front and Reverse View of the Food Truck

Over-land Trucking and Freight: Relevant Costs for Decision Making

Thomas L. Albright, Naval Postgraduate School; Paul Juras, Babson College; and Russ Elrod
Arab Cartage and Express Co.

OVER-LAND TRUCKING AND FREIGHT HAS A long-established and mutually beneficial business relationship with a major international automotive parts company, FHP Technologies. Management at FHP has approached Over-land with a request to provide additional routes that are important to the efficiency of its supply chain. Over-land's management wishes to nurture the business relationship with FHP but is concerned about the available capacity to service the new routes, potential risks, and profitability associated with FHP's request.

The case is suitable for an introductory managerial accounting course at both the undergraduate and graduate levels. It is designed to be used to reinforce the concepts of cost behavior and cost-volume-profit (CVP) analysis and to introduce the concept of capacity.

Keywords: cost behavior, breakeven, point of indifference, relevant costing, capacity.

Over-land Trucking and Freight: Relevant Costs for Decision Making*

Thomas L. Albright
Naval Postgraduate School

Paul Juras
Babson College

Russ Elrod
Arab Cartage and Express Co.

ABSTRACT

Over-land Trucking and Freight has a long-established and mutually beneficial business relationship with a major international automotive parts company, FHP Technologies. Management at FHP has approached Over-land with a request to provide additional routes that are important to the efficiency of its supply chain. Over-land's management wishes to nurture the business relationship with FHP but is concerned about the available capacity to service the new routes, potential risks, and profitability associated with FHP's request.

INTRODUCTION

Alan James founded Over-land Trucking and Freight in 1968 and has grown the business into a sizeable operation with 90 trucks and 180 trailers. His largest customer, FHP Technologies, has submitted a proposal to him to add delivery routes that would improve the efficiency of FHP's supply chain. Alan was not certain that Over-land could handle the additional routes since the company currently was operating at (or near) full capacity.

FHP offered a total of $2.15 per mile (including fuel service charge and miscellaneous fees) for the new route. But Alan knew that to accept the offer he would have to add more trucks and perhaps incur additional debt. The question was whether the rates offered by FHP were high enough to offset the associated risks of growing the fleet. Although the business had been grown organically through the years by reinvesting profits, it incurred debt from time to time to replace older equipment (usually in blocks of five trucks). Alan knew the slim profit margins associated with trucking, coupled with a downturn in the economy, could spell disaster if saddled with too much debt. See Exhibits 1 and 2 for the company's most recent statement of income from operations and the balance sheet, respectively.

Roger Simmons, Over-land's operations manager for the past 16 years, had been reviewing the FHP proposal and approached Alan. "Alan, we need to discuss this offer from FHP. I think it is a great opportunity for our company, and we need to find a way to make it work." Within 10 minutes Alan and Roger were in a closed-door meeting discussing the pros and cons of FHP's offer. Roger began by stating the obvious: "Alan, this is a huge opportunity for us to grow the business. Not to mention, as FHP becomes more dependent on our services, we will be in a stronger position to negotiate future rate increases. I know you are opposed to debt, and I understand the risks of carrying more debt, but there is more than one way to grow our fleet. If you would consider using independent contract drivers, we could grow the fleet enough to accept FHP's offer without incurring more debt."

Alan cringed at the thought of using independent contract drivers. Although independent contractors owned their own trucks, Alan viewed them as difficult to deal with and not worth the headache. "Roger, I hear you, but this new route will not last a week if we cannot give FHP great service. Independent contractors call the shots, not us. They own the rig and will sit at home if they want to. I would rather deal with our own company's rigs and drivers. The rewards just do not justify the risks of damaging our relationship with FHP."

The views expressed in this document are those of the author and do not reflect the offical policy or position of the U.S. Department of Defense or the U.S. government.

"But I am not sure we should take on any more debt at this point to purchase additional rigs. The economy is in the tank, and it is a bad time for us to leverage the balance sheet any further. Roger, my success in this business was not built by jumping on every offer that came along. Sometimes you have to say no, even to your biggest customer. Unless you can find a way to squeeze out more capacity within our current fleet, I just do not think we can accept FHP's offer at this time," Alan concluded.

As the two men left the room, Roger was convinced that Alan was wrong. Roger knew that Alan was leaving money on the table. He just needed to prepare a financial analysis that would prove it. Was it possible to squeeze out more capacity from an already fully utilized fleet? Perhaps they could shift trucks from another account. Was taking on more debt truly "risky" given the profit potential of this new route? Roger knew he had to make a convincing argument before FHP took its offer to another truck line.

INDUSTRY TERMS

- A tractor-trailer rig is a truck that consists of a tractor attached to a trailer. The tractor typically is powered by a diesel engine.

- A flatbed trailer is long flat platform with no sides.

- A dry van trailer is a boxed cargo compartment designed for nonrefrigerated freight.

- Trucking companies often have a revenue-generating load in one direction but need a revenue-generating contract for the return trip. The return trip is known as a backhaul. Often trucking companies contract with freight brokers to acquire backhauls.

INDUSTRY BACKGROUND AND COST STRUCTURE

Trucking firms generate a variety of revenue types from hauling goods for their clients. Presented next is a brief overview of key types of revenues included in the 2013 income from operations of Over-land Trucking and Freight.

Line haul revenue is earned from hauling freight.

Fuel prices in recent years have been volatile. Because trucking companies are exposed to fuel price volatility when they sign a long-term contract with their customers, they may charge an additional fee associated with fuel costs when prices exceed predetermined levels. Thus, the primary purpose of the **fuel surcharge (FSC) revenue** is to protect the truck line from fuel price increases during the contract term.

Included in miscellaneous revenue are the following:

Storage fees are collected when Over-land stores a loaded trailer on its lot for a customer.

Lumper revenue is collected if a driver assists with unloading a trailer.

Certain flatbed loads, such as drywall, unpainted steel, and some types of wood products, that would be damaged by rain must be covered. Trucking companies typically charge a **tarping fee** for such loads.

Additional insurance is required when transporting **high-value cargo**. Practices vary throughout the industry. If a load is above a company's standard cargo insurance limits, many companies simply will not haul it. Trucking companies that are willing to bind additional cargo coverage normally do so for a fee that covers only the extra cost of insurance. (Alternatively, this revenue line item could have been booked as a reduction to the "Insurance" expense account.)

Loads transported on flatbed trailers must be secured by straps or chains. These types of loads often are associated with higher worker's comp claims. Thus an extra **strapping and chaining fee** is charged only for a flatbed load.

If a truck sits idle at the dock for more than two hours, customers can be charged a fee that is classified as detention revenue. Placing a **detention revenue** clause in the contract encourages customers to load trailers efficiently in order to avoid further constraints on Over-land's tractor capacity.

TYPES OF BUSINESS ARRANGEMENTS WITH DRIVERS

Over-land has potentially two arrangements with drivers. They are classified as employees or as independent operators. Employees receive traditional employee benefits and a Form W2 for tax purposes. These persons are typically engaged in work for the company that is considered "permanent."

Alternatively, independent operators are not considered employees and receive a Form 1099 (rather than a Form W2) for tax purposes. These operators typically provide the tractor but generally do not provide the trailer. In addition to driver salaries and depreciation on trucks, expenses incurred by independent contractors include:

- Tags (known as International Registration Plan (IRP)) – The independent contractor buys the IRP tag for the tractor, while the shipping company buys the tags for the trailer.
- IRS Form 2290 – Heavy Road Use Tax.
- Diesel fuel, engine fluids, and all maintenance-related parts and items.

- Physical damage insurance.
- Non-trucking "bobtail" Liability Insurance (needed for when the truck is not transporting a trailer).
- Tolls and scale fees.

For an example of a publicly traded transportation company that primarily uses independent operators, visit Landstar Trucking Company's website at www.nonforceddispatch.com/landstar.php.

For a description of a publicly traded transportation company that primarily owns its rigs and employs company drivers, see J. B. Hunt Transportation Services' Form 10K at www.sec.gov/Archives/edgar/data/728535/000143774914002605/jbht20131231_10k.htm. Read the discussion in Item 1-Business.

Independent contractors generally control their own working hours, unlike an employee. Further, independent contractors' work generally is considered temporary, rather than permanent (unlike for an employee). In the trucking industry, an independent contractor often signs a one-year contract for a temporary job. But an employee is hired permanently under the assumption that he or she will make deliveries until further notice. This arrangement constitutes a permanent job.

CAPACITY ISSUES AND INDUSTRY PRACTICES

Over-land Trucking typically assigns one driver to one tractor. But this practice can constrain the available hours the tractor can operate. For example, laws require a driver to take a 10-hour break after 11 hours of driving. Further, a driver cannot work more than 70 hours in an eight-day period without taking a 34-hour break. To improve tractor utilization by avoiding constraints based on legal driving time requirements, some trucking companies use "slip seating." This is a practice that permits greater tractor utilization by placing a fresh driver behind the wheel at the end of the former driver's shift. Slip seating is similar in practice to an airline company that keeps its planes flying longer by inserting fresh flight crews as the previous crew goes off duty. It also is efficient to utilize "team drivers" that are commonly husband-wife teams. One person drives while the other sleeps. Relative to a single driver, this arrangement basically doubles the amount of miles driven in a given week. Typically, teams are paid more, but additional line haul revenues offset the extra labor costs.

Another strategy to improve tractor utilization is to use trailer pools, commonly referred to as "drop and hook" systems. For example, trucking companies will leave an empty trailer with customers, who will load it with products as units are produced. When the trailer is filled, a tractor arrives, drops an empty trailer to replace the trailer just filled, then immediately hooks onto the loaded trailer and departs. Tractor utilization improves because tractors are not sitting idle while a customer loads a trailer. This approach is economically feasible because trailers are far less expensive to purchase and operate than tractors.

Most trucking companies keep some tractors "on the fence" as spares, in case one breaks down. There is considerable disagreement, however, over what constitutes too many spares. Some owners believe a truck line should put all available equipment on the road and rent a tractor if a spare is needed. Others disagree and maintain a small number of tractors in reserve. Currently, Over-land Trucking and Freight keeps a small number of tractors and trailers out of service but prepared for duty in case a rig breaks down. Some managers believe this policy is an expensive luxury and that some of these idle rigs could be used to add the new routes requested by FHP. When estimating a tractor's practical capacity, management at Over-land use 85% of total potential miles driven in a period. Theoretical (or 100%) capacity utilization is virtually impossible in the industry because of factors such as traffic and loading delays.

THE PROPOSAL AND RELATED ISSUES

Management at FHP has asked Over-land to consider adding two dry van loads per week; each load would require 1,500 round-trip miles. Because FHP is a long-term client with a strong financial position, the company's management has asked for a very favorable rate of $2.15 per mile including FSC and all miscellaneous fees. Roger believes the potential volume of freight from FHP can be used to grow Over-land's business and profitability. There is also risk associated with not taking the new lines. If Over-land does not accept the new routes, another trucking line will, thus building loyalty with FHP.

FHP is a stable, solvent company that presents no question of collection, thus ensuring a reliable cash flow. If FHP decides to restructure its supply chain in the future, Over-land could find itself in the undesirable position of holding dedicated assets (trucks and trailers) for routes that no longer exist. The owner's aversion to increased debt levels further exacerbates concerns about acquiring additional fixed assets. Perhaps Over-land could service the initial demand with existing equipment. But, as additional routes are added in the future, Over-land must acquire more tractor-trailer rigs or consider outsourcing the miles by using independent contractors.

Exhibit 1 presents Over-land Trucking and Freight's income from operations for the year ending December 31, 2013. This statement is not prepared in accordance with

Generally Accepted Accounting Principles (GAAP) but presents costs by behavior. Exhibit 2 presents Over-land Trucking and Freight's balance sheet for the year ending December 31, 2013.

Exhibit 1
Income from Operations

(All financial information in the case has been scaled and disguised for educational purposes.)

Over-land Trucking and Freight
Income from Operations
For the year ending December 31, 2013

Revenue	FYE 12/31/2013	Per Mile
Line Haul	$20,925,280	$1.86
Fuel Surcharge	4,950,160	0.44
Miscellaneous	450,120	0.04
Total Revenue	$26,325,570	$2.34
Variable Expenses		
Insurance	675,120	0.06
Fuel	8,775,190	0.78
Oil Lubricants	112,700	0.01
Tolls	112,550	0.01
Parts and Small Tools	787,630	0.07
Hourly Wages: Drivers	4,950,160	0.44
Trailer Pool Expense	255,120	0.02
Total Variable	15,638,480	1.39
Fixed Expenses		
Insurance		
General Liability	112,620	0.01
Physical Damage	225,010	0.02
Workers Compensation	226,000	0.02
Health Insurance	224,500	0.02
Security	111,750	0.01
Depreciation	2,137,500	0.19
Salaries, Benefits (Garage)	675,000	0.06
Salaries, Benefits (Office)	1,012,520	0.09
Bad Debt Expense	113,500	0.01
Permits	111,520	0.01
Rental Equipment	1,013,000	0.09
Payroll Taxes	562,500	0.05
Accounting Fees, Supplies, Computer Maintenance	112,350	0.01
Miscellaneous	337,510	0.03
Total Variable	6,975,280	0.62
Income from Operations	$3,681,810	$0.33

Note: Per-mile values are based on 11,250,000 miles and have been rounded to two decimal places.

Exhibit 2
Over-land Balance Sheet

Over-land Trucking and Freight
Balance Sheet
For the year ending December 31, 2013

Assets		
Current Assets		
Cash	$200,000	
Accounts Receivable	300,000	
Total		$500,000
Property Plant and Equipment		
Land	1,000,000	
Buildings	3,000,000	
Accumulated Depreciation Buildings	(1,250,000)	
Tractors, Trailers, and Equipment	18,650,000	
Accumulated Depreciation	(4,750,000)	
Total		$16,650,000
Total Assets		$17,150,000
Liabilities and Equity		
Current Liabilities		
Accounts Payable	150,000	
Taxes Payable	65,000	
Current Portion of Long-Term Debt	35,000	
Total Current Liabilities		$250,000
Long-Term Liabilities		
Notes Payable	1,865,000	
Total Long-Term Liabilities		$1,865,000
Total Liabilities		$2,115,000
Owner's Equity		
Contributed Capital	3,550,000	
Retained Earnings	11,485,000	
Total Owner's Equity		$15,035,000
Total Liabilities and Owner's Equity		$17,150,000

THE DECISION

Over-land's management is considering the proposal from FHP. There are many issues involving strategy, cost, risk, and capacity. Prepare a recommendation to management. Use the following questions to guide your analysis.

1. Assume Over-land could service the contract with existing equipment. Use Exhibit 1 to identify the relevant costs concerning the acceptance of FHP's request to add two additional loads per week. Which costs are not relevant? Why?

2. Calculate the contribution per mile and total annual contribution associated with accepting FHP's proposal. What do you recommend? (Use 52 weeks per year in your calculations.)

3. Consider the strategic implications (including risks) associated with expanding (or choosing not to expand) operations to meet the demands of FHP. Analyze this question from a conceptual point of view. Calculations are not necessary.

4. After a closer examination of capacity, management believes an additional rig is required to service the FHP account. Assume Over-land's management chooses to invest in one additional truck and trailer that can serve the needs of FHP (at least initially). Assume the annual incremental fixed costs associated with acquiring the additional equipment is $50,000. Further, FHP would agree to pay $2.20 per mile (total including FSC and miscellaneous) if Over-land would sign a five-year contract. What is the annual number of miles required for Over-land to break even, assuming the company adds one truck and trailer? What is the expected annual increase in profitability from the FHP contract? (Use 52 weeks per year in your calculations.)

5. Over-land has business relationships with independent contractors, though Alan is reluctant to use them. Another possibility for expanding capacity is to outsource the miles requested by FHP. One of Over-land's most reliable independent contractors has quoted a rate of $1.65 per mile. As with question 4, assume FHP would agree to pay $2.20 per mile if Over-land would sign a five-year contract. Further, assume Over-land would incur incremental fixed costs of $20,000 annually. These costs would include insurance, rental trailers, certain permits, salaries and benefits of garage maintenance, and office salaries such as billing. How many annual miles are required for Over-land to break even if the miles are outsourced? What is the

expected annual increase in profitability from the FHP contract? What are your conclusions?

6. **a.** Why might Over-land use an independent operator if the variable cost per mile is higher than if the company had purchased a rig and hired a driver?

   b. At what point would management be indifferent between the scenarios illustrated in questions 4 and 5? Based on your analysis, would you recommend adding capacity by purchasing an additional rig or by utilizing the services of an independent contractor? Why?

7. The case references J. B. Hunt and Landstar as two publicly traded companies that have two very different cost structures. This is true because the companies practice two different philosophies for using (or not using) owner operators (e.g., independent contractors). Speculate about the company that may produce higher profits in periods of high economic demand. Why? Speculate about the company that may have a less risky cost structure in poor economic times. Why?

8. All organizations have the potential to perform work, which is determined by the types of resources and the organization's capacity. Effective use of resources can be critical to a firm in any competitive market. In their efforts to efficiently use capacity, managers may ask questions such as: What portion of the available capacity is in use? Of the capacity in use, what portion is used productively? How can we increase the productive use of capacity? Why is a portion of available capacity not in use? Can we eliminate unused capacity? Over-land's management is no different. In fact, management is not exactly clear about how to view capacity. Discuss the challenges that Over-land's management faces with defining and managing capacity. Consider various definitions of capacity, such as theoretical, practical, normal, and actual capacity. Based on the facts presented in the case, prepare an estimate of capacity for Over-land (assuming one driver per rig without slip seating or team driving).

Patterson Manufacturing

Shane Moriarity, University of Oklahoma and Unitec New Zealand; Andrew Slessor, Unitec New Zealand

A SUBSIDIARY HAS BEEN ASKED to recommend a plan for improving their profitability. They have proposed to outsource the production of its largest-selling product, thereby reducing its cost and allowing more competitive pricing. Students are asked to evaluate the proposal and recommend to management whether the proposal should be adopted.

The case is suitable for an advanced undergraduate managerial accounting course or an MBA accounting course. It would be helpful for at least some of the students to have completed a management class with topics on business strategy.

Keywords: make or buy analysis, strategy, problem identification.

The Association of
Accountants and
Financial Professionals
in Business

Patterson Manufacturing

Shane Moriarity
University of Oklahoma and Unitec New Zealand

Andrew Slessor
Unitec New Zealand

INTRODUCTION

The vice president at your company, Columbia Holdings, has given you a new assignment: "Recently I asked the folks at Patterson Manufacturing to develop a strategy for improving their profitability. They have responded with a proposal. I want you to evaluate the proposal: Is it viable? Is it sustainable? Visit their operations and bring back a recommendation."

As you travel to the site you review a brief history of the firm. Patterson Manufacturing was founded in a small northeastern city more than a century ago. Wesley Patterson started the firm alongside a fast-moving stream that provided mechanical power to drive cutting tools, grinders, lathes, and polishers. These tools were used to produce precision parts other manufacturers needed. The firm quickly established a reputation for producing high-quality products to exacting tolerances. The firm prospered.

Wesley studied the industries he served to develop new products that could fill his customers' emerging needs. He often met with customers to design unique products for them. He referred to his approach as providing "customer-driven creative solutions." He also kept abreast of new manufacturing materials and technology to ensure his products were of the highest quality.

The firm grew steadily and, by 1925, was (and still is) the community's largest employer. Wesley donated the land that is now the city's central park. He also paid for constructing the first municipal buildings. More recently, the company

was the primary donor for the construction of the municipal library and the local hospital. And the taxes paid by the firm and its employees are responsible for an excellent array of community services, including the Patterson Sports Complex and Patterson Community Center.

The Great Depression in the 1930s brought hard times to the company, yet none of its employees were discharged. Instead, the firm and its employees cooperated to spread the available work among its employees by reducing each individual's working hours (and wages). During that time, the firm also suspended paying dividends to its owners. After the company returned to prosperity in the 1940s, it continued to emphasize customer-driven creative solutions, and its loyal workforce enthusiastically overcame product design challenges.

Wesley passed leadership of his business to his son, who later passed it down to Wesley's grandson, and then to Wesley's great granddaughter, Jessica Patterson. But five years ago, when Jessica wanted to retire, there was no heir willing to take over the business. Consequently, the plant was sold to your employer, Columbia Holdings.

BACKGROUND

Columbia invests in family-owned businesses with a strong presence in niche markets. Columbia retains existing management and local business practices but provides centralized services, such as finance, accounting, insurance, and corporate-level management. Patterson has remained profitable since the acquisition, but its return on investment has been declining.

Your first stop at the Patterson complex is a meeting with the controller. He provides some additional background: "Jessica, like her predecessors, spent most of her time with customers developing new products to meet customer needs. She didn't concern herself with costs. Customers were willing to pay for products that solved problems. Upon Jessica's retirement, Columbia appointed Paul, our former production manager, to CEO. Paul has done wonders in rationalizing and standardizing our product lines. He substantially reduced manufacturing costs, which led to record profits in the two years following the sale of the company. Those early results have apparently set high expectations for our continuing performance. Our proposal will help move us toward meeting those expectations," he said.

"Our proposal is to stop manufacturing our largest-selling product, the Gudgeon EH40, and instead acquire it from an overseas supplier," continued the controller. "This product currently represents 30% of our total sales revenue and production volume. But sales have been declining because competitors are offering a similar product at lower prices. We think that by reducing our price by 5% we can increase our unit sales volume by 15%. The increased volume coupled with a lower product cost from the offshore supplier should nearly double our firm-wide profit."

The controller also provided some supporting documents. Exhibit 1 summarizes operations for the five years since Patterson Manufacturing was sold to Columbia Holdings. Year 1 represents the first full year after Jessica retired, and Year 5 is the year that just past. Exhibits 2, 3, and 4 provide an income statement for Year 5, the current employee staffing levels by job title, and a detailed price proposal from the overseas supplier.

The controller continued: "The analysis is pretty straightforward. Sales of the Gudgeon EH40 were $27 million last year. The direct material costs came to $14.3 million, while overhead costs of $4.2 million were allocated to the product. But only $2.9 million of the overhead will be avoided if we stop manufacturing the Gudgeon EH40. The remaining overhead costs are nearly all fixed and not subject to reduction in the near future. Our direct selling costs consist mostly of an 8% commission paid to sales representatives. In addition, there's a $2 million advertising allowance devoted to promoting the Gudgeon EH40 in trade magazines."

He also said, "By outsourcing the Gudgeon EH40, we can release three administrative managers, eight administrative support staff, 128 general production personnel, and 10 supervisors. The firm will incur a one-time charge of $1 million for severance pay and pension contributions for dismissed employees. We'll also need to spend $200,000 for the construction of receiving facilities for the outsourced product."

The controller continued: "The supplier's cost quotation (Exhibit 4) needs to be adjusted for the expected 15% increase in volume. The cost for materials and labor will increase proportionately, but the overhead and 'other' costs are unlikely to be affected. The supplier's mark-up will be 10% of the new total cost. In addition to the product cost, Patterson will incur transportation costs to get the product from the manufacturer to our warehouse. The transportation costs are variable and would have been $0.6 million for the volume of product in Year 5."

THE TASK

After his brief overview, the controller hands you the exhibits and says, "You should go through the numbers yourself to ensure that my projection for the increase in profit is correct."

As you make your way to an empty office to review the numbers, the marketing manager approaches you. She pleads, "Don't let them do this. The proposed action will deal a devastating financial blow to our community. Wesley Patterson would have never approved such a move. He loved this town."

REQUIRED

1. Using the controller's projections, prepare an analysis of the expected effect of outsourcing the product on Patterson's profitability.

2. Would it be a viable alternative to produce the product locally and lower the price to achieve the increase in sales volume?

3. Does the firm have an obligation to maintain employment levels in the town?

4. What risks are associated with the proposal?

5. Make a recommendation to your vice president on whether the proposal should be accepted. Provide your reasoning and any suggestions for additional or alternative actions that Patterson should take.

Exhibit 1:
Patterson Manufacturing Five-Year Summary of Operations

	Year 5	Year 4	Year 3	Year 2	Year 1
Total Revenues	$90.2	$94.9	$99.1	$106.2	$111.4
Net Income	$3.1	$3.8	$4.4	$7.3	$7.5
Domestic Sales	$74.7	$76.9	$79.3	$85.0	$88.1
International Sales	$15.5	$18.0	$19.8	$21.2	$23.3
Sales of Established Products*	$73.9	$75.1	$74.4	$76.3	$76.6
Sales of New Products*	$16.3	$19.8	$24.7	$29.9	$34.8
Research and Development	$0.9	$1.1	$1.5	$1.2	$1.3
Return on Assets	2.0%	2.3%	2.7%	4.1%	4.2%
Number of Employees	480	485	502	492	510

Note: Dollar figures are in millions.
*Established products are those that have been marketed for five years or more. New products have been marketed for less than five years.

Exhibit 2:
Summary Income Statement for Patterson Manufacturing

	Year 5
Sales	$90.2
Cost of Goods Sold (COGS)	74.3
Gross Margin	15.9
Administrative Costs	1.6
Selling Costs	11.2
Operating Income	**$ 3.1**

Note: Dollar figures are in millions. Interest expense and income taxes are only shown on Columbia's consolidated financial statements.

Exhibit 3:
Distribution of Current Patterson Employees by Job Title

Job Title	Number of Employees	Average Salary Per Employee
Administrative Manager	10	$45,000
Administrative Staff	24	32,000
Production Supervisor	29	50,000
General Production Personnel	417	37,000

Exhibit 4:
Off-Shore Supplier's Price Proposal for the Volume of Product in Year 5

Material Costs	$12.7
Labor Costs	1.8
Overhead Costs	2.7
Other	1.5
Total	18.7
Profit Mark-Up (10%)	1.9
Total Price	**$20.6**

Note: Dollar figures are in millions. The total price is quoted for supplying the quantity of product Patterson sold in Year 5. The quoted price is FOB the supplier's manufacturing plant.

Pikesville Lightning: Evaluating Strategic Business Expansion Opportunities

Thomas G. Canace, Wake Forest University; Paul E. Juras, Babson College

GREG STORM, OWNER OF PIKESVILLE LIGHTNING, IS STRIVING TO make his organization a market leader by finding unique ways to grow the business. He views his accountants as consultants who not only have the technical skills to provide financial and analytical information, but who also have the strategic thinking to provide valuable input to him and the business leaders to help improve the profitability and expansion potential of the business. This case asks the student to play the role of a member of the accounting team and perform some financial and strategic analysis of operating results. The student is also asked to view the role of accountant as that of a strategic business partner by making a specific strategic recommendation to improve the operating results of the organization.

This case is intended for use in upper-level undergraduate or introductory-level graduate management accounting courses. The assignments could be modified for use in an introductory undergraduate managerial accounting course, and suggested modifications for such use are presented within the teaching note.

Keywords: cost behavior, budgeted income statement, and strategic analysis.

The Association of
Accountants and
Financial Professionals
in Business

Pikesville Lightning:
Evaluating Strategic Business Expansion Opportunities[1]

Thomas G. Canace
Wake Forest University

Paul E. Juras
Babson College

INTRODUCTION

Greg Storm, team owner, has often been quoted as saying, "I don't own a baseball team; I sell hot dogs!" This line ties in well with the recent strategy of minor league organizations to transform games into an "affordable family experience" offering much more entertainment than just the game. Still, Storm is a visionary who values outside-the-box thinking and who continually strives to be a market leader in finding unique ways to grow his business. Storm needs help "hitting a home run," because base hits alone would not revolutionize the industry or provide long-term, sustainable growth for the seasonal business.

BACKGROUND

In 1882, the Northwestern League of baseball was organized. Soon after its inception, however, league officials signed an agreement with the National League and the American Association that established territorial rights and essentially assigned "major" or "minor" league status to teams. From this agreement, the Northwestern League became the first recognized minor league in baseball. Further agreements established the rights of major league teams to draft minor league players, resulting in the "farm system" where players

trained for the major leagues in obscure one-horse towns with little pizzazz.

Such organized baseball was confined to the northeastern United States at first, but quickly expanded throughout the country by the turn of the century. Although the number of minor league clubs had decreased considerably by the mid-twentieth century, by the 1980s minor league baseball had exploded, with attendance exceeding 20 million for the first time since 1950. This success prompted the business relationship between the two leagues that exists today under the Professional Baseball Agreement. Under the new agreement set forth in the 1990s, the majors continued to pay a large share of the operational expenses, but minors were now required to share ticket revenues and establish minimum standards at their ballparks. To this day, many fans and observers are unaware that the major league organization has full authority to decide who plays for the minor league team for the season. In fact, many farm clubs have commented that it is not unusual for them to learn their final rosters about one month before the start of the season. Of course, while the minor league owners have limited control over the baseball operations, all clearly recognize that they

---

[1] This case was prepared to provide an opportunity for students to interpret, analyze, evaluate, synthesize, and communicate a solution to a management accounting problem.

are still running a business that must thrive at the local level, and the operating performance of these organizations has been anything but "minor."

In fact, thanks to the strategic thinking and entrepreneurial spirit of a new breed of team owners, these teams are run like top-flight professional clubs, playing in uniquely designed ballparks while also offering a new entertainment alternative for families. These owners have recognized that, while on the surface, their mission is to "play ball" by preparing young players for the big leagues, more importantly their profitability depends largely upon their successful establishment as an entertainment venue. Many observers have often made the analogy that minor league teams compete with movie theaters for entertainment revenue, charging a flat-rate admissions fee but hoping to expand the bottom line by providing ancillary food and entertainment services. Hence, while winning games is key to filling the ballpark at the major league level, operating success for minor league teams is driven more by affordability and alternative non-baseball entertainment.

THE PIKESVILLE LIGHTNING

The Pikesville Lightning organization is a minor league baseball team based in Pikesville, Ohio, and plays in the Central Division of the Eastern League. Since the 1976 season, the team has been the AAA affiliate of the Pittsburgh Pirates, and currently plays in Waterfall Stadium, a state-of-the-art facility built in 2006 near Cleveland. Storm Enterprises is the primary owner of the organization, and maintains full ownership of park vending and entertainment operations. Food and entertainment revenue is so vital to the overall profitability of the organization that owner Greg Storm has often been quoted as saying, "I don't own a baseball team; I sell hot dogs!" This line ties in well with the recent strategy of minor league organizations to transform games into an affordable family experience with much more entertainment offered than just the game. In addition to the wide array of foods, drinks, and snacks, Storm designed the ballpark with kids in mind by providing various forms of entertainment around the perimeter of the park. To keep parents and children coming back to the park, Storm firmly believes that team success on the diamond must be complemented by family fun at every game. Table 1 provides a sample of some strategic initiatives he has put in place during the season to entertain fans (Table 1).

Storm is a visionary who values outside-the-box thinking and who continually strives to be a market leader in finding unique ways to grow his business. While many minor league organizations have also found ways to improve attendance and loyalty during the season, Storm has made it very clear to his employees that he does not want to be limited by the seasonality of the business.

Table 1

Top Initiatives of Pikesville Lightning

Panel A – Game Day Events for All

1. Post-game fireworks and concert
2. Kids Happy Hour – free hour in FunZone for kids only
3. Surprise Major League visitor from the past
4. Meet-the-players night
5. Become a general manager for the weekend
6. Road trip give-away – travel with the team to a road game
7. Win a 1-hour shopping spree in the Lightning Shop
8. All-star kid of the game – one child selected before each game based upon pre-entry.
9. The Magical Family – one family selected to sit with team
10. Mascot encounter – sit with the "Lightning Bolt" team mascot

Panel B – Special Request Game Day Experiences

1. Birthday party – food, swimming, FunZone games and special VIP treatment
2. Ceremonial first pitch – includes cap, autographed baseball, and team picture with you
3. Corporate outings and parties
4. Buy-a-box: Rent the owners' box for a night for your event.

EXPANDING PROFITABILITY

In recognition of his stretch goal for the business, Storm developed a first-step initiative to bring some of this ballpark experience into the homes of fans even during the off season to keep fans thinking about the team. The company obtained an exclusive franchise from its manufacturer to purchase "POG" ovens (branded with the Pikesville Lighting team logo for distribution via phone and Internet orders. A "POG" is a special type of hot dog sold at the ballpark that has become a hit with Pikesville fans of all ages, and has even been labeled "out of this park" by many sports vending companies. These ovens were special because they were smaller replicas of the ovens used at the park.

With fiscal 2010 on the horizon, Storm, a chief financial officer (CFO) earlier in his career, has asked the divisional accounting team to begin planning profitability from oven sales. To provide the necessary data to prepare the budgeted financials for fiscal 2010, the accounting team pulled together some volume data, accessed the general ledger to pull financial data, and summarized some key elements of the cost structure (Table 2).

Table 2
Selected Financial and Other Data

Panel A – Volume Data for Hot Dog Oven Business

Quarter	Units Sold	Kilowatt Hours	Quarter	Units Sold	Kilowatt Hours
FY2006:			FY2008:		
Q1	9,100	4,300	Q1	10,000	4,000
Q2	14,700	5,250	Q2	16,000	5,000
Q3	16,900	6,310	Q3	18,000	6,000
Q4	14,800	10,011	Q4	15,000	10,000
FY2007:			FY2009:		
Q1	9,500	11,777	Q1	11,000	12,000
Q2	15,100	10,966	Q2	17,000	11,000
Q3	17,000	9,120	Q3	20,000	9,000
Q4	15,000	8,320	Q4	13,000	8,000

Table 2
Selected Financial and Other Data (continued)

Panel C: Other Summary Data

Cost of Goods Sold has historically amounted to $35 per oven sold, while sales commissions represent 6% of sales. These figures aren't expected to change for fiscal 2010. Storm has also advised the team that advertising expenses must remain flat relative to the prior year, while administrative salaries and insurance expenses are each subject to inflationary increases of 3%. Cost data for the prior 16 quarters is available for these items in the general ledger, as shown in Panel B. Cost data for shipping, electricity, maintenance, and depreciation are available for the prior 16 quarters in the general ledger as well. The sales and operations teams have also provided relevant volume data over the last 16 fiscal quarters, as shown in Panel A.

Management has also planned to build up the balance sheet during the first quarter of fiscal 2010 with capital expenditures of $500,000 for additional trucks to assist in the ground distribution of the product and with a $1 million investment in POG ovens. (The division's fixed-asset policy is to take a full year's worth of depreciation on assets purchased during the year, regardless of the date of acquisition.) The trucks are expected to have a useful life of 10 years. For planning purposes, the division doesn't tax-effect its financials because taxes are calculated at a corporate level and allocated to the divisions based upon overall performance. Engineers expect to use 13,000 kilowatt hours during the first quarter of fiscal 2010.

In planning for the first quarter of fiscal 2010, Storm was interested in three scenarios for the budgeted financials: (1) Base Case: Assume 12,000 ovens sold at a price of $100 per oven; (2) Market Penetration Strategy: Assume the company can sell 10% more ovens by offering a 5% price discount; (3) Market Premium Strategy: Assume the company loses 15% of its planned customers if it attempts to sell the ovens at a 15% premium and spending $5 more per unit to make the logo bigger.

As an aid in planning, Storm described a unique income statement format he wanted the accountants to use when preparing the budgeted information for his review. He referred to it as a "Hybrid P&L" because it was comprised of the GAAP-based and contribution margin based income statement. To ensure there was no miscommunication, he illustrated the concept for them on a piece of paper as shown in Table 3:

Table 3
Illustration of Hybrid Income Statement

Hybrid P-and-L

	Sales
Less:	
	Cost of Goods Sold
Equals:	
	Gross Profit
Less:	
	Operating expenses: **Variable**
Equals:	
	Contribution Margin
Less:	
	Operating expenses: **Fixed**
Equals:	
	Operating income

A VISION FOR THE FUTURE

Future Expansion Initiatives

While Storm considered his first initiative a "step in the right direction," he was already starting to think ahead to the next breakthrough. Unlike his peers in the world of team ownership, he really did not want to take time off during the off season while there could be a wealth of unexplored opportunities awaiting him. He valued his accounting team as consultants and was eager to receive their input about the strategic direction of team marketing and entertainment events. Once again, he wanted to consider off-season initiatives as a way to expand the seasonality of the business. But this had to be bigger than the POG oven initiative. He wanted to capitalize on his facilities' investments and really get the fans involved to provide a year-long experience. He knew this would get a great deal of attention from the local media, and could even hit the national radar screen as an innovative breakthrough.

From a business standpoint, since much of the capital infrastructure became idle during the off season and some of the operating expenses were fixed, he believed that a high proportion of new revenue from off-season ventures could drop to the bottom line and expand his overall profitability.

---

2 The division's fixed asset policy is to take a full year's worth of depreciation on assets purchased during the year, regardless of the date of acquisition.

Table 2
Selected Financial and Other Data (continued)

Panel B – General Ledger Data

Raw Download from Oracle General Ledger						*Raw Download from Oracle General Ledger*				
Current data						Current data (07/05/2010 13:05:04)				
GL Account Retrieval		year/quarter/account				GL Account Retrieval		year/quarter/account		
Func. Currency		usd				Func. Currency		usd		
Profit Center		1000 Pikesville - Oven				Profit Center		1000 Pikesville - Oven		
Distr. Channel		10 Final customer sales				Distr. Channel		10 Final customer sales		
Product		PG-101 POG Warmer Oven PLIGHT 101				Product		PG-101 POG Warmer Oven PLIGHT 101		
Page feed	1 of 2					Page feed	2 of 2			
Lead column	GL number	Actual	Fiscal year	Quarter		Lead column	GL number	Actual	Fiscal year	Quarter
insurance	000100100	5,000	2006	1		shipping	000100122	110,000	2008	1
insurance	000100100	5,000	2006	2		shipping	000100122	176,000	2008	2
insurance	000100100	5,000	2006	3		shipping	000100122	198,000	2008	3
insurance	000100100	5,000	2006	4		shipping	000100122	165,000	2008	4
insurance	000100100	5,000	2007	1		shipping	000100122	121,000	2009	1
insurance	000100100	5,000	2007	2		shipping	000100122	187,000	2009	2
insurance	000100100	5,000	2007	3		shipping	000100122	220,000	2009	3
insurance	000100100	5,000	2007	4		shipping	000100122	143,000	2009	4
insurance	000100100	6,250	2008	1		depreciation	000100123	32,655	2006	1
insurance	000100100	6,250	2008	2		depreciation	000100123	32,655	2006	2
insurance	000100100	6,250	2008	3		depreciation	000100123	32,655	2006	3
insurance	000100100	6,250	2008	4		depreciation	000100123	32,655	2006	4
insurance	000100100	8,737	2009	1		depreciation	000100123	32,655	2007	1
insurance	000100100	8,737	2009	2		depreciation	000100123	32,655	2007	2
insurance	000100100	8,737	2009	3		depreciation	000100123	32,655	2007	3
insurance	000100100	8,737	2009	4		depreciation	000100123	56,000	2007	4
admin. salaries	000100110	18,000	2006	1		depreciation	000100123	56,000	2008	1
admin. salaries	000100110	76,099	2006	2		depreciation	000100123	56,000	2008	2
admin. salaries	000100110	76,099	2006	3		depreciation	000100123	56,000	2008	3
admin. salaries	000100110	78,689	2006	4		depreciation	000100123	56,000	2008	4
admin. salaries	000100110	78,689	2007	1		depreciation	000100123	70,000	2009	1
admin. salaries	000100110	82,455	2007	2		depreciation	000100123	70,000	2009	2
admin. salaries	000100110	82,455	2007	3		depreciation	000100123	70,000	2009	3
admin. salaries	000100110	86,555	2007	4		depreciation	000100123	70,000	2009	4
admin. salaries	000100110	138,016	2008	1		utilities	000100184	17,850	2006	1
admin. salaries	000100110	138,016	2008	2		utilities	000100184	20,099	2006	2
admin. salaries	000100110	138,016	2008	3		utilities	000100184	23,100	2006	3
admin. salaries	000100110	138,016	2008	4		utilities	000100184	33,024	2006	4
admin. salaries	000100110	140,777	2009	1		utilities	000100184	32,550	2007	1
admin. salaries	000100110	140,777	2009	2		utilities	000100184	31,000	2007	2
admin. salaries	000100110	140,777	2009	3		utilities	000100184	28,999	2007	3
admin. salaries	000100110	140,777	2009	4		utilities	000100184	25,997	2007	4
advertising	000100121	192,506	2006	1		utilities	000100184	18,000	2008	1
advertising	000100121	192,506	2006	2		utilities	000100184	21,000	2008	2
advertising	000100121	192,506	2006	3		utilities	000100184	24,000	2008	3
advertising	000100121	192,506	2006	4		utilities	000100184	33,000	2008	4
advertising	000100121	197,896	2007	1		utilities	000100184	35,000	2009	1
advertising	000100121	197,896	2007	2		utilities	000100184	33,000	2009	2
advertising	000100121	197,896	2007	3		utilities	000100184	30,000	2009	3
advertising	000100121	197,896	2007	4		utilities	000100184	27,000	2009	4
advertising	000100121	203,883	2008	1		maintenance	000100191	6,980	2006	1
advertising	000100121	203,883	2008	2		maintenance	000100191	7,800	2006	2
advertising	000100121	203,883	2008	3		maintenance	000100191	9,040	2006	3
advertising	000100121	203,883	2008	4		maintenance	000100191	11,650	2006	4
advertising	000100121	210,000	2009	1		maintenance	000100191	7,869	2007	1
advertising	000100121	210,000	2009	2		maintenance	000100191	11,250	2007	2
advertising	000100121	210,000	2009	3		maintenance	000100191	9,980	2007	3
advertising	000100121	210,000	2009	4		maintenance	000100191	9,200	2007	4
shipping	000100122	100,100	2006	1		maintenance	000100191	6,500	2008	1
shipping	000100122	161,700	2006	2		maintenance	000100191	7,500	2008	2
shipping	000100122	185,900	2006	3		maintenance	000100191	8,600	2008	3
shipping	000100122	162,800	2006	4		maintenance	000100191	11,700	2008	4
shipping	000100122	104,500	2007	1		maintenance	000100191	12,000	2009	1
shipping	000100122	166,100	2007	2		maintenance	000100191	11,800	2009	2
shipping	000100122	187,000	2007	3		maintenance	000100191	10,000	2009	3
shipping	000100122	165,000	2007	4		maintenance	000100191	9,600	2009	4

He was excited about these prospects especially because he knew that no other team owners were considering such a strategy, so this would give him a first-mover advantage. Storm was routinely heard saying, "We are limited only by our own creativity," and now he would put this phrase to test with his accounting team in the hopes of making history in the world of minor league baseball entertainment.

Enhancing Organizational Strategic Financial Management

In addition to creating a new strategic breakthrough for his organization, Storm was interested in developing a framework for governing the ongoing strategic financial management of his business. Without such a framework, he believed his accounting organization would not be empowered to unleash its strategic contribution to the business, but would forever be seen only as the "number-crunchers." Given his roots in accounting and finance, he wholeheartedly believed that the growth and prosperity of his business depended upon adopting a better business partnering model. Such a model would rein in the intelligence of his accountants to add value beyond the traditional transaction processing and would enable them

to become strategic advisors continuously working toward business solutions.

Recently, he recalled that, early in his career, he was exposed to a framework that he had never implemented for his business: the C-framework for the strategic business partner (SBP) role (Table 4). He decided to present this framework to his accounting organization. He wanted to place the onus on them to bring this framework to life by "fitting" it to their situation and organization, however. As he began introducing the framework to them, he emphasized that such a governing model would provide a tangible way to consciously think about the importance of strategic financial management through business partnering, and to avoid "slipping" back into a role that fails to see past the mere production of the fundamentals.

He explained that, at the top of the framework, there were several dimensions along which individuals could assist the CFO in becoming a better partner to the overall business (CFO levers). These dimensions serve as inputs. First, the accounting organization could act as catalysts in leading change for the business by helping to introduce and implement new strategies. Second, they could take

Table 4
The C-Framework for the SBP Role

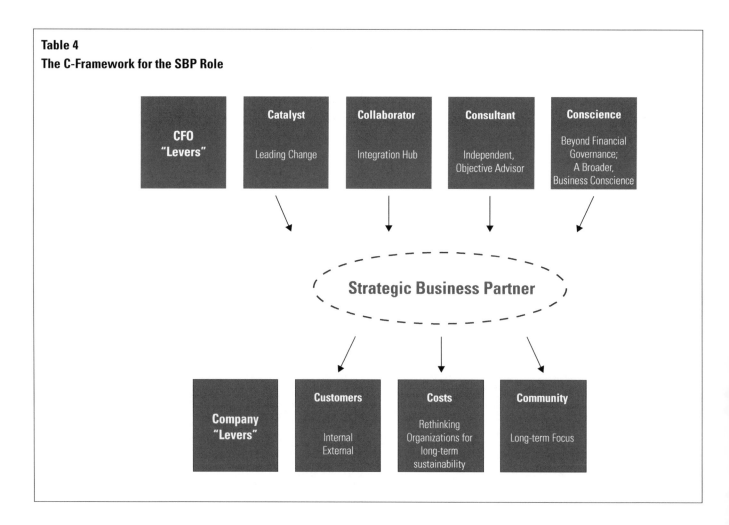

on the role of collaborator by serving as a hub to integrate the functional aspects of the business such as purchasing, sales, human resources, and information technology. Third, the accountants would assume the role of consultant by acting as an independent, objective advisor to the business leaders. Finally, recent scandals have made it clear that the accounting organization must provide a conscience to the business – not only with respect to the reported financials but also by advising how strategy could have broader ramifications.

By acting as a catalyst, collaborator, consultant, and conscience for the business to partner with the business leaders, each of the dimensions should ultimately impact the company along several dimensions (company levers) that serve as outputs. First, each action at the CFO level should positively impact the customers of the organization – both internal partners who rely on information and advice from the accountants and the external revenue-generating fans. Second, each CFO lever should assist the business in achieving a cost structure that allows for long-term sustainability. No business can live for the present without considering ramifications for the future. Finally, the first-tier levers should work toward the advancement and benefit of the local and larger community.

Storm declared that, once developed and tailored to the Pikesville organization, the framework would be lived by the accounting team every day and the entire business would reap the rewards of linking the financial function into the strategic aspects of the decision making. They would "C" themselves as business partners in every task they perform for the business. To motivate them toward this goal, he reminded them that their current task of developing the off-season initiative was a prime example of how they already go beyond just "counting beans" and have begun to step into a role of helping to run the business.

THE CHALLENGE

It was clear to the accounting team that Storm had high expectations for their work and for the future of his organization. Storm challenged them to "hit home runs" with their thinking, for base hits alone would not revolutionize the industry or provide long-term, sustainable growth for the seasonal business.

He viewed his accountants as consultants who not only had the technical skills to provide financial and analytical information, but who also had the strategic thinking to provide valuable input to him and the business leaders to help improve the profitability and expansion potential of the business. He was confident that, by performing the work he was asking them to do, they, too, would begin to view themselves as strategic financial managers – business partners – who would support and assist with the decision making of the business.

Storm asked the team to prepare a report for his review. He wanted the report to address the following current issues and future prospects that could propel the business toward long-term growth:

- Provide an executive summary that outlines the current situation, key metrics from your financial analysis, and your strategic recommendations for the business.

- Financial Analysis – Using statistical and financial methods, provide an analytical assessment of the planned performance for the POG oven segment including

  - A table that outlines the cost behavior of each element of the cost structure;

  - A hybrid-format budgeted income statement for Q1FY2010 [provide supporting analysis];

  - Outline the benefits and usefulness of Storm's hybrid income statement approach.

- Strategic Analysis – Future Expansion

  - Outline your advice to Storm about one specific high-impact potential off-season expansion strategy to be employed for achieving greater profitability. Include in your discussion an assessment of the resources (e.g., operating, capital, financing, personnel, and external consultants) necessary to execute the strategy.

- Strategic Analysis – Employing the C-framework

  - Use the C-framework to outline your advice to Storm about how to improve its strategic financial management function. Include a thorough discussion of the framework by linking each CFO-lever input to each of the three company-lever outputs.

IV. Risk Management and Internal Controls

The Le-Nature's Inc. Fraud: What Happened and Why?

Michael C. Knapp and Carol A. Knapp, University of Oklahoma

LE-NATURE'S INC. WAS A PENNSYLVANIA-BASED BEVERAGE COMPANY founded in 1989 by CEO Gregory Podlucky, who oversaw a large-scale financial fraud based on bogus sales revenues from the late 1990s through 2006. This case uses the Le-Nature's fraud as a vehicle to introduce students to the fraud triangle, the Committee of Sponsoring Organizations of the Treadway Commission (COSO) internal control framework, and how management accountants can contribute to strong internal controls, fraud prevention, and an ethical climate that encourages good overall corporate governance. Case questions require students to relate the Le-Nature's case to these topics and make recommendations on how Le-Nature's could have improved its corporate governance practices and avoid this massive fraud. Students are also required to explore the ethical responsibilities of corporate accountants and other parties involved in the accounting and financial reporting process by referring to the IMA Statement of Ethical Professional Practice.

Students in undergraduate upper-level cost accounting courses, advanced management accounting courses, or those in a graduate-level MBA or master of accountancy program should understand the pervasive and adverse effects that fraud can have on an organization.

Keywords: fraud, internal control, enterprise risk management, corporate governance, professionalism, independent audits, beverage industry.

Le-Nature's Inc. Fraud: What Happened and Why?

Michael C. Knapp
McLaughlin Chair in Business Ethics and
Professor of Accounting
University of Oklahoma

Carol A. Knapp
Assistant Professor
University of Oklahoma

INTRODUCTION

After graduating from West Virginia University in 1984 with a degree in accounting and finance, Gregory Podlucky decided to work with his father Gabriel, who had a small business empire in western Pennsylvania that included a chain of auto parts stores, an ethanol fuel company, several real estate properties, and the Jones Brewing Company, best known for its line of Stoney's beers.

In 1989 Gregory Podlucky decided to strike out on his own. Using the funds he obtained from cashing out his ownership interest in his father's businesses, Podlucky established a water bottling venture in Latrobe, Pa., the hometown of golfing great Arnold Palmer. In 1992, entrepreneur and former CPA Podlucky expanded his product line to include a wide range of flavored water, fruit, and tea drinks.

Despite being in the hypercompetitive beverage industry, Podlucky's company, which he ultimately named Le-Nature's Inc., grew rapidly. By 2006, the company was the 33rd largest beverage producer in the United States, with annual reported sales approaching $290 million and a workforce of several hundred employees. One year earlier, Podlucky had rejected a $1.2 billion offer to sell Le-Nature's. Instead of selling, Podlucky decided to take his company public. Unfortunately for him, his fellow investors, and his company's many creditors, that dream was never realized.

STRATEGIC FINANCING

Podlucky served as Le-Nature's chief executive officer (CEO) and relied principally on his family and wide circle of friends and business associates to staff the company's other key positions as it expanded over the years. He hired his brother Jonathan to serve as Le-Nature's chief operating officer (COO) and placed his 22-year-old son Jesse in charge of the day-to-day accounting for Le-Nature's large subsidiary that produced bottled tea products. Among the friends that he appointed to management positions at Le-Nature's was Robert Lynn, who held different titles during his years with the company, including executive vice president of sales.

Despite serving as Le-Nature's CEO, Gregory Podlucky was also heavily involved in the company's routine accounting functions.[1] Tammy Andreycak, another close friend of Podlucky, held the title of director of accounting, and was the organization's chief accountant. But Andreycak was a single mother who did not have a college degree or formal training in accounting. According to company insiders, her primary role within Le-Nature's was serving as Podlucky's confidante. When dealing with third parties, Podlucky often referred to Andreycak as his secretary.[2]

A shortage of capital is a common problem for rapidly growing small companies. Therefore, Podlucky relied on a variety of different strategies to finance his company's expanding operations. During the 14 years that he served as Le-Nature's CEO, the articulate and outgoing Podlucky raised almost $1 billion of debt and equity capital for the company.

In 1999, Podlucky retained a financial consulting firm to identify potential investors for Le-Nature's. In 2000 and 2002, that consulting firm arranged for two investment funds to collectively purchase eight million shares of Le-Nature's preferred stock, which they had the right to convert into the company's common stock. If the two funds had exercised the convertibility option, they would have controlled 45% of Le-Nature's outstanding common stock. Instead, Podlucky owned all of his company's outstanding common stock throughout its existence.

The sales of preferred stock raised nearly $30 million for Le-Nature's. Those transactions directly affected Le-Nature's corporate governance structure because each of the investment funds that purchased the preferred stock had the right to appoint an individual to the company's board of directors. The majority of the board consisted of "inside" directors including Podlucky, his brother Jonathan, and other senior company executives.

Podlucky also used long-term equipment leasing as a financing technique. In one such transaction, Podlucky retained a North Carolina leasing agent to contract with a Wisconsin-based company that was a subsidiary of a German manufacturing firm. The German firm manufactured equipment Le-Nature's used in its bottling operations. With the North Carolina leasing agent serving as an intermediary, Le-Nature's leased the equipment from the Wisconsin subsidiary of the German firm. The leasing agreement required Le-Nature's to make a large escrow deposit with the leasing agent; Le-Nature's borrowed the funds to make that deposit from a U.S. lender. In total, Podlucky financed the acquisition of approximately $300 million of equipment in this manner.

Podlucky used conventional long-term borrowing arrangements as the primary method for raising funds for his company. Wachovia, a diversified financial services firm based in North Carolina, arranged or underwrote approximately $500 million of long-term debt for Le-Nature's.[3] In 2005, for example, Wachovia marketed a $150 million bond issue for the company. The high-yield or "junk" bonds were sold primarily to pension and retirement funds such as CalPERS (California Public Employees Retirement System), the nation's largest pension fund.

Podlucky relied heavily on Le-Nature's audited financial statements to borrow funds for his company. For example, in the case of the $150 million bond issue, Wachovia included Le-Nature's audited financial statements with the promotional materials for those bonds. Likewise, Moody's Investors Services accessed and relied on Le-Nature's financial statements to assign credit ratings to those bonds—and the company's other outstanding debt obligations.

SUSPICIONS AND RESIGNATIONS SPARK INVESTIGATION

In August 2003 Le-Nature's independent audit firm, Ernst & Young (EY) was completing its review of the company's financial statements for the second quarter of fiscal 2003. During the EY quarterly review, a standard procedure was to ask a client's senior executives whether they suspected or were aware of any fraudulent activity within the organization. When Richard Lipovich, the EY audit engagement partner, posed that question to John Higbee, Le-Nature's CFO at the time, Higbee candidly replied that he had significant doubts about the reliability of his company's recorded sales figures. Lipovich received similar responses from Le-Nature's chief administrative officer (CAO) and its vice president of administration (VPA). The day after communicating their concerns to Lipovich, the three company officials submitted letters of resignation to Gregory Podlucky.

In their resignation letters, the three former executives suggested that Podlucky was "engaging in improper conduct with Le-Nature's tea suppliers, equipment vendors, and certain customers."[4] Higbee—who had served for 20 years as an audit partner with Arthur Andersen & Co., including 16 years heading up the audit practice for that firm's Pittsburgh office—reported that Podlucky had repeatedly refused to provide him with documentation supporting key transactions reflected in Le-Nature's accounting records. He considered Podlucky's failure to provide such documentation "an astonishing and extremely improper restriction for any executive officer to impose upon a company's chief financial officer."[5] Those restrictions made it impossible for Higbee to satisfy his CFO-related corporate governance responsibilities.

Higbee also identified what he considered to be several material weaknesses in Le-Nature's internal controls. Those weaknesses included Podlucky's "absolute control" over the company's "detailed financial records" and the lack of "checks and balances" for key assets of the company, such as the large escrow deposits for its long-term equipment leases and its product inventories.[6]

The startling statements by Higbee and his two former colleagues in their resignation letters prompted Lipovich to write a letter to Le-Nature's board of directors. In that letter, Lipovich requested that Le-Nature's retain an independent law firm to investigate and file a report regarding the allegations made by the three former company executives. Lipovich informed Le-Nature's board that EY would not be associated with any of the company's financial statements until the law firm completed its investigation, EY reviewed the report, and EY determined if it had to undertake any other investigative procedures.

Le-Nature's board responded to Lipovich's letter by creating a Special Committee to investigate the allegations made by the three former executives. That committee was made up of the outside members of the company's board, which included the directors appointed by the investment funds that had purchased Le-Nature's preferred stock. The Special Committee retained an independent law firm, K & L Gates (one of the 10 largest legal firms in the United States) to supervise that investigation. In turn, K & L Gates hired an independent accounting firm, Pascarella & Wiker, to assist in the investigation.

In late November 2003, K & L Gates submitted a draft copy of its report to Podlucky, who was not a member of the Special Committee. The CEO provided feedback regarding the report to the law firm. One week later, K & L Gates provided a revised copy of the report to the members of the Special Committee. The report "found no evidence of fraud or malfeasance,"[7] although it did identify multiple internal control weaknesses. Among the suggestions made to remedy those internal control weaknesses were strengthening the segregation of duties for key transactions such as equipment leases and inventory purchases, adopting more rigorous documentation standards for those transactions, and establishing an audit committee consisting of outside directors.

The outside directors on the Special Committee accepted the findings of the investigative report and indicated that they would work with the other members of Le-Nature's board of directors to address the identified internal control problems. Shortly thereafter, Le-Nature's dismissed EY as its independent audit firm and retained BDO Seidman, which would ultimately audit the company's 2003 through 2005 financial statements.

FRAUD ALLEGATIONS RESURFACE

Following the 2003 investigation, Gregory Podlucky rededicated himself to enhancing his company's stature and size in the beverage industry. Le-Nature's impressive financial data caught the attention of several private equity funds in 2005 when Wachovia prepared and distributed a confidential memorandum to sell the company to the highest bidder. The initial bid received for the company was $1.2 billion. To the disappointment of the company's preferred stockholders, Podlucky rejected that offer. The preferred stockholders claimed that Podlucky intentionally sabotaged the sale of Le-Nature's by refusing to allow the potential buyer access to the company's accounting records. Podlucky

dismissed that allegation and instead maintained that he had rejected the buyout offer because the price had been too low.

In May 2006, the preferred stockholders filed a lawsuit against Le-Nature's, Podlucky, and other top executives to force an outright sale of the company. Despite that lawsuit, Podlucky began preparing an initial public offering (IPO) for Le-Nature's with the assistance of K & L Gates. At the same time, Wachovia was in the process of arranging more than $300 million of additional long-term loans for Le-Nature's.

Podlucky's plans for his company were disrupted when allegations of an accounting fraud within Le-Nature's resurfaced. The CEO responded to those allegations by pointing to the fact that his company's financial statements had received an unqualified audit opinion each year from Le-Nature's independent auditors. Podlucky also insisted that "the financial stability of Le-Nature's has never been stronger"[8] and boldly predicted that Le-Nature's sales would nearly quadruple over the next four sing from approximately $290 million to more than $1 billion annually. In October 2006, Le-Nature's preferred stockholders requested a restraining order against the company in a petition they filed with a Delaware court. In the petition, the preferred stockholders referred the court to a fraudulent equipment leasing transaction arranged by Le-Nature's. One of the lenders that provided the financing for the company's long-term leases had determined, with the assistance of a handwriting expert, that certain documents for the given transaction had been forged. The forged documents had resulted in $20 million of the lease escrow deposit financed by the lender being improperly transferred to Le-Nature's.

The Delaware court issued the requested restraining order, evicted Podlucky from the company's corporate headquarters, and appointed Steven Panagos of Kroll Zolfo Cooper (a consulting firm specializing in corporate turnarounds and restructuring) to serve as the custodian of Le-Nature's assets and operations. Less than one week later, Panagos filed an affidavit with the court that presented evidence of a massive accounting fraud within the company. He also reported that he had found evidence that Podlucky had "frantically shredded company documents"[9] before he was forced to leave Le-Nature's corporate headquarters. Even more troubling was the custodian's discovery that the company had been maintaining two sets of accounting records.

Panagos' affidavit spurred Le-Nature's creditors to file a petition to initiate involuntary bankruptcy proceedings against the company. A federal bankruptcy judge approved that petition and appointed a bankruptcy trustee to take control of Le-Nature's for the purpose of liquidating it and pursuing any viable legal claims against individuals or entities involved in undermining the company.

FRAUD ON A GRAND SCALE

Investigations of Le-Nature's accounting records by the company's court-appointed custodian, bankruptcy trustee, and law enforcement authorities revealed the sordid details of the brazen accounting hoax Podlucky initiated in the late 1990s. The individual who would prove to be most helpful in unraveling the fraudulent scheme was Andreycak, Le-Nature's director of accounting and Podlucky's most trusted associate. After pleading guilty to multiple criminal charges, Andreycak agreed to cooperate with law enforcement authorities investigating the Le-Nature's scandal. A federal judge would subsequently note that Andreycak and Podlucky were the only "two people aware of the magnitude of the [Le-Nature's] fraud."[10]

James Garrett, a federal prosecutor with the U.S. Department of Justice assigned to the Le-Nature's case, characterized the fraud masterminded by Podlucky as a "financial mirage" the likes of which he would not even dream could be created."[11] In 2002, the company had reported sales of more than $135 million when the company's actual sales were less than $2 million. Three years later, in 2005 (the fiscal year before the fraud was uncovered) Le-Nature's audited financial statements reported revenues of $287 million when the company's actual revenues were less than $40 million. A large portion of the bogus revenues booked by Le-Nature's was cycled through its tea subsidiary. From 2000 through 2006, that subsidiary reported sales of $240 million while its actual sales during that period were less than $100,000.[12]

Podlucky and his co-conspirators used Le-Nature's graphics department to prepare a slew of bogus purchase orders, sales invoices, and other fake documents to sustain the accounting fraud. The bogus documents allowed the conspirators to conceal Le-Nature's enormous volume of fictitious revenues from the company's lenders, independent auditors, and regulatory authorities. As determined by one of Le-Nature's lenders, the conspirators also used forged documents to improperly transfer deposits held in escrow by a leasing agent to Le-Nature's. In turn, that leasing agent provided confirmations to Le-Nature's independent auditors that intentionally overstated the dollar amount of deposits being held by his firm on behalf of the company.

Le-Nature's maintained two completely separate accounting systems during the course of the massive accounting fraud. One system accumulated the company's actual transaction data but only Podlucky and Andreycak could access this system. The other accounting system contained primarily fraudulent financial data. The company's independent auditors were never aware of the accounting system that had actual transaction data. Podlucky was also successful in concealing that accounting system from law firm K & L Gates and accounting firm Pascarella & Wiker, that were involved in the Special Committee fraud investigation of 2003.

Podlucky used Le-Nature's phony financial statements to convince third parties to loan funds to the company. He then siphoned off large amounts of those borrowed funds for his personal use. Because the stolen funds had to be repaid, it was necessary for Podlucky to continually borrow additional amounts. This cycle of repaying stolen funds with new loans caused law enforcement authorities to characterize his fraud as a Ponzi scheme.

As pointed out by Le-Nature's court-appointed bankruptcy trustee, the 2003 Special Committee investigation tragically backfired on the company's preferred stockholders and creditors, who were the primary victims of Podlucky's scam. The "no fraud" conclusion of the investigative report submitted to the Special Committee allowed Podlucky and his co-conspirators to continue "looting" the company "and wasting corporate funds on avoidable transactions" for three more years.[13]

Federal law enforcement authorities placed a final price tag of nearly $700 million on Podlucky's long-running scam. U.S. District Judge Alan Bloch, in a decision that was largely symbolic, imposed a $661 million restitution order on Podlucky. That figure included the huge losses suffered by Le-Nature's enormously unprofitable business operations and the funds embezzled and squandered by Podlucky and his family members.

Podlucky used the embezzled funds to finance a lavish and ostentatious lifestyle. An audit of Podlucky's personal finances revealed that in one year he spent $45,000 on shoes; his corporate salary at the time was $50,000. When he lost control of Le-Nature's, Podlucky was building a palatial, 25,000-square-foot home near the company's headquarters that had a price tag approaching $20 million. Investigators discovered nearly $30 million of jewelry (purchased with Le-Nature's funds) in a secret room within the company's corporate headquarters. Years later, authorities recovered additional jewelry worth millions of dollars, when members of the Podlucky family attempted to sell it through Sotheby's auction house. Law enforcement authorities seized other extravagant Podlucky personal assets, including a small fleet of luxury automobiles and an immense model train collection that he had acquired at a cost of $1 million.

The lynchpin of the Le-Nature's fraud was the fatal flaw in the company's corporate governance system that allowed Podlucky to single-handedly manipulate and distort the company's reported financial results. Outside of the company,

Podlucky was perceived as a gregarious, well-meaning individual who was heavily involved in charitable, religious, and political organizations and activities. Internally, Podlucky (a very large man) was known for his overbearing and volatile disposition. Podlucky used his domineering personality to control his subordinates.

During their testimony in various court proceedings, Podlucky's former colleagues alluded to his "foul-mouthed, dictatorial style" that he used to "bully" them into submission.[14] In one particularly revealing anecdote that they reported, Podlucky forced a fellow executive to take off his (Podlucky's) shoes, shine them, and then put them back on his feet. The executive was also forced to tie the shoes and adjust Podlucky's socks.

Podlucky's son Jesse also eventually faced criminal charges for his role in the Le-Nature's fraud. A principal element of his attorneys' defense strategy was the fact that the young accountant had been controlled and manipulated by his tyrannical father throughout his life, which allegedly reduced Jesse's responsibility for his misdeeds. Jesse's attorneys reported that because of Podlucky's "erratic" and "uncontrollable temper," his children had lived under a "reign of terror" in the Podlucky household.[15] Jesse recalled one scene in which his father hurled his own birthday cake against a wall and referred to his children with a derogatory epithet. In another incident, Jesse recalled that he was beaten so badly by his father that his face was "almost unrecognizable."[16]

JUDGMENT DAY

In October 2011, Podlucky appeared before federal Judge Alan Bloch during his sentencing hearing after pleading guilty to mail fraud, income tax evasion, and conspiracy to commit money laundering. While addressing Judge Bloch, Podlucky stated, "I am appalled by my actions, Lord, I mean, Your Honor."[17] Later in the hearing, Podlucky referred to himself as a "filthy rag" and pleaded with the judge to give him a noncustodial sentence so that he could create a charity to cater to the needs of federal prison inmates. Judge Bloch ignored Podlucky's tearful contrition and sentenced him to 20 years in federal prison for his egregious crimes.

Seven of Podlucky's relatives and business associates also received prison sentences for their roles in the Le-Nature's fraud. Despite his attorneys' efforts to blame his criminal behavior on his overbearing father, Jesse received a nine-year prison sentence after being convicted of money laundering. A similar conviction for Karla Podlucky, who was Podlucky's wife and Jesse's mother, resulted in a four-year prison sentence. The money laundering charges against Jesse and Karla stemmed from their involvement in covertly selling jewelry that had been purchased with Le-Nature's corporate funds. The two had used the proceeds from the sale of the jewelry for a variety of improper expenditures, including the payment of Podlucky's legal bills and the purchase of an $80,000 Mercedes-Benz automobile for Jesse.

Podlucky's close associate Andreycak received a five-year prison term despite her extensive cooperation with law enforcement authorities investigating the Le-Nature's fraud. After pleading guilty to one count of bank fraud, Podlucky's brother Jonathan, Le-Nature's former COO, received a sentence of five years. Like Jesse and Karla, Lynn (Le-Nature's former executive vice president of sales) opted for a jury trial rather than pleading guilty to the criminal charges filed against him. Following his conviction on 10 fraud charges, Lynn received a 15-year prison sentence. Another former Le-Nature's executive, Andrew Murin, received a prison sentence of ten years after pleading guilty to bank fraud, while a similar plea by one of Le-Nature's former leasing agents, Donald Pollinger, resulted in a five-year prison sentence.

DISCUSSION QUESTIONS

1. The fraud triangle identifies conditions or circumstances that are often precursors to financial fraud. Define the three categories of fraud risk factors that are included in the fraud triangle and provide specific examples of each.

2. Using the fraud triangle, identify fraud risk factors that were present in the Le-Nature's case. What implications did these factors have for the reliability of Le-Nature's accounting and financial reporting process?

3. The Committee of Sponsoring Organizations of the Treadway Commission (COSO) internal control framework identifies the five principal components that should be present in an organization's system of internal control. Name and briefly describe each of those components.

4. Relying on the COSO framework, identify specific flaws that were present in Le-Nature's internal control. How were principles of COSO's internal control framework violated by Podlucky and his co-conspirators? How did the deficiencies in Le-Nature's internal controls contribute to the failure of third parties (including Wachovia, leasing companies, and the company's independent auditors) to uncover the Le-Nature's fraud?

5. What stakeholders were negatively affected by Le-Nature's lack of internal controls and its leaders' criminal behavior? How so?

6. Identify specific work roles assumed by management accountants in business organizations and explain how the individuals occupying those roles contribute to internal controls, fraud prevention, an ethical climate and thus to good overall corporate governance.

7. Several accountants or individuals with accounting backgrounds were involved in the Le-Nature's debacle. These individuals included Higbee, Lipovich, Andreycak, Podlucky, Podlucky's son Jesse, and the individuals assigned to the Pascarella & Wiker investigative team. Evaluate the overall professionalism of each of those individuals by applying the four standards discussed in the IMA Statement of Ethical Professional Practice that can be found at www.imanet.org/docs/default-source/press_releases/statement-of-ethical-professional-practice_2-2-12.pdf?sfvrsn=2.

ENDNOTES

[1] Richard Gazarik, "Lawsuit Alleges Fraud in LeNature's Dealings," TribLIVE, May 1, 2008, http://triblive.com/x/pittsburghtrib/news/westmoreland/s_565150.html#axzz3sQEQUslS.

[2] Joe Mandak, "Witness in Pa. Soft Drink Fraud Case Gets 5 Years," Assoicated Press, 3 January 2012, http://news.yahoo.com/witness-pa-soft-drink-case-gets-5-185137723.html.

[3] Wachovia was acquired by Wells Fargo in late 2008 during the height of the 2008-2009 financial crisis that gripped the U.S. economy.

[4] *Mark Kirschner v. K & L Gates LLP, et al*, Superior Court of Pennsylvania, 46 a.3d 737 (2012), 2012 PA Super 102, July 19, 2012.

[5] *Ibid.*

[6] *Ibid.*

[7] *Ibid.*

[8] Richard Gazarik, "Greg Podlucky Had Visions of Taking Le-Nature's's to the Top," TribLIVE, November 19, 2006, http://triblive.com/x/pittsburghtrib/news/westmoreland/s_480492.html#axzz3sQEQUslS.

[9] *Ibid.*

[10] Joe Mandak, Joe Mandak, "Robert Lynn, Former Chief Revenue Officer of Le-Nature's, Sentenced to 15 Years in Prison for Massive Accounting Fraud," Huff Post, January 3, 2012, http://huffingtonpost.com/2012/01/03/robert-lynn-le-nature_n_1181909.html.

[11] Joe Mandak, CNS News, "Ex-Pa. Soft-drink CEO Gets 20 Years in Prison," CNSNews.com, October 23, 2011, http://www.cnsnews.com/news/article/ex-pa-soft-drink-ceo-gets-20-years-prison.

[12] *USA v. Karla Podlucky*, U.S. Court of Appeals for the Third Circuit, Docket No. 12-2469, May 27, 2014.

[13] *Mark Kirschner v. K. & L Gates LLP, et al.*, 2012.

[14] Joe Mandak, CNS News, 2011.

[15] *USA v. G. Jesse Podlucky*, U.S. District Court for the Western District of Pennsylvania, Case 2:11-cr-00047-ANB, Document 201, April 19, 2012.

[16] *Ibid.*

[17] Joe Mandak, CNS News, 2011.

West Coast Equestrian Association

Doug Kalesnikoff, Vince Bruni-Bossio, and Suresh Kalagnanam, University of Saskatchewan

WEST COAST EQUESTRIAN ASSOCIATION (WCEA) IS THE DISGUISED NAME OF a real 35-year-old not-for-profit organization that provides support to equestrian sport and recreation. This case study is based on the personal experience of one of the authors who advised the organization on strategy and governance. The fraud depicted in this case is based on a real event that was reported in the local media. It took place in a small local organization where the financial executive left the country with more than a million dollars. By blending the issues from two real organizations into this case, we want to convey that: (1) trust is an important factor in every organization, especially small organizations that suffer from a lack of resources, and (2) not-for-profit organizations are especially vulnerable to fraud because the board of directors of not-for-profit organizations place a significant amount of trust on the executive director and other staff for internal controls.

The case is best suited for an advanced undergraduate course or master's level courses in fraud, auditing, management accounting/control, and governance and also for capstone case courses that integrate multiple topic areas. The case is based on a not-for-profit organization, but it does not require in-depth knowledge of accounting for not-for-profit organizations.

Keywords: governance, not-for-profit organizations, fraud, internal controls.

The Association of
Accountants and
Financial Professionals
in Business

West Coast Equestrian Association

Doug Kalesnikoff
Assistant Professor
University of Saskatchewan

Vince Bruni-Bossio
Assistant Professor
University of Saskatchewan

Suresh Kalagnanam
Associate Professor
University of Saskatchewan

INTRODUCTION

It was May 15, 2014. The sun was shining as Doug Lawrence smiled and watched Excalibur, his favorite horse, running circles in the field outside his house. Doug loves horses, which is why he decided to volunteer as chair of the board of the West Coast Equestrian Association (WCEA). The WCEA has been around for 35 years, and Doug remembered when his dad would take him to WCEA events. As Doug thought about recent events at WCEA, his smile disappeared, and he looked very concerned. WCEA was not doing well. Membership and participation was up, but Doug had recently become aware of many internal problems at multiple levels and substantial sums of money that apparently went missing. WCEA was, in fact, very close to folding because of fraud allegations, management control, and governance issues.

Less than a month ago, Doug had received a telephone call from a staff member of WCEA that the executive director of 21 years, Marvin Pendleton, had disappeared. Doug had taken it upon himself to make some inquiries. Marvin's spouse was distraught. She claimed that, when she arrived home one day, Marvin was nowhere to be found. She saw that some of his clothes were missing, along with his passport. She had reported Marvin as a missing person to the police. The police undertook an investigation and found that Marvin had boarded a flight to San Salvador on April 3, 2014, the day of his disappearance.

Furthermore, the police reported that his traveling companion was Joan Walton, the auditor for WCEA.

Upon hearing this news, Doug grabbed a copy of the 2013 audited financial statements that had been approved at the last board of directors meeting. He read WCEA's statement of operations and statement of financial position (see Tables 1 and 2) and tried to verify the balance in WCEA's bank account and investments. Much to his horror, Doug found that the bank's year-end account balance was only $45,354, compared with the $102,473 that was reported in the financial statements. Even worse, he could not find any reference to an investment account, and none of the current staff knew anything about any investment account. Doug obtained a copy of the bank statement for the three months since year-end and found that 17 unexplained checks of $2,000 had been written in the weeks leading up to Marvin's disappearance, and the bank account had been depleted to less than $10,000.

Doug had no accounting training, but even he could see that the organization suffered from a lack of proper record keeping. WCEA only had one laptop, which held some accounting records and files, and an old desktop computer that contained other files. The only other filing system consisted of two storage rooms filled to the ceiling with boxes of materials. To make matters worse, the WCEA board of directors had never seen a budget and was only provided with financial statements on an annual basis. Moreover, no one in the organization, including board members, had any understanding of the operations or finances of the organization. Doug sighed, looked back at Excalibur, and thought to himself, "I had blind trust in Marvin. I just did not think that things were this bad."

The directors met in an emergency meeting to review their liability insurance policy. The policy covers the directors for errors and omissions due to theft or fraud up to $100,000, provided that the directors were not negligent. Thus, the directors could be held culpable for any losses exceeding $100,000 and for all loses if they were found to be negligent.

HISTORY

The organization started 35 years ago as a grassroots nonprofit organization to support equestrian sports and recreation on Canada's west coast. Over the decades, the organization has developed into one with a membership base growing from 2,300 in 2012 to 2,500 in 2013, with reported annual revenues of about $750,000 per year. To facilitate this growth, WCEA has held membership fees firm at $220 per year for the past five years. Memberships are renewable annually by March 31. A membership receipt is issued to each member, as they are eligible to receive a discount in insurance premiums for horses.

SERVICES

WCEA wants to grow and provide more services and programs to equine owners that support their interests. WCEA programs cover a wide range of equestrian activities, which include initiatives for beginners and advanced riders. Included in these services are certification and education programs. 2013 was the first year that at least one certification or education program was delivered each month of the year, and two programs were delivered in each of the summer months (June, July, and August). This surpassed the previous record of 11 program deliveries in 2012. Each participant of these programs paid a fee of $150 per session, and attendance is generally between 20 and 30 participants. Since many participants cannot claim these program fees for tax purposes, only a fraction of the participants ask for a receipt.

The organization also receives donations from bequests and from collection boxes placed in chain stores that sell sporting goods.

WCEA also sells merchandise such as t-shirts, belt buckles, coasters, and art depicting equestrian settings. These items are priced at a 50% markup from cost.

WCEA is also funded by a grant of $225,000 ($220,000 in 2012) from Western Sport Lotteries. The grant is contingent upon receiving audited financial statements.

Although the grant and some of the membership program fees and donations are received in the form of checks, many of the remaining receipts are handled in cash.

GOVERNANCE

Doug had always been unclear about the role of the board. The WCEA board has always consisted of horse enthusiasts who want to promote equine activities but have little understanding of accounting or controls. Board members had always been more interested in pursuing activities such as coaching, promoting, veterinary care, and so on than they were in performing their jobs as board members.

The board has 14 members. They serve four-year staggered terms, and elections are held every year at the annual general meeting. The former executive director offered very little transparency into board activities, and, in fact, used this lack of information to control the board. The executive director developed unique rules over the years that limited the sharing of information between administration and the board. This included a rule stating that board members were not allowed to enter the executive director's office.

The former executive director was seldom questioned by the board. Since most board members were specialists in their own equine areas, they did not want to be distracted from doing what they loved most. This resulted in most board members being happy to have such a strong executive director in place because it meant they did not have to attend as many meetings or deal with "all that financial stuff."

The result of this secrecy was that many board members could not comment on or answer questions regarding what the organization was doing. This impacted WCEA's members, who felt that board members were either clueless, did not care, or that the organization was hiding things.

Another issue was that board directors lacked any formal training pertaining to their roles and responsibilities. WCEA also had very few governance policies. Instead, it had a brief orientation book that only dealt with Robert's Rules of Order, which discussed concepts such as how to make a motion and vote on issues. There were almost no policies detailing the actual job responsibilities of the board.

Concerned about the lack of oversight at the board level, Doug decided to research the topic of governance. He reviewed a binder full of material that he had received in a course on governance during his university days and made some notes. The results of his research and accompanying notes are in Figure 1.

REQUIRED

Doug has now contacted you in your capacity as a professional accountant. A second emergency meeting is to be held in two days. Doug would like you to write up a discussion memo outlining:

1. An estimate of how much money might be missing.
2. What management controls could be put in place to help prevent this from happening again?
3. What changes in the governance policies should be considered by the organization? This should include a review of the fiduciary duties that a board must follow and make recommendations about how WCEA can ensure that it meets its responsibilities at this level.

Table 1: WCEA's Statement of Operations

For the year ended December 31, 2013

		2013	2012
Revenue			
	Memberships	$435,098	$465,444
	Grants	225,000	220,000
	Donations	29,350	26,998
	Education programs	38,876	30,643
	Sales	24,567	22,113
	Other	13,453	10,087
		$766,344	$775,285
Expenses			
	Salaries and benefits	$360,435	$351,989
	Director Insurance	12,209	12,334
	Education programs	46,089	39,854
	Advertising and promotion	159,366	170,564
	Office administration	97,654	94,544
	Rent	45,342	43,094
	Cost of sales	25,987	24,098
	Audit fees	6,500	6,000
	Meeting costs	5,643	4,339
	Amortization	4,097	3,976
	Other	554	476
		$763,876	$751,268
Excess (Deficiency)		$ 2,468	$ 24,017

Table2: WCEA's Statement of Financial Position

As at December 31, 2013

		2013	2012
Current Assets			
	Bank	$102,473	$103,486
	Accounts receivable	5,987	4,665
	Prepaid expenses	12,098	11,543
		120,558	119,694
Capital Assets		17,989	16,917
Investments		100,000	100,000
		$238,547	$236,611
Current Liabilities			
	Accounts payable	$ 21,098	$ 14,543
	Accrued liabilities	5,800	5,300
	Unearned membership fees	108,775	116,361
		135,673	136,204
Net Assets		102,875	100,407
		$238,547	$236,611

Figure 1: Notes from the Governance Manual

What is Governance?

Governance is "the exercise of authority, direction and control of an organization in order to ensure that its purpose is achieved."[1] Governance seeks to answer the following questions:

- Who is in charge of what?
- Who sets the direction and the parameters within which the direction is to be pursued?
- Who makes decisions about what?
- Who sets performance indicators, monitors progress, and evaluates results?
- Who is accountable to whom and for what?

Key Components of Governance

Governance Structure

Good governance starts with a proper organizational structure. It is also very important that the board understands the difference between an operational committee (a committee that assists with operations) and a standing committee (a board level committee), as well as the reporting relationship as illustrated here:

(Doug reflected on past confusions within WCEA about committees. Many board directors did not understand that, when serving on an operational committee, they could not use their board director status to influence the committee. In fact, as members of an operational committee, board directors were under the direction of the executive director. Conversely, when board directors were members of standing committees, such as the Governance committee or the Finance & Audit committee, they had the right to ask for clarification from the executive director in completing these functions. In the past, however, Board directors serving on standing committees had been too willing to abdicate responsibilities by handing over their duties to the former executive director.

("What a mess," Doug thought, "we need to train our board members on when to put on their operational committee hats and when to put on their governance hats.")

Fiduciary Duties[2]

Board members must know, understand, and legally fulfill the following fiduciary duties, or they could be found liable.

Duty of Due Diligence: This includes being informed about the requirements of the relevant laws and becoming familiar with the organization's articles, bylaws, and governing policies. It also means being aware of the organization's mission, vision, and values and being informed about the organization's programs and activities.

(Currently, there were no written policies to guide board directors. Although bylaws exist, Doug wondered how many of the board directors had actually read them even once.)

Duty of Care: This includes being prepared and willing to participate fully in board (and committee) decision making. Board directors are required to act ethically and be open and transparent. The idea here is that each board director should look after the organization with care and attention as if he or she were the owner. This was really about acting in good faith.

(Doug recalled that most meetings were short and hardly involved any decision making.)

Duty of Loyalty: This is really about doing what was in the best interest of the organization. It means putting aside personal interests and ensuring that confidentiality is maintained. Full disclosure of any potential conflicts of interest was integral to the Duty of Loyalty.

(Doug believed that the board had the right intentions, but many directors did not understand how to act in the best interest of the organization. For example, most board directors did not realize that they created a conflict-of-interest situation by advocating only for those equine initiatives that they were personally invested in.)

---

[1]Note: Much of the discussion about "what is governance?" is adapted from: Mel D. Gill, *Governing Results: A Director's Guide to Good Governance*, Trafford Publishing, Crewe, U.K., 2005.

[2]Material in this section is adapted from: "Primer for Directors of Not-for-Profit Corporations: Rights, Duties and Practices," Ch. 2, Industry China, 2002, www.ic.gc.ca/eic/site/cilp-pdci.nsf/vwapj/Primer_en.pdf/$FILE/Primer_en.pdf.

Out of Control: Lax Procedures at National Capital Trust?

Ron Messer, Kwantlen Polytechnic University

THIS CASE STUDY IS BASED ON A REAL FINANCIAL INSTITUTION and requires students to identify weaknesses in the internal control processes described, which relate to the operations of a trust company. Students will also determine the appropriate controls that need to be in place and their purpose and will need to make suggestions for audit tests that will identify whether any improprieties have occurred. This case is particularly timely, as the aging baby boomer generation places significant assets in the care of third parties. It's based on actual events that resulted in significant loss to a financial institution, as well as a great deal of negative publicity. To maintain confidentiality, the names of the trust company and persons involved have been changed.

The case is intended for a course in auditing, risk management, or advanced management accounting. It is most appropriate once students have discussed the nature and purpose of internal controls within an organization.

Keywords: internal controls, fraud, audit, risk management.

Out of Control: Lax Procedures at National Capital Trust?

Ron Messer, CA, CMA (Canada)
Kwantlen Polytechnic University
Vancouver, Canada.

INTRODUCTION

As manager of the Finance department for National Capital Trust, Miriam Richardson was in charge of financial functions at the institution. It was her job to ensure that clients' funds were managed properly. In August 2013, Miriam noticed several unexplained changes in various accounts, including some accounts that were worth millions of dollars. Small sums of money were being withdrawn frequently, and large undocumented credit card purchases were being made. The Legal Services department also reported that an unusually large number of amendments were being made to client wills. With all this going on, Miriam was concerned about the safety of the customers' assets.

BACKGROUND

National Capital Trust (NCT) was formed in the 1970s to provide trustee services for elderly clients. Even as it grew and subsequently offered additional services to its customers, NCT remained first and foremost a trust company. As its aging client base grew, more assets were being placed in the hands of NCT's professional staff. As a trustee, the company provided security for money held in its accounts, items in safety deposit boxes (such as jewelry), investment portfolios, and real estate assets. To do this, NCT was assigned power of attorney (POA) over the client's assets

through a document completed by the client or a family member. Clients' bills were paid with funds held in the trust, and their assets were managed so that they could maintain a comfortable lifestyle.

Miriam was concerned that financial safeguards had not kept pace with the rapid growth in NCT's assets. Fraud was always a possibility when dealing with assets held in trust. In fact, the company's external auditors and regulatory authorities had identified weaknesses in the internal controls on several occasions. Unfortunately, very few of these issues were addressed. As one senior manager said, "We trust our employees." In addition, Miriam's department was constantly backlogged with work, and the shortage of workers with the necessary skills made it difficult to find qualified candidates to hire.

BUSINESS PROCESS

NCT has four client-facing departments: Client Services, Finance, Investments, and Legal Services (see Figure 1). The processes at the company relating to trust accounts involve client enrollment, administration procedures, and transaction controls. Figure 2 provides an overview of the processes relating to client accounts, while Figures 3 and 4 contain a sample of job descriptions and NCT policies and procedures.

CLIENT ENROLLMENT

For an individual to enroll with NCT, an application form needs to be completed in the Client Services department. This typically is done by a family member of the elderly customer. The customer's assets are catalogued by a representative of NCT who goes to the individual's home to take an inventory of valuables. In the past, two individuals usually went and catalogued everything, but staff shortages resulted in only one bank representative now being sent. Assets that get catalogued could include jewelry, collectibles, and—not uncommonly—loose cash. The assets are then placed in a secure location at NCT (or sometimes offsite), and a POA is assigned to the trustee to make prudent financial decisions on the client's behalf. Assets are held in trust until the client dies. At that time, they are distributed based on the terms of the will. The Legal Services department coordinates client POA documents and wills.

ADMINISTRATION PROCEDURES

NCT assigns a case worker from its Client Services department to each new customer. It is the case worker's job to contact clients periodically to ensure their wellbeing. For example, if the individual is in a care facility, the case worker ensures the person is properly fed, clothed, and bathed.

A financial representative in the Finance department works with the case worker to ensure that all financial issues, such as paying bills and making small purchases (e.g., a television for personal use), are handled properly. It is the financial representative's job to ensure the propriety of any payments made, including providing appropriate supporting documentation for any disbursements. In most cases, family members aren't interested in caring for their elderly parents. As a result, the case worker becomes the main personal contact for many clients, and close ties frequently develop between client and case worker.

TRANSACTION CONTROLS

Prior to a payment being made, a pre-audit is done on the disbursement to ensure that (1) it relates to the correct client, (2) the funds are taken from the right account, (3) the necessary approvals have been obtained, and (4) appropriate supporting documentation is provided. Payments can be made by way of petty cash, check, or by using a client's credit card. Payments are authorized by the case worker and approved by the financial representative. The Finance department requires supporting documentation

for the disbursement, but it is not always provided. Case workers can make small payments using petty cash, which is taken directly from the client's bank account. Because of the small dollar value of these disbursements, supporting documentation usually is not provided to the financial representative who approves the transactions.

The Finance department receives cash from client investments (such as dividend checks, interest on bonds, and certificates of deposit, as well as rent from real estate holdings). Incoming mail is opened by the client's financial representative. Any cash or checks received are deposited into the appropriate account by the financial representative and recorded by both the Investments department and the Finance department. NCT's auditors had noted that a bank reconciliation of the cash received and cash deposited was required but not always completed on a timely basis.

NEW HIRE

A new case worker was hired in January 2013 to alleviate staff shortages and deal with the large backlog of work, particularly in client enrollment. She seemed to be the ideal candidate. She had relevant work experience, proper academic qualifications, and had performed well on aptitude tests. In addition, phone calls placed to her references resulted in glowing reports.

NCT's Human Resources (HR) department was tasked with verifying the candidate's credentials. Unknown to the HR person checking her qualifications, the person who provided confirmation of the candidate's prior work experience also served as a reference and was a close personal friend of the applicant. Also unknown to HR was the fact that her qualifications came from an obscure college located outside the country. A photocopy of her degree had been accepted as evidence of education. These vetting procedures were not normal practice for HR, but the department was short-staffed and busy trying to fill numerous positions. The urgency to fill the case worker position and time constraints led to the relaxed standards.

ASSIGNMENT

In August 2013, Miriam noticed that some of the client accounts were becoming seriously depleted for no apparent reason. In addition, clients' petty cash accounts were being used more often than usual. The Legal Services department notified Miriam of changes to clients' wills that, while not unusual, were not frequent occurrences. Miriam wanted to investigate these apparent anomalies and make the necessary changes.

Your assignment is to address each of the following questions:

1. In general, what are the major objectives of internal control? What is their purpose?

2. What are the risks associated with providing financial services such as those of a trustee? Classify each risk as (1) high, (2) medium, or (3) low.

3. Review the processes outlined in the case and indicate where:

   a. Controls should be in place but do not exist and

   b. Controls are in place but are not working effectively.

4. For each of the controls that are in place, or should be, identify whether that control is preventive or detective.

5. Was NCT's senior management adequately performing its fiduciary responsibilities on behalf of its clients? (See Figure 5.) Give an example of how it was, or was not, meeting its responsibilities.

6. What are the ethical responsibilities of senior management toward its clients?

7. How would you test whether inappropriate activity (potential fraud) had occurred?

REAL-LIFE RESULTS

In this real-life business situation, fraud was uncovered after Miriam's suspicions caused her to approach senior management with her concerns. The company spent more than $1 million to assess the extent of the fraud. Although the financial institution desperately wanted to avoid any negative publicity, news of the incident was reported and caused significant embarrassment. All misappropriated funds were eventually recovered, and the perpetrator was sent to jail for several years.

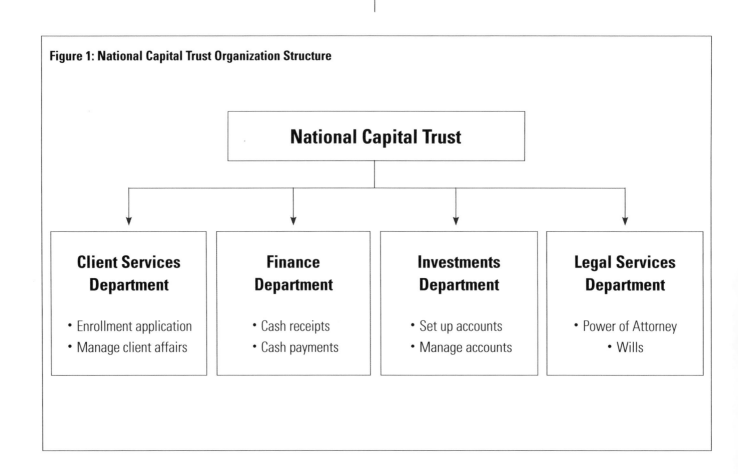

Figure 1: National Capital Trust Organization Structure

National Capital Trust

Client Services Department	Finance Department	Investments Department	Legal Services Department
• Enrollment application • Manage client affairs	• Cash receipts • Cash payments	• Set up accounts • Manage accounts	• Power of Attorney • Wills

Figure 2: Processes for Client Accounts

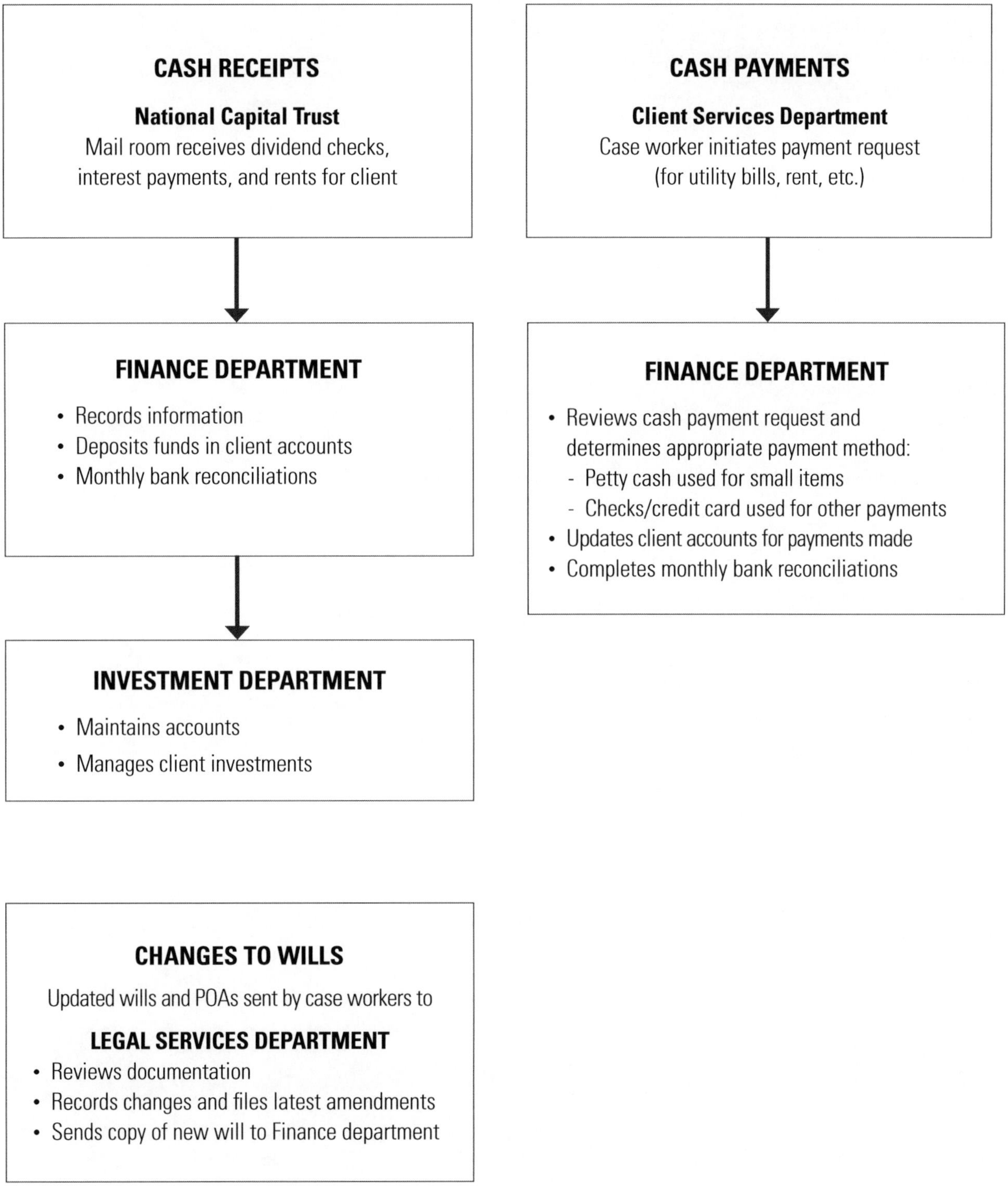

CASH RECEIPTS

National Capital Trust

Mail room receives dividend checks, interest payments, and rents for client

↓

FINANCE DEPARTMENT

- Records information
- Deposits funds in client accounts
- Monthly bank reconciliations

↓

INVESTMENT DEPARTMENT

- Maintains accounts
- Manages client investments

CASH PAYMENTS

Client Services Department

Case worker initiates payment request (for utility bills, rent, etc.)

↓

FINANCE DEPARTMENT

- Reviews cash payment request and determines appropriate payment method:
  - Petty cash used for small items
  - Checks/credit card used for other payments
- Updates client accounts for payments made
- Completes monthly bank reconciliations

CHANGES TO WILLS

Updated wills and POAs sent by case workers to

LEGAL SERVICES DEPARTMENT

- Reviews documentation
- Records changes and files latest amendments
- Sends copy of new will to Finance department

Figure 3: Manager Job Descriptions (excerpts)

Manager Client Services

Key responsibilities include:

- Process intake forms for new clients
- Custody, record, and safeguard client assets (jewelry, collectibles, etc.)
- Coordinate case workers and clients
- Hire/train new case workers

Manager of Finance

Key responsibilities include:

- Security over cash receipts and payments on behalf of clients
- Pre-audit of client payments before disbursement
- Maintain accurate and complete client financial records and bank accounts
- Manage client petty cash funds

Manager of Investments

Key responsibilities include:

- Safeguard client investments (securities, real estate, etc.)
- Ensure appropriate returns on client assets, in compliance with investment policies
- Prepare quarterly client investment statements
- Liaise with the Finance department

Manager of Legal Services

Key responsibilities include:

- Represent clients in court proceedings (e.g., will variation disputes)
- Process files and maintain security over all legal documents
- Manage/review client POAs and wills and ensure they are current and authorized
- Act as executor for deceased clients

Figure 4: NCT Policies and Procedures (excerpts)

Petty Cash
Petty cash funds are to be used for purchases costing $50 or less, chargeable to a client account. All such purchases must be supported by a paid invoice or a receipt. A petty cash fund is an imprest fund. This means that the fund is always at the same value. The cash on hand at all times, the cash on hand, plus vouchers or invoices representing amounts paid from petty cash, plus the amounts awaiting reimbursement, must equal the value of the fund. The petty cash fund is subject to audit on a periodic basis.

Payments on Behalf of Client
Receipts provide documentation for purchases made by check or credit card. The overriding expectation is that receipts or paid invoices are to be submitted as documentation for these purchases.

Receipt and Safeguarding of Cash
The mail room will forward all client correspondence to the Finance department, where the financial representative responsible for a client will open the mail. Cash received must not be left unattended during the day. Funds should be stored overnight (or during the day when unattended) in a cashbox within a locked cabinet or safe to which there is restricted access. Ideally, one person should be held responsible for the safekeeping funds. Deposits of funds are to be made daily.

Client Bank Accounts
Bank reconciliations should be completed on a timely basis (monthly) for all client accounts and should be reviewed and approved by a supervisor.

Signing Authorities
All client funds must be administered through the client bank account(s) maintained by the Finance department. The following persons are authorized to sign all checks on all bank accounts for their clients: (1) financial representative or (2) case worker.

Security of Credit Card Information
National Capital Trust is bound by contract and by law to keep confidential any credit card information received from clients or any other party. All copies of credit card receipts should be sent with cash transmittals or tallies to the Finance department, which then stores these documents in a secure location until the documents can be destroyed.

Figure 5: NCT Corporate Governance (excerpts)

The Board of Directors will be composed of 12 members. Four committees will be formed from these members:

Compensation Committee (4 members)

This committee makes recommendations on the amount of remuneration paid to the CEO and senior executives, including base salaries, bonuses, and other compensation.

Audit and Risk Management Committee (4 members)

The audit and risk management committee will be responsible for approving the company's financial statements and liaising with the external auditors. The committee is responsible for developing and implementing an appropriate risk management strategy, including ensuring good internal control practices, which should encompass, but is not limited to, the following:

• Proper segregation of duties.

• Maintaining complete and accurate client records along with supporting documentation.

• Safeguarding client and company assets.

• Proper and timely authorization of transactions and reconciliation of accounts.

• Creating an internal audit function. (Note: To date, this has not been done by the committee.)

Audit committee members must be independent in their dealings with NCT. This includes any relationship for which they could receive a financial gain. At least one of the members of the committee must be financially literate.

Capital Projects Committee (4 members)

The committee is tasked with the review and approval of all major capital projects, including expansion and refurbishment of NCT facilities.

Strategy Committee (4 members)

The committee is tasked with developing and implementing corporate strategy on an annual and long-term basis.

The Moulder Company: Alternative Strategies for Toxics Use Reduction

George Joseph and Mark Myles, University of Massachusetts Lowell

MOULDER CO. IS A U.S.-BASED MANUFACTURER OF STADIUM SEATING. This case illustrates the use of capital budgeting to respond to environmental regulatory issues from a business perspective, integrating environmental concerns with business priorities. Increasingly, stakeholder pressures, cost containment, and potential product development opportunities increase the motivation for companies to address environmental issues proactively. The case addresses the complexity surrounding environmental investment decisions, with factors such as environmental cost identification, capital budget criteria, and integration of environmental factors such as risk and taxation that facilitate a more detailed analysis of pollution prevention options. Overall, the case provides a forum to illustrate how management accountants can play a significant role in supporting the increasing complexity of environmental regulation.

The case could be used in an MBA-level or master's-level course or an upper-level undergraduate management accounting course that integrates sustainability and managerial accounting concepts.

Keywords: environmental costing, capital budgets, toxics regulations, risk analysis, tax implications.

The Association of
Accountants and
Financial Professionals
in Business

The Moulder Company: Alternative Strategies for Toxics Use Reduction

George Joseph
Associate Professor of Accounting
University of Massachusetts Lowell

Mark Myles
Training Program Manager Toxics Use Reduction
Institute University of Massachusetts Lowell

INTRODUCTION

Moulder Company was founded in 1922 by William A. Moulder III, son of a shipping magnate from Framingham, Mass. Moulder left Framingham and moved to Western Massachusetts to seek his fortune in wood products manufacturing. For decades, Moulder Company specialized in value-added products, such as fine-milled lumber, doors, and specialty moldings. In the 1950s, he expanded Moulder Co.'s product line to include a Seating Division that focused on stadium seating. William Moulder ran the company until he retired in the late 1970s, and his son-in-law, Wilson Jacobs, took over as President. Jacobs expanded the company and organized it into four divisions. The Seating Division eventually became the largest and most profitable part of the company.

Both Moulder and his successor Jacobs viewed environmental management expenditures as a burden on the business that reduced profits and inhibited productive investment in a new plant and equipment. Yet the industrial environment had undergone changes because of increased environmental activism that was particularly intense in the New England region. A recent news article became a wake-up call for the Moulder Co. enterprise. A community activist group with strong connections to the local newspaper and other regional environmental groups had begun scrutinizing the company. Shortly thereafter, the local paper ran a front-page article featuring Moulder Co.'s Toxics Release Inventory (TRI) reporting data and its environmental impacts.[1]

Jacobs finally hired Terry Wilbur, a full-time environmental manager with several years of experience in the field. Wilbur took over the duties of several engineers, who had performed the work in their spare time, with a mandate to ensure compliance while "keeping environmental spending within reasonable limits." Wilbur realized the mandate would be difficult to fulfill given the significant environmental risks. Regulators were increasingly assertive, and stakeholders were more vocal. Additionally, guidelines under the Massachusetts Toxics Use Reduction Act (TURA) suggested a proactive pollution prevention (P2) approach, which also could unveil strategic possibilities that forward-thinking companies could use.[2]

Soon after beginning his new role, Wilbur set up the Environment, Health, and Safety (EH&S) team. Drawn primarily from the Seating Division and Corporate Services (see Figure 1 for organizational chart), the core members of the EH&S team included Wilbur; Phil Bingham, the controller who oversaw all accounting and tax functions at Moulder; and Paul Grimes, the staff accountant who was recently hired to support operational accounting and internal reporting.

At the first meeting, the EH&S team invited all members of the Engineering, Production, and Controller Divisions to explore options and develop an actionable plan. Again Wilbur highlighted the importance of P2.[3] He explained that P2 was basic to nearly all emerging trends in environmental rulemaking and regulatory compliance and included initiatives such as product design changes and technology or process

Figure 1
Moulder Company Organizational Chart

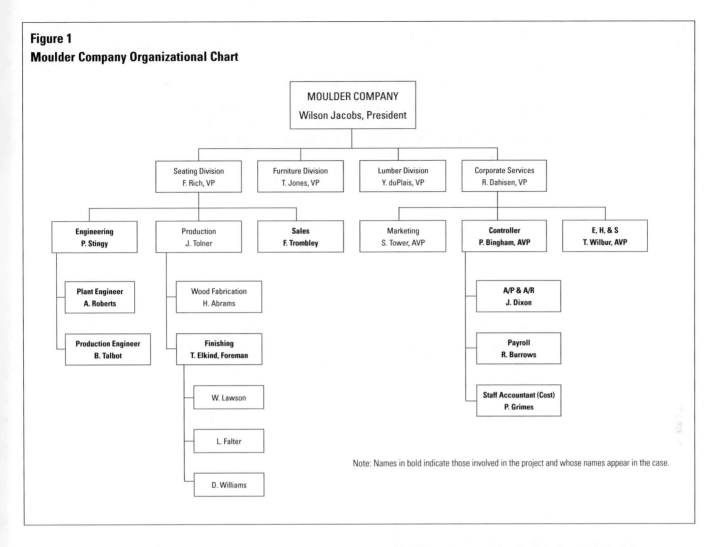

Note: Names in bold indicate those involved in the project and whose names appear in the case.

modifications that involved substituting toxic chemicals with safer alternatives. Wilbur pointed out that more facilities were affirming the benefits of P2 that source reduction led to cost savings in areas such as reduced capital investment for end-of-pipe control, lower waste-disposal costs, lower costs for complying with environmental regulations, less need for worker protective equipment, and lower annual operating and maintenance costs. In addition, P2 also encompassed good operating practices such as waste segregation (separating recycling and other forms of waste), preventive maintenance, training and awareness programs, and production scheduling.[4]

The audience responded with both enthusiasm and apprehension. This was a whole new perspective to the audience, and they quickly realized that it called for significant change in procedures and outlook. Nevertheless, all were aware that the time had come to address the regulators' concerns, particularly volatile organic compound (VOC) and hazardous air pollutant (HAP) emissions.[5] The difficult question now was where to begin, so Wilbur began to assess environmental concerns at Moulder Co.

SEATING DIVISION AND FINISHING PROCESSES

Moulder's Stadium Seating Division produces two product lines: bleachers and stadium chairs. Bleachers are manufactured from flat boards while the stadium chairs require specialized manufacturing processes because of the complex shapes of the arms, backs, and seats.

BLEACHER

STADIUM

Most pollutants (particularly VOCs) emerged during the finishing processes, with larger proportion from the stadium chairs. Moulder Co. uses two types of finishing operations: (1) Manual application of coatings for the flat boards used in the bleacher seating and (2) spray application for the complex wooden shapes of the stadium chairs. Wilbur focused his P2 assessment on the spray finishing of the arms, backs, and seats of the stadium chairs since this accounted for the highest use of coating materials.

The finishing process would begin after the wooden components of the stadium chairs were assembled onto metal frames and then carried into a large ventilated spray booth. Typically three or four coats were applied with high volume, low pressure (HVLP) spray guns: stain, sealer, and two lacquer topcoats. After each coat, the part was carried to a flash-off area to dry, then to a prep area for sanding before being returned to the spray booth for the next coat. The spray gun assembly (lines, nozzles, and so on) were cleaned with a hydrocarbon solvent, such as toluene, at the end of each shift and whenever lacquer pigments were changed. Because these solvents emit VOCs, the paint booths were equipped with filtered ventilators. Spray operators were outfitted with protective suits and full-head respirators to meet the U.S. Centers for Disease Control and Prevention (CDC) National Institute for Occupational Safety and Health (NIOSH) guidelines.[6] The spray booth had a coated paper liner that was able to be stripped and replaced as needed.

All stadium seating was custom made-to-order with different finishing specifications that required various finishing times and quantities of materials. Depending on the work flow and order backlog, workers moved back and forth between the bleacher and the stadium chair finishing operations.

The coating materials, purchased in 55-gallon drums, were moved to the production area as needed, and the contents were transferred into the spray dispensers. Employees were responsible for cleaning the spray equipment with solvent after each shift or for coating changeovers. They obtained solvent from a 55-gallon drum stored near the work area. When drums were empty, the person who emptied them would contact the store room for replacements.

Used solvent was dumped into an open drum, which was then resealed and sent to a centralized waste disposal holding area. Contaminated rags and spray booth liners were also deposited into drums and sent to the waste disposal holding area. Maintenance staff was responsible for calling a certified hazardous waste hauler to pick up the drums when the holding area approached capacity. Figure 2 outlines the steps in the stadium chair finishing process.

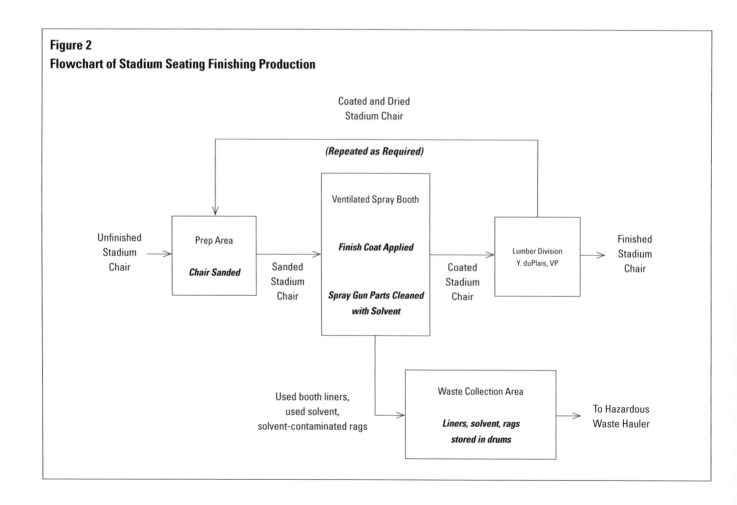

Figure 2
Flowchart of Stadium Seating Finishing Production

Financial feasibility was a crucial component of Wilbur's mandate to explore pollution prevention options. Wilbur soon realized that the cost system was not equipped to provide the granular information to analyze environmental costs. The current management accounting system provided an aggregated picture of direct labor and materials costs by job. Bingham noted that the cost classification system had applied a traditional approach to costs, without any consideration of environment-related factors. The next important step was to gather the required information for the financial analysis.

The meeting brought many key elements into focus. Before adjourning the meeting, two teams were assigned to prepare reports for the next meeting. Wilbur would oversee both: Grimes's team would gather cost information on current finishing operations in the stadium division, and Bingham's team (including Pete Stingy from the Engineering division and Flora Trombley, the sales manager) would explore alternatives to the stadium chair finishing operations.

COLLECTING THE COST INFORMATION

Grimes reviewed the financial records with the finishing processes to identify a list of annual operating costs associated with finishing the stadium chair products. The records provided information on coating materials, production labor, and maintenance (primarily cleaning solvents). Grimes realized that there were other finishing costs within the overheads but was not sure how to identify or classify them. Wilbur and Grimes went to work examining the records and interviewing the operations personnel, and they identified the other costs for finishing, namely solvent disposal, rag and spray booth disposal, electricity for ventilation, heating oil, environment compliance, and employee and EH&S team training. Grimes then began gathering the costs, another significant challenge involving further interviews of personnel involved in activities associated with finishing. The foreman, Tim Elkind, kept track of the total number of hours worked at each area. He had assigned finishers on a rotating basis to track the amounts of each type of finishing material used for each job.

Wilbur handled most of the environmental compliance work—tracking hazardous waste, labeling it, liaising between divisions, and more—but acknowledged that he had not yet kept very good track of the amount of time he spent within each division, much less on any specific activity. Wilbur needed an estimate of his own time spent on compliance, and, after some reflection, estimated that "I spend about an eighth of my time on compliance activities for stadium chair finishing operations."

It was particularly difficult to estimate cleaning solvent use. Alan Roberts, the plant engineer, recalled that, "We used a total of about five to six drums per month for all operations, but we do not track solvent use for stadium chair finishing." After a pause, he added: "Probably half of what is used for stadium chair finishing ends up as fugitive emissions or is absorbed by cleaning rags."[7]

Roberts estimated such "fugitive emissions" amounted to "about a drum per month for stadium chair finishing." Disposal cost for rag and spray booth liner was $10,000 per year for stadium chair finishing. EH&S team training cost for the finishing line was about $2,000 per person. Moulder Co. trained two employees per year.

The energy costs for finishing stadium chairs posed another challenge. A quick call to Bill Talbot, the production engineer, confirmed that a portion of the heating oil bill could be linked to stadium seating. He estimated that such heating oil cost attributable to stadium chair finishing was the increased ventilation requirements to contain "fugitive emissions." Such ventilation costs resulted in an overall increase in the heating costs of about 25%. In addition, he also estimated that the portion of electricity bill attributable to stadium chair finishing ventilation was about 10%.

Grimes compiled the information from the team's records and discussions with other employees, adding a checklist for computing the current costs for stadium chair finishing (see Appendix A).

POLLUTION PREVENTION OPTIONS

Meanwhile, the second team had begun to conduct extensive research into options to the current sealer and lacquer finishing. Emphasizing the need to meet the TURA guidelines, the team came up with three options for the stadium chair.

Project A involves switching from sealer and lacquer coatings that average 26% solids to coatings with 35% solids. To enable proper application of the material with HVLP guns, Moulder Co. would have to heat the coatings in-line and would need to work with its equipment supplier to modify the spray gun caps, nozzles, and tips. These high-solids coatings with HVLP spray guns contain approximately 40% fewer VOCs and 80% fewer HAPs.

The second option, Project B, involves a more significant switch from nitrocellulose-based to water-based coatings. While the potential environmental gains are significant, the financial benefits are less certain, and Wilbur is also concerned about quality issues. Some customers ("Customer S" in particular) make it clear that they prefer the high gloss of the conventional nitrocellulose lacquer. Nevertheless, the water-based coatings would reduce VOCs and HAPs by more than 75% and would eliminate the need to use chlorinated solvents for clean-up.[8] The water used for cleaning the spray equipment would require some type of treatment to allow its discharge under an existing National Pollutant Discharge Elimination System (NPDES) permit, but Wilbur didn't anticipate any problems with that, other than a potential additional permit fee of about $500 per year.

The third option, Project C, emerged from a suggestion from an employee who had previously worked for a competitor in the Northwest. It involves the possibility of installing a state-of-the-art ultraviolet coating system. Although such systems had been installed in the industry primarily to coat flat boards, such as those used on the bleacher seating, new equipment had been introduced by one vendor to enable the use of ultraviolet coating on the more complex dimensions of other wood seating and furniture.[9] The technology looked promising but did not yet have an extensive track record for the type of application Moulder Co. was considering. Moreover, an automated system would require a significant up-front investment. Yet it did have the potential to generate major savings in materials and labor and provide significant environmental advantages.

Wilbur's research team examined the alternative projects in detail, considering the differences in technology and its impact on the cost elements identified earlier. Their summary estimates are explained in Appendix B.

PREPARING THE FEASIBILITY REPORT

At the next meeting, the two teams discussed their findings. Wilbur explained the need to prepare a feasibility report that integrated all the research and analysis. This report was to be presented to the management team headed by Jacobs and would need to highlight the technical, financial, and qualitative aspects of alternatives to the existing system. Technical aspects included reliability and effectiveness of new equipment in meeting pollution and toxics use targets, while qualitative factors include the impacts of the new processes on product and environment quality. While the engineering team focused primarily on technical and qualitative aspects, the financial component, as Wilbur observed, provided a basis for determining the viability of technical and qualitative aspects of the analysis. Financial feasibility for new investments was determined through a capital budgeting process based on company-wide criteria.

Bingham remarked that capital budgeting at Moulder Co. had always been a fairly informal process. Equipment investments required a five-year payback, while smaller equipment required three years. The hurdle rate (cost of capital) for all divisions was set at 20%. All long-term analysis assumed an economic lifetime of 10 years, using the straight-line method for depreciation. Bingham noted that the hurdle rate included a risk premium, particularly given uncertainties in regulatory mandates for toxics emissions. Wilbur then reviewed the alternative project options. He suggested that a discount on risk premium was in order if toxics emissions could be reduced significantly. In particular, Project C could warrant such a discount given its potential of eliminating the use of toxics in the Toxics Release Inventory, thereby transforming stakeholder perceptions of the company. There was also the possibility that improved quality and stakeholder appreciation could have a positive impact on the prices of some orders. Trombley pointed out that product enhancement from Project C processes might lead to an overall increase in annual cash flow from increased prices and sales, while adoption of Project B would cause customers who prefer the high-gloss finish ("Customer S") to seek other alternatives.

CONCERNS AND FUTURE CHALLENGES

The meetings had raised awareness of the new realities of the regulatory environment for toxics. Without a doubt, change was inevitable. Significant concerns now emerged about cost allocation for the different job orders that varied with finishing details. Trombley expressed her concern that the prices did not sufficiently reflect the specific requirements of some customers. The Production Engineers inquired about the need to determine environmental costs that may occur during other phases of the product cycle and other products (e.g., the bleacher product). Clearly there was concern that not all environment costs were identified, that some remained hidden. While the early concern was the need to control costs, Bingham now understood the need to make changes to the cost systems, including adding more relevant cost classifications. Clearly that involves significant time and effort and, most importantly, attaining clear directives from top management.

The new initiatives had raised an awareness of the impact of the firm's operations on the employees and society. Society's concerns, such as resource usage, health hazards from contaminants, climate change, and other such externalities largely overlooked in the past, were now part of the conversation. Wilbur realized that much remained to be done for Moulder Co. to adapt to the environmental risks in the emerging regulatory environment, not the least of which was getting buy-in from top management. Nevertheless, he was optimistic. They had gotten off to a good start!

SUGGESTED DISCUSSION QUESTIONS

Assume you are part of Wilbur's EH&S team responsible for preparing the feasibility report that would justify a course of action. Answer the questions below as a basis for preparing the report:

1. To perform the financial analysis, compare Projects A, B, and C by using payback period, net present value (NPV), and internal rate of return (IRR). Consider tax implications on operating cash flows, including the impact of depreciation tax shield assuming that all assets have a 10-year useful life and tax rate of 25%. (Hint: To calculate cash outflows, adjust tax deductions; depreciation tax shield is considered separately.)

    Present sensitivity analysis of NPV for Projects B and C, considering the following:
    - Risk assessment considered in cost of capital hurdle rates: Wilbur assessed that Project B merited a 1% discount and Project C merited a 2% discount because of reduced hazards from toxics emissions.
    - Sales impacts on projects as indicated by Trombley: Trombley's projections showed an estimated $6,000 net decrease in annual cash flow in Project B from loss of "Customer S" and an estimated $20,000 net increase in annual cash flows for Project C from changes in sales and selling prices.

2. Compare the alternatives by integrating any qualitative and technical aspects of the project that might argue for or against its implementation. Indicate your preferred option in the context of the three components of the feasibility report and explain your reasons for choosing that option. Consider the implications of the cost accounting systems, particularly any observed weakness.

3. The discussions during the meeting also exposed weaknesses in the cost accounting system. Describe how the cost system could be adapted to support environmental costing (review relevant readings on environmental management accounting from the Reference List), emphasizing how the system could develop and support:

    a. Cost classifications to identify and measure environmental impacts of toxics,
    b. Cost allocation (applying Activity-Based Costing) to improve pricing and cost controls for multiple products, and
    c. Management of environment costs and decision making through improved measurement of cost.

REFERENCE LIST

Environmental Protection Agency (EPA), "An Introduction to Environmental Accounting As A Business Management Tool: Key Concepts and Terms," June 1995, http://1.usa.gov/1HWWaNs.

IMA (Institute of Management Accountants), *Implementing Activity-Based Costing*, Statements on Management Accounting, 2014, www.imanet.org/docs/default-source/thought_leadership/internal_measurement_systems/implementing_activity_based_costing.pdf?sfvrsn=2.

IMA (Institute of Management Accountants), *Enterprise Risk Management: Tools and Techniques for Effective Implementation*, Statements on Management Accounting, 2014, www.imanet.org/docs/default-source/thought_leadership/governance_systems/erm_tools_and_techniques.pdf?sfvrsn=4.

ISO (International Organization for Standardization), "Environmental management: The ISO 14000 family of International Standards," 2009, www.iso.org/iso/theiso14000family_2009.pdf.

United Nations Division for Sustainable Development, "Environmental Management Accounting Procedures and Principles," 2001, New York, N.Y., www.un.org/esa/sustdev/publications/proceduresandprinciples.pdf.

APPENDIX A

INFORMATION FOR COMPUTING CURRENT COSTS
Robert Burrows from the Payroll department had information on compensation, including:

	Rate (including all benefits)
Vice Presidents	$60,000 annual salary
Assistant Vice Presidents (EH&S Team Manager)	$50,000 annual salary
Engineering Staff	$45,000 annual salary
Foreman	$20 per hour
Office Staff	$15 per hour
Finishers	$15 per hour

Moulder Co. operated for 50 weeks during the year. An average work week consisted of 40 hours.

Tom Elkind, finishing foreman, had the following information:

"A total of 12 people are employed in the bleacher finishing and stadium chair finishing operations." The Weekly Summary Labor Report for stadium chair finishing looks like this:

Week Ending	5/4	5/10	5/17	5/24	5/31	6/7	6/14	6/21	6/28	7/5
Total Hours	340	345	305	290	295	330	325	315	335	320

Janet Dixon from Accounts Receivable and Accounts Payable/ Purchasing had the following information on the costs of chemical items to be used:

Item	Cost (including taxes)
Stain	$6.00 per gallon
Lacquer	$7.10 per gallon
Sealers	$5.00 per gallon
Solvent	$0.85 per pound (11 pounds per gallon)
Solvent Disposal	$1.10 per pound (11 pounds per gallon)
Electricity	About $4,000 per month
Heating Oil	About $6,000 per month

Coating materials used per year for stadium chair finishing:

Coating	Gallons
Stain	6,500
Sealer	8,000
Lacquer	10,000

CHECKLIST FOR COMPUTING CURRENT COSTS

Stadium chair finishing operations costs will include:

- **Coating Materials** – Dixon has provided the required information.
- **Production Labor** – Use weekly labor report to calculate average weekly hours worked.
- **Cleaning Solvent Costs for Maintenance** – Cleaning solvent for maintenance is twice the quantity of fugitive emissions, therefore two drums of cleaning solvent are required (55 gallons each) for regular maintenance.
- **Cleaning Solvent Disposal Costs** – One drum of solvent is filled with remaining solvent waste and requires disposal. The other drum is fugitive emissions.
- **Rag and Liner Disposal Costs** – Given in text.
- **Electricity** – Dixon has provided the required annual cost. Talbot estimated 10% for stadium chair finishing.
- **Heating Oil** – The average monthly heating oil includes the 25% increases in heating costs for ventilation. Only assign this 25% incremental cost of additional ventilation for stadium finishing operations.

- **Environmental Compliance** – Calculate Wilbur's time on stadium chair finishing.
- **Training Costs** – Calculated based on Roberts's estimates.

APPENDIX B: POLLUTION PREVENTION OPTIONS

The research team came up with three options (Projects A, B, and C) for the stadium chair, with careful consideration of cost implications and the use of toxic items listed under the Toxic Reduction Inventory, and presented them to Wilbur.

Project A – High-solids coatings with HVLP spray guns would have costs and savings as listed here:

- **Coating materials** – The higher-solids coatings are about double the cost of the low-solids coatings on a per-gallon basis, but less material is used to achieve the same finished thickness. Combined with the elimination of the second top coat, total quantity of coating purchased was expected to decline, but the total cost was projected to be about 10% more given the higher cost of the high-solids coatings. The supplier expected the price differential to decrease as more companies switched to higher-solids coatings.
- **Production labor** – The higher-solids coating would eliminate the need for a second top coat in most cases and thus would reduce labor by about 4,500 hours per year on constant volume. The sealer coat, however, would be more difficult to sand, requiring orbital rather than block sanders and an additional 1,000 hours of labor per year.
- **Maintenance** – Cleaning solvent requires an increase of about 30% more due to higher viscosity of the material.
- **Solvent disposal** – Increases disposal by one half of the increase in cleaning solvent (i.e., by 15%).
- **Rag and spray booth liner disposal** – No significant change.
- **Utilities (Electricity)** – Heating the coatings requires an additional $1,000, and increased air flow in the sealer flash-off area requires an additional $500.
- **Heating oil** – Increased air flow in the sealer flash-off area requires an extra $3,000.
- **Environmental compliance** – No significant change.
- **Training** – Extra production training in the first three to six months of operations would cost $5,000, and annual costs for training are unchanged.
- **Rework** – Rework incre ases to $15,000 per year because there is less margin for error with a single, heavier topcoat.
- **Plant and equipment** – An upgrade to the flash-off area and to modify spray-gun equipment costs an additional $30,000.

Project B – Water-based coatings option would have estimated cost items as follows:

- **Coating materials** – The water-based coatings cost approximately 10% more than what Moulder Co. was currently using, but Wilbur expects the relative difference to decrease.

- **Production labor** – Reduce labor to 500 hours per year.

- **Maintenance** – Using a water-based cleaning solvent would eliminate the need for a chlorinated solvent and would reduce cost by 20%.

- **Rag and spray booth liner disposal** – Cost would be reduced by 20%.

- **Utilities (Electricity)** – The ventilation requirements would be reduced by 25%.

- **Heating oil** – Heating oil requirements would be reduced by 25%.

- **Training** – Extra production training in the first three to six months of operations would cost $5,000, and annual training costs would be cut in half.

- **Water treatment** – Installing new lines and tankage would cost $75,000 initially, and then chemicals would cost $2,000 per year.

- **Environmental compliance** – Wilbur estimated that he would save about two hours per week if he eliminated using solvent at this operation but would add about an hour to check on the water treatment and discharge.

- **Permit fee** – Potential additional permit fee of about $500 per year.

Project C – Ultraviolet coatings option costs and savings were estimated as follows:

- **Coating materials** – The UV coatings cost more on a per-gallon basis, but personnel would use considerably less because the coatings have a higher percentage of solids, and over-spray is captured and recirculated into the spray equipment, virtually eliminating waste. Wilbur projected a reduction of about 30% in the cost of coating materials.

- **Production labor** – The automated system would enable the reassignment of at least two employees to other operations.

- **Maintenance** – UV coatings would reduce the amount of cleaning solvent required for clean-up by 90%.

- **Solvent disposal** – The use and disposal of solvent would be reduced by 90%.

- **Rag and spray booth liner disposal** – Would be reduced by 90%.

- **Utilities (Electricity)** – The ventilation requirements would be reduced by 25%. UV lamps would cost about $5,000 annually to operate.

- **Heating oil** – The ventilation requirements would reduce heating oil use by 25%.

- **Environmental compliance** – Would be reduced by 50%.

- **Training** – Extra training in the first three to six months of operations would cost $10,000. More production training on an annual basis would cost $3,000 per year.

- **Plant and equipment** – $350,000 for equipment and $130,000 for installation, phased start-up, and lost production during changeover.

ENDNOTES

[1] A TRI relates to the mandated list of toxic chemicals that companies need to report as mandated by federal law. For more information, see www2.epa.gov/toxics-release-inventory-tri-program.

[2] While TURA is the regulation in Massachusetts for toxic chemicals pollution prevention, provisions under TURA specifically relate to chemicals in the TRI list and changes to that list over time. When complying with TURA, companies effectively reduce their compliance burden on federal requirements under TRI reporting. More information on TURA is available from Massachusetts Department of Environmental Protection (MassDEP) at www.mass.gov/eea/agencies/massdep/toxics/tur.

[3] P2 stands in contrast to common environmental management methods like end-of-the-pipe pollution control and environmental remediation. The latter approach works at the facility boundary to clean up toxics that the operation has generated before they enter the general environment. Stack scrubbers and hazardous waste collection for special treatment are typical end-of-pipeline pollution control measures. On the other hand, P2 seeks to reduce or eliminate pollution problems at their source. More information on P2 is available from the EPA website at www.epa.gov/p2.

[4] For an example, see Edward C. Moretti, "Reduce VOC and HAP Emissions," *CEP Magazine*, June 2002, www.aiche.org/resources/publications/cep/2002/june/reduce-voc-and-hap-emissions.

[5] VOCs are emitted as gases from certain solids or liquids. They include a variety of chemicals, some of which may have short- and long-term adverse health effects. HAPs are air pollutants listed by the Environmental Protection Agency (EPA) and promulgated by the Clean Air Act Amendments of 1990 to achieve maximum achievable control.

⁶The CDC's guidelines for organic solvents are available at www.cdc.gov/niosh/topics/organsolv.

⁷The EPA defines fugitive emissions as "Those emissions which could not reasonably pass through a stack, chimney, vent, or other functionally equivalent opening" (see title 40 of the Code of Federal Regulations, sections 70.2 and 71.2). See "Memorandum on Fugitive Emissions" at www.epa.gov/region07/air/title5/t5memos/fug-def.pdf.

⁸For more about chlorinated solvents, see www.worker-health.org/chlorinatedsolvents.html.

A Declaration of War: A Case of Competition in the Video Game Industry

Nicholas J. Fessler, The University of Texas at Tyler

THIS CASE PLACES STUDENTS IN THE CONTEXT OF THE VIDEO GAME INDUSTRY and a developing competition between the best-selling video game in history, the Active Duty series, and Video Game Entertainment's directly competing product, the TrueWar series. The industry is enormous—the best-selling video games have higher sales than the best-selling movies, and video game development costs (all of which are incurred prior to earning any revenue) can amount to hundreds of millions of dollars. Many students participate in this segment of the entertainment industry as consumers. This fictionalized case helps students better understand the business behind the entertainment.

This case is perhaps best suited for use in a junior-level cost accounting course for accounting majors, but it has also been successfully used in a master of accountancy course. Instructors can use the case to discuss accounting topics such as what-if analysis, transfer pricing, return on investment (ROI) calculations, and product line evaluation (the purchase of a subsidiary business).

Keywords: video game industry, parent and subsidiary, what-if analysis, return on investment, transfer pricing.

The Association of
Accountants and
Financial Professionals
in Business

A Declaration of War: A Case of Competition in the Video Game Industry

Nicholas J. Fessler
The University of Texas at Tyler
College of Business and Technology
Department of Accounting, Finance, & Business Law

The author is grateful to graduate students Trevor Arnold and Tim Rost for much research and assistance with this project and to Margaret Shackell and the editors and reviewers for many helpful comments.

BACKGROUND OF VIDEO GAME ENTERTAINMENT

Video Game Entertainment (VGE) is currently one of the largest video game producers in the industry. It has roots in California when it was founded, funded, and incorporated in 1982 by Jim "Hawk" Stevens.

With the cash he earned from a lucrative IPO, Stevens incorporated VGE and personally funded VGE for the first six months. Stevens wanted to properly credit and compensate the talent that produced games, giving them the same respect that artists in other media enjoy. He envisioned VGE as a publishing company that would be known for its quality and professionalism, working with the best independent talent to make the computer game industry equivalent to film, books, or music.

By the 1990s, VGE had grown significantly and began to acquire successful game developers. This practice allowed VGE to "gain development expertise, proprietary technology, intellectual property and a competitive advantage," rather than rely on independent game development companies.[1] And even more importantly, it prevented other publishers from obtaining the content from the best developers. The developers benefited by gaining access to resources (including funding for new game development), new technology, and extensive marketing.

ACQUIRING DIGITAL CREATIONS AND ITS *TrueWar* SERIES

TrueWar is a video game series created by German video game developer Digital Creations, which was started in 1988 by four developers who came from the same town. They were still in college when they made their first video game and did not even intend it to be a commercial product. Instead, the game turned out better (and more popular) than they expected.

Years later, in 2000, Digital Creations bought another Germany-based developer, Gold Medal Games, which had just developed and released a first-person shooter (FPS) action game. FPS is a video game genre that centers the gameplay on gun and projectile weapon-based combat through first-person perspective. For instance, the player experiences the onscreen action through the eyes of a protagonist, which differs from the third-person, over-the-shoulder onscreen view used in third-person video games. Gold Medal Games already had its next FPS game under development when Digital Creations acquired the company. This game became the first game to use the name *TrueWar* and was Digital Creations' big breakthrough.

It took only the first two games of the series, *TrueWar Allies* and *TrueWar: Bravo Company: Jungle*, to attract VGE's attention. In 2004 VGE publicly announced its intent to purchase Digital Creations. The acquisition process began in 2003 when VGE started acquiring the bulk of Digital Creations' stock through open market purchases in 2003, 2004, 2005, and 2006. And in 2006, the acquisition of Digital Creations for $93 million was complete.

VGE had published all of Digital Creations' *TrueWar* titles and acquired Digital Creations so that it could become a "fully integrated VGE studio dedicated to growing the *TrueWar* franchise and developing new products for the PC, next-generation consoles, and other new platforms." Digital Creations' CEO Patrick Mandorff felt that "being part of the VGE studio team is a great step forward that will help us continue to deliver new games and new franchises to Digital Creations' fans."

A DECLARATION OF WAR

Speaking at an advertising conference in New York City, Jonathan Sebastian III, CEO of VGE, went on record stating: "This November, we're launching *TrueWar III*. It's going up against the next *Active Duty*, which is presently the number one game in the industry, a game that last year did $400 million in revenue on day one. *TrueWar III* is designed to take that game down." He continued by comparing the upcoming holiday's battle between the two games to the Red Sox/Yankees rivalry in baseball and said gamers can expect to see massive advertising campaigns for both titles. "Everybody loves a heavyweight fight, and that's what this is going to be. We are here to compete. We know we have a big competitor, but we have the superior game engine, superior development studio, and a flat-out superior game."

These statements represented a veritable declaration of war against the most successful video game franchise in history. It certainly began a war of words with the CEO of *Active Duty's* publisher, but Sebastian's words clearly represented a statement of intent to compete more vigorously with its largest competitor. How large? Developed and published by Calling Card, the most recent game in the series, *Active Duty: Code Black*, that was released the prior year had tallied more than $650 million in worldwide revenue during the first five days after its release. This feat bested any prior release of any entertainment product, including movies, books, and video games. It took Code Black six weeks to reach sales of $1 billion.

A VGE EXECUTIVE MEETING

The week after Sebastian's declaration of war with Calling Card and *Active Duty*, VGE executives met to discuss financial results and to evaluate the performance of its video game developers. The VGE Executive Committee members were well aware of the inherent riskiness of the industry. Additionally, they were familiar with the performance of their competitors—the enormous profitability of Calling Card and the substantial losses of Serial Games (SG), another big competitor. Also present at the Executive Committee meeting was VGE's Executive Vice President and CFO Jerry Brown.

During the meeting, Sebastian suggested that VGE was in an excellent position. "Our traditional games with consoles and PCs remain a growth business, growing at the high single digits to low double digits, while social and mobile games are seeing explosive growth in the double and triple digits."

But, Brown was concerned—very concerned, in fact. He was concerned that the charismatic and sometimes impulsive CEO had, in such a public way, challenged the most successful video game franchise in the history of the industry and its publisher. He was concerned about the added pressure this challenge placed on VGE and its video game developers at Digital Creations, who were now in the unenviable position whereby developing anything less than the best-selling game in history could be considered a failure. To Brown, this seemed immeasurably unreasonable.

Keeping these concerns to himself for the moment, Brown did say: "Our business is intensely competitive and 'hit' driven. If we do not deliver 'hit' products and services, or if consumers prefer our competitors' products or services over ours, our operating results could suffer.

"Competition in our industry is intense, and we expect new competitors to continue to emerge throughout the world. Our competitors range from large established companies, like Calling Card, to emerging start-ups. In our industry, though, many new products and services are regularly introduced, only a relatively small number of hit titles account for a significant portion of total revenue for the industry. We have significantly reduced the number of games that we develop, publish, and distribute. In fiscal year 2010, we published 54 primary titles, and in fiscal year 2011, we published 36. In fiscal year 2012, we expect to release approximately 22 primary titles. Publishing fewer titles means that we can concentrate more of our development spending on each title, and driving hit titles often requires large marketing budgets and media spending.

The underperformance of any single title, like *TrueWar*, can have a large adverse impact on our financial results. Also, hit products or services offered by our competitors may take a larger share of consumer spending than we anticipate, which could cause revenue generated from our products and services to fall below expectations.

"So, yes, I agree that we are currently in a good market position. But given our strategy to reduce the number of titles we publish, we need to be absolutely sure we pick the right ones," Brown finished. VGE had a number of large-scale game development projects in the works, but one of the largest projects is the production of *TrueWar III*.

RISK IN THE VIDEO GAME INDUSTRY

Brown is familiar with the riskiness of the video game industry and the performance of VGE's competitors. But the level of success experienced by Calling Card is not typical for the industry. Video game development costs are high and growing higher. Development costs for the average game for Microsoft's Xbox 360 or Sony's PS3 range from $15 million to $30 million.[2] And most games simply are not profitable. It is estimated that only 4% of games are produced, and only 20% of games that make it to retailers actually realize a profit.[3]

Because such a high percentage of games are unprofitable, many publishers like VGE are hesitant to publish new games (also known as new IPs, or Intellectual Properties). Instead publishers often put greater confidence in established, highly successful game franchises. For many genres, typically one, two, or a series of titles are dominant. Because many gaming consumers buy only the top game in a genre, any competing games are likely to have poor sales in comparison.[4] Therefore, publishers are reluctant to release a game into a genre that is dominated by a different publisher, unless the new game is unique enough to separate itself from competitors.

Because video games are so expensive to develop, the development of each represents a high level of risk to VGE. For example, DangerZone—a video game development company that was acquired by VGE's competitor SG in 2008 for $682 million—had some of the largest game budgets in the industry. Examples include:

- *Magic Swords*. DangerZone spent an estimated $130 million developing it. The sequel, *Magic Swords 2*, was not expected to cost as much, but it still had a large development budget.

- *The Empire of Sand (TES)*. Many in the video game industry believed this game would be one of the most expensive games in the history of the industry. An SG insider estimated that SG and DangerZone had already incurred more than $300 million on the project. These costs included a large licensing fee, voiceacting (*TES* was the first game of its kind to use full voiceacting instead of only text for onscreen conversations), and a large development team.

The costs of video game development are effectively fixed (and sunk) from the perspective of a video game publisher. All expenses associated with the development of the game and prerelease advertising represent the bulk of all costs associated with a game's release and are incurred prior to any revenues being received from game sales. For example, SG struggled to recover those substantial investments. As a result, SG experienced net losses of $1.1 billion in 2009 and $677 million in 2010. While its financial performance during the subsequent year improved, SG still was not profitable.

STRUCTURE OF THE VIDEO GAME INDUSTRY

The video game industry is composed of three sets of firms: the publishers (e.g., VGE), the developers (e.g., Digital Creations), and the platform holders (e.g., Microsoft (Xbox 360) and Sony (PS3)).[5] The publishers typically provide the funding/budget, promotion, marketing, distribution, and support, whether the game development studio is external (to the publisher) or internal (like Digital Creations for VGE). The developers are the idea makers and the workers responsible for game conception, prototype, design, technology, and development and implementation. A technology platform is required to play video games, so the platform holders are the console companies that control nearly every aspect of games on their platforms. For instance, the publisher and developer could require permission from the platform holder to begin developing a game, and the platform holder would submit a finished game to a certification process before it could be sold. Alternatively, personal computers (PCs) are an open platform with a low barrier for entry to developers but higher competition for customers.

A publisher in the video game industry purchases the rights to publish a new game that has been created by a developer, much like how a book publisher purchases the rights from an author to publish the book. This is the same relationship between VGE and Digital Creations: The developer (Digital Creations) creates the video game, while the publisher (VGE) markets the game and arranges for its manufacture, distribution, and sale.

The relationship between publishers and developers, however, could feel strained. There is a clear cultural difference between publishers, which are stereotypically business men or accountants who do not necessarily care about games the way developers do, and the developers, which are people who enjoy playing video games and have creative and technical expertise.[6] At least one video game developer thought that publishers were largely at fault for a worrying increase of Western game development studios that went bankrupt.[7] The argument was that "ignorant" publishers could make "ruinous" requests of developers, which would cause a game to tank, but then were in a position to blame the game's failure on the developer, which was often contractually bound to say nothing. So the publisher could continue unscathed, ready to do the same to the next development studio, while the affected development studio often went out of business.

Most typically, the publisher would share revenue with the developer: The developer assumes the production costs while the publisher assumes the marketing and distribution costs.[8] The publisher typically pays the developer royalties for a game based on a percentage of the game's net sales revenue after deductions, such as taxes, shipping, insurance, and returns—a calculation often described as "net receipts"[9] or "adjusted gross receipts."[10] But developer royalties could sometimes cover marketing costs if it is written in the contract, but such contracts are considered "exploitative" because contractual deductions include expenses that are not under the control of the developer (like marketing, advertising, and promotion expenses). Such contracts leave the publisher in control of determining the amount of "adjusted gross receipts," and ultimately give the publisher control of determining how much royalty income to pay the developer.

The royalty paid to independent video game developers could vary anywhere from 10% to 70% of the amount paid to the publisher. Yet royalties are often paid to the developer only after the publisher has first recouped any advances paid to the developer.[11] Additionally, contracts between publisher and developer could include step ups in rates based on hitting certain sales goals or milestones.[12]

Publishers take on a lot of risk when they choose to fund a project, but many developers feel that they also take a disproportionate cut of the revenue.[13] If a developer could afford to do so, it should stay independent to control its own development and schedule of the game. Alternatively, if the developer receives no advance funds against the royalty from the publisher, all development risk resides with the developer, which funds the entire development process. Therefore, some developers think that a publisher contract *is* worth it (in order to receive publisher advance funding), despite the obvious drawbacks (most notably, a loss of control of the publication process).[14] If possible, it is advisable for developers to have a lawyer and accountant on hand when negotiating and reviewing a contract with a publisher.[15] Because Digital Creations is wholly owned by VGE, some of these tensions are diminished.

VGE'S PUBLISHING PROCESS

VGE follows a standard process for publishing a new video game. In most cases, VGE receives a loan request from a subsidiary developer for a new game development project. The developer makes a presentation outlining the game details, including the concept, story, game play, and genre, as well as an estimate of costs, including staffing, technology needs, and length of development.[16]

VGE then performs its own market research and cost analysis to determine the potential profitability of the new game. In market research, VGE determines the potential success of the game based on an analysis of its target audience, the saturation of the game's genre, and the estimated marketing expenses that would be incurred. The market analysis gives a rough estimate on potential sales revenue that a new game might generate. VGE looks at the potential sales of the game and the loan amount then uses its judgment to decide whether or not to approve the development loan.

If the loan request is approved, VGE typically assigns a producer or team of producers to the project.[17] The producer is responsible for making sure that development stays on schedule and on budget. Any additional changes to the schedule or budget must be approved by the producer.[18] Significant changes must be approved by VGE management; management informs producers prior to development what constitutes a "significant change."

Once a development loan is approved, the developer begins the actual work of creating the new game. Because console manufacturers (such as Microsoft and Sony) set certain requirements for games to be released on their consoles, VGE works with the developer to ensure these requirements are met during production. In cases where the game is being developed by an outside company, VGE typically advances the development costs to the developer in the form of milestone payments—paid at various predetermined stages in the game's development.[19]

The producer is in close contact with VGE's marketing team to develop a marketing plan for the game.[20] Marketing is an essential part of the video game development process. The trend in the video game market is to spend as much on marketing a new game as actually developing it.[21] Marketing a video game includes magazine ads, television spots, trade shows, internet forums, and/or a game demo.[22] Some games are making use of "adver-gaming," when advertisements are put into the games themselves. In-game advertisements are becoming increasingly feasible and popular because so many games are played online. The Internet connectivity required for online gaming allows new advertisements to be placed in older games. Constant communication between the producer and the marketing function is essential.

After the game has gone through rigorous testing and the marketing plan has been set in motion, the distributor is sent a master copy, the game manual, and box art that has been created by the marketing team in collaboration with the developer.[23] In most cases, the distributor is the console manufacturer (such as Microsoft and Sony). The distributor copies and packages the game and ships it to retailers. The cost of producing and distributing these copies is borne by the publisher.

VIDEO GAME COST BREAKDOWN

Console games for Xbox 360 and PS3, for example, typically sell for $60 to consumers. The cost breakdown, detailed next, shows where the $60 paid by the consumer goes (see Exhibit 1). It does not portray how transactions are recorded.[24]

Exhibit 1: Video Game Cost Breakdown Summary

Purpose	Amount	Paid By	Paid To
Retailer (Profit)	$15	Consumer	Retailer
Returns/PP/MDF	7	Publisher	Retailer
Distribution/COGS	4	Publisher	Media Manufacturer
Platform Royalty Fee	7	Publisher	Platform Holder
Publisher	27	Publisher	Internal
Total Cost to Consumer	$60		

Notes on terminology:

Retailers include stores such as GameStop, Walmart, and Amazon.

Returns are money paid to retailers for product returns.

PP is "price-protection" or money paid back through the chain if/when the publisher reduces the price of the video game.

MDF is "marketing and development funds" or money paid to retailers for promotions such as TV ads, local flyers, and in-store marketing displays.

Distribution costs are for shipping and warehousing.

COGS (Cost of Goods Sold) is the cost of manufacturing the physical DVD, the instruction manual, and the case.

The *Platform Royalty Fee* is paid to Microsoft or Sony, as applicable.

The *Publisher* pays royalties to the developer out of the remaining amount.

Games for PCs typically sell for $50. PC sales differ from console sales because the majority of PC game sales involve no physical product. Instead customers purchase and download games via websites, such as SteamPowered.com. In this case, publishers receive $35 for the sale of every PC game, while the website owner receives $15 (in this case, the website is the retailer).

Video games could have digital sales, often described as Downloadable Content (DLC). DLC also could refer to additional game content sold after the original game release. The publishers receive 70% of the revenues from digital sales, and the download source (e.g., Microsoft (Xbox 360), Sony (PS3), or Steam (PC)) keeps the remaining 30%. Thus, for DLC priced at $20 to the customer, the publisher receives $14.

CONSOLE RELEASES

Digital Creations created and released several games under VGE's ownership. The seventh-generation consoles (at the time, commonly referred to as "next gen") were kicked off by the release of Microsoft's Xbox 360 in 2005 and Sony's PlayStation 3 (PS3) in 2006. This was the first console generation really capable of running *TrueWar* games, and Digital Creations took advantage of the opportunity to release the games summarized in Exhibit 2. (See Exhibits 3-8 for breakdown and statistics of VGE's other console games.)

Exhibit 2: Console Video Game Releases

***True War: Alpha Company* (2008)**

	Later became available for digital download for $20	
Loan:	$25 million	
Marketing:	$30 million	

***True War: WWII* (2009)**

	Only sold via digital download for $15	
Loan:	$6 million	
Marketing:	$4 million	

***True War: Bravo Company* (2009)**

Sales:	3.2 million copies PC	
	3.8 million copies Xbox 360	
	3 million copies PS3	
	290,700 copies sold via digital download for $20	
Loan:	$60 million	
Marketing:	$45 million	

***True War: Bravo Company: Jungle* (2010)**

	Only sold via digital download for $15	
Sales:	1.1 million copies	
Loan:	$10 million	
Marketing:	$5 million	

Exhibit 3: VGE Income Statement: *TrueWar: Alpha Company*

Revenue:

Xbox 360 sales ($27 per unit sold × 1.4 million)	$37,800,000	
PS3 sales ($27 per unit sold × 1.01 million)	27,270,000	
Digital download ($14 per download × 107,900)	1,510,600	
Total Revenue		**$66,580,600**

Expenses:

Digital Creations royalties

Xbox

First million units sold (1 million × $27 × 25%)	$(6,750,000)	
Remainder units sold (400,000 × $27 × 26%)	(2,808,000)	
Total	**$(9,558,000)**	

PS3

First million units sold (1 million × $27 × 25%)	$(6,750,000)	
Remainder units sold (10,000 × $27 × 26%)	(70,200)	
Total	**$(6,820,200)**	

Games on Demand (107,900 × $14 × 50%)	$(755,300)	
Total Digital Creations Royalties		$(17,133,500)
Marketing		$(30,000,000)
Total Expenses		**$(47,133,500)**
Income		**$19,447,100**

Exhibit 4: Digital Creations' Return on Game Development

TrueWar: Alpha Company

Digital Creations royalty income	$17,133,500
VGE loan	(25,000,000)
Excess/Unpaid portion of loan (Digital Creations)	$(7,866,500)

VGE's Return on Loan Investment
TrueWar: Alpha Company

Net income	$19,447,100
Excess/Unpaid portion of loan	(7,866,500)
Total return on project (VGE & Digital Creations)	$11,580,600

Exhibit 5: VGE Income Statement: *TrueWar: WWII*

Revenue:

Digital downloads ($10.50 per unit × 1.5 million)	$15,750,000	
Total Revenue		**$15,750,000**

Expenses:

Digital Creations royalties (1.5 million × $10.50 × 50%)	$(7,875,000)	
Total		$(7,875,000)
Marketing		$(4,000,000)
Total Expenses		**$(11,875,000)**
Income		**$3,875,000**

Exhibit 6: Digital Creations' Return on Game Development

TrueWar WWII

Digital Creations royalty income	$7,875,000
VGE loan	(6,000,000)
Excess/Unpaid portion of loan (Digital Creations)	$1,875,000

VGE's Return on Loan Investment
TrueWar WWII

Net income	$3,875,000
Excess/Unpaid portion of loan	1,875,000
Total return on project (VGE & Digital Creations)	**$5,750,000**

Exhibit 7: VGE Income Statement: *TrueWar: Bravo Company*

Revenue:

Xbox 360 sales ($27 per unit sold × 3.8 million)	$102,600,000	
PS3 sales ($27 per unit sold × 3 million)	81,000,000	
PC sales ($35 per unit sold × 3.2 million)	112,000,000	
Digital download ($14 per download × 290,700)	4,069,800	
Jungle ($10.50 per unit sold × 1.1 million)	11,550,000	
Total Revenue		**$311,219,800**

Expenses:

Digital Creations royalties

Xbox

First million units sold (1 million × $27 × 27.5%)	$(7,425,000)	
Second million units sold (1 million × $27 × 28.5%)	(7,695,000)	
Third million units sold (1 million × $27 × 29.5%)	(7,965,000)	
Remainder units sold (800,000 × $27 × 30.5%)	(6,588,000)	
Total	**$(29,673,000)**	

PS3

First million units sold (1 million × $27 × 27.5%)	$(7,425,000)	
Second million units sold (1 million × $27 × 28.5%)	(7,695,000)	
Remainder units sold (1 million × $27 × 29.5%)	(7,965,000)	
Total	**$(23,085,000)**	

PC

First million units sold (1 million × $35 × 27.5%)	$(9,625,000)	
Second million units sold (1 million × $35 × 28.5%)	(9,975,000)	
Third million units sold (1 million × $35 × 29.5%)	(10,325,000)	
Remainder units sold (200,000 × $35 × 30.5%)	(2,135,000)	
Total	**$(32,060,000)**	

Digital download (290,700 × $14 × 50%)	$(2,034,900)	
Jungle units sold (1.1 million × $10.50 × 50%)	$(5,775,000)	
Total Digital Creations Royalties		**$(92,627,900)**
Marketing (Bravo Company)		$(45,000,000)
Marketing (Bravo Company: Jungle)		$(5,000,000)
Total Expenses		**$(142,627,900)**
Income		**$168,591,900**

Exhibit 8: Digital Creations' Return on Game Development

TrueWar: Bravo Company

Digital Creations royalty income	$92,627,900
VGE loan	(70,000,000)
Excess/Unpaid portion of loan (Digital Creations)	$(22,627,900)

VGE's Return on Loan Investment

TrueWar: Bravo Company

Net income	$168,591,900
Excess/Unpaid portion of loan	22,627,900
Total return on project (VGE & Digital Creations)	$191,219,800

ROYALTY AGREEMENT BETWEEN VGE AND DIGITAL CREATIONS

The contract between VGE and Digital Creations does not include marketing expenditures when determining "net receipts." Instead, VGE is responsible for paying for promotion expenses out of its portion of the revenues, while Digital Creations is responsible for all development costs.

At VGE, the royalties typically first go toward paying back the development loan. Only after the development loan is repaid does the developer (in this case, Digital Creations) actually receive royalty revenue. It is unlikely that a developer would receive any additional development loans if it had trouble repaying development loans in the past. Alternatively, developers with a history of creating profitable games could warrant minimum guaranteed royalty payments. In these cases, a publisher and a developer agree on a minimum guaranteed royalty payment prior to the release of the game. The minimum guaranteed royalty payment is essentially recorded as a prepaid asset by the publisher.

The royalty percentage to be paid by VGE to Digital Creations is determined at the beginning of the agreement. The royalty share is effectively an expense that reduces VGE's profit. Additionally, VGE increases Digital Creations' royalty percentage every time game sales meet an "additional royalty threshold." There is a threshold for each SKU,[25] meaning that there is an independent threshold for each released version of the game (for example, Xbox 360, PS3, and PC). Each time the threshold for a specific SKU is met, Digital Creations receives a prescribed royalty percentage increase. For example, when *TrueWar: Alpha Company* reached 1,000,001 units sold, that one unit (and the next 999,999 units) received a royalty of 26%—1% higher than the first one million units sold. The 2,000,001 unit sold had a royalty of 27%. Royalty percentages and thresholds are specific to each individual game and are detailed in Exhibit 9. The royalty revenue is first applied toward paying off the

development loan made to Digital Creations. Only after the loan is repaid is royalty revenue paid to Digital Creations.

Exhibit 9: VGE and Digital Creations Royalty and Loan Agreements

	Loan Amount	Royalty %	Royalty Threshold	Increase %
TrueWar: Alpha Company	$25 million	25%	1 million	1%
TrueWar: WWII	$6 million	50%	N/A	N/A
TrueWar: Bravo Company 2	$60 million	27.5%	1 million	1%
TrueWar: Bravo Company: Jungle	$10 million	50%	N/A	N/A
True War III	$100 million	29%	1 million	1%

Because *TrueWar WWII* and *TrueWar: Bravo Company: Jungle* were only distributed digitally, VGE was able to earn a larger portion of each sale. *TrueWar WWII* and *TrueWar: Bravo Company: Jungle* also had unique royalty agreements: Digital Creations earned 50% of VGE's revenue from those games (the royalty percentage) but received no additional royalty share for meeting a new threshold. Both games sold for $15, and VGE received 70% of each download ($10.50).

A year or more after their release, both *TrueWar: Alpha Company* and *TrueWar: Bravo Company* were also released digitally on consoles via services provided by the console manufacturers. Both games sold for $20, and VGE received 70% of each download ($14). Once again, Digital Creations earned 50% of VGE's revenue from game sales (the royalty percentage) but received no additional royalty share for meeting a new threshold.

DIGITAL CREATIONS' NEWEST PROJECT: *TrueWar III*

Digital Creations' newest project is *TrueWar III*. This is a large-scale project for Digital Creations. It has been nearly five years since Digital Creations released *TrueWar II*, and the expectations from the development team and PC gamers are extraordinarily high. Digital Creations received a $100 million loan from VGE for the development of *TrueWar III*. *TrueWar III* is intended as the true successor to *TrueWar II* and will be available on both PC and console.

VGE plans to spend at least $100 million on a marketing campaign for *TrueWar III*. Therefore, along with the $100 million loan to Digital Creations, VGE anticipates spending a total of $200 million on the development and advertising of *TrueWar III*. The unit sales for all of Digital Creations' recent projects, including forecasts of *True War III*'s most realistic case, worst case, and best case sales, are found in Exhibit 10.

Exhibit 10: *TrueWar* Unit Sales Information	
TrueWar: Alpha Company	**Worldwide Total**
Xbox 360	1,400,000
PS3	1,010,000
Digital download	107,900
TrueWar WWII	
Total Sales (digital download only)	1,500,000
TrueWar: Bravo Company	
Xbox 360	3,800,000
PS3	3,000,000
PC	3,200,000
Games on Demand (digital download)	290,700
Jungle DLC (digital download, all platforms)	1,100,000
TrueWar III:	
Most Realistic Case: 11 million units sold	
Xbox 360	4,180,000
PS3	3,300,000
PC	3,520,000
TrueWar III:	
Worst Case: 7 million units sold	
Xbox 360	2,660,000
PS3	2,100,000
PC	2,240,000
TrueWar III:	
Best Case: 15 million units sold	
Xbox 360	5,700,000
PS3	4,500,000
PC	4,800,000

A GROWING CONCERN

At VGE's Executive Meeting, CFO Jerry Brown feels a growing concern: "We have a lot of capital tied up in game development. The industry trends toward larger and larger game budgets. This is likely because of the fact that publishers like us are stricter on which games will be developed and published. We [at VGE] are publishing fewer titles and therefore investing more heavily in each individual release.

"As you know, we have already approved Digital Creations' $100 million loan for its new game, *TrueWar III.* Although I am a fan of the series, *TrueWar* has substantial competition, particularly since the series is directly competing against the best-selling video game franchise in history: *Active Duty.* The last video game published by Digital Creations, *TrueWar: Bravo Company*, was not even in the top 5 games in the genre, based on total unit sales. The *Active Duty* series is on top in that genre, and they have been able to release a game every year.

"Why should we continue funding and marketing Digital Creations' projects in a market dominated by *Active Duty*? Would we be better off focusing our development and marketing efforts in other genres and/or markets? We have already committed $100 million to the development of *TrueWar III*, not including our marketing costs, and for a new video game release we have historically spent an amount equal to development costs. Given the relatively poor showing of Digital Creations' last product, we can cut our losses, minimize marketing expenses for *TrueWar III*, and focus our attention on our other products. I continue to wonder if the Digital Creations acquisition was really a worthwhile investment. More importantly and relevant to the current discussion, however, should we continue to support Digital Creations' development efforts?" Brown finished.

CEO Jonathan Sebastian thought for a moment before speaking. "We must be sure that our focus meets the needs of the changing, growing market. We are building the strength of our most important IPs, and for VGE, this means about a dozen very substantial IPs. Each of these will be transformed into year-round businesses with major packaged goods launches, social launches, downloadable content, and microtransactions. Our most important IPs include *TrueWar*. Digital Creations and its *TrueWar* franchise are very important to us.

"Sales forecasts for *TrueWar III* demonstrate it is a viable title in the genre. Independent companies have projected sales figures of eight million and 11 million copies. I think *TrueWar III* will sell more than either of these projections. *TrueWar: Bravo Company* sold more than nine million units, so we must only sell an additional two million units to reach the higher forecast," Sebastian said.

Despite Sebastian's obvious enthusiasm, Brown remained skeptical but said nothing more. Given that VGE was reducing the number of titles it was releasing, using one of those titles to directly attack the most successful video game in history seemed unwise and perhaps was an invitation for financial failure for *TrueWar III*.

DECISIONS ABOUT DIGITAL CREATIONS

When Brown returned to his office, he convened a meeting of some of his staff, determined to explore more thoroughly his concerns about Digital Creations. Brown had joined VGE just a few months ago after holding CFO positions at technology and clothing companies, so he had not participated in any earlier decisions regarding Digital Creations. First he wanted to reinvestigate the decision to fund *TrueWar III* to see if he agreed with the decision. Second, despite the fact that VGE anticipated spending $100 million on marketing for *TrueWar III,* the bulk of those funds have not yet been spent. Therefore, he wanted to determine how much he thought would be appropriate for VGE to spend on marketing for *TrueWar III.* Third, he wanted to learn more about the relationship between VGE and Digital Creations, including (but not limited to) the contract and the structure of the royalty fees. He was not sure what he would learn but knew that the royalty fee structure, for example, was critical to the profitability of both VGE and Digital Creations, particularly because Digital Creations was a foreign subsidiary. Finally, Brown wanted to reinvestigate the purchase of Digital Creations to determine its value to VGE—had the purchase been a good investment from the perspective of VGE?

Brown decided that he wanted fresh eyes to perform the analysis, someone who had not been involved with the purchase of Digital Creations and had not previously been involved with analysis of Digital Creations' financial performance. So he looked right at you, recent graduate and the newest member of the finance team at VGE, and gave you a special project.

FACT AND FICTION

This case is based on real companies, utilizing public information about the companies and their competing products. For example, many statements made by the CEO and CFO were obtained either from text in the company's 10-K or from quotes made by the CEO in conversations with investors and analysts. Gaps in the public information were estimated (and are, therefore, fictionalized). All names in the case were changed for anonymity.

CASE REQUIREMENTS

1. Should VGE have approved the development loan for *TrueWar III?*
   To answer this question, prepare what-if analysis of the most realistic case, worst case, and best case scenarios (see Exhibit 10). Begin by preparing what-if analysis of the **most realistic case** scenario:
   a. Calculate total revenue for Xbox 360, PS3, and PC sales of 11 million units.
   b. Calculate Digital Creations' total royalties for each separate console. Be sure to incorporate the royalty increase threshold.
   c. Calculate nonroyalty costs (for example, marketing costs).
   d. Using the information from 1a-1c, create an income statement.
   e. Determine how much (if any) Digital Creations owes VGE on its development loan for *TrueWar III* (this is a simple comparison of Digital Creations' royalty income to the amount of the loan from VGE to Digital Creations). Was Digital Creations able to repay its loan from VGE?
   f. Calculate VGE's return on loan investment for TrueWar III. This is the sum (or net) of the project's net income/loss (calculated in 1d) and the excess/unpaid portion of the loan (calculated in 1e).
   g. Under these assumptions, should VGE have approved the loan for TrueWar III?
   h. Repeat steps 1a-1g to prepare what-if analyses for the **best case** and **worst case** scenarios with estimated sales of 15 million and 7 million units, respectively (see Exhibit 10). Also calculate Digital Creations' return on game development and VGE's return on loan investment for these scenarios.

2. How much should VGE spend on marketing for *TrueWar III?* Are any of the scenarios unprofitable? If so, does this influence your recommendation?

3. How does the transfer price (i.e., royalty payments) influence an evaluation of the performance (i.e., profitability) of Digital Creations? What could (or should) VGE do with Digital Creations if *TrueWar III* proves unprofitable? What other issues should Jerry Brown consider with regard to the structure of the royalty payments from VGE to Digital Creations?

4. Is the investment in Digital Creations worth what VGE paid to purchase it? Is the cycle of releases really working for Digital Creations? Hint: Can you estimate the return on investment (ROI, calculated as a percentage) for each of the three games individually? Collectively (i.e., can you estimate the ROI for VGE's purchase of Digital Creations)?

5. Now that you have completed the analysis requested by Brown, what will you say when you present it to him? Do you think Brown's concerns about Digital Creations and *TrueWar III* are well-founded—that is, should he be concerned?

ENDNOTES

[1] Nik Shah, "The Video Game Industry From a VC Perspective," MBA Fellows Project, Glassmeyer/McNamee Center for Digital Strategies, 2005.

[2] Kris Graft, "Budgets For Games Going in 'Reverse Direction,'" Gamasutra, August 24, 2010.

[3] Don Reisinger, "Why Most Video Games Aren't Profitable," CNet, November 24, 2008.

[4] Shah, March 2005.

[5] Steve Rabin, *Introduction to Game Development*, Cengage Learning, Boston, Mass., June 2010.

[6] David Sherlock, "When Developers Take Control from Publishers," December 28, 2013, http://paddytherabbit.com/when-developers-take-control-from-publishers.

[7] Anonymous Game Developer, "We Need Better Video Game Publishers," April 15, 2013, http://kotaku.com/we-need-better-video-game-publishers-472880781.

[8] Howard Tsao, "Thinking through Publishing Contracts: Tips and Lessons Learned," Gamasutra, July 26, 2012.

[9] Simeon Pashley, "Avoiding Game Development Contract Pitfall – Royalties," May 26, 2010, http://gamelinchpin.com/2010/05/avoiding-contract-pitfalls-royalties.html.

[10] Tsao, July 2012.

[11] Dale Dietrick, "Cost Components that Make up a Typical Video Game's Retail Price," December 31, 2009, www.daleisphere.com/cost-components-that-make-up-a-typical-video-games-retail-price.

[12] Ralph Edwards, "The Economics of Game Publishing," IGN, May 5, 2006.

[13] Zachary Knight, "Game Developer Refuses Publishing Offer; Realizes It's Better To Stay Independent," Tech Dirt, August 27, 2012.

[14] Pashley, May 2010.

[15] Ivan Ertlov, "Insider Tipps: Publishing Contracts and Publishing Deals Feature," MODDB, December 18, 2011.

[16] Erik Bethke, *Game Development and Production*, Wordware Publishing, Inc., Plano, Texas, January 2003.

[17] Shah, March 2005.

[18] Michael E. Moore and Jeannie Novak, *Game Development Essentials: Game Industry Career Guide*, Cengage Learning, Boston, Mass., October 2009.

[19] Edwards, May 2006.

[20] Bob Bates, *Game Design*, Cengage Learning PTR, Boston, Mass., September 2004, p. 242.

[21] Kris Graft, August 2010.

[22] Bates, 2004, p. 241.

[23] Bethke, 2003, p. 295.

[24] Dietrich, December 2009.

[25] SKU (Stock Keeping Unit) – a number or code used to identify each unique product or item for sale in a store or other business.

SuperHeroes LLP: A Super Management Control Case

Norman T. Sheehan and Ganesh Vaidyanathan, University of Saskatchewan

THIS SHORT, ILLUSTRATED CASE involves designing a management control system for a recently incorporated group of super-heroes who sell their unique, creative crime-fighting services to a large, crime-ridden metropolis. While the superheroes have managed to reduce the metropolis's crime rate, they also have caused significant collateral damage to its citizens and property in the process. Students are asked to devise a management control system that best controls the superheroes' actions without jeopardizing their ability to effectively fight crime. The case was written to introduce students to the use and development of management control systems, but it also provides instructors with an opportunity to discuss why and how management controls vary across firms. Student feedback indicates that the innovative context, concise length, and graphic format of the case gains and retains their interest and thus enhances the students' potential for learning about management control systems.

This very unique case has been used successfully in an undergraduate required senior-level management control class and a required MBA strategy tactics and implementation class.

Keywords: merchant's management control framework, Simons' Levers of Control framework, control system contingencies, knowledge-intensive firms, graphic teaching case.

The Association of
Accountants and
Financial Professionals
in Business

SuperHeroes LLP: A Super Management Control Case

Norman T. Sheehan
University of Saskatchewan

Ganesh Vaidyanathan
University of Saskatchewan

INTRODUCTION

Prepare for the in-class discussion of the case by reviewing a brief description of Kenneth A. Merchant's management control system or Robert Simons' Levers of Control framework, and then prepare the case pre-assignment questions that follow. Then, read the short, graphic case and answer the questions provided.

For more information, read Merchant's Control in Business Organizations, *Ballinger Publishing Company, Cambridge, Mass., 1985, and Simons'* Performance Measurement and Control Systems for Implementing Strategy, *Prentice Hall, Upper Saddle River, N.J., 2000.*

MERCHANT'S MANAGEMENT CONTROL SYSTEM

Merchant's framework focuses on eliminating three barriers that prevent employees from successfully executing their organizations' strategies:

1. Employees lack direction in the sense they don't know what is expected of them.
2. Employees know what is expected of them but aren't motivated to complete the activities.
3. Employees know what's expected of them and are motivated, but personal limitations, such as lack of training, prevent them from successfully completing the activities.

To address these barriers to effective strategy implementation, Merchant proposes that managers use one or more of the following management controls: results, action, and/or personnel and culture.

Results controls. To tackle problems relating to lack of employee motivation and direction, Merchant recommends managers apply results controls. Results controls clearly communicate to employees what they must accomplish to effectively execute the organization's strategy and allow employees to determine how to best to reach their goals. Employees are rewarded when they reach the specified outcomes. Performance measurement tools, such as key performance indicators (KPIs), clearly communicate to employees the activities that need to be completed in order to execute the organization's strategy, and the prospect of earning rewards for successfully completing these activities enhances employees' motivation. Examples of results controls are KPIs, such as customer satisfaction with product quality or number of product defects per batch.

Action controls. Merchant recommends using action controls to address management control problems that relate to employees' lack of direction. Action controls are intended to constrain employee actions by clearly directing employees on what they should and should not do. Examples of action controls include supervision; pre-action reviews, which require employees to seek approval prior to undertaking an activity; action accountability, which involves having standard operating procedures; and codes of conduct that clearly delineate those activities that employees aren't allowed to engage in, such as using company assets for personal use or bribing public officials.

Personnel and culture controls. In order to address issues relating to employees who lack direction, motivation, or have personal limitations, Merchant recommends personnel and culture controls. Personnel controls rely on employees' desire to self-police their actions. Merchant's personnel controls include hiring ethical and competent employees, providing training to employees, and designing jobs so that employees can succeed. Cultural controls rely on peer pressure to influence individual employee's actions. An example of culture controls is when managers not only "talk the talk" but also "walk the walk" (i.e., lead by example) and intra-organizational employee transfers as a way to transfer productive cultures to other units.

In order to effectively remove the barriers that may prevent employees from successfully executing the organization's strategy, Merchant recommends that managers first apply personnel and cultural controls, as they have fewer negative side effects and are less intrusive than action and results controls. If managers judge that personnel and culture controls are inadequate (i.e., the firm has assets that are easy to steal), then Merchant recommends introducing action controls (such as securely storing valuable assets), and finally, results controls (such as using KPIs to measure performance).

SIMONS' LEVERS OF CONTROL FRAMEWORK

Robert Simons' Levers of Control framework consists of four controls that work together to help managers implement their organization's strategy: diagnostic, boundary, belief, and interactive. The four controls increase the alignment between the activities outlined in the organization's strategy and the activities performed by its employees.

Diagnostic controls involve developing performance measures based on the organization's strategy, setting targets, outlining initiatives to reach targets, and then paying bonuses when successful. If the performance measures align with the strategy and are met, then the strategy should be successfully implemented. A downside of diagnostic controls is that it's difficult to perfectly align the measures and budgets with the organization's strategy, and the pressure to deliver the results specified by the plan may lead employees to cut corners. Because of the pressure that diagnostic controls place on employees to succeed, managers need to employ boundary controls to ensure their employees don't overstep any ethical or legal boundaries.

Boundary controls outline those activities that aren't allowed, such as bribing officials or private use of company assets. Examples of boundary controls include codes of conduct and mission statements that specify which activities aren't allowed. While boundary controls outline what employees should not do, they don't encourage employees to do the right things for the organization. For this, firms need belief controls.

Belief controls serve to inspire employees to create value for their organizations because they believe in what the organization is trying to accomplish. While the organization's culture is the manifestation of the belief controls, managers can influence culture by formalizing the organization's values and live by them to set an example for their employees. Other tactics that reinforce the belief controls are rewarding individuals who epitomize the organization's formal beliefs and only hiring new employees based on their fit with the organization's values.

Interactive controls monitor the environment for changes that may harm the firm, and then update the organization's strategy to address these threats.

SUPERHEROES LLP PRE-ASSIGNMENT CASE QUESTIONS

After reading the SuperHeroes LLP case, prepare the following questions prior to class discussion of the case:

1. What is the role of management control systems in organizations?
2. Describe each element of a management control system.
3. Why do different types of firms require different management control systems?

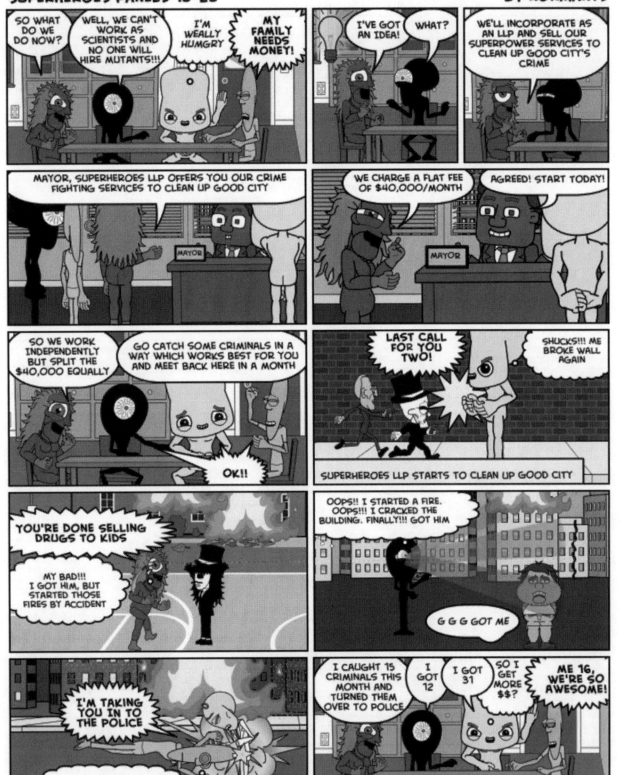

WWW.BITSTRIPS.COM

WWW.BITSTRIPS.COM

SINCE WE AGREE ON SUPERHEROES LLP'S STRATEGY AND THE NEED TO EXPAND OUR GROUP, WE JUST NEED A PLAN TO EFFECTIVELY EXECUTE THE STRATEGY.

I KNOW A PROFESSIONAL ACCOUNTANT WITH SUPER MANAGEMENT CONTROL POWERS, THE CONTROLLER, WHO MAY BE ABLE TO HELP US. LET'S ASK HIM TO FORMULATE A PLAN TO EXECUTE OUR STRATEGY

DO IT! WE NEED TO PRESENT A PLAN TO THE MAYOR NEXT WEEK

CONTROLLER, CAN YOU HELP SUPERHEROES LLP? WE DON'T EVEN KNOW WHAT THE MAYOR WANTS

I WOULD LOVE TO HELP. LET ME SEE. THERE ARE 12 OF YOU NOW, AND YOU'VE INCORPORATED AS AN LLP WITH CATRIX AS CEO, YES?

MEETING IN THE CONTROLLER'S OFFICE

OK, I NEED TO ASK YOU SOME QUESTIONS BEFORE WE CAN START. FIRST, WHO ARE SUPERHEROES LLP ACCOUNTABLE TO? AND WHAT IS IT ACCOUNTABLE FOR?

SECOND, WHAT KEEPS YOU, CATRIX, AWAKE AT NIGHT? WHAT CAN GET IN THE WAY OF SUPERHEROES LLP SUCCESSFULLY EXECUTING ITS STRATEGY?

THIRD, WHAT ARE YOUR FIRM'S VALUES? WHAT COMPASS GUIDES YOUR DECISIONS? AND MORE IMPORTANTLY, HOW WILL YOU GET THE GROUP TO LIVE BY THOSE VALUES?

FOURTH, WHAT IS THE BEST WAY FOR SUPERHEROES LLP TO GET PAID BY THE CITY? TO ANSWER THAT YOU NEED TO MEASURE YOUR BENEFIT TO GOOD CITY. YOU KNOW SUPERHEROES LLP CONTRIBUTES MORE TO GOOD CITY THAN JUST TURNING BAD GUYS OVER TO THE POLICE TO BE PROSECUTED.

AND WHAT IS THE BEST WAY TO COMPENSATE EACH OF THE 12 SUPER HEROES? GUFFAW IS CATCHING TWICE THE CRIMINALS, BUT GETS THE SAME PAY. IS THAT FAIR TO HER/HIM?

THIS WILL BE A TOUGH ASSIGNMENT AS ALL 12 OF YOU ARE TALENTED INDIVIDUALS THAT USE HIGHLY UNIQUE AND CREATIVE WAYS TO CATCH CRIMINALS.

SO HOW CAN SUPERHEROES LLP BEST CONTROL ITS MEMBERS ACTIONS WITHOUT JEOPARDIZING ITS RESULTS? LET'S GET TO WORK AND DRAW UP A PLAN FOR THE MAYOR!

PART 2: APPLICATION

SUPERHEROES LLP CASE ASSIGNMENT QUESTIONS

1. Develop a management control system for SuperHeroes LLP by answering the following questions:

   a. Who is SuperHeroes LLP accountable to? And what is it accountable for?

   b. What keeps SuperHeroes LLP's CEO, Catrix, awake at night? In other words, what can get in the way of SuperHeroes LLP successfully executing its strategy of cleaning up Good City and keeping it safe from criminals?

   c. What are SuperHeroes LLP's values? What compass guides its decisions? And more importantly, how should the CEO get the other superheroes to live by these values?

   d. What is the best way for SuperHeroes LLP to get paid by the city? As part of your answer, develop a performance measurement system for SuperHeroes LLP. What is the best way to compensate each of the 12 superheroes?

2. Do you feel that the control system you have just developed meets the objective of cleaning up Good City and keeping it safe from criminals while minimizing property damage and casualties to its citizens? Before answering this question, refer back to the description of Kenneth Merchant's management control system provided in part 1 of the case to verify that your proposed control system for SuperHeroes LLP adequately addresses each element in the control framework.

V. Strategic Cost Management

The Gatekeepers: A Case on Allocations and Justifications

David Hurtt, Bradley Lail, Michael Robinson, and Martin Stuebs, Baylor University

THIS CASE CHALLENGES STUDENTS' ABILITY TO JUSTIFY DIFFICULT accounting choices and subsequently consider the ramifications of those choices. We provide two different scenarios that examine the responsibilities, incentives, and issues faced by accountants—the gatekeepers in many reporting environments. The first scenario is a familiar academic reporting task in which students assess group performance and allocate points to members. The second is a similar task within the segment reporting environment in which costs are allocated to the reporting units. A summary exercise then requires students to link these scenarios. The open-ended nature of the case allows its use in multiple courses and at various levels of accounting education. Ultimately, the case will encourage students to behave more like managers, make tough choices where guidelines are vague, and assess the consequences of their actions.

The case is best suited for an upper-level, undergraduate managerial accounting course, although it could be modified for use in other courses.

Keywords: allocations, decision justification, ethical dilemmas, group projects, segment reporting, responsibility accounting.

The Association of
Accountants and
Financial Professionals
in Business

The Gatekeepers:
A Case on Allocations and Justifications

David Hurtt
Associate Professor of Accounting
Baylor University

Bradley Lail
Assistant Professor of Accounting
Baylor University

Michael Robinson
Professor of Accounting
Baylor University

Martin Stuebs
Associate Professor of Accounting
Baylor University

INTRODUCTION

This case provides an opportunity for you to make accounting allocation choices, justify those choices, and subsequently consider their ramifications. In this case study, we present students with two different scenarios—one takes place in an academic setting, and one in a business setting—that examine the incentives and reporting issues faced by managers and accountants as *gatekeepers* of their reporting environments. For each scenario, you will read the case materials and then answer the "Questions for Analysis." Each scenario presents you with an allocation task. In the first scenario, an allocation task in an academic setting, you will assess group members' contributions to a project and allocate points across the group. These point allocations contribute to determining individual group member's grades. The second scenario is also an allocation task but in a business setting—specifically the segment reporting environment. Here the task is to allocate indirect costs across reporting segments. For advanced reading, consider Accounting Standards Codification (ASC) Topic 280, "Segment Reporting," which can help guide you in the degree of flexibility, if any, allowed in determining how to allocate costs across segments.[1]

SCENARIO 1—STUDENT REPORTING ISSUES: GROUP POINT ALLOCATIONS

"I think we have a good paper here," said Ron during the final team meeting of the semester. The team—composed of Ron (the team leader), Tom, James, and Jen—was putting the finishing touches on their project, a paper that Ron considered to be quite good.

"I wish I could have worked more on this project," said Tom. It had been a tough year outside of school for Tom. He is a single father, and his daughter has had some health struggles that have occupied much of Tom's time. "Nevertheless, I feel as if I have learned a great deal and really appreciate the support that you all have given me."

"We were all busy," replied James, a basketball player on the school team and a good friend of Ron's. "I had to miss a couple of the team meetings to play in those away games, but I do not know what I would have done in your situation, Tom."

Jen responded, "I think we have made a really strong team and have probably done more than most of the other teams from what I hear. I also think if this had been an individual project rather than a group project, I would not have learned as much or done as well. Hang in there, Tom. We've got you covered!" Jen and Ron had picked up the slack for Tom and James and were primarily responsible for keeping the project on track.

Ron continued, "Don't forget, we each have to complete the team evaluation. Professor Brown stated that the group point allocations must sum to 1,600 points for our group. If allocated evenly, each group member receives 400 points (or 100%). It has been great working with each of you, and I hope we can work together again."

As Ron stated, the last step in the group project is for each member of the team to prepare an evaluation that Professor Brown will use to weight the project grades. The peer evaluations should be based on both the individuals' contributions to the project and their contributions to the team. The instructor requires that the individual student weightings sum to 400 points across the entire group, with each group member delineating points across the four members. Each student's overall weighting is determined by summing the points assigned to him or her (including the self-evaluation) and dividing by four—the number of group members—to obtain a weighting percentage. The student's final project grade is based on this weighting. For example, if the group receives a grade of 90% on the project and one of the group member's contribution totals 440 points (the sum of the points assigned to that student by the four group members), the weighting percentage would be 110% (440 points / 4 members), and the individual would receive a grade of 99% (90% × 110% = 99%). A team member with a weighting percentage of 90% (360 total points assigned to that student by the four group members / 4) would receive a grade of 81% (90% × 90% = 81%).

To help decide how to allocate the 400 points across the four group members, Ron had kept track of the following information on group member performance throughout the semester (shown in Table 1).

Table 1: Group Member Performance Measures

Group Member	Time Invested in Group Work (minutes)	Pages of Final Group Work Produced
Ron	250	18
Tom	150	10
James	200	7
Jen	400	15
Total	1,000	50

Ron had enjoyed working with this group and was proud of the 50-page final report that the group produced. He viewed himself as an effective group leader who had appropriately coordinated and delegated tasks. Still, he was struggling with the point allocation.

SUGGESTED DISCUSSION QUESTIONS FOR SCENARIO 1

1. Allocate the 400 points according to time invested, and then allocate the points according to pages produced. Decide how you would allocate the points to group members if you were Ron, using whatever means you believe to be appropriate. Justify your final allocation decision.

2. What role does Ron play in evaluating and reporting other students' performances? What responsibilities does Ron have in this role and to whom?

3. What incentives or pressures might cause a student like Ron to not perform the duties you identified in Question 2?

4. What characteristics would help Ron report appropriate point allocations to other students even in the presence of conflicting incentives? Hint: Refer to the *IMA Statement of Ethical Professional Practice* to help Ron identify appropriate reporting responsibilities and characteristics.[2]

5. How will Ron's reporting decisions affect the quality of information given to his instructor?

SCENARIO 2—SEGMENT REPORTING ISSUES: STRATEGIC COST ALLOCATIONS

The upcoming four days of Wayne's vacation had never looked so good. The end truly was near. There were only a few loose ends for Wayne to tie up, but first he needed to have a quick conversation with his boss.

"Mr. Wilkinson, thanks for the call earlier. I am sorry it has taken me a while to get back to you. I have my group hard at work. The end of the year is almost here," Wayne said.

Wayne heads the investor relations team, which is working on putting together the company's financial statements. The investor relations department serves as the intermediary between the executive team and the institutional investors, analysts, and large banks that anxiously await the finalized financial statements each year. Wayne's team must understand the numbers and eloquently explain them to outsiders.

"Wayne, this year has been very challenging for us, both strategically and operationally," said Mr. Wilkinson, one of the company's executives. "We have good people doing great work for the company. The numbers from the accountants look good and reflect our success, but we need them to look as nice as they possibly can—within the letter of the law, of course!" Mr. Wilkinson stated.

Wayne responded, "I can assure you that my team has done everything it can to accommodate our analysts and other constituents. Our last task is to allocate indirect costs across the segments."

Mr. Wilkinson replied, "Those allocations are critical, Wayne. You know how much outside folks care about segment information and use it to build forecasts and assess the future of our company." He was correct. Segment reporting results receive a large amount of attention by the analysts, and Wayne's investor relations team is continually asked to drive down the revenues and expenses to the segments whenever possible. It is obvious to Wayne that these segment results matter as much as the consolidated ones.

"I can assure you that we are very aware, Mr. Wilkinson," Wayne said. "And my concern, as always, is how to best decide which costs should be assigned to which operating segments. Some of the headquarters' costs and the company's research and development expenses, among others, belong to many departments." If the investor relations team does not do its job well, not only will Mr. Wilkinson and the executives be disappointed, but interested parties who desire quality financial disclosures could be misled. This allocation exercise of indirect costs carries some significant pressures that Wayne's team members must be willing to handle.

"I recognize the challenge, but no one is better situated to allocate these costs than you and your team. The segment managers are aware that whatever decisions you make are final, and they must manage appropriately, especially if they want that year-end bonus!" Mr. Wilkinson explained. He continued, "All the executive team expects from you is to fairly report each segment's results. Let the segment managers handle the subsequent day-to-day decisions. That is not your concern."

"No problem, sir. When we are finished I will have those numbers sent up to you."

"I want that on paper, Wayne. You know how I feel about spreadsheets."

"Of course, sir." Wayne smiled and hung up.

Every year it takes a monumental effort from Wayne and his investor relations team to finalize the financial statements. Wayne's final task of updating the segment-reporting footnote to the financial statements is not as easy as it used to be. Revenues are easily traceable to each segment, but expenses are often shared by these segments, so how the team allocates them is often a challenging process to justify. In addition, the new segment reporting rules allow much greater flexibility in how segment performance is presented.[3] In the cost allocation process, expenses can be shifted among operating segments and between operating segments and nonoperating segments. The goal of the new standard for segment reporting is to enable managers to disclose segment performance in the most transparent manner. Managers can choose which segments to disclose and the corresponding measure of performance as long as they match the internal reporting of the company. Greater discretion can lead to better information, but it also can open the door for manipulation (and misleading financial statements).

Such flexibility in reporting seems like a good thing, but the allocation process causes Wayne some grief. How his team allocates expenses that are not directly related to one particular segment can become a political process. Segments can be made to look better (or worse) based on how the costs are allocated. The edict from the executive team seems clear: Report "fairly" and "as nice as possible." Mr. Wilkinson's words make financial reporting partly an application of marketing strategy. Wayne's angst is understandable.

Wayne's company is broken down into three operating segments based on the three major product lines of the company (Mechanical, Innovation, and Enterprise) and a fourth corporate-level segment that typically is assigned all expenses not belonging to the three operating segments. All revenues and many product-related costs (including salaries) are directly identified with the appropriate operating segment. The challenge is how to handle indirect costs of resources that are shared by two or more segments, such as human resources or research and development. Each of these costs alone is significant enough to influence the operating margins of the segments. The investor relations team must justify that its allocation decisions are based on a rational methodology that is acceptable to both upper management and the segment managers, who are intensely interested in the final operating margins of their segments. The good news is that no matter how Wayne allocates these costs, total company income is unchanged. He wants to avoid any political debates and remove any appearance of bias in the final allocation of indirect costs.

This year, the investor relations team must consider how to allocate $1,474,000, which represents 16.5% of total revenues. These costs include charges for research and development, human resources, and information technology. One obvious option is to not allocate any of these costs, which would be advantageous for all operating segments from a profitability perspective. Consider the Enterprise

Table 2: Segment Reporting Disclosure

Segment	Revenue	Direct Expenses	Profit Before Allocation	Profit Margin
Mechanical	$6,952,000	$4,792,000	$2,160,000	31%
Innovation	1,265,000	658,000	607,000	48%
Enterprise	623,000	677,000	(54,000)	(9%)
Corporate/Other	68,000	912,000	(844,000)	0
Pre-Allocation Total	**$8,908,000**	**$7,039,000**	**$1,869,000**	**21%**
Indirect Expenses:				
Research and Development			$559,000	
Human Resources			664,000	
Information Technology			251,000	
Allocable Costs			**$1,474,000**	
Company Profit			**$395,000**	**4%**

segment, a recently added product line for which the executive team has high hopes. Currently the segment is operating at a small loss. Management's concern for the profitability of Enterprise will be exacerbated to the extent indirect costs are allocated to the segment.

The Mechanical segment is the typical cash cow that makes steady and predictable profits; it has provided significant support to the company for many years. The product line of the segment is highly competitive, but Mechanical has continued to be an industry leader through strong management policies and strategic direction. The size of Mechanical (78% of total sales) and steady cash flows make any allocations to or from this segment barely noticeable. Wayne's good friend Thomas runs Mechanical's operations, and Wayne knows Thomas has benefitted financially from the segment's profitability.

Finally, the Innovation segment also has been a huge success story. Lack of competition has made this particular product line highly profitable over the last two years. Being part of the company's leadership team and working directly with the executives on a regular basis, Wayne knows their desire is to keep the success of Innovation under the radar for as long as possible. The segment's profit margin of 48% is unheard of across the industry, and much of that is due to the lack of competitors. If new companies enter Innovation's space, its competitive advantage probably will not be sustainable.

Some of his graduate accounting and finance courses have taught Wayne that segment results are key inputs for analysts when developing forecasts of future performance. As the analysts speak, the market follows. Wayne's responsibility is

to the company as a whole, but he recognizes the importance of each segment to the company.

As the team members entered the room to make their important allocation decisions and finalize the financial reports, their conversation turned to the task at hand, but their minds seemed someplace else. Charles, a veteran member (and pessimist) of the group, reminded everyone that, "Last year's allocation process was a nightmare. It seemed that all we accomplished was to make other people mad at us."

Wayne sensed the glum mood in the room but still felt the need to remind the team of the consequences of their allocation decisions. Segment income is a key input not only to analysts' forecasts of future performance but also for the evaluation of segment manager performance (and bonus awards). Wayne then responded to Charles' comment: "Yes, this is an unenviable task, but Mr. Wilkinson just reminded me how impressed he is with our work. Still, I am thankful that segment reporting is the last thing we do before year-end."

SUGGESTED DISCUSSION QUESTIONS FOR SCENARIO 2

1. U.S. Generally Accepted Accounting Principles (GAAP) provides many areas in which managerial discretion is allowed. Why does such discretion exist, and what are some specific reporting issues under GAAP where discretion exists? Under ASC 280-10, the FASB has specified segment reporting guidelines. Where is discretion available within segment reporting?

2. Based on the information presented in the scenario, do you personally consider segment reporting a critical disclosure? What facts in the case lead you to that conclusion?

3 What role does Wayne and his investor relations team play in reporting financial performance? What responsibilities and individual characteristics would you consider most important for investor relations team members in this role? What incentives and pressures does Wayne's team face in carrying out this role and these responsibilities? As with Ron in Scenario 1, refer to the *IMA Statement* to make your decision.

4. Consider the $1,474,000 in indirect research and development, human resources, and information technology costs shown in Table 2. Should Wayne's team allocate these costs to the three operating segments? Why or why not? If the team decides to do so, what factors should it consider in deciding *how* to allocate the costs?

5. What specific bases (possibly not from the case) might the team consider to allocate the indirect costs shown in Table 2? How would you allocate the costs? Justify your decision.

6. Are post-allocation profit margins relevant for assessing the performance of segments and their managers? Why or why not?

SUMMARY: ANALYSIS OF REPORTING ENVIRONMENTS

Reporting the information used to allocate resources and costs is an important role and responsibility for managerial accountants. Now that you have practiced making allocation decisions in the first two scenarios, it is time to draw connections between the scenarios and uncover some important lessons for you as an accounting professional. The intention of this case is to cultivate a greater understanding of the issues related to allocating resources and costs and reporting information. Figure 1 presents a general reporting process. Three parties are involved in different roles in the general reporting process: the reporter, the reportee, and the report user(s). The reporter assesses the performance of the reportee and issues a report as a result of this assessment. Report users use this report to analyze the reportee's performance.

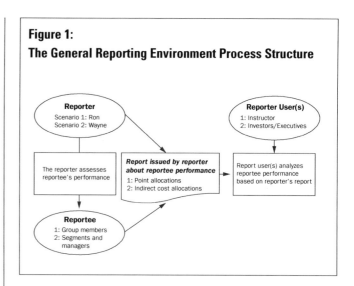

Figure 1:
The General Reporting Environment Process Structure

The first scenario in this case deals with the academic reporting environment in which Ron (the reporter) assesses the performance of fellow group members (the reportees). Based on his assessment, Ron issues a point allocation (report). His instructor and others (report users) use the reported point allocation to analyze the students' (reportees') performance. In the second scenario, Wayne (the reporter) assesses the indirect costs of segments and segment managers (the reportees). Based on his team's assessment, Wayne allocates indirect costs among segments and reports the segments' performance (report). Investors, company executives, and others (report users) use the reported segment performance, including the indirect cost allocations, to analyze the performance of company segments, segment managers, segment employees, and products (reportees). Table 3 summarizes the similar corresponding reporting parties and activities across the academic setting (Scenario 1) and the business setting (Scenario 2).

Table 3: Comparison of Different Reporting Environments

Item Environment	Academic Reporting Environment	Business Reporting Environment
Report	Point allocation reports	Cost allocations and financial performance reports
Reportee	Group members	Segments and segment managers
Reporter	Student (Ron)	Accountant (Wayne)
Report User	The class instructor	Investors and creditors (outside the company), executives (inside the company), and others

You began to think about these ideas when you identified the reporting role and reporting responsibilities of Ron and Wayne and his investor relations team. Reported information can be extremely powerful and therefore valuable. In the academic reporting environment, reported grade information has the power to affect numerous decisions. Hiring, graduate school admissions, and scholarship awards are a few examples of such decisions. Information reporting provides the reporter and reportee with an opportunity to gain an informational advantage over the report user by influencing the information presented to the report user. Because of the reported information's value, both the reporter and the reportee have incentives to manipulate the information in order to maximize their personal benefits. These incentives can create conflicts of interest and ethical dilemmas for reporters to forsake their reporting duties in pursuit of personal gain. In Scenario 1, Ron can manipulate reported point allocations for personal benefit. Similarly in Scenario 2, Wayne can strategically manipulate allocated indirect cost information for his benefit.

Students currently are in the academic reporting environment but eventually will become a reporter in a business reporting environment. Natural parallels exist between the academic and the business reporting environments. The intention of this case is to promote a greater understanding of the importance of the role and responsibilities of information reporters and the issues related to reporting information, whether in the academic setting or business setting.

SUGGESTED DISCUSSION QUESTIONS

1. **Identify:**
   - Reporter responsibilities: What are the ethical responsibilities of reporters/managerial accountants when preparing reports?
   - **Incentives:** What incentives or pressures might cause a managerial accountant/reporter to not perform these responsibilities?
   - **Characteristics:** What characteristics do you think help a managerial accountant/reporter perform these responsibilities even in the presence of conflicting incentives?

2. **Ethical issues:** What are the key ethical issues and conflicts of interest that the reporter/managerial accountant faces in a reporting environment?

3. **Advice:** What guidelines would you create to help the reporter/managerial accountant make decisions and handle reporting environment issues? Use the *IMA Statement* as a reference.

4. **Reporting failures and costs:**
   - **Failures:** Identify some reporting failures. For example, Enron's financial statement fraud is a notable example of a reporting failure in the financial reporting environment. Can you think of others? You can consider the financial reporting environment and other reporting environments such as academia, government, tax accounting, and managerial accounting.
   - **Costs:** What are some of the costs of the reporting failures you identified? Who bears these costs?
   - **Reporter's role and importance:** How important is the reporter's job in these reporting environments? What happens if the reporter does not perform his or her job well?

ENDNOTES

[1] ASC 280, "Segment Reporting," can be found on the on the Financial Accounting Standards Board (FASB) website at https://asc.fasb.org. Login is required.

[2] *IMA Statement of Ethical Professional Practice*, IMA® (Institute of Management Accountants), Montvale, N.J., 2005, www.imanet.org/docs/default-source/generalpdfs/statement-of-ethics_web.pdf?sfvrsn=2.

[3] The requirements for segment reporting can be found under ASC Topic 280, "Segment Reporting."

Product Costs: Application in an Insurance Company

Scott McGregor, Western Connecticut State University

COST ACCOUNTING TEXTBOOKS TYPICALLY FOCUS ON manufacturers and provide less emphasis on applying cost accounting practices in service companies. But understanding the costs to sell, produce, and administer products is extremely important in both service and manufacturing industries. Many service companies, such as banks and insurance companies, have very large administrative functions and use cost accounting principles as a means to understand costs and to improve cost effectiveness and profit margins. The case is based on an actual project that updated the product cost allocation process at a large insurance company (case uses a fictional company name and accompanying data).

The case is designed to be used in an undergraduate cost accounting course. The case may also be used in an undergraduate or graduate management accounting course.

Keywords: cost allocations, product costs, activity-based costing (ABC).

The Association of
Accountants and
Financial Professionals
in Business

Product Costs: Application in an Insurance Company

Scott McGregor
Western Connecticut State University

INTRODUCTION

Greg McAndrews has recently been hired as Vice President for Expense Management at a large insurance company. His responsibilities include the process for allocating expenses to products. Through discussions with his staff, he has learned that there is a great deal of discontent with the expense allocation process. He decided that one of his top priorities will be to analyze the product costing process and make necessary corrections.

Greg is a CMA® (Certified Management Accountant) and CPA (Certified Public Accountant) with an undergraduate degree in accounting and a Master of Business Administration (MBA). Although he has worked in various roles with progressing responsibilities throughout his 12-year career, Greg has never been directly responsible for expense allocations. He has read numerous articles on the current applications of cost accounting techniques in service industries, including activity-based costing (ABC). He believes that he has a good understanding of cost accounting techniques and is eager for his team to improve the expense allocation process.

COMPANY OVERVIEW

AXE Life Insurance Company is among the leading life insurance companies in the United States. AXE Life employs more than 5,000 people and has assets in excess of $17 billion and annual premiums ("revenue") in excess of $10 billion. The company is well established with a long successful history.

AXE Life sells individual life insurance products, individual annuities, and group annuities. The individual products, both life and annuity, are sold through insurance agents. The group annuity products are sold by banks and brokerage firms. The group business represents approximately 40% of total sales, and the individual business represents the remainder. The company continually develops new products, both life and annuity, typically bringing one or two new products to market each year. The company currently has 17 different life and annuity insurance products.

AXE Life has a functional organization structure with Sales, Marketing, Finance, IT, and Service departments representing a functional discipline. The Service department has a joint management team but has separate functions to service annuity products and life insurance products. All other departments provide support to both life and annuity products. Because of the size of the functional departments and their annual expense budgets, there are financial support roles in each department. The financial support staffs provide budgeting and financial analysis support to the departments.

LIFE INSURANCE TERMS, PRODUCTS, AND PROCESSES

The two primary types of products sold and serviced by life insurance companies are life insurance and annuities. These two products have different characteristics. In general, life insurance is used for financial protection and annuities for retirement savings. A life insurance policy provides a payment to the beneficiary upon the death of the insured. An annuity provides a stream of periodic payments to the customer upon attaining a specified age.

A life insurance policy is usually sold to customers to provide financial protection for their families in the event of the insured's death. If the policy provides coverage for the full life of the insured, it is called whole life insurance. If the insurance coverage is only for a specified period, it is called term life insurance. For life insurance, customers most often pay the cost of the policy ("premiums") over a long period of time. During the period of time that the policy's coverage is active, the policy is considered to be "inforce." The process involved with life insurance begins with the sale of the policy, often through a life insurance agent. The life insurance agent meets with the potential customer and gathers personal information, which is collected using an application for insurance. Potential customers also will provide medical information and are often subjected to a medical examination. The application containing personal information and medical information is submitted to the Underwriting department, which is responsible for deciding whether a policy should be issued and the appropriate premium for the policy.

After the company and the customer agree on the policy's terms and conditions, the company issues the physical policy. Most life insurance companies have service departments that have an "issuance" function that performs this activity. After the policy has been issued, the company collects the premiums, answers ongoing customer questions, and terminates the policy if the insured decides to cancel the policy or fails to pay the premium. These functions also are performed in their service departments. Then, when the insured dies, the insurance company pays the benefits specified in the insurance policy to the beneficiary—this process is performed by the Claims department.

Premiums under an annuity product may be paid in a lump sum or periodically over a number of years. The insurance company invests these funds and provides either a set return ("fixed annuity") or a return that varies with investment performance ("variable annuity"). For individual annuity sales, the issuance and premium collection processes are very similar to the processes for life insurance policies. For group annuity products, the sales process is completed by a licensed representative of a bank or brokerage firm instead of an insurance agent. But the other activities are consistent with individual annuity sales.

Although many of the processes are similar for life and annuity products, insurance companies often have separate Service departments performing functions for annuities products since there are activities associated with the products that differ. For example, when an annuity policy is canceled, or surrendered, the customer receives a payment that represents the premiums they have paid in addition to investment returns less a surrender fee. Most life insurance companies have a separate unit within its Service department that performs the surrender function. Once a customer reaches the age specified in the annuity contract, the company begins making a series of periodic payments, which is performed by the annuity Service department.

CURRENT COSTING SYSTEM

The vast majority of AXE Life's financial reporting is prepared at a company level, although there are periodic reports on product results. AXE Life allocates all expenses to products. All expense allocations are prepared within the expense management function in the Finance department with little input from the finance staff in the functional departments.

AXE Life has a cost center structure with approximately 1,000 cost centers. In its hierarchy, multiple cost centers make up a functional center (see Figure 1). Each of these functional centers is part of a department. A manager may be responsible for one or more cost centers, a higher-level manager for a functional center, and an executive-level manager for departments. One of the performance measurement factors for cost center managers is how effectively they manage the expenses of the cost center against the budget. For managers of functions, their performance measurement includes how effectively they manage the expenses of all of the cost centers within their function. For the executives managing the business departments, their cost effectiveness is measured on all of the cost centers and functions within their department.

Responsibility and accountability for expenses is based on responsibility center. There is no accountability for the expenses at the product level nor is there direct measurement or accountability for the cost effectiveness of any activities associated with the sale or service of the company's products.

Figure 1. Illustration of the Hierarchy of Departments, Functions, and Cost Centers

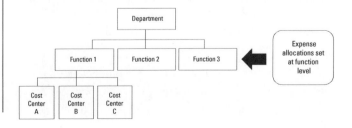

Expense data is captured at the cost center level, and the basis for allocating expenses is set at a functional center level. Because of the large number of cost centers and the lack of attention on cost allocations, Greg finds that cost driver information often is not used or is unavailable at the cost center level. The current system makes use of more generalized expense allocation bases, such as assets or sales, and uses that basis to allocate expenses of all cost centers within the functional center. These allocation bases may differ from the cost driver (the activities that actually drive expenses). For example, the expenses of the underwriting function within the Service department are allocated to products based on life insurance sales, even though the cost driver is the number of life insurance applications.

Even when cost driver information is available at a cost center level it can vary with the allocation basis for expense since the same basis is used for all cost centers within the functional center. Due to the limited time available to analyze the inputs and results of the process, the basis of expense allocations to products is only reviewed on an annual basis. Greg finds that much of the cost center information has not been updated in years.

During Greg's first month, he reviews AXE Life's process of allocating costs and finds that the current process takes up to three business days to complete during each monthly close, with significant manual intervention required. The expense allocation process is performed using a spreadsheet that was developed eight years ago, and the process requires a series of iterations. Under the current process, the staff accountant receives a downloaded file of cost center expenses on the day after the monthly expense accounting close is complete. She also receives information on the sales volume (in U.S. dollars) during the month, the annual premium for the policies inforce, and the amount of assets under management. These measures serve as the bases to allocate expenses to products.

The staff accountant enters the volume information for the allocation bases (sales, assets, premium) for the month into the spreadsheet. She imports the cost center expenses into the spreadsheet to populate the cost centers with the expenses for the month. She runs a series of Microsoft Excel macros to allocate the expenses to product. The staff accountant then reconciles the allocations to ensure that all expenses have been allocated.

The costs for the Sales department, Marketing department, and Service department related to issuing new policies (new customers) are allocated to product based on sales volume. The total annual premium per product is used to allocate the costs for the service functions including those related to supporting and terminating customers and the costs for the claims function.

After the costs are allocated to products, the process is considered complete. There are no rates per policy or per function calculated as part of the process. Additionally, there is no study of the time or cost required for activities. Table 1 shows the outcome of the expense allocations for the most recent month (July 2012) using the current cost allocation process.

Table 1. Panel A: Monthly Expense Results
Expenses July 2012

Expenses by Department	
Sales	$ 30,700,125
Marketing	5,524,850
Finance	8,624,567
Customer Service	15,750,225
Information Technology	11,424,525
Human Resources	3,942,563
Executive	2,512,235
Corporate & Other	4,046,032
Total	**$82,525,122**

Table 1. Panel B:
Expenses July 2012 under Current Cost Allocations

Product	Product Expense
Whole Life Series 1	$ 2,212,742
Whole Life Series 2	2,598,048
Variable Life Series 1	3,718,892
Variable Life Series 2	3,983,063
Term Life 2000	1,315,393
Term Life New Horizon	1,627,201
Flexible Life	1,719,782
Secure Life	7,018,232
Brokerage Annuity	10,457,380
Fixed Annuity, Brokerage	3,298,115
Happy Life Annuity	12,849,825
Bankers Choice	1,958,313
Fixed Annuity, Bank	4,161,012
Individual Fixed Annuity 1	6,646,289
Individual Fixed Annuity 2	6,775,007
Individual Fixed Annuity 3	1,431,363
Life Style Annuity	10,754,464
Total Allocated	**$ 82,525,122**

Table 1. Panel C:
Product Allocations by Department, Current System

Product	Sales	Service	Marketing	IT	Finance	All Other	Total
Whole Life Series 1	$568,673	$972,669	$104,376	$211,240	$160,037	$195,746	$2,212,742
Whole Life Series 2	614,643	1,306,637	81,388	234,203	168,655	192,523	2,598,048
Variable Life Series 1	1,024,239	1,416,358	232,353	372,157	294,340	379,445	3,718,892
Variable Life Series 2	1,373,039	761,773	397,999	482,686	406,466	561,101	3,983,063
Term Life 2000	391,680	446,071	81,663	143,664	111,570	140,745	1,315,393
Term Life New Horizon	586,255	338,417	114,267	216,523	165,901	205,837	1,627,201
Flexible Life	279,446	962,249	146,498	85,970	91,727	153,893	1,719,782
Secure Life	1,520,900	3,049,065	698,525	486,402	485,649	777,691	7,018,232
Brokerage Annuity	4,731,929	959,177	341,303	1,856,485	1,259,212	1,309,274	10,457,380
Fixed Annuity, Broker	1,161,666	573,359	336,322	408,455	343,836	474,476	3,298,115
Happy Life Annuity	4,897,700	1,790,417	1,142,659	1,773,658	1,411,813	1,833,579	12,849,825
Bankers Choice	494,749	563,186	294,031	145,714	167,162	293,470	1,958,313
Fixed Annuity, Bank	1,912,221	283,261	163,261	745,479	512,342	544,447	4,161,012
Ind. Fixed Annuity 1	3,230,604	310,625	137,274	1,285,402	846,537	835,846	6,646,289
Ind. Fixed Annuity 2	3,268,866	402,744	114,201	1,305,252	853,169	830,776	6,775,007
Ind. Fixed Annuity 3	740,165	27,522	783	300,243	189,736	172,914	1,431,363
Life Style Annuity	3,903,351	1,586,694	1,137,947	1,370,992	1,156,416	1,599,065	10,754,464
Total Allocated	**$30,700,125**	**$15,750,225**	**$5,524,850**	**$11,424,525**	**$8,624,567**	**$10,500,830**	**$82,525,122**

Table 1. Panel D: Cost Driver Information, Current Allocations

Department/Function	Description of Activities	Cost Driver	Products Supported	Allocation
Marketing				
Marketing Management	Manage marketing dept.	Marketing Campaigns	All	Sales
Marketing Department Staff	Marketing campaigns	Marketing Campaigns	All	Sales
Happy Retirement Annuity Campaign	Costs for media campaign	Media campaign	Happy Retirement Annuity	Sales
Secure Life Insurance Campaign	Media campaign for secure life product	Media campaign	Secure Life	Sales
Total Company Ad Campaign	Media campaign for company	Media campaign	All	Sales
Customer Service – Life				
New Business Management	Manage new business	New policy volume	Life (all)	Sales
Applications	Review applications	Number of applications	Life (all)	Sales
Underwriting	Underwriting applications	Number of applications	Life (all)	Sales
Policy Issuance	Issuing new policies	Number of policies issued	Life (all)	Sales
e-Issuance	Tech support for e-applications	Number of e-applications	Life (all)	Sales
Customer Service Management	Manage customer service	Number of policies	All	Premium
Call Center	Staff in call center	Number of phone calls	All	Premium
Life Insurance Inforce Maintenance	Servicing life policies	Number of policies	Life (all)	Premium, life
Claims Management	Manage staff for claims	Number of claims	Life (all)	Premium, life
Life Insurance Claims Adjusters	Adjudicate claims	Number of claims	Life (all)	Premium, life
Life Insurance Claims	Issue claim checks	Number of claims	Life (all)	Premium, life
Customer Service – Annuity				
New Business Management	Manage new business issuance	New policies sold	Annuities (all)	Sales
Applications	Reviewing applications	Number of applications	Annuities (all)	Sales
Policy Issuance	Staff issuing new policies	Number of policies issued	Annuities (all)	Sales
e-Issuance	Tech support for e-applications	Number of e-applications	Annuities (all)	Sales
Annuity Inforce Maintenance	Service all annuity products	Number of policies	Annuities (all)	Premium, annuity
Annuity Surrenders	Issue surrenders	Number of surrenders	Annuities (all)	Premium, annuity
Information Technology				
IT Management	Manage staff for IT	Number of systems/projects	All	Assets
Financial Management Systems	Managing financial systems	Number of systems/projects	All	Assets
Human Resource Systems	Manage HR systems	Number of systems/projects	All	Assets
Life Insurance Claims Systems	Managing life claim system	Number of systems/projects	Life	Assets
Life Policy Systems	Managing life systems	Number of systems/projects	Life	Assets
Annuity Systems	Managing annuity systems	Number of systems/projects	Annuity	Assets
Annuity Projects	Projects for annuity products	Project hours	Annuity	Assets
Life Insurance Projects	Projects for life products	Project hours	Life	Assets
Financial Systems Update	Project for upgrading financial system	Project hours	All	Assets
Controller	Accounting staff	Number of reports	All	Assets
Actuarial	Actuarial staff	Number of reports	All	Assets
Financial Planning and Analysis	Financial analysts and budget analysts	Number of analysis and reports	All	Assets
Expense Management	Cost accounting staff	Number of reports	All	Assets

Table 1. Panel D: Cost Driver Information, Current Allocations (continued)

Department/Function	Description of Activities	Cost Driver	Products Supported	Allocation
Human Resources				
HR Management	Manage staff	Employees	All	Assets
Compensation and Payroll	Executive and employee compensation	Employees	All	Assets
Staffing and Recruiting	Recruit for all company positions	Open positions	All	Assets
Sales				
Sales Management	Manage sales function for company	Sales	Life and annuity (all)	Sales
East Region	East coast sales staff and management	Sales for region	Life and annuity (all)	Sales
Midwest Region	Midwest sales staff and management	Sales for region	Life and annuity (all)	Sales
South Region	Sales staff and management for south	Sales for region	Life and annuity (all)	Sales
West Region	Sales staff and management for west coast	Sales for region	Life and annuity (all)	Sales
Facilities				
Facilities Management	Manage staff for Facilities	Number of employees/sq. ft.	All	Assets
Facilities Staff	Maintenance and other Facility staff	Number of employees/sq. ft.	All	Assets
Corporate Unallocated Rent	Rent for entire corporate office	Number of employees/sq. ft.	All	Assets
Treasurers				
Treasurer	Manage staff for Treasurer's dept.	Assets	All	Assets
Cash Management and Banking	Manage cash & banking relationships	Number of bank accounts	All	Assets
Investments	Manage investments	Invested assets	All	Assets
Executive & Corporate				
Office of the CEO	CEO and support staff		All	Assets
Corporate	Expenses not chargeable to any business area		All	Assets

In discussions with his team, Greg finds that the team does not fully understand how the information is used and its importance. Also, he learns that they are frustrated with the time required to complete the expense allocation process and complain that they do not have adequate time to review results or maintain the inputs for the expense allocation process. Greg believes that the expense allocation process could be accomplished in one business day instead of three. If processing time can be reduced, Greg anticipates the staff would be afforded more time to analyze the results and maintain the cost allocation information used in the process.

OBJECTIVES OF THE PRODUCT COST ALLOCATIONS

In his discussion with the staff, Greg learned that they receive limited information after recording the monthly product expenses. Their understanding is that the product expense allocation is coupled with claims information and premium revenue information to determine the profitability of each product. This process of reporting on product profitability is completed within the Actuarial department. To better learn what the objectives of the expense allocation process should be, Greg meets with the actuaries to find how the product expense information is used and gathers their concerns with the current process.

Sal Enrich, the company's chief actuary, discusses how his department uses the expense allocation information. Sal explains that the product-based expenses are critical for determining product profitability and for setting the pricing for products, both of which are vital to the company's success. The Actuarial department is the sole provider of product profitability information for the company. Sal explains that no individual manager is directly responsible for individual product profitability and that his department is in charge of monitoring product profitability, and the results are shared with executive management. Sal emphasizes that executive management looks to his department to ensure that products' profitability information is correct. Executive management uses the information to determine which products to emphasize in the sales process and the insurance agents receive larger commissions on the sale of more profitable products.

Sal details how the actuaries take the product expense information, revenue, mortality results (death benefits), sales commissions, and other nonoperating expenses to determine the profitability of each product. Since the product expense information is a significant component in determining the profitability of each product, misstating it could lead the company to cease selling a profitable product or to oversell an unprofitable product.

Sal further explains that the product expenses are a critical component in determining the appropriate pricing for each of AXE Life's existing products. Additionally, when new products are developed, the actuaries rely on the historical unit costs for similar products. Thus, if the product expenses are inaccurate, they could over-price or under-price a product, which would hurt AXE Life's long-term profitability.

Sal believes that the cost information is inadequate in meeting the needs of his department and AXE Life. Sal expresses concern that the cost system is inaccurate, and the information is not available in a timely fashion. As a result, Sal's staff spends hours analyzing the data and making adjustments, all within a compressed time frame. He outlines the format the actuaries would prefer the cost information to be organized, with the following broad categories of expenses organized along the major activities associated with a product:

- Cost to develop the product
- Cost to market the product
- Cost to sell the product
- Cost to issue the product
- Cost to service the product
- Overhead expenses (other administrative expenses)
- One-time expenses (such as special projects) and nonrecurring expenses

After the meeting, Greg decides that the expense allocation system needs immediate attention. He assembles a small project team and, during the first meeting, outlines the features of a useful cost system:

- Timely, accurate information
- Ability to use the information for product pricing, product profitability, and management decision making

Greg also lists the shortfalls of the current system:

- Requires significant manual intervention using spreadsheets
- Long processing time
- Expense allocations based on general factors (e.g., sales at the functional level)
- Outdated or nonexistent cost driver information for cost centers
- Lack of reporting (limited monthly information, no comparison of budget to actual results)
- Lack of cost information based on activity
- Lack of information on the time to complete each activity
- No identification of direct costs vs. indirect costs
- No identification of expenses as variable or fixed

PROJECT OVERVIEW

Greg and two staff members make up the primary project team. The team decides that the first two shortfalls (significant manual intervention and long processing time) can be improved by eliminating the current spreadsheet approach and replacing it with cost allocation software.

After the team has selected software to support their process, the next step is the most critical aspect of the project: solve the lack of sufficient and updated information to allocate expenses to products. To assist in improving and updating the cost driver information, the team decides to involve the financial support staff in the various functional departments since they have a better understanding of the activities in the respective departments they support and can easily meet with employees performing the activities. They put in place a project plan that includes the following actions for the initial phase of the project:

- Review available cost accounting software packages.
- Prepare a project proposal including estimates of cost and benefits.
- Submit the project plan and receive approval.
- Engage finance support staff to update all cost center/cost driver information.
- Purchase and install software.
- Load cost center data.
- Test it.
- Implement it.

The team sets a four-month time frame for the project with the goal to have the new process in place for the next calendar year. They also include as deliverables using the new process for the preparation of the current year's annual product expenses and the annual budgeted product expenses for the next calendar year.

During the first month of the project, Greg and his team review software products. After narrowing their choices, the team conducts an in-depth review of four potential software products. The team chooses a package from ABC Software, Inc. as its preferred software product. This product will not only support the department's ability to allocate the expenses quickly and accurately, but it also can support activity-based costing, which will be the second phase of the project. The team prepares a project proposal and receives approval from executive management to undertake the project.

Greg and his staff meet with the finance support staff from the various departments to put in place a process to update the information associated with the expense allocation process, including the cost driver information.

Greg explains the importance of the information to the company and the value of the involvement of the financial support staff. He also seeks management's input as how to best implement a process to ensure the information is consistently updated on an ongoing basis.

The group is receptive and agrees to the following actions:

- Complete an update of the cost center information within the next 30 calendar days.
- Provide activity and driver information for each new cost center that is added.
- Annually update all of the cost center information as part of the annual budget cycle.

The financial support staffs are given a grid to use while collecting data on each cost center, which includes:

- Function center number,
- Functional center,
- Cost center number,
- Cost center name,
- Activity,
- Cost driver, and
- Products supported.

ABC Software, Inc. completes the installation of the cost allocation software during week three of the four-month project. During week four, the project team loads all of the cost centers into the ABC software. By the end of the first month of the project, all of the finance support staff submits the updated cost center/cost driver information. For the next month, the project team loads all of the cost center information, including activities and cost drivers. For the first test of the system, the team loads the expense information for July 2012.

RESULTS OF THE FIRST TEST OF REVISED PROCESS

The team collects the volumes of activity (Table 3) and expenses for July 2012. Using the new process, the product allocations are completed with a summary of the results from Table 2. Panels A and B show the total expenses and the product expenses after allocation. Table 2, Panel C, shows a table with the grid completed for each of the functional centers within each department. The expense details for those functional centers for July 2012 allocated to product are provided in Table 2, Panel D.

Table 2. Panel A: First Test of Revised Cost Allocation Process Expenses by Department July 2012		Table 2. Panel B: Expenses by Product July 2012 under Revised Cost Allocations	
Expenses by Department		**Product**	**Product Expense**
Sales	$30,700,125	Whole Life Series 1	$ 3,186,824
Marketing	5,524,850	Whole Life Series 2	2,945,549
Finance	8,624,567	Variable Life Series 1	4,105,859
Customer Service	15,750,225	Variable Life Series 2	5,571,684
Information Technology	11,424,525	Term Life 2000	3,245,164
Human Resources	3,942,563	Term Life New Horizon	2,432,906
Executive	2,512,235	Flexible Life	2,611,487
Corporate & Other	4,046,032	Secure Life	8,255,685
Total	**$82,525,122**	Brokerage Annuity	6,523,542
		Fixed Annuity, Brokerage	4,239,529
		Happy Life Annuity	12,511,268
		Bankers Choice	3,539,366
		Fixed Annuity, Bank	3,407,226
		Individual Fixed Annuity 1	3,969,907
		Individual Fixed Annuity 2	4,068,980
		Individual Fixed Annuity 3	1,336,349
		Life Style Annuity	10,573,797
		Total Allocated	**$ 82,525,122**

Table 2. Panel C: Product Allocations by Department, Revised Allocations

Product	Sales	Service	Marketing	IT	Finance	All Other	Total
Whole Life Series 1	$584,062	$1,290,124	$157,635	$660,831	$300,011	$194,161	$3,186,824
Whole Life Series 2	458,626	1,155,822	141,994	661,092	312,748	215,267	2,945,549
Variable Life Series 1	1,307,471	1,159,683	244,710	662,657	389,270	342,067	4,105,859
Variable Life Series 2	2,238,117	1,476,626	357,415	663,911	391,954	443,660	5,571,684
Term Life 2000	453,580	1,653,389	142,181	660,064	203,902	132,048	3,245,164
Term Life New Horizon	641,752	522,565	164,365	660,891	244,317	199,017	2,432,906
Flexible Life	831,076	683,788	186,295	659,410	171,900	79,019	2,611,487
Secure Life	3,835,669	2,076,504	700,018	802,403	394,015	447,075	8,255,685
Brokerage Annuity	1,880,550	804,511	318,840	659,270	1,153,987	1,706,385	6,523,542
Fixed Annuity, Broker	1,832,987	722,040	315,451	642,840	350,779	375,431	4,239,529
Happy Life Annuity	6,182,754	1,767,557	1,019,206	803,455	1,108,043	1,630,254	12,511,268
Bankers Choice	1,662,587	611,271	286,676	639,859	205,039	133,933	3,539,366
Fixed Annuity, Bank	936,802	403,131	197,700	646,664	537,723	685,205	3,407,226
Ind. Fixed Annuity 1	784,688	333,724	180,019	652,790	837,212	1,181,475	3,969,907
Ind. Fixed Annuity 2	661,673	542,029	164,320	653,015	848,223	1,199,720	4,068,980
Ind. Fixed Annuity 3	5,226	35,638	87,150	641,612	290,755	275,968	1,336,349
Life Style Annuity	6,402,505	511,823	860,875	653,761	884,688	1,260,144	10,573,797
Total Allocated	**$30,700,125**	**$15,750,225**	**$5,524,850**	**$11,424,525**	**$8,624,567**	**$10,500,830**	**$82,525,122**

Table 2. Panel D: Cost Driver Information, Revised Allocations

Department/Function	Description of Activities	Cost Driver	Products Supported	Allocation
Marketing				
Marketing Management	Manage Marketing dept.	Marketing Campaigns	All	Sales
Marketing Department Staff	Marketing campaigns	Marketing Campaigns	All	Sales
Happy Retirement Annuity Campaign	Costs for media campaign	Media campaign	Happy Retirement Annuity	Direct to Happy Retirement
Secure Life Insurance Campaign	Media campaign for secure life product	Media campaign	Secure Life	Direct to Secure Life
Total Company Ad Campaign	Media campaign for total company	Media campaign	All	Sales
Customer Service – Life				
New Business Management	Manage new business	New policy volume	Life (all)	# of new policies
Applications	Review applications	Number of applications	Life (all)	# of applications
Underwriting	Underwriting applications	Number of applications	Life (all)	# of applications
Policy Issuance - Life Insurance	Issuing new policies	Number of policies issued	Life (all)	# of polices issued
e-Issuance	Tech support for e-applications	Number of e-applications	Life (all)	# of e-applications
Customer Service Management	Manage customer service	Number of policies	Life and annuities (all)	# of policies
Call Center	Receive incoming calls	Number of phone calls	Life and annuities (all)	# of phone calls
Life Insurance Inforce Maintenance	Servicing life policies	Number of policies	Life (all)	# of life policies
Claims Management	Manage staff for claims	Number of claims	Life (all)	# of claims
Life Insurance Claims Adjusters	Adjudicate claims	Number of claims	Life (all)	# of claims
Life Insurance Claims	Issue claim checks	Number of claims	Life (all)	# of claims
Customer Service – Annuity				
New Business Management	Manage new business issuance	New policies sold	Annuities (all)	# of new policies
Applications	Reviewing applications	Number of applications	Annuities (all)	# of applications
Policy Issuance	Staff issuing new policies	Number of policies issued	Annuities (all)	# of polices issued
e-Issuance	Tech support for electronic applications	Number of e-applications	Annuities (all)	# of e-applications
Annuity Inforce Maintenance	Service all annuity products	Number of inforce policies	Annuities (all)	# of policies
Annuity Surrenders	Issue surrenders	Number of surrenders	Annuities (all)	# of surrenders
Information Technology				
IT Management	Manage staff for IT	Number of systems/projects	All	Assets
Financial Management Systems	Managing financial systems	Number of systems/projects	All	Assets
Human Resource Systems	Manage HR systems	Number of systems/projects	All	Assets
Life Insurance Claims Systems	Managing life claim system	Number of systems/projects	Life	Life claims
Life Policy Systems	Managing life systems	Number of systems/projects	Life	Life policies
Annuity Systems	Managing annuity systems	Number of systems/projects	Annuity	Annuity policies
Annuity Projects	Project for new annuity product	Project hours	Happy Retirement Annuity	Annuity policies
Life Insurance Projects	Project for new life product	Project hours	Secure Life Insurance	Life insurance policies
Financial Systems Update	Project for upgrading financial system	Project hours	All	Assets
Controller	Accounting dept.	Number of reports	All	Assets
Actuarial	Actuarial staff	Number of reports	All	Assets
Financial Planning and Analysis	Financial analysts and budget analysts	Number of analysis and reports	All	Assets
Expense Management	Cost Accounting staff	Number of reports	All	Assets

Table 2. Panel D: Cost Driver Information, Revised Allocations (continued)

Department/Function	Description of Activities	Cost Driver	Products Supported	Allocation
Human Resources				
Human Resource Management	Manage staff for HR	Employees	All	Assets
Compensation and Payroll	Executive and employee compensation	Employees	All	Assets
Staffing and Recruiting	Recruit for all company positions	Open positions	All	Assets
Sales				
Sales Management	Manage sales function for company	Sales	Life and annuity (all)	Sales
East Region	East coast sales staff and management	Sales for region	Life and annuity (all)	Sales
Midwest Region	Midwest sales staff and management	Sales for region	Life and annuity (all)	Sales
South Region	South sales staff and management	Sales for region	Life and annuity (all)	Sales
West Region	West coast sales staff and management	Sales for region	Life and annuity (all)	Sales
Facilities				
Facilities Management	Manage staff for facilities	Number of employees/sq. ft.	All	Assets
Facilities Staff	Maintenance and other facility staff	Number of employees/sq. ft.	All	Assets
Corporate Unallocated Rent	Rent for entire corporate office	Number of employees/sq. ft.	All	Assets
Treasurers				
Treasurer	Manage staff for Treasurer's dept.	Assets	All	Assets
Cash Management and Banking	Manage cash & banking relationships	Number of bank accounts	All	Assets
Investments	Manage investments	Invested assets	All	Assets
Executive & Corporate				
Office of the CEO	CEO and support staff		All	Assets
Corporate	Expenses not chargeable to any area		All	Assets

Table 3: Actual Cost Driver Volumes for July 2012

in millions

Product	Policies Issued	Apps	Inforce Policies	e-Apps	Phone Calls	Claims	Surrenders	Annuity Checks	Assets	Annual Premium	Sales
Whole Life Series 1	1,025	1,425	332,500	125	1,520	1,240	—		$1,850	$507	$16
Whole Life Series 2	720	785	280,250	525	816	1,517	—		2,050	726	13
Variable Life Series 1	1,475	1,752	225,000	—	710	910	—		3,258	678	36
Variable Life Series 2	2,125	3,150	75,000	—	1,215	1,175			4,225	158	61
Term Life 2000	650	720	331,250	625	915	2,885			1,258	207	123
Term New Horizons	525	650	91,501	65	362	575			1,895	118	178
Flexible Life	715	755	147,250	70	1,665	615			753	469	23
Secure Life	2,150	2,252	252,500	775	5,517	2,410			4,258	1,309	108
Brokerage Annuity	1,150	1,175	88,125	—	4,175	—	1,415	12,125	16,250	1,823	53
Fixed Annuity, Broker	1,125	1,150	72,500	250	3,215	—	715	14,141	3,575	521	52
Happy Life Annuity	3,850	4,005	115,050	350	6,152	—	875	11,250	15,525	1,229	176
Bankers Choice Annuity	725	755	62,500	—	3,150	—	2,102	15,010	1,276	668	45
Fixed Annuity, Bank	625	650	25,250	120	1,185	—	1,650	5,500	6,526	270	25
Individual Fixed Annuity 1	525	550	42,500	—	1,275	—	125	10,101	11,251	475	21
Individual Fixed Annuity 2	375	415	85,750	415	2,282	—	450	19,252	11,425	891	18
Individual Fixed Annuity 3	10	10	8,520	10	115	—	10	1,010	2,628	91	0.1
Life Style Annuity	1,105	1,215	40,248	—	615	—	445	5,250	12,000	550	175
Total	**18,875**	**21,412**	**2,275,694**	**3,330**	**34,884**	**11,327**	**7,787**	**93,639**	**$100,000**	**$10,690**	**$850**

ASSIGNMENT

1. Discuss some of the alternatives and factors that Greg should consider when developing the expense allocation system. What are some of the costs and benefits of the alternatives?

2. As shown in Table 1, Panel C, AXE Life is allocating all expenses of all departments to products. Are there any potential problems caused by allocating all expenses to products?

3. Review the basis for the expense allocations under the current system (Table 1, Panel D) and identify functional centers that are using expense allocation bases that may be inconsistent with the activities that drive costs for that function. Using the information provided, suggest changes to the expense allocations for each function.

4. Table 2 shows the results of the test month of the first iteration for the system. Greg has confirmed that all expenses were allocated. Review the expense allocations used in the first test and discuss the functional centers in which the expense allocation bases have been improved and those that still may need improvement.

5. Table 4 shows the cost centers for the Life Insurance Projects functional center and a description of the activities in each cost center that make up that functional center. Based on this information, is the proposed basis for allocating expenses for these cost centers accurate? Why? How could it be improved?

6. Discuss the steps Greg should take to complete the project and then maintain the expense allocation process going forward. Based on the data provided, what additional steps can be taken to improve the product expense allocation process at AXE Life?

PHASE II: ACTIVITY-BASED COSTING

Greg charges the project team to begin work on the second phase of the project, which is to use the expense allocation process to begin to develop activity-based costs. As an initial step, the team reviews the information provided on the activities performed by each of the functions as shown in Table 2, Panel D, and categorizes the activities as unit, batch, product, and facility.

7. Activities can be categorized as unit, batch, product, and facility. Provide the definitions of each of these categories and then use the information in Table 2, Panel D, to categorize the activities as unit, batch, product, or facility.

8. As its next step, the team gathers information in Table 5 and calculates a rate for each of the functions based on the associated volumes. Use the information in Table 5 to calculate cost rates for the functions identified. Is this information sufficient for decision making? Why or why not?

Referring back to his discussion with the chief actuary, Greg identifies two activities to begin developing activity-based costs: the cost to issue life insurance products and the cost to service them. The project team defines the activities encompassing the cost to issue a policy as the cost to receive and process applications, underwrite policies and print, and collate and mail policies (termed "issuance"). The cost to maintain policies is defined as the cost of storing policy information, updating policy information as needed, responding to requests for service on insurance policies, the payment of claims and benefits, and the associated computer costs.

Table 4: Cost Level Data for Life Insurance Projects Function				
19008 Life Insurance Projects				
Cost Center Number	**Cost Center**	**Products Supported**	**Activity**	**Expense**
19008-001	Whole Life Series 2 Update	Whole Life Series 2	Update system to reflect 2012 changes in policy conditions	$ 12,425
19008-002	Variable Life Series 2 Update	Variable Life Series 2	Update system to reflect 2012 changes in policy conditions	11,429
19008-003	Term Life New Horizon Update	Term Life New Horizon	Update system to reflect 2012 changes in policy conditions	13,152
19008-004	Secure Life Project	Secure Life Project	System modifications for new secure life product	101,444
			Total	**$ 138,450**

Table 5: Cost and Volume Data

Department/Function	Driver	Volume	Expense
New Business Life	New life policies	9,345	$ 191,525
New Applications	Number of life applications	11,489	815,251
Policy Underwriting	Number of life applications	11,489	1,610,825
Policy Issuance – Life	Number of life policies issued	9,385	1,155,424
e-Policy Issuance – Life	Number of electronic life policies	2,185	172,515
New Business Annuity	New annuity policies	9,490	397,125
New Applications	Number of annuity applications	9,925	1,215,241
Policy Issued	New annuity policies	9,490	1,192,500
e-Policy Issuance – Annuity	Number of electronic annuities	1,145	173,525
Customer Service Management	Number of policies (all)	2,275,694	1,156,250
Call Center	Number of calls	34,884	910,257
Life Inforce Management	Number of life policies	1,735,251	1,115,497
Annuity Inforce Management	Number of annuities	540,443	1,485,273
Annuity Surrenders/Payments	Number of annuities	101,426	415,125
Claims Management	Number of life claims	11,327	1,101,010
Life Claims Adjusters	Number of life claims	11,327	1,415,000
Life Claims Support	Number of life claims	11,327	1,227,904
Life Claims System	Number of life claims	11,327	1,215,250
Life Insurance System	Number of life policies	1,735,251	1,229,850
Annuity System	Number of annuities	540,443	$1,201,525

As its first step, the team is going to focus on developing the costs to receive life insurance applications manually and issue a life insurance policy. During July 2012, the company received 11,489 applications and issued 9,385 life insurance policies. Not all applications are issued policies, thus the team must calculate the cost to receive and process the applications and adjust those costs to reflect that approximately one out of five applications does not result in a policy being issued.

9. Use the information provided in Table 6 to calculate the cost to issue a life insurance policy, including receiving and processing applications for each product.

10. Use the information from Table 7 to calculate the costs to service and maintain a policy for each product. Assume that AXE Life has defined the cost to service and maintain a policy as the customer service costs, call center costs, and costs to adjudicate and pay claims. What do you notice about the costs per policy? Is there other information that would make this analysis more useful?

11. An activity-based costing system would provide AXE Life with an understanding of the costs to develop, sell, and service their products. How can AXE Life use this information to improve the efficiency and cost effectiveness of their operations?

12. Greg also read an article that stated that using time-driven activity-based costing reduces the time and complexity associated with implementing an activity-based costing system. Based on his understanding, Greg believes that using a time-driven system may be an efficient way of implementing activity-based costing. Describe how Greg can create an activity-based costing system and include the steps necessary if the team follows (a) the traditional approach to activity-based costing and (b) a time-driven activity-based costing approach.

Table 6: Cost to Receive and Process Life Insurance Application – July 2012

Volumes for Cost Drivers

Applications   11,489

New Life Policies   9,385

Function	Variable	Fixed	Total	Characteristics of Costs
New Business – Life (Management): Manage new policy underwriting and issuance				
Salaries & Benefits		112,522	112,522	Fixed within range of +/- 20% of current levels
Supplies		4,252	4,252	Fixed within range of +/- 20% of current levels
Depreciation – Furniture		10,200	10,200	Fixed within range of +/- 20% of current levels
Leased PCs		14,650	14,650	Fixed within range of +/- 20% of current levels
Allocated Rent		15,250	15,250	Fixed within range of +/- 20% of current levels
All Other		34,651	34,651	Fixed within range of +/- 20% of current levels
Total		**$191,525**	**$191,525**	
New Applications: Receive and review new life policy applications				
Salaries & Benefits	225,125	252,500	477,625	Hourly, part time considered variable; others are within a range of +/- 20% of current levels
Supplies	62,150		62,150	Vary with applications
Depreciation – Furniture		32,500	32,500	Fixed within range of +/- 20% of current levels
Leased PCs		52,500	52,500	Fixed within range of +/- 20% of current levels
Allocated Rent		65,250	65,250	Fixed within range of +/- 20% of current levels
All Other		125,226	125,226	Fixed within range of +/- 20% of current levels
Total	**$287,275**	**$527,976**	**$815,251**	
Policy Underwriting: Review and underwrite new life policies				
Salaries & Benefits	375,125	512,500	887,625	Hourly, part time considered variable; others are within a range of +/- 20% of current levels
Medical reports	215,047		215,047	Vary with applications
Supplies	61,250		61,250	Vary with applications
Depreciation – Furniture		51,500	51,500	Fixed within range of +/- 20% of current levels
Leased PCs		62,500	62,500	Fixed within range of +/- 20% of current levels
Allocated Rent		125,250	125,250	Fixed within range of +/- 20% of current levels
All Other		207,653	207,653	Fixed within range of +/- 20% of current levels
Total	**$651,422**	**$959,403**	**$1,610,825**	
Policy Issuance: Process and issue new life policies				
Postage & Mail Costs	37,540		37,540	Vary with applications
Salaries & Benefits	412,525	125,862	538,387	Hourly, part time considered variable; others are within a range of +/- 20% of current levels
Supplies	72,175		72,175	Vary with applications
Depreciation – Furniture		56,750	56,750	Fixed within range of +/- 20% of current levels
Leased PCs		82,500	82,500	Fixed within range of +/- 20% of current levels
Allocated Rent		145,250	145,250	Fixed within range of +/- 20% of current levels
All Other		260,362	260,362	Fixed within range of +/- 20% of current levels
Total	**$484,700**	**$670,724**	**$1,155,424**	

Table 7: Cost to Service Life Insurance Policies

Function	Variable	Fixed	Total	Characteristics of Costs
Customer Service Management: Manage customer service support of existing policies				
Salaries & Benefits	254,750	495,250	750,000	Hourly, part time considered variable; others are within a range of +/- 20% of current levels
Supplies	21,520		21,520	Fixed within range of +/- 20% of current levels
Depreciation – Furniture		55,425	55,425	Fixed within range of +/- 20% of current levels
Leased PCs		47,500	47,500	Fixed within range of +/- 20% of current levels
Allocated Rent		82,500	82,500	Fixed within range of +/- 20% of current levels
All Other		199,305	199,305	Fixed within range of +/- 20% of current levels
Total	**$ 276,270**	**$879,980**	**$1,156,250**	
Call Center: Respond to customer inquiries				
Salaries & Benefits	415,150	42,520	457,670	Hourly, part time considered variable; others are within a range of +/- 20% of current levels
Supplies	21,514		21,514	Vary with applications
Depreciation – Furniture		62,520	62,520	Fixed within range of +/- 20% of current levels
Leased PCs		55,125	55,125	Fixed within range of +/- 20% of current levels
Allocated Rent		90,500	90,500	Fixed within range of +/- 20% of current levels
All Other		222,928	222,928	Fixed within range of +/- 20% of current levels
Total	**$436,664**	**$250,665**	**$910,257**	
Life Inforce Management: Provide service to all existing policies (changes in beneficiary, address, questions)				
Salaries & Benefits	514,250	120,125	634,375	Hourly, part time considered variable; others are within a range of +/- 20% of current levels
Supplies	44,450		44,450	Vary with policies
Depreciation – Furniture		71,500	71,500	Fixed within range of +/- 20% of current levels
Leased PCs		61,750	61,750	Fixed within range of +/- 20% of current levels
Allocated Rent		95,120	95,120	Fixed within range of +/- 20% of current levels
All Other		208,280	208,280	Fixed within range of +/- 20% of current levels
Total	**$558,700**	**$348,495**	**$1,115,475**	
Claims Management: Manage claims process				
Salaries & Benefits	417,500	215,250	632,750	Hourly, part time considered variable; others are within a range of +/- 20% of current levels
Supplies	21,250		21,250	Vary with policies
Depreciation – Furniture		81,742	81,742	Fixed within range of +/- 20% of current levels
Leased PCs		91,250	91,250	Fixed within range of +/- 20% of current levels
Allocated Rent		111,500	111,500	Fixed within range of +/- 20% of current levels
All Other			162,518	Fixed within range of +/- 20% of current levels
Total	**$438,750**	**$499,742**	**$1,101,010**	
Claims Adjusters: Adjudicate claims				
Salaries & Benefits	607,150	333,525	940,675	Hourly, part time considered variable; others are within a range of +/- 20% of current levels
Supplies	41,525		41,525	Vary with policies
Depreciation – Furniture		101,525	101,525	Fixed within range of +/- 20% of current levels
Leased PCs		100,752	100,752	Fixed within range of +/- 20% of current levels
Allocated Rent		117,850	117,850	Fixed within range of +/- 20% of current levels
All Other		112,673	112,673	Fixed within range of +/- 20% of current levels
Total	**$648,675**	**$653,625**	**$1,415,000**	

Table 7: Cost to Service Life Insurance Policies (continued)

Function	Variable	Fixed	Total	Characteristics of Costs
Life Claims Support: Support claims adjusters, process and issue all claims checks				
Postage & Mail Costs	91,425		91,425	Vary with claims paid
Salaries & Benefits	481,500	112,525	594,025	Hourly, part time considered variable; others are within a range of +/- 20% of current levels
Supplies	41,525		41,525	Vary with applications
Depreciation – Furniture		91,250	91,250	Fixed within range of +/- 20% of current levels
Leased PCs		77,141	77,141	Fixed within range of +/- 20% of current levels
Allocated Rent		99,750	99,750	Fixed within range of +/- 20% of current levels
All Other		23,788	232,788	Fixed within range of +/- 20% of current levels
Total	**$614,450**	**$613,454**	**$1,227,904**	
Life Insurance Systems: System and IT personnel that supports life insurance policies				
Salaries & Benefits	115,400	411,500	526,900	Hourly, part time considered variable; others are within a range of +/- 20% of current levels
Supplies	11,750		11,750	Vary with applications
Depreciation – Furniture		66,271	66,271	Fixed within range of +/- 20% of current levels
Leased PCs		77,141	77,141	Fixed within range of +/- 20% of current levels
Allocated Rent		61,250	61,250	Fixed within range of +/- 20% of current levels
All Other		471,938	471,938	Fixed, mostly system maintenance charges
Total	**$127,150**	**$1,088,100**	**$1,215,250**	
Life Claims Systems: System and IT personnel that support life insurance claims				
Salaries & Benefits	115,400	372,500	487,900	Hourly, part time considered variable; others are within a range of +/- 20% of current levels
Supplies	33,250		33,250	Vary with applications
Depreciation – Furniture		88,815	88,815	Fixed within range of +/- 20% of current levels
Leased PCs		91,250	91,250	Fixed within range of +/- 20% of current levels
Allocated Rent		91,475	91,475	Fixed within range of +/- 20% of current levels
All Other		437,160	437,160	Fixed, mostly system maintenance charges
Total	**$148,650**	**$1,081,200**	**$1,229,850**	

ADDITIONAL READING

Robert S. Kaplan and Steven R. Anderson, "Time-Driven Activity-Based Costing," *Harvard Business Review*, November 2004.

Mohan Nair, "Activity-Based Costing: Who's Using It and Why?" *Management Accounting Quarterly*, Spring 2000, pp. 29-33.

Anna Szychta, "Time-Driven Activity-Based Costing in Service Industries," *Social Sciences/Socialiniai Mokslai*, 2010, pp. 49-60.

Dynamic Medical Solutions: Expanding the Application of Cost Management Principles to Channel and Customer Profitability Analysis

Casey J. McNellis and Ronald F. Premuroso, University of Montana

THIS CASE DESCRIBES THE SALES OF DYNAMIC MEDICAL SOLUTIONS (DMS), a medical products supplier (as a retailer of products manufactured by others), whose reimbursements for sales made to customers eligible for Medicare and Medicaid appear to be in violation of government reimbursement guidelines. The case is an illustration of one of the major emerging trends in management accounting: expansion of profitability analysis from cost allocations focused primarily on product costs to sales channels and/or customer types, including the allocation of nonproduct costs.

This real-world case requires students to first understand the dilemma faced by the company, including information regarding certain products and sales channels and related product cost data, departmental processes, and related operating expenses from its latest year of operations. The student's task is to evaluate alternatives the company should consider with regard to cost allocations to specific products and sales channels along with their resulting impact on product pricing and channel profitability. Students will then be in a position to make recommendations ensuring both qualitative and quantitative compliance with government regulations for Medicare and Medicaid reimbursements.

This case study is intended for students enrolled in upper-division or graduate-level cost management courses in either an undergraduate or graduate accounting program. The case can also be used in an advanced managerial accounting MBA course.

Keywords: product line profitability analysis, Medicare, Medicaid, good cause.

The Association of
Accountants and
Financial Professionals
in Business

Dynamic Medical Solutions: Expanding the Application of Cost Management Principles to Channel and Customer Profitability Analysis

Casey J. McNellis, Ph.D., CPA
University of Montana

Ronald F. Premuroso, Ph.D., CPA, CFE
University of Montana

COMPANY INTRODUCTION AND CASE BACKGROUND

Dynamic Medical Solutions (DMS) is a small company that sells (as a retailer of products manufactured by others) durable and nondurable medical products to customers in seven states across the United States. Some of the popular durable products sold by the company are hospital beds, diabetic footwear, and mobility equipment (i.e., wheelchairs, scooters, etc.). A large portion of the company's business involves the sale of durable and nondurable medical supplies including nutrition supplements, gloves, and personal care products used in patient care. All of the products carried by DMS are over-the-counter items and thus do not require a physician's prescription.[1] Like most companies in the medical products supply industry, DMS serves a multitude of customers, including those with (1) no insurance (i.e., cash and carry), (2) Medicare and Medicaid benefits (i.e., government programs),[2] and (3) private insurance. Accordingly, DMS has a billing department internally for customers with such benefits and insurance. Many customers, including those enrolled in government programs and those who pay for products out of pocket (i.e., cash and carry) are elderly and/or reside in assisted-living facilities. The company employs sales representatives who visit these facilities and interact with the customers and their caregivers on a regular basis and establish the ordering process for the customers via phone or fax. Customers also are able to purchase goods at one of the company's five retail stores via the company's website or through the phone/fax process with a sales representative.

In regard to cash and carry customers, DMS strives to offer competitive prices as the company is directly competing with large national retail stores that offer many types of medical products and operate on small profit margins. Serving cash and carry customers is fairly straightforward, involving no other considerations beyond the typical sales initiation (i.e., visits from a sales representative), point-of-sale sales, and warehouse shipping or customer pick-up processes.

On the other hand, serving government programs customers is more restrictive and requires an extensive number of internal processes and procedures. The prices charged to these customers (i.e., the reimbursement amount) are set by the program entity (i.e., Medicaid or Medicare). Most importantly, the process of selling goods involves additional mandated (by law) considerations beyond the normal cash-and-carry process, including the written verification of medical necessity from the customer's physician, the processing of insurance claims, and the substantiation of product delivery. For many of the nondurable medical supplies, such as nutrition supplements and gloves, the process is even more cumbersome as these products are supplied to customers on a monthly basis. Accordingly, proof of medical necessity for these products also has to be updated on a recurring basis. This involves additional interaction by the company with primary care physicians and Medicare/Medicaid representatives, as well as increased processing of paperwork.

Sales to customers using private insurance comprise an immaterial amount of the company's revenues. Most private insurance companies cover only a minor amount of the charges for the products offered by DMS, often after a government program has been billed first and has paid for the majority of the charge billed by DMS.

Table 1 provides a breakdown of DMS's sales for the most recent financial year, along with other relevant financial information (excluding an immaterial amount for private insurance-related sales).

Table 1: DMS Sales by Customer Type and Other Financial Information

	Sales	% of Total Sales
Government Programs Sales	$3,000,000	75.0%
Cash and Carry Sales	$1,000,000	25.0%
Total Net Sales	**$4,000,000**	**100.0%**
Cost of Sales	($1,300,000)	32.5%
Gross Profit	**$2,700,000**	**67.5%**
Operating Expenses	($2,200,000)	55.0%
Operating Income	**$ 500,000**	**12.5%**

The company's operations are divided into five departments: Customer Service, Shipping, Billing, Compliance, and Administration. Table 2 includes a breakdown of the operating expenses by department along with a brief description of the general functions carried out by each department for the most recent financial year.

Table 2: Department Operating Expenses and Descriptions

Department	Operating Expenses	Description of Functions
Customer Service	$660,000	Process sales orders; support customer base
Shipping	$870,000	Prepare orders for shipment; track shipments to delivery
Billing	$120,000	Submit insurance claims; monitor customer eligibility for government programs
Compliance	$120,000	Monitor company policies regarding government programs
Administration	$430,000	Perform bookkeeping, payroll, and marketing functions; heat, light, and power; insurance expenses; execute strategic plan
Total Operating Expenses	$2,200,000	

REGULATORY ENVIRONMENT

As Table 1 depicts, DMS's primary source of sales are from customers who are eligible for assistance from government-related healthcare programs. As such, the company's success is largely based on understanding government regulations, policies, and procedures governing Medicare and Medicaid programs, including reimbursements.

Because of past alleged abuses of these government insurance programs by healthcare providers, Federal and state authorities have enacted several regulations under the Social Security Act for providers like DMS involved with submitting reimbursement claims under government programs. For example, the Department of Health and Human Services (HHS) has the power to revoke a company's privileges to serve Medicare and Medicaid customers if the company has been involved in criminal activity, patient abuse, and/or healthcare fraud. Additionally, the Act also allows HHS to prohibit a company from engaging in business activities with Medicare and/or Medicaid if the company submits product reimbursement claims for government programs customers significantly higher than amounts charged to cash and carry customers. Specifically, Section 1128(b) of the Act states that HHS:

"…may exclude…from participation in any Federal health care program…any individual or entity that the Secretary determines…has submitted or caused to be submitted bills or requests for payment (where such bills or requests are based on charges or cost) under Title XVIII or a State health care program containing charges (or, in applicable cases, requests for payment of costs) for items or services furnished **substantially in excess** of such individual's or entity's **usual charges** (or, in applicable cases, substantially in excess of such individual's or entity's costs) for such items or services, unless the Secretary finds there is **good cause** for such bills or requests containing such charges or costs." (Emphasis added.)

The language of this regulation was further interpreted in a proposal by the Office of the Inspector General (OIG) in June 2007.[3] The phrase "usual charges" was suggested to include "charges billed directly to cash paying patients" (i.e., cash and carry customers). The term "substantially in excess" was defined by the OIG proposal as charges exceeding "120 percent of an individual's or entity's usual charges." Finally, the OIG proposed that "good cause" for "substantially in excess" charges could be established in a number of ways, including, for example, evidence of "increased costs associated with serving Medicare or Medicaid beneficiaries."

DMS'S DILEMMA

DMS sends a member of the management team to a government programs seminar, where firms are provided information and guidelines regarding Federal regulations governing Medicare and Medicaid reimbursements. The team member is amazed by the number of regulations governing these programs, including the one mentioned earlier. Because the team member is not familiar with the methods that ensure DMS is in compliance with these regulations, he holds a meeting with the rest of the management team to discuss the regulations. The management team agrees it is necessary to hire a healthcare consultant to review DMS's policies, procedures, and billing practices for products sold to customers under government programs.

After examining DMS's operations in some detail, the healthcare consultant hired by DMS informed management of a grim, unexpected finding: DMS's product pricing appeared to be in violation of Federal regulations governing Medicare and Medicaid reimbursements. The aforementioned regulation was the issue referenced by the healthcare consultant in determining DMS was potentially in violation of the Federal Act. The consultant examined all of the company's products and determined many of them had Medicaid reimbursement rates "substantially in excess" of prices charged to cash and carry customers. According to the consultant, DMS would likely have to change its pricing structure and/or potentially eliminate the sale of certain products sold by the company to remedy the violation. Accordingly, the company was advised to employ one of the following courses of action: either raise cash and carry prices for products not complying with the 120% proposed "rule," or eliminate sales of the two selected products to cash and carry customers. Discouraged by the findings and faced with uncertainty and potentially disastrous consequences, the DMS management team members contemplated their next moves.

DMS'S INITIAL CONCERNS AND RESPONSE

Given the substantial portion of DMS's sales from customers eligible for government program reimbursements, the issue of product pricing is therefore critical to the company. Prices offered to cash and carry customers must be competitive, yet they must be within a certain percentage of government program reimbursement claims in order for DMS to comply with government regulations. As such, pricing decisions have the potential to not only adversely impact DMS's market share of cash and carry customers but also may put the company's ability to sell and receive reimbursement for these products under the respective government programs in jeopardy.

Unhappy with these two alternatives suggested by the consultant, company officials began compiling product pricing and costing data, as well as observing and documenting key operational aspects of the business to determine the extent of the problem revealed by the consultant and to develop potential alternative courses of action.

SELECTED PRODUCT PRICING DATA

The first two products examined by management were the nutrition supplement and nondurable gloves, two products eligible for reimbursement under government insurance programs. Table 3 includes selected information for these two products in the latest financial year.

Table 3: Information for Selected Products Offered by DMS		
	Nutrition Supplement (1 can)	**Nondurable Gloves (1 box)**
Retail sales price (paid by cash and carry customers)	$1.54	$6.95
Maximum permitted selling price to government*	$2.20	$8.82
Product cost	$0.66	$2.65
Product sales as a % of cash and carry sales	3%	4%
Quantity of product sold to cash and carry customers	19,480 cans	5,755 boxes
Product sales as a % of government programs sales	6%	6%
Quantity of product sold to government programs customers	81,800 cans	20,408 boxes

*This maximum permitted selling price to the government applies to all companies in general under specific regulations pertaining to these products issued by the government.

BUSINESS OBSERVATIONS

Management was inclined to believe disproportionate shares of company resources were being devoted to serving government program customers, especially in the case of nutrition and nondurable products (i.e., gloves), which involved additional processing costs in order to comply with regulations. But they had no formal evidence to support this belief and thus needed to obtain relevant information about the efforts being exerted to serve the two different customer types: cash and carry and government programs. As a first step, the officials observed employees from each department to obtain an understanding of the sales and order fulfillment processes, separately, for the cash and carry and government program customers. Information about these processes from new sales origination all of the way through billing are detailed in Table 4.

As part of these observations, company employees from selected departments were asked to keep track of the amount of time they spent on the different types of customer orders and related activities for a one-month period. Because of increased work demands at the time the study was performed, similar time data was not immediately obtained from employees working in the Shipping or Administration departments. The results are presented in Table 5.[4]

Table 4: Summary of Relevant Portions of Company Processes	
New sales origination	**Cash and carry**: A company salesperson visits nursing homes, hospitals, and assisted-living facilities, speaking with potential customers and guardians. The salesperson takes orders and phones/faxes them to warehouse customer service representatives. **Government programs:** Same as cash and carry.
Recurring sales	**Cash and carry:** A customer service representative contacts customers and takes sales orders. **Government programs:** Same as cash and carry.
Order fulfillment	**Cash and carry:** A representative from customer service enters the order into the company's accounting system. The system produces a pick slip, which is forwarded to Shipping. The employees in Shipping fill the order, which is then given to a third-party courier for delivery. A copy of the pick slip is sent back to the customer service representative. **Government programs:** Per regulations, DMS must obtain a valid identification card proving the customer's eligibility for the government program. To establish medical necessity, a doctor's order is required to be submitted with each order. A customer service representative prepares fax inquiries to the customer's physician (to establish medical necessity) and to the customer for valid proof of eligibility (if a copy was not obtained by the salesperson). Upon receipt of this documentation, the order is entered into the accounting system. The system produces a pick slip, which is forwarded to Shipping. The employees in Shipping fill the order, which is then given to a third-party courier for delivery. A copy of the pick slip is sent to a Billing representative. Shipping employees track shipments with the courier's website to confirm delivery.
Billing	**Cash and carry:** A representative from customer service examines the pick slips sent back from Shipping and prepares an invoice to the customer. The customer has 30 days to pay the invoice. **Government programs:** A representative from Billing prepares a government program claim and submits it. The reimbursement usually takes between 15-60 days.
Other	**Government programs: Renewals for nutrition and nondurable goods:** Periodically, a customer's physician order and proof of eligibility documentation are required to be renewed. A billing representative tracks these customers and prepares renewal requests when appropriate. **Government programs: Oversight:** Per regulations, DMS is required to have a compliance program staffed with a compliance officer, whose sole responsibility is to oversee compliance issues and related employee training.
Retail store and website transactions	Customers also visit the company's retail stores and website on their own. For cash and carry customers, the retail store process in similar to point-of-sale transactions of major retail stores. For website sales, a sales representative is not involved. Rather, the customer places the order, which is then sent to a customer service representative. At that point, the customer service representative processes the order in the same way as described under "Order fulfillment." Transactions with government programs customers visiting the retail stores are still processed in accordance with the steps above. But no sales representative is involved in the transaction. In general, government programs customers do not place orders via the company website.

Table 5: Results of Employee Study and Selection of Operating Cost Allocation Bases		
Department	Average % Time – Government Programs	Average % Time – Cash and Carry
Customer Service	85%	15%
Shipping	No Data Available	No Data Available
Billing	100%	0%
Compliance	100%	0%
Administration	No Data Available	No Data Available

CASE QUESTIONS

1. Why are government regulators sensitive to the amount of claims submitted to the government insurance programs in comparison to retail prices?

2. Why potentially could/would government programs reimbursement amounts exceed the retail sales prices for products?

3. Consider the information provided for the two products shown in Table 3. In accordance with the OIG's suggestions for "substantially in excess," are the government programs reimbursement rates for each product presently "substantially in excess" of the "usual charges"? Provide the details of your calculations in your submission.

4. Assuming at least one of the products violates the OIG's suggestion for "substantially in excess," discuss the impact of the following three potential solutions to this dilemma on DMS's market share, operations, exposure to liability, and so on. In your assessment, consider the future financial implications of the three alternatives along with the assumptions you have made in your analysis.

   a. Raise prices charged to cash and carry customers such that the government programs reimbursement rate is no more than 20% higher than the newly calculated amount.

   b. When submitting government program claims, request reimbursement amounts below the maximum allowable reimbursement rates in order to be within 20% of the prices charged to cash and carry customers.

   c. Attempt to establish "good cause." Refer to some of the principles and concepts you have learned or are learning in your cost management course (for example, Customer Profitability Analysis and allocations of overhead) in establishing "good cause." Provide details of your calculations, which will aid DMS in establishing "good cause" and apply them to the two specific products shown in Table 3. (Hint: This will require you to perform cost allocations and select appropriate bases for the allocation(s).) What are your revised total cost per unit and overall profit margin amounts on the two products?

5. Looking back at your calculations and analyses performed in question 4c, do you believe the company can establish and support "good cause' in submitting claims for the maximum allowable rates offered by government programs? In answering the question, first consider the qualitative evidence you have already developed. Second, develop a quantitative analysis appropriate to use in establishing or supporting your qualitative evidence.

6. In anticipation of the regulating agencies performing an investigation into the pricing structure of DMS, identify the strengths and weaknesses of the work performed by DMS in response to the consultant's findings as well as the analysis you provided in the previous questions. How should DMS address the weaknesses in preparation for the audit?

ENDNOTES

[1] On the other hand, customers with private insurance or access to government medical programs are required to provide evidence of medical necessity, which is often indicated by physician orders, for reimbursement.

[2] Medicare is a national social insurance program administered by the U.S. Federal Government since 1966, which guarantees access to health insurance coverage for U.S. citizens age 65 or older who have worked and paid into the program. Medicaid is a U.S. government insurance program for all U.S. citizens whose income or personal resources are unable to pay for their personal healthcare.

[3] Department of Health and Human Services (HHS) and the Office of the Inspector General (OIG), "Medicare and State Health Care Programs: Fraud and Abuse; Clarification of Terms and Application of Program Exclusion Authority for Submitting Claims Containing Excessive Charges," Federal Register Volume 72, No. 116, June 18, 2007.

[4] The firm does not have any type of bank borrowings or debt, and thus there is no interest expense in overhead-related expenses to consider.

Product Costing at Fine Foods: Is it a Symptom or the Problem?

David Axelsson, Marcus Fogelkvist, and Gary M. Cunningham

THIS CASE FOCUSES ON ISSUES THAT APPEAR TO BE problems but are symptoms of more fundamental problems. These are common issues in management accounting and management control situations. It also provides a good overview of product costing and performance evaluation, accounting for special orders, and agency costs and benefits including nonquantifiable costs and benefits. The case is based on an actual food processing company that had these issues. It can be used to cover manufacturing accounting in many other contexts as well.

This case is designed primarily for master's degree students taking advanced management accounting or management control courses. It can also be used in advanced undergraduate classes in management accounting in which students have had a prior background in basic cost and management accounting concepts.

Keywords: symptoms vs. problems, product costing, performance evaluation, special orders, nonquantifiable agency costs and benefits.

The Association of
Accountants and
Financial Professionals
in Business

Product Costing at Fine Foods:
Is It a Symptom or the Problem?

David Axelsson is the accountant and controller for an expanding wholesaler, board member for a family business, and member and vice-chairman of the board of directors for a local bank.

Marcus Fogelkvist is the international research and development group controller for a large hard goods manufacturing multinational company.

Gary M. Cunningham, Ph.D., is Professor Emeritus and Research Fellow at Gävle University in Gävle, Sweden.

INTRODUCTION

Kay Smith is the manager of Strategic Marketing Unit Two (SMU2) at Fine Foods, Inc., a provider of branded, high-quality food products. Smith is unhappy with what she perceives to be unfair and inappropriate product costing for her unit, especially for what Fine Foods considers to be special orders. Smith's education, experience, and expertise as a food scientist and process engineer have earned her considerable respect at Fine Foods, but she has limited accounting knowledge, which holds her back from expressing her serious concerns. Therefore, Smith asked you, a recent accounting graduate, to develop a draft memorandum, a slide presentation, and a glossary of terms to help her make her case more forcefully to management.

FINE FOODS, INC.

Fine Foods, Inc., rooted in the upper Midwest United States, produces a wide range of food products in a competitive industry. Almost all of its products are sold under the Fine 'n' Fast brand name, which is widely recognized for its high quality and has a loyal customer following. Most products are packaged in sizes for end-consumption and are sold through supermarkets,

convenience shops, and similar outlets. Depending on the nature of the product and consumer preferences, products are sold frozen, refrigerated, canned, boxed, or packaged in other ways. Some items, such as individual packets of ketchup, mayonnaise, and mustard, are sold to fast food restaurants and similar outlets. The company also sells half-gallon containers—branded with the company logo—of salad dressings, ketchup, mustard, and similar items with a plastic pump so that restaurant customers can serve themselves at salad bars and similar places. Other products are sold, often in bulk, to institutional users, such as large food service groups, caterers, and the like. These products may or may not be branded. A small portion of sales is made to other food producers, for example, salad dressing packets are sold to producers of packaged fresh salad greens; Fine Foods does not deal with fresh products.

Fine Foods is owned by Great Plains Capital, a private equity firm. Great Plains Capital gives Fine Foods almost complete freedom and control over management, product selection, performance evaluation, and so forth. Because it is privately owned, external financial reporting is not mandatory, nor is there any obligation to use any set of financial accounting standards for internal reporting. Any external financial reporting is on a group or consolidated basis and performed by Great Plains Capital.

Great Plains Capital also owns Fine Foods Canada, Ltd., which sells products almost exclusively in Canada, with primary operations nearby in the prairie provinces. There is no mutual ownership or management connection between Fine Foods and Fine Foods Canada. Because the two companies produce many identical products using the Fine 'n' Fast brand, they do share recipes and process technology. Fine Foods also produces some products for Fine Foods Canada that do not have sufficient market size in Canada to justify separate production. Great Plains Capital also owns smaller companies with the Fine 'n' Fast name that are mostly importers of Fine 'n' Fast products in countries outside of the U.S. and Canada where high-quality, branded North American food products have niche markets. These products are produced by Fine Foods.

Fine Foods is organized into three Strategic Marketing Units (SMUs) based on the markets they serve. SMU1 serves supermarkets and similar outlets. SMU2 serves mostly institutional customers who order in large volumes and often in bulk quantities. SMU2 also sells special orders from time to time that involve unbranded bulk products that are exported. SMU3 serves affiliated Fine Foods companies in other countries, mostly for import into those countries; governmental organizations that sell food and have food service facilities, such as military organizations; and similar customers that have special contracting requirements.

Products sold by all three SMUs are manufactured by the same production facilities, including warehouses, food preparation and cooking facilities, and packaging facilities. The SMUs also share most headquarters activities, such as information technology, accounting and other administration, human resources, and similar activities. SMU1 and SMU2 have their own marketing and sales departments, while SMU3 does not have separate departments for these tasks. Figure 1 shows an organizational chart for Fine Foods.

COST ALLOCATION

Smith strongly and persistently tells you that she believes her unit is being treated unfairly in the way costs are allocated to products. In particular, she has a problem with the product cost allocation for special orders of product MP, a basic product that is widely consumed in North America. SMU2 is the only unit filling special orders, and almost all of the special orders are for product MP. While all three units sell product MP, it represents a significantly larger percentage of total sales for SMU2 than it does for the other two units. SMU1 and SMU3 do not perceive a product costing problem because a substantial portion of their sales come from other products, which means the product costs for product MP are not a major part of their cost of sales.

After talking with Smith, you review what you learned in your accounting classes about product costing and special orders. With this knowledge, you set out to conduct an in-depth look at product costing and accounting for special orders at Fine Foods, especially in SMU2.

THE PRODUCTION PROCESS

In order to learn about product costing at Fine Foods, you decide that first you need to understand the physical flow of products through production lines. A simplified diagram of the product MP production process, which is typical of many of the company's products, is shown in Figure 2.

Basic raw food items begin production with preliminary inspection, sorting, and so forth. The raw material then goes to the first stage of preparation, which can involve chopping and peeling, as well as some preliminary cooking. After possible temporary storage, additional ingredients are added, such as seasonings, flavorings, and so on, and then the final cooking and processing occurs. The prepared product is then packaged, frozen, stored temporarily (if necessary), and then shipped to the customer.

PRODUCT COSTING

The management of Fine Foods believes that it must allocate *all* costs to its products in order to get a true and accurate measure of each product's profitability. Here is a look at the product costing procedure that would apply to product MP, as well as virtually all other products. Product MP is one of several different products that comes from the same initial raw material but are then processed and sold in different configurations and package sizes.

Raw material, packaging material, and direct production salaries are added to determine what Fine Foods calls *direct calculated costs*. Electricity, steam, water, and warehouse costs are then allocated based on estimates and a mark-up to cover spoilage and other incalculable costs. This calculation gives an amount the company calls *variable manufacturing costs*. Material costs are determined based on the cost required for one unit of product. Direct salaries are determined by the amount of time normally required for one unit multiplied by the hourly labor cost.

Fine Foods allocates what it considers to be *fixed production costs* in a complicated process. A list of what Fine Foods considers to be fixed production costs is shown in Table 1.

Costs for production management, steam boilers, and quality are shared by different factories. Estimates are made about usage of these activities, and costs are allocated to factories based on these estimates. If only one factory uses a service, the entire cost of the service is allocated to that factory. When these and other costs are assigned to factories, two approaches are used for further allocation to product groups (such as salad dressings, canned soups and vegetables, and puddings) and products:

- All costs for steam boilers, building maintenance, vehicles, and sanitation are allocated directly to products using net weight or gross weight.
- Remaining factory costs are first allocated to product groups. One allocation is a fixed percentage based on estimates that do not change for each product group. Other costs are allocated based on the weight, labor time, and production time of the product produced. If the allocation of remaining factory costs is a fixed percentage, then allocation to products is based on production time.
- For special orders (virtually all product MP), the total *freight out* is accumulated for a month and then allocated based on the weight of product shipped. The estimated freight cost is included in the sales price. Similar procedures are followed for other products, for which Fine Foods pays the freight.

Media and sales promotion costs for SMU1 and SMU2 are allocated to product groups and to individual products based on weight of product sold.

Fine Foods allocates what it calls *other fixed costs* in two ways:

- Sales and marketing costs, which are incurred only in SMU1 and SMU2, are allocated to products based on sales volume.
- Costs for top management, business administration, information systems, human resources, supply management, and logistics are allocated in two steps. Costs are first allocated to cost centers based on number of employees, labor time, production time, or set percentages. Then costs are further allocated to products based on gross sales, amount of time spent on internal reviews, number of marketing campaigns, quantity sold, number of orders, net weight of product delivered, or equally to each product.

Smith is concerned that the amount of costs allocated to special orders for product MP is excessive and therefore causing her unit to be viewed less favorably than the other units. Among other things, she believes allocations based on weight are unfair because product MP is a relatively dense, bulky, and heavy product that, while profitable, has a relatively low profit per pound compared to other products.

SPECIAL ORDERS

Because of Smith's concerns, you further explore what Fine Foods considers to be *special orders*. According to Smith, a special order is one in which the contract specifies that it can be rejected within one year before delivery, otherwise it is not special. Such special orders constitute 2% of total revenues for Fine Foods.

Virtually all of the special orders are for product MP and for a food distributor in Mexico. Product MP is not a normal part of the diet of Mexican people, but there is a niche market for it. The market is not large enough to motivate a Mexican food production company to produce the item, but Fine Foods is motivated to provide the items to Mexican food suppliers as so-called special orders because the company is already producing the product for a variety of customers in the U.S. and Canada. It is packaged unbranded for sale in Mexico because it will be used primarily by institutional food preparers; it is shipped frozen in 10-pound packages.

The raw material used to make product MP can be kept in storage for a fairly long time under proper conditions, and there is always a ready stock on hand because it is used in many other products. Once product MP is produced, it can be kept frozen for up to one year. These factors provide a high degree of flexibility in scheduling production to meet such special orders. Production of product MP can be readily scheduled when there is idle production capacity. Sometimes requests for these special orders come unexpectedly; other times, SMU2 approaches the customer to indicate that idle capacity is planned. Typically, orders are in relatively large quantities.

SMU2 accepts special orders when the contribution margin (CM1) is positive. Fine Foods defines CM1 as net sales minus variable manufacturing costs, fixed manufacturing costs, and freight out (see Table 2). Smith is convinced that decisions to accept the special orders are good for the company and contribute to Fine Foods' overall profitability, but she is frustrated at the impact on the results of her unit's operations.

PERFORMANCE EVALUATION IN FINE FOODS

Halfway through your project, you discuss it with friends and colleagues who are also recent accounting graduates. As you describe Smith's concerns with Fine Foods' product costing, as well as your frustration with analyzing and developing recommendations, one friend interrupts to say that the product costing problem appears to be only a symptom of a larger issue. Your friend had recently covered the issue of symptoms vs. underlying problems in her management control class, and it seemed to her that the major issue is performance evaluation of the SMUs, not product costing.

Somewhat skeptical, you look at some of your textbooks and other sources to brush up on performance evaluation. Then you explore performance evaluation at Fine Foods. You begin by speaking to Peter Jones, the controller of Fine Foods, who explains how the company computes CM1, CM2, CM3, CM4, and operating profit for each unit (see Table 2). Jones says the SMUs have the ability to control the costs of their divisions, and other costs are allocated easily and fairly. Targets are established for CM1, CM2, CM3, CM4, and operating profit, and the numbers are reviewed monthly to see if corrective action is necessary. Evaluation of performance against the targets is made at the end of the year.

Smith, however, tells you that the primary evaluation for the SMUs is operating profit. Jones and another unit controller confirm it. Smith feels the method used by Fine Foods to calculate operating profit does not reflect the true performance of the SMUs because unit management cannot control several of the cost elements included in the calculation. Further, she believes using operating profit as the primary indicator for evaluating units has a negative motivational effect on the employees of her unit.

YOUR REPORT

PART 1: PRODUCT COSTING

1. Develop a glossary of terms and definitions for Smith to use in her presentation and discussions to ensure consistency and mutual understanding of terms. In addition to definitions, provide a brief description of the applicability of terms to Fine Foods. The glossary should include, but not be limited to:

- Cost Object
- Cost Driver
- Product vs. Period Costs
- Fixed vs. Variable Costs
- Direct vs. Indirect Costs
- Incremental vs. Common Costs
- Relevant vs. Irrelevant Costs
- Controllable vs. Uncontrollable Costs
- Dual Allocation (sometimes called Departmental Costs)
- Volume Allocation
- Activity-Based Costing

2. Write a draft of a memorandum that Smith can present to her colleagues and management to support her case. The memo should include, but not be limited to, an analysis of current product costing approaches used at Fine Foods, changes she should recommend, and the extent to which the recommended changes would resolve her concerns.

PART 2: SPECIAL ORDERS

Write a draft of a memorandum that Smith can present to her colleagues and higher management that focuses on what Fine Foods calls special orders. The memo should include, but not be limited to:

- A description of the accounting and other considerations with respect to special orders.
- A brief definition of the terms "byproducts" and "joint products" and the extent to which these items apply to special orders at Fine Foods.
- Identification of all the benefits that Fine Foods receives from special orders.
- An analysis of the way Fine Foods handles its special orders and any recommended changes.

PART 3: PERFORMANCE EVALUATION

1. Develop a glossary of terms and definitions for Smith to use in her presentation and discussions to ensure consistency and mutual understanding of terms. In addition to definitions, provide a brief description of the applicability of terms to Fine Foods. The glossary should include, but not be limited to:

- Types of responsibility centers:
  - Cost Centers
  - Revenue Centers
  - Profit Centers
  - Investment Centers
- Computation methods of monetary amounts to evaluate performance:
  - Contribution Margin
  - Operating Profit
  - Return on Investment
  - Residual Income and EVA®
- Agency Costs

2. Prepare a draft of a memorandum for Smith to present to her colleagues and management that includes, but is not limited to:

- What roles do performance evaluation and reward systems play in organizations? Discuss individual vs. team-based performance evaluation in this context.

Are these roles relevant for all types of organizations and employees? To what extent, if any, do these roles apply to Fine Foods?

- Discuss basic concepts of performance evaluation, particularly results control. Discuss issues of financial vs. nonfinancial performance in this context.
- What types of responsibility centers are the SMUs in Fine Foods? Are these appropriate types of responsibility centers for Fine Foods? Why or why not?
- Identify potential agency costs that might occur within Fine Foods. Discuss performance measurement (monitoring) and incentive systems as mechanisms to decrease agency costs at Fine Foods. Identify and discuss any recommendations to implement a reward system. Analyze the extent to which your recommendations would solve the issues that concern Smith and would decrease agency costs.
- Analyze the performance evaluation approaches at Fine Foods. Identify and discuss any changes you might recommend, and the extent to which these changes would resolve the issues Smith raised.

PART 4: CONCLUSION AND RECOMMENDATIONS

1. Prepare a draft memorandum for Smith to present to her colleagues and to higher management that gives recommendations for changes and discusses their benefits for the company as a whole.
2. Prepare a draft of an executive summary of the entire memorandum (Parts 1-4).
3. Prepare a slide presentation for Smith to use when presenting the memorandum to her colleagues and higher management.

This case study was originally used in the 2013 IMA Student Case Study Competition and has been modified for classroom use.

Figure 1
Fine Foods, Inc. Organization Chart

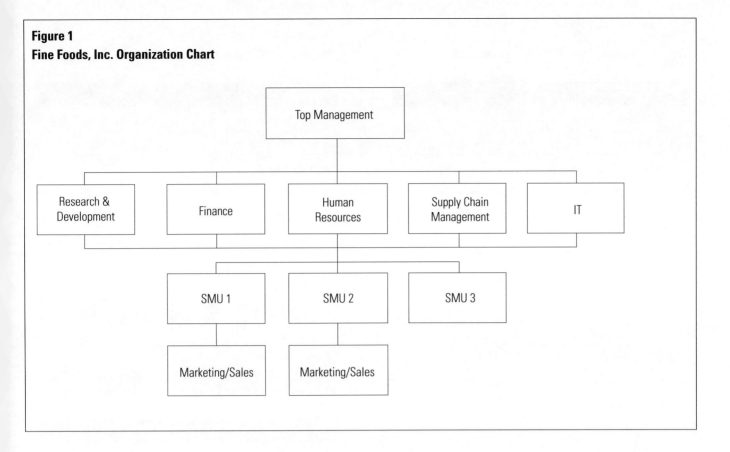

Figure 2
Production Process for Product MP

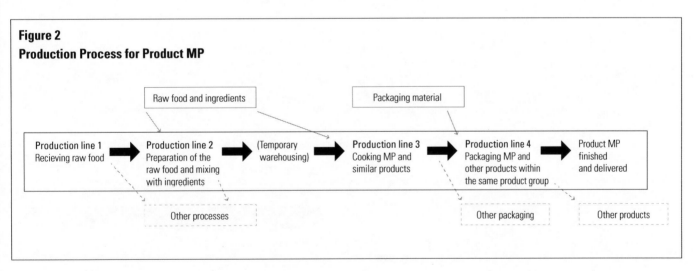

Table 1
Fixed Production Costs Allocated to Products

Workshop Storage
Environment
Electricity
Maintenance Mechanics
Quality
Engineering
Production Line Maintenance
Production Line Cleaning
Lower Production Management
Handling Raw Material Department
Production Office Services
Production Manager and Related Costs
Warehouse/Storage
Internal Logistics/Resource Planning
Sanitation
Vehicles
Building Maintenance
Steam Boiler

Table 2
Contribution Margins and Operating Profit

Gross Sales
(Standard discounts)
(Activity discounts)
(Special discount activities for customers)
Net Sales
(Variable manufacturing cost)
(Fixed manufacturing cost)
(Freight out)
Contribution Margin 1
(Media)
(Sales promotion)
Contribution Margin 2
(Marketing and sales)
Contribution Margin 3
(Top management)
(Business administration)
(Information system)
(Human resources)
(Supply chain)
(Production)
(External logistics for finished goods)
(Mark up - Manufacture expenditures)
(Other fixed costs)
Contribution Margin 4
(Structural costs)
(Total depreciation)
Operating Profit

TransGlobal Airlines

Shane Moriarity, Laura Hopkins, and Andrew Slessor, Unitec New Zealand

A GOVERNMENT-OWNED, MONOPOLY AIRLINE IS scheduled to be privatized. A group of young managers has banded together to undertake an analysis of the current situation and recommend a post privatization strategy. Using data gathered by the group, students are asked to prepare an analysis of market segment profitability. In addition they are asked to estimate the breakeven passenger volume for one of its routes. After doing a SWOT (strengths, weaknesses, opportunities, threats) analysis, students are asked to prepare and present a recommendation for a strategy to the firm's executive committee.

This case was written specifically for use in the Institute of Management Accountant's Student Case Competition. The intent of the case is to encourage students to take a broad view: integrating various cost/managerial analyses to guide a recommendation for future strategy. It provides students with the opportunity to work in a team and to prepare a formal presentation to management. The case requires familiarity with activity-based costing, breakeven analysis, and preparing a SWOT analysis. Thus, it would be appropriate for use in an upper division cost/managerial accounting course near the end of the term. It could also be used in a capstone course by putting more emphasis on the development of strategy recommendations.

Keywords: activity-based costing, SWOT analysis, and strategy recommendation.

The Association of
Accountants and
Financial Professionals
in Business

TransGlobal Airlines

Shane Moriarity
Unitec New Zealand

Laura Hopkins
Unitec New Zealand

Andrew Slessor
Unitec New Zealand

"We are facing a major change in our firm's operating environment," the CEO of TransGlobal Airlines declared at the opening of a hastily called executive committee meeting. *"We need to adopt a survival strategy, now! Noah built the ark when the weather was fine. He didn't wait for the rain to come."*

TransGlobal Airlines is the government-owned, national flag carrier of a small republic. While nominally a democracy, the country in which TransGlobal is located has been ruled by the same president for more than 40 years. During this time, tight controls were placed on all aspects of the economy. Increasingly, the country's wealth was concentrated in the hands of a few powerful supporters of the president. The economy stagnated, and basic infrastructure fell into disrepair. Recent violent protests, however, have led the aging president to announce his retirement. He has scheduled an election to be held in three months' time. At stake in the election will be the presidency as well as all the seats in the legislature. Several political parties have been organized and are fielding viable candidates. All the major parties agree that opening the economy to competition is necessary for the country's financial recovery.

THE CURRENT SITUATION

"As you know," TransGlobal's CEO continued, "we have enjoyed monopoly status on all domestic routes under the current government. That has made life pretty comfortable for us. Unfortunately, that also means we've served our markets without much thought to the quality of the service or facilities that we provide. But last night each of the three major presidential candidates indicated that, if elected, he/she will privatize our company and open our market to competition. Their plans are similar. Trans-Global Airlines will become an independent corporation. Some of the corporate stock will be distributed to current employees based on salary and length of service. But most of the shares will be distributed to the local government bodies whose communities we serve. These shares will be allocated based on the volume of service we currently provide to each community. A temporary advantage for our current management team is that none of these bodies has any experience running an airline. In addition, no single shareholder will initially have a controlling interest. Thus our management team should have a pretty free hand in running the company for the next several months. The new company's shareholders, however, will have the right to sell their shares. It seems likely that many will choose to sell and that a private investor or group of investors will eventually gain effective control. Thus our time to shape our own destiny may be short."

The CEO then held up the diagram in Figure 1 and summarized current operations. "Domestically, TransGlobal operates out of a primary hub in our capital city (SOF) and two subsidiary hubs in PLO and VAR. The company serves six international destinations, four large domestic cities (including the two subsidiary hubs), and five small regional cities from SOF. There is direct service between PLO and VAR. In addition, there are six small regional cities served from PLO and four regional cities served from VAR. Table 1 provides our schedule of daily flights.

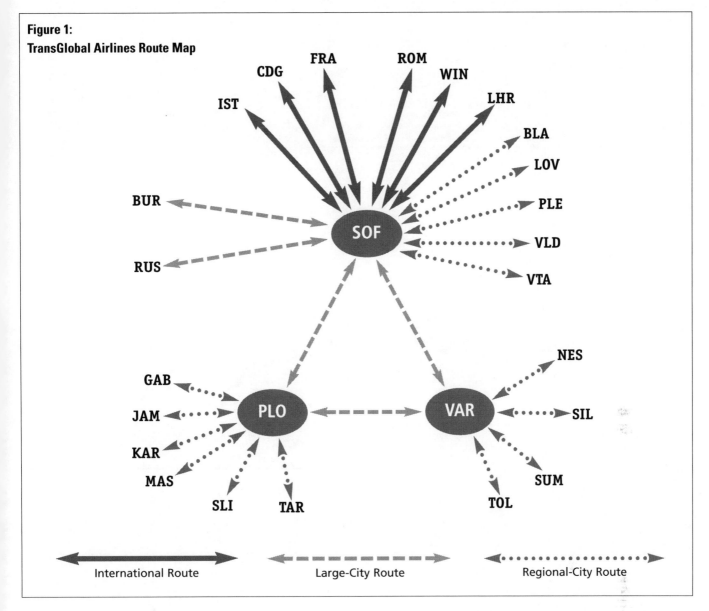

Figure 1:
TransGlobal Airlines Route Map

IST CDG FRA ROM WIN LHR

BUR RUS SOF BLA LOV PLE VLD VTA

GAB JAM KAR MAS PLO SLI TAR VAR NES SIL SUM TOL

International Route   Large-City Route   Regional-City Route

At present, there is reciprocal service on the international routes but without 'beyond rights.' That is, for each international destination that we serve, an airline from the destination country (usually the flag carrier) is allowed to serve SOF. But those carriers aren't allowed to serve any domestic cities beyond SOF. Similarly, we serve only one city in each of our international destinations.

The competitive change that will occur is that the reciprocal carriers will be offered 'beyond rights' so they can serve any of our destinations. This right will include carriage of passengers from one domestic city to another. The offer of 'beyond rights,' of course, will be subject to our gaining similar rights in the corresponding international market."

In my opinion, we have one of two ways to go. We can try to be a major, full-service carrier, or we can focus on being a low-cost carrier for our local markets. We need to decide which approach is more viable. Do we expand our international

reach, or should we focus on improving our local services?" With that question left unanswered, the CEO handed the meeting over to the chief financial officer (CFO).

"Reviewing the current situation, I am pleased to report that we are in a strong financial position." The CFO explained: "With the exception of a couple of quarters when fuel prices spiked, we've been consistently profitable. We're also in the enviable position of owning our own aircraft, and yet we have almost no debt. This situation is the result of our policy of acquiring aircraft only when the government has had the funds to buy them outright. On the other hand, it also means that some of our aircraft are quite old."

"Our fare structure is very simple," the CFO continued. "We match the hard-currency denominated prices charged by our competitors on the international routes. We have a slight advantage because government employees have access only to the local currency, the Krevna [abbreviated

Table 1:
TransGlobal Airlines Daily Flight Schedule

All flights operate 365 days per year

Home City	Destination	One-Way Distance (Miles)	Market Segment*	Equipment**	Round-Trip Flights Per Day	Annual Passenger-Miles-Flown (Millions)
SOF	CDG	2,800	I	JJ	1	480.3
	FRA	2,500	I	JJ	1	465.3
	IST	1,800	I	JJ	1	329.8
	LHR	3,200	I	JJ	1	630.7
	ROM	1,200	I	JJ	1	223.3
	WIN	3,500	I	JJ	1	608.1
	BUR	280	C	MJ	2	32.7
	PLO	240	C	MJ	6	98.9
	RUS	270	C	MJ	2	32.7
	VAR	260	C	MJ	6	103.7
	BLA	125	R	TP	4	7.7
	LOV	160	R	TP	3	6.3
	PLE	170	R	TP	2	4.2
	VLD	140	R	TP	2	2.2
	VTA	130	R	TP	6	3.9
PLO	VAR	225	C	MJ	4	60.5
	GAB	180	R	TP	2	2.1
	JAM	170	R	TP	2	2.2
	KAR	200	R	TP	3	8.8
	MAS	130	R	TP	3	4.6
	SLI	170	R	TP	4	3.9
	TAR	120	R	TP	2	1.2
VAR	NES	190	R	TP	4	6.7
	SIL	125	R	TP	2	1.6
	SUM	120	R	TP	4	2.5
	TOL	135	R	TP	2	1.2
						3,125.1

*I=International,   C=Large City,   R=Regional City   **JJ=Jumbo Jet   MJ=Medium Jet   TP=Turboprop

Kr], which we readily accept at the official exchange rate. Depending on the status of the international money markets, our competitors sometimes impose a surcharge on payments made in Krevna. The result is that we feel only moderate pressure on prices on these routes, and we currently average Kr 165 for a one-way international flight.

"Fares on domestic flights are negotiated annually with our government's Aviation Oversight Agency. Government policy has been to allow us a 'reasonable' overall profit. We use two types of aircraft on our domestic routes: medium-sized jets on the large city routes and turboprops for the regional cities. Customers find the turboprops less desirable, so we charge lower fares on them. Right now the agreed fare structure is Kr 89 for a one-way ticket on a medium-sized jet and Kr 49 for a one-way flight on a turboprop. This two-tier fare structure simplifies marketing but doesn't reflect differences in distances traveled on each route."

The CFO then handed out Table 2 and said, "I hope this document will help you understand how we perform. The top part is last year's income statement. In the second part I've divided the costs and revenues by our three major market segments: international routes, large-city routes, and regional-city routes. It was easy to identify revenues by market segment. Costs, however, were more difficult. To split the costs, I allocated aircraft operating costs to each segment based on the relative number of passenger-miles-flown in each market. [Passenger-miles-flown is the industry's measure of volume. Ten passenger-miles-flown could represent one passenger flying 10 miles, five passengers flying two miles, or some other similar combination.] I used passenger-miles because the aircraft operating costs depend on both the distances flown and the number of passengers carried. The other costs we incur are primarily related to the number of passengers served, so I used last year's passenger counts to split those costs. The numbers in Table 2 are approximations, but they clearly show that we're operating at a loss in the market segment where we face competition. Our challenge will be to stay profitable when competition expands to our domestic market."

As the meeting ended, the CEO said, "For our next meeting, I want each of you to give some thought to the challenges we face. I intend to start next time with a SWOT analysis in which we catalogue our strengths, weaknesses, opportunities, and threats. I hope that exercise will then help us identify a viable strategy for our future. In the short run, I think survival is our paramount goal. As most of you know, the failure rate is quite high for former monopolies suddenly thrust into a competitive market. But we need to consider our longer-term strategy also."

Table 2:
TransGlobal Airlines Last Year's Income Statement
(in Millions)

Revenues		Kr 316.9
Aircraft costs		
Fuel	Kr 158.1	
Aircraft depreciation	44.4	202.5
Flight personnel costs		
Pilot crew	24.8	
Cabin crew	17.7	42.5
Ground costs		
Gate rental	2.8	
Ground staff	6.1	8.9
Corporate costs		
Marketing	21.5	
General administration	17.4	38.9
Net income		Kr 24.1

Condensed Income Statement by Market Segment
(in Millions)

	International	Large City	Regional City	Total
Revenues	Kr 180.7	Kr 116.9	Kr 19.3	Kr 316.9
Aircraft operating cost	177.4	21.3	3.8	202.5
Other costs	35.3	42.3	12.7	90.3
Net Income	Kr (32.0)	Kr 53.3	Kr 2.8	Kr 24.1

THE CHALLENGE

You are a manager in the Financial Services Department at TransGobal Airlines. A few days after the meeting, several of the younger company managers stopped by your office. "You know, most of the other managers are fairly old, set in their ways, and have never worked in a competitive environment. I don't think many of them will survive the changeover," one of your colleagues said. Another commented, "Their departures will open up career opportunities for those of us who can adapt, assuming we do. I suggest we work together as a team to analyze the situation and come up with recommendations in time for the next executive committee meeting. That will increase our chances of being appointed to leadership positions in the transition process." There was quick agreement on a plan of action: One member of the team would gather more detailed data on operations, and two others would gather further descriptive information on the firm's market. The team agreed to meet the following Friday.

Table 3

TransGlobal Airlines Summary of Selected Cost and Operating Data

Average Passenger Loads and Distances

	ONE-WAY FLIGHTS PER DAY	ANNUAL PASSENGER-MILES (MILLIONS)
International (Jumbo Jet) 250 passengers flying 2,500 miles	12	2,737.5
City (Medium Jet) 90 passengers flying 250 miles	40	328.5
Regional (Turboprop) 12 passengers flying 150 miles	90	<u>59.1</u>
Total		3,125.1

Annual Fuel Costs

		Millions
International	Kr 10,000 per flight + Kr 0.02 ppm = Kr 43.8 + Kr 54.7	Kr 98.5
City	Kr 2,500 per flight + Kr 0.015 ppm = Kr 36.5 + Kr 4.9	41.4
Regional	Kr 500 per flight + Kr 0.03 ppm = Kr 16.4 + Kr 1.8	<u>18.2</u>
Total		Kr 158.1

Aircraft Fleet

	SEATING CAPACITY	AVERAGE AIRCRAFT AGE (YEARS)	ORIGINAL COST (MILLIONS)	USEFUL LIFE	ANNUAL DEPRECIATION (MILLIONS)
6 Jumbo Jets	300	7	Kr 600	20	Kr 30.0
10 Medium Jets	100	14	250	20	12.5
25 Turboprops	25	22	57	30	<u>1.9</u>
Total					Kr 44.4

Annual Cost for Pilots

MARKET SEGMENT	CREWS NEEDED PER YEAR	NUMBER OF PILOTS PER CREW	AVERAGE SALARY	TOTAL COST (MILLIONS)
International	24	3	Kr 175,000	Kr 12.6
City	40	2	100,000	8.0
Regional	30	2	70,000	<u>4.2</u>
Totals				Kr 24.8

A crew flies one one-way international flight per day. Crews for the large-city routes fly one round-trip flight per day. The regional crews fly three round trips per day. But crews don't work every day, so there needs to be an allowance for holidays, sickness, and so on. Thus the firm hires an equivalent of twice the number of crews needed per day.

Table 3 continues on next page

Table 3

TransGlobal Airlines Summary of Selected Cost and Operating Data

Continued from previous page

Annual Cost for Cabin Crews

MARKET SEGMENT	CREWS NEEDED PER YEAR	NUMBER OF ATTENDANTS PER CREW	AVERAGE SALARY	TOTAL COST (MILLIONS)
International	24	10	Kr 50,000	Kr 12.0
City	40	3	40,000	4.8
Regional	30	1	30,000	0.9
Totals				Kr 17.7

Cabin crews put in the same amount of flight time as pilots.

Gate Charges

TYPE OF GATE	NUMBER OF GATES	AVERAGE GATE RENTAL	ANNUAL COST (MILLIONS)
International Destinations	6	Kr 150,000	Kr 0.9
International Gates at SOF	3	200,000	0.6
City Gates at SOF	3	100,000	0.3
Other City Gates	5	60,000	0.3
Regional Gates at SOF	4	50,000	0.2
Other Regional Gates	20	25,000	0.5
Totals			Kr 2.8

Gates are dedicated to each type of aircraft. Thus there is no sharing of gates among the three market segments. There is one large-city gate at BUR, PLO, and RUS, and there are two large-city gates at VAR. Each regional city has one gate. There are three regional-city gates at PLO and two at VAR.

Ground Staff Salaries

LOCATION OF STAFF	NUMBER OF LOCATIONS	TOTAL NUMBER OF EMPLOYEES	ANNUAL AVERAGE SALARY	COST (MILLIONS)
International Destinations	6	24	Kr 50,000	Kr 1.20
Primary Hub (SOF)	1	40	42,000	1.68
PLO	1	20	40,000	0.80
VAR	1	12	40,000	0.48
BUR & RUS	2	8	35,000	0.28
Regional Destinations	15	60	27,000	1.62
Total				Kr 6.06

An informal time study shows that the staff at the primary hub spend 30% of their time servicing international flights, 40% on domestic large-city flights, and 30% on regional flights. The staff at PLO spend 40% of their time devoted to large-city flights and 60% to regional-city flights. The staff at VAR spend 50% of their time on large-city flights and 50% on regional flights.

Table 4
TransGlobal Airlines
Further Information on Our Services and Competition

Our customer base is pretty thin. Few of our citizens can afford to travel for personal reasons.

We serve far more small regional locations than most other national airlines. The government directed that some of our routes be undertaken to boost local economic development. Another factor is the abysmal condition of most of our country's roads. Few of our customers are willing to undertake the rigors of intercity road travel if they can avoid it.

We have the annual passenger volumes for each route, but we don't know how those loads are distributed throughout the week. I was told that patronage is light on our domestic weekend services.

Our firm hasn't conducted formal customer surveys, but the general impression from friends and colleagues is that we are below average in customer satisfaction. Our lack of domestic competition has allowed us to get away with offering pretty basic service. For example, we don't have entertainment systems in any of our aircraft, our spacing between seats is tight, and there is no beverage service on domestic flights. Our on-time performance is far below industry standards.

On the other hand, our safety record is very good. Because there is little pressure to adhere to our published schedule, flights are routinely delayed or cancelled whenever there's an indication of an equipment malfunction. Our only accidents to date have been quite minor. Our worst accident occurred a couple of years ago when a plane hit a cow on one of the regional runways while landing. There were a few minor passenger injuries but nothing serious. Yet we got a lot of unwanted "humorous" attention from the news media.

This raises another negative: Our ground facilities are generally in pretty poor condition. This is especially true at the regional destinations. Ground facilities are owned by the local government bodies, and we pay rent for their use. But little of our rent money has gone into maintaining the facilities.

Our international flights leave early in the morning so travelers can reach their destination in time to conduct business during the day or to catch connecting flights if they are travelling farther. Our planes then sit idle at the destination airport until about 6 p.m. local time when they return home. Our competitors for the most part fly here only in the late afternoon and then return to their home country in the early evening. They don't want to have a plane sitting here idle overnight or during the day. Thus we operate our international morning flights at near capacity.

The information provided in Tables 3 and 4 was distributed on Friday afternoon. "I haven't had a chance to analyze the information," the person who gathered the data in Table 3 said. "Unfortunately, I also haven't been able to get as much detailed information as I would have liked. But the executive committee meeting is on Monday, so we need to proceed with what we have now."

"We share your concern. We also would have preferred to get more information," one of the people responsible for Table 4 added. "But we hope what we found is useful."

You then suggest, "Let's spend the weekend at my house going through this material. We can start by digging into the financial details. I suggest we examine the relative profitability of the market segments and determine our breakeven passenger volume for one of our routes, say the SOF to PLE regional route. These exercises should familiarize us with our basic cost structure. Then let's prepare a SWOT analysis as requested by the CEO. But our most important task is to come up with a recommendation for a strategy. We will also need an impressive presentation to get top management's attention."

THE ASSIGNMENT

- Form your team.
- Prepare an analysis of the profitability of each market segment.
- Determine the breakeven passenger volume for the SOF to PLE route.
- Prepare a SWOT analysis for the firm.
- Recommend a strategy for the firm.
- Prepare a formal presentation for the executive committee.

Alternative Costing Methods: Precision Paint Shop's Dilemma

Eileen Peacock, AACSB International; Paul Juras, Wake Forest University

IN THIS CASE, STUDENTS ARE PRESENTED AN OPPORTUNITY to identify the various roles a costing system can play in supporting strategic management decisions. The setting is a privately held custom coater of automotive components to original equipment manufacturers (OEMs). Historically the company took just about all the work it was offered, and management was using a form of standard costing to evaluate product profitability. Demand was increasing, but along with the increase in volume came a decrease in profits and management could not understand why. There had been a recent switch to an ABC system to better understand the costs associated with painting the various products, but management was unsure if this system provided the information they needed for effective decision making. Throughput costing based on Theory of Constraints (TOC) and Resource Consumption Accounting (RCA) have now been offered as alternatives for supporting strategic decision making and the students are asked to help management make a decision about their costing system.

The case can be used in an undergraduate cost accounting course, an introductory management accounting course at the MBA level, or a cost analysis course in an MBA or graduate program in accounting curriculum.

Keywords: costing system, activity-based costing, resource consumption accounting, and theory of constraints.

The Association of
Accountants and
Financial Professionals
in Business

Alternative Costing Methods: Precision Paint Shop's Dilemma

Eileen Peacock
AACSB International

Paul Juras
Wake Forest University

"We invested a great deal of time and money into developing the activity-based costing (ABC) system, and now I am not sure if it provides the information we really need for long-term decision-making purposes," Amy Wesling, plant manager of Precision Paint Shop's (PPS) Southern Plant, told her administrative team. "The ABC data helped us understand our costs better, but now I'm wondering if it's the right information to serve as the basis for helping us achieve our strategic goals."

COMPANY DESCRIPTION

Precision Paint Shop (a fictionalized version of an actual Midwest company) is a privately-held custom coater (painter) of automotive components for original equipment manufacturers (OEMs) and tier 1 and tier 2 suppliers. The company has annual revenues of $90 million per year, with $35 million in sales from the Southern plant, which specializes in spray topcoat applications.

PPS specializes in the application of a series of coatings. Raw metal parts are received on consignment from the customer, finished with the desired application(s) of paint and other coatings, and shipped back to the same customer. The product lines consist of a large number of combinations of paint colors, types of coating, and paint finishes. Figure 1 provides a diagram of the production process, and "PPS's Production Process" (Sidebar 1) provides a narrative of the production process.

Historically, PPS accepted most of the work assignments offered. Prices were market driven, and management used a form of standard costing to evaluate product profitability. Over the past three years demand had significantly

increased, especially in the higher-grade coatings. In fact, the product mix flip-flopped from 80% low-gloss (LG) finish two years ago to 85% high-gloss (HG) finish in the current year. Unfortunately, along with the increase in volume came a decrease in profits.

The immense number of combinations of coatings and color created complexity for the company. Also, the parts to be painted varied in size and shape, further complicating the painting process. The end result was that four characteristics—coating, color, shape, and size—were instrumental in determining the complexity of the operation. This variety initiated a mix of activities unique to each job. The very nature of the painting process and the need for a near-100% perfection level in the industry resulted in a high level of inspections, refinishing, rework, and scrap. Complexity had driven up overhead costs, leaving direct materials accounting for only 26% of total manufacturing costs.

THE COSTING SYSTEM

Recently had PPS moved away from a conventional standard costing system to ABC. The change was made to better understand the costs associated with painting the various products. The ABC analysis revealed the fundamental differences that existed between the different mixes of product characteristics. Table 1 provides an illustrative comparison of two versions of a bumper: an LG finish and an HG finish. After the ABC analysis, Chad Leaders, plant accountant, provided a report showing a significant change in the reported profitability levels of the various product lines. Table 2 summarizes the types of changes that took place.

Once implemented, the ABC information was used to negotiate product pricing and to report financial performance.

PLANNING FOR CAPACITY USE

The conveyor line was definitely a constraining resource of the painting process. Through her knowledge of theory of constraints (TOC), Mandy James, production supervisor, had developed a method for factoring in the various process elements into demand levels on conveyor capacity. Using bumpers as an example, she presented the template appearing in Table 3, and compared an LG bumper to an HG bumper. The template starts with the quality issue. The greater the percentage of defects, the lower the yield rate (YR) for a production run. The more complex shapes and finishes have lower yield rates than those that are less complex. LG bumpers currently have a YR of about 95%, while HG bumpers run about 92%.

Defective products can be worked on in-house, and some can be recovered. For bumpers, the recovery rate (RR) is about 5% of units started. Since the recovered bumpers are brought up to an acceptable quality level, they contribute toward meeting customer demand and put no further demand on the conveyor capacity. The YR and RR can be combined to determine how many products must be processed to generate one unit of acceptable quality, which is called the run factor (RF). The RF is equal to $1/(YR+RR)$. If $YR+RR=1$, as with the LG bumper, then only one unit must be put on the conveyor to ultimately yield one unit of acceptable quality. The RF for the HG bumper is 103% (computed as $1/(92\% + 5\%)$), meaning PPS must paint 103% of the total bumpers required to yield enough bumpers of acceptable quality to satisfy customer demand.

Since the conveyor line is the constraint, the time a product spends on the conveyor is an important issue. Line speed can vary from 10 to 18 feet per minute, depending on the size and shape of the product being painted. Mandy considers 18 feet per minute to be the standard time unit for the conveyor line. A complexity factor (CF) ranging between 1 (for fastest line speed) and 1.8 (for slowest speed) is determined for each product family and added to the calculation of demand. The CF is computed by dividing the standard line speed of 18 feet per minute by the line speed required for the specific product, so a faster line speed results in a CF closer to 1. The line speed of the HG bumper is currently 12 feet per minute, resulting in an CF of $18/12 = 1.5$. The CF is then multiplied by the RF to get the total constraint demand factor (DF).

The DF is actually a demand placed on the conveyor per unit of finished good of a particular part type. Because parts can vary in shape and size, PPS needed a standard unit of measure to compare product profitability that factored in the total demand placed on the conveyor. The square footage of each part was chosen as the measurement unit because it represents the surface area of each part that's coated. As a result, the DF is divided by the total square footage of a particular part (e.g., a bumper) to yield the bottleneck demand factor (BDF), which is the demand factor per square foot of a particular size, shape, and finish. The profit level per square foot of finished good is divided by the BDF to yield the profit per throughput unit (P/TU) on the conveyor. Table 3 shows the LG bumper has a lower profit per unit ($10 per bumper, or $1 per sq. ft.), but after adjusting for the respective demands on the conveyor, the LG bumper has a higher P/TU.

DECISION POINT

Management of PPS used ABC to obtain a better understanding of the "true" cost of the products in order to help make better pricing decisions. Management now wants to be more proactive in the use of costing information to help develop and implement organizational strategy in an environment where the demand exceeds current productive capacity. Based on the opening question posed by Amy, PPS's management was attempting to move away from merely trying to assign costs more accurately to using the cost information to support strategic decision making. Specifically, Amy wants to make strategic decisions about which product lines to promote and pursue. She is aware of the ABC process of assigning cost of resources to activities, but considers this an operational rather than strategic issue. She isn't clear about whether ABC supports strategic decision making.

Mandy pointed out that the conveyor line was being fully utilized and jobs were being turned down because of the capacity constraint. She thought the capacity issue should drive any strategic decisions and that Amy should adopt the principles of TOC and throughput costing for strategic decision making. Mandy supported her position with the following example. "HG bumpers are a big part of production," she said. "We evaluated whether or not to increase the line speed when HG bumpers are being painted. The increase in speed will reduce the yield rate from 92% to 90%. There will be more defects, but the RR will increase to 6%, and, as Table 3 shows, the P/TU will increase and the finesse costs per unit would actually decline." (See Sidebar 2, "Finessing.")

Chad disagreed with Mandy's recommendation. Using Table 1, Chad noted that the HG finishes have higher reject rates, require additional painters, more colors, more inspections and maintenance costs, and slower line speed. The HG products are also treated as they pass through Stations 3 and 4. Since some of the costs related to resource demands are fixed costs, throughput costing shouldn't be used because these fixed costs would be ignored. He offered an alternative, resource consumption accounting (RCA), which he had heard about at a recent local IMA chapter meeting. He thought RCA might be what Amy needed, but he wasn't entirely sure. Chad presented Amy with a brief description of the costing method. (See Sidebar 3, "Basics of RCA.") He offered to learn more about RCA by attending a continuing education session offered by IMA, but Amy wanted more information before making the investment in having Chad attend the session.

SUGGESTED RESOURCES

Chwen, Sheu, Ming-Hsiang Chen, and Stacy Kovar. "Integrating ABC and TOC for Better Manufacturing Decision Making." *Integrated Manufacturing Systems*, May 2003, pp. 433-441.

Grasso, Lawrence P. "Are ABC and RCA Accounting Systems Compatible with Lean Management?" *Management Accounting Quarterly*, Fall 2005, pp. 12-27.

Keys, David, and Anton van der Merwe. "Gaining Effective Organizational Control with RCA." Strategic Finance, May 2002, pp. 41-47.

Resource Consumption Accounting Institute website, http://www.rcainstitute.org

van der Merwe, Anton, and David Keys. "The Case for Resource Consumption Accounting." *Strategic Finance*, April 2002, pp 31-36.

SIDEBAR 1: PPS'S PRODUCTION PROCESS

PPS operates two 8-hour shifts, 240 days per year. The paint process involves a monorail conveyor line that moves at line speeds of 10-18 feet per minute, depending on the application and part complexity. The total paint cycle time is about 2.5 hours. The production schedule is created based on customer requirements, line speed, minimum lot (or batch) size, and the availability of racks. The material handlers bring the raw parts and racks to the line and loaders rack each part, making sure it is racked properly so that when it enters the E-coat tank a proper electrical ground is attained.

THE PAINT PROCESS

The part is first treated with chemicals (pre-treatment stage), a sequence of washing and rinsing to remove any grease or dirt and to prepare the part for paint adhesion with a phosphate spraying. Next, the part is submerged in a 20,000-gallon e-coat tank. As it comes out of the tank, it is sprayed with fresh, deionized water to rinse off any "dragout" paint clinging to the parts, thereby eliminating appearance defects. The part then moves through four paint booths. Depending on the part type, however, all four booths may not be used.

- Booth 1 has five automatic spray guns that apply primer. A part may or may not receive a primer coating, which provides additional protection against chipping and rusting.
- Booth 2 has two manual sprayers as well as automatic sprayers that paint basecoat or enamel topcoat.
- Booth 3 has one manual sprayer and an automatic spray gun that apply clearcoat. Only high-gloss products receive the glossy, shiny clearcoat finish.
- Booth 4 has two manual sprayers and automatic spray guns that also apply clearcoat for parts that require two coats.

While low-gloss products are being painted, booth 3 and booth 4 painters are idle and the spray guns are turned off. Depending on the product line, the part receives a basecoat (high gloss) or an enamel topcoat (low gloss). After these processes, the paint is cured in another oven. As the product arrives back at the unload/load area, it is date-stamped, unracked onto a floor conveyor, inspected, unloaded, and packaged.

THE SETUP PROCESS

A five-minute setup "gap" is required when changing paint colors. This gives line workers the time to change the tooling racks, modify the line speed, purge the line of the old paint, and run the new paint through the system.

As the setup gap nears the paint booths, paint containers with the required colors are transported to the paint booth. While the last part from the prior color is painted, the paint lines are quickly purged of the old paint, flushed with solvents to clean the paint lines, and new paint is sprayed through the spray guns to obtain the desired consistency. As the gap ends and the raw parts appear, the painting begins again.

QUALITY ASSURANCE OR REWORK PROCESS

The primary sources of rejections are: dirt and dust in the manual hand sprayers, old equipment, and the nature of the industry. High-gloss products, which are much more expensive to reprocess, have substantially higher rejection rates than low-gloss products.

Rework mostly requires sanding. The product is sanded down to the e-coat primer and then moved to the line for reprocessing. Some products are sent to an outside stripper. Some defects can be corrected by finessing, which eliminates the need for complete reprocessing. Finessing allows the defect to be buffed out on parts that have the clearcoat glossy finish. Parts are considered "saved" when they can be unloaded along with the other painted good parts.

SIDEBAR 2: FINESSING

Currently PPS finesses approximately 100,000 bumpers per year, or about 5% of bumpers run on the conveyor. If the line speed is increased, the decline in the yield rate would create about 20,000 additional bumpers that the finesse department could work on. The finesse department can handle 125,000 units per year when operating at maximum efficiency, and the variable costs for finesse are less than $0.02 per unit, so the increase in units worked wouldn't generate much change in the total costs even though the computed cost per unit does change. The table provides the supporting detail.

Finesse Cost Per Unit at Various Defect Levels

	Annual Cost	Units	Cost Per Unit
Current Defect Level	$480,000	100,000	$4.800
Defect Level with Increased Line Speed	$480,400	120,000	$4.003
Practical Capacity to Handle Defects	$480,500	125,000	$3.844

SIDEBAR 3: BASICS OF RCA

Resource consumption accounting (RCA) is based on costing methods developed by German companies and the activity costing philosophy of ABC. RCA takes a resource-based view of an organization and looks closely at the quantity of resources consumed and the underlying nature of the cost of those resources. Some of the key characteristics of RCA are the treatment of idle capacity, the use of costs other than historical, and the ability to group and track cost information at various levels. This comprehensive management accounting system can lead to improved decision support by providing more accurate product costs and a better understanding of the interrelationships between processes and costs.

Table 1
Summary of Items Affected by the Need for High- or Low-gloss Finish on a Bumper

	High Gloss	Low Gloss
Rejection Rate	high	low
Number of Colors	high	low
Batch Size	low	high
Number of Painters	high	low

Table 2
Number of Products That Had Changes in Calculated Profit Margin from Standard Costing to ABC

Negative Margin	Positive Margin
← 3 became more negative	5 became more positive →
	7 → moved from negative to positive
1 → became less negative	← 10 became less positive

Table 3
Using Capacity Demand to Rank Profitability

Product	Yield Rate (YR)	Recovery Rate (RR)	Run Factor (RF) = 1/(YR + RR)	Speed	Complexity Factor (CF) = 18/speed	Demand Factor (DF) = (RF x CF)	Sq. Ft. per Unit of Product (Sq. Ft.)	(BDF) Bottleneck Demand Sq. Ft. = (DF/Sq. Ft.)	Profit per Unit of Finished Product	(P/TU) Adjusted Product Profit per Throughput Unit Profit per Sq. Ft. /BDF
Compare Two Bumper Finishes										
Low-Gloss Bumper	95%	5%	100%	15	1.20	1.20	10	.120	$10.00	$8.33
High-Gloss Bumper	92%	5%	103%	12	1.50	1.55	10	.155	$12.00	$7.76
Evaluate a Process Change										
Current Process High-Gloss Bumper	92%	5%	103%	12	1.50	1.55	10	.155	$12.00	$7.76
Change Speed and YR	90%	6%	104%	13	1.38	1.44	10	.144	$12.00	$8.32

Figure 1
Diagram of the production process

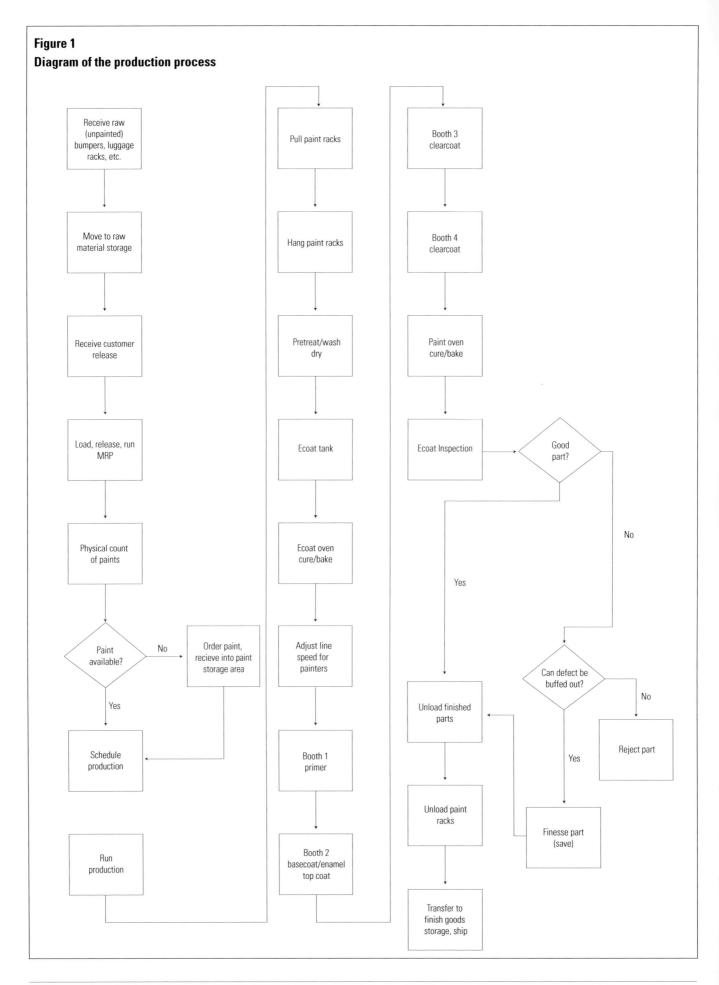